GEORGE HUDSON

George Hudson

The Rise and Fall of the Railway King:
A Study in Victorian Entrepreneurship

A. J. Arnold and S. McCartney

Hambledon and London
London and New York

102 Gloucester Avenue
London, NW1 8HX

175 Fifth Avenue
New York
NY 10010

First Published 2004

ISBN 1 85285 401 4

A description of this book is available from the
British Library and from the Library of Congress.

Typeset by Carnegie Publishing, Lancaster,
and printed in Great Britain by Cambridge University Press.

Distributed in the United States and Canada
exclusively by Palgrave Macmillan,
a division of St Martin's Press.

Contents

Illustrations

Introduction

George Hudson was one of the most prominent figures in the social and political circles of the nineteenth century. His fame came from a series of spectacular business achievements in the growth industry of the day, the railways: no-one else could match his acumen, vision and commercial judgement. His 'very nod' could raise shares ten per cent in the market and he had a major impact on the whole investment mania of the mid 1840s. His ability, fame and charisma made him an eagerly sought-after companion at social events everywhere.

In the ten years that followed the opening of the Stockton and Darlington railway in 1825, more than fifty railway Acts were passed by Parliament, authorising the construction of five hundred miles of track. The railways, constructed piecemeal through private initiatives, were to become the most powerful industry of the century and one that would bring unprecedented change to the world in which Victorian people lived.

The new transport system also transformed the investment opportunities facing a middle class that was far more affluent, now that the privations of the French wars had receded. The industrial revolution of the late eighteenth century might have been a period of greater innovation but it certainly required far less capital. Even in the nineteenth century, manufacturers who wanted to develop their businesses would generally look to the financial support of wealthy local families. Here, the ties of kinship, neighbourhood and long acquaintance bound both investor and entrepreneur in a relationship that ensured a close understanding of the risks and benefits.

The railway age was quite different, with a requirement for enormous amounts of capital, on a scale that went far beyond the remit of purely local wealth. The government was well aware of this and recognised the unique importance of the railways. While business investors generally put their personal wealth at risk if things went wrong, in the railways, investors were usually able to limit their risk to the agreed amount of their investment.

Large numbers of widely dispersed potential investors still had to be reached and their interest attracted, however, and George Hudson had the skills appropriate to the age. Unlike Brunel or the Stephensons, he had no great technical ability, but he did have the talents needed to move capitalism

on to a larger scale of operations. He had an extraordinary eye for possibilities and a sense of the dramatic, focused with great skill through public
oratory, the press and the new journals for investors. His schemes were no
mere puffs; his prodigious energy, drive and organisational competence
brought demonstrable results to convince even the sceptical. He was, in
short, the first person who really knew how to attract and use other people's
money.

He was also highly successful in politics. After utterly dominating the
affairs of his adopted home city of York, he moved on to become MP for
Sunderland and a leading member of the Tory protectionists under Lord
George Bentinck. He loved to socialise and no-one else in the north of
England could compete with the brilliance and dazzle of his social occasions.
He was genuinely close to landed families in the north of England and for
a time he was also feted in London society although, as a 'nouveau' he
never achieved a secure position in the affections of the socially elevated.

Nonetheless, his combination of political importance, energetic socialising
and self-promotion through the press meant that his appeal to investors,
whether in the railways, in banking or in dock construction became highly
personalised, blurring the distinction between Hudson and 'his' companies.

In 1845, at the zenith of his success, one of Hudson's supporters noted
that 'he wields at command and presides over an amount of pecuniary
capital exceeding that of any other man in the empire'. This *personal* control
over enormous and unprecedented resources was to have important implications for the way that capitalism developed. At the same time, few of the
restrictions that are such a familiar feature of our world were placed on
his dealings. Auditing was almost non-existent and organisational controls
were still rudimentary in the extreme. His fellow-directors found it virtually
impossible to hold out in disputes against his manifest competence, mastery
of detail and public standing, although his high profile and bombastic
manner also led to numerous attacks by those who rejected his highly
personalised bandwagon.

Victorian entrepreneurs were in many cases well rewarded, if their efforts
served the interests of the state or if they owned businesses that were
commercially successful. In the case of the relatively new, limited liability
companies, however, this was not the case. Directors were usually paid only
modest fees, appropriate to the exercise of a watching brief over shareholder
interests. Victorian times are often seen as quintessentially entrepreneurial,
yet the rewards for managerial enterprise in the new limited liability
businesses were tiny compared with their level today, when share options
have become commonplace and performance related payments to directors
and 'fat-cat' salaries have become a public scandal.

Even when the companies Hudson managed were extremely profitable, they never paid him what his enterprise was worth. Frustrated at the limited rewards to be obtained from activities that were making other people extremely rich, he began to misuse his position in order to make money for himself and enjoyed a period of quite dazzling success and popularity until revelations of dishonesty and false accounting turned the public against him.

The story of George Hudson's life is one of initial spectacular achievement; his energy and enterprise generated vast new wealth during the heady days of the railway construction era. The 'get-rich-quick' ethos of the railway mania period, which he exemplified, generated huge sums for those who invested in stocks and shares, including many from the new middle classes who had developed a taste for railway speculation. The representatives of old wealth took their share of these spoils but they were also nervous of so much new money and disapproved of the brash new world of commerce that no longer knew its place. When George Hudson's downfall was attributed to his lack of gentlemanly honour they quickly distanced themselves from the scandal and him.

The exposure of his failings was attended by the most enormous public interest and there was a vigorous debate in the press. Hudson was of course the author of his own misfortune but some of his contemporaries recognised that many of his shortcomings were also failures of the system, the predictable outcome of the 'get rich quick, money for nothing' mentality that had become so pervasive. The *Times* saw the system as one 'without rule, without order, without even a definite morality' and thought the tendency to blame an individual such as Hudson both highly distasteful and hypocritical.

The penalties for impropriety and failure were far more severe in the nineteenth century than they are today; Hudson was pursued for debts arising from his years as a railway chairman, for over twenty years until the year of his death, by his successor on the board, a member of the landed gentry who was determined that Hudson should pay for his misdeeds. As William Gladstone wrote, after Hudson's death:

> The world in its vices is cruel, I wis,
> But the world in its virtue – God save me from this.

Nineteenth century politics and business life were often confrontational and Hudson was anything but diplomatic in his personal style. The language of those involved was robust by present-day standards, but there has been an unfortunate tendency to take the comments of his critics at face value, without reference to the context in which they were made. Captain Watts, for example, famously characterised Hudson as 'crowing on the dunghill of his own plenitude', but Watts, as both a staunch supporter of the rival Stockton and Darlington line and a noted eccentric was far from being a reliable witness. While the angry denunciations of Hudson by the Liberal politicians of York in 1839 do tell us something about Hudson's approach, due allowance should also be given to the considerable pique of the Liberals and to their own (understandable) desire to damage the person most responsible for their own sudden loss of political influence.

Perhaps because his life was so dramatic and his personal style so polemical, Hudson has often been portrayed in simple terms as either a heroic or as an almost villainous figure. Hudson's combative nature, the defensive snobberies of a London society unused to 'new wealth' and the dramatic nature of his downfall meant that he was the subject, and often the butt, of numerous colourful stories. Many were, however, merely apocryphal or humorous.

His first biographer, R. S. Lambert in 1934, was very well disposed towards him, felt that he had been punished unreasonably by Victorian society as a scapegoat for the faults of a system and consequently overlooked some of his undeniable failings. A. J. Peacock, on the other hand, who wrote extensively about Hudson during the 1970s and 1980s, has been almost obsessively critical and negative about the means and reality of his achievements.

These achievements were, in fact, very substantial and Hudson's extraordinarily eventful life has much to tell us about the values, motivations and prejudices of the society in which he lived. He is also too important a part of the evolution of capitalism for his story to be told in an overly partisan manner and our intention has been to write a dispassionate biography that also pays due attention to the context and pressures under which he operated, in the hope of providing the reasonably full and balanced portrayal of his life, personality and achievements that his impact on Victorian society deserves.

Towards that end we would like to offer our thanks to a number of people for their help in the writing of this book, to David Smith of G. H. Smith and Son of Easingwold for access to his holding of Hudson family private papers, to A. J. Peacock of York and Peter Hawkins of Clapham for their helpful advice, to John Kirman of Garbutt and Elliott of York for showing us round Hudson's former house in Monkgate and to Alf Abbott, Harry Collett and Peter Thornton, all of Whitby, for sharing their interest in George Hudson with us. Above all we would like to thank to our families for their enthusiasm and encouragement and also acknowledge the generous assistance we received from the staff of a large number of reference libraries, museums and archives in York, Whitby, Newcastle, Sunderland and London.

1

First Steps

George Hudson became initially famous, and then notorious, during an era in which inventors, engineers and entrepreneurs changed their world with a speed that has never been matched. In this age of great endeavour, Hudson was a pivotal figure, the first of a new breed of business tycoons. His upbringing and early years were not, however, typical of the other great innovators of his time, many of whom grew up in politically radical, nonconformist, middle-class urban families and developed technical skills suited to the opportunities of the new age.

George Hudson was born on 10 March 1800, the fifth son and seventh of ten children of tenant farmer John Hudson (1756–1808) and his wife Elizabeth Ruston (1768–1807).[1] Hudson's career has sometimes been told as a tale of 'rags to riches' but his early upbringing was modestly respectable.

His family had been farming part of the Cholmley estate in Howsham, a small village on the Derwent in the East Riding of Yorkshire, a few miles north east of York, for nearly two hundred years. They were not rich but they had a good standing in the locality. Hudson's father, besides running the farm, was a minor local dignitary, bearing the title of Chief Constable of the Wapentake of Buckrose.[2] The family lived in a solid, broad-fronted stone farmhouse, pleasantly situated, near the bottom of an incline leading to the gates of Howsham Hall, the family home of the Cholmleys, who owned much of the land in that area.[3] This beautiful Jacobean hall was clearly visible, some two hundred yards from the Hudsons' farmhouse; these surroundings together with his upbringing as a farmer's son may well have helped to predispose George Hudson towards the farming and land-owning interests he would support so vigorously and consistently in his maturity.[4] He was baptised and brought up in the Church of England and appears to have remained faithful to his early religious upbringing throughout his life.[5]

Both George's parents died when he was still very young; his mother (of consumption) in 1807 and his father the following year. His elder brothers took on the responsibility of running the farm. A turning point in the young George Hudson's life came when he was fourteen or fifteen. He left home for the nearest city, York, to be apprenticed to a linen draper in College Street. The reasons for his move, which must have cost a good

deal of money, are unclear. One of his biographers suggests that he may
have been escaping from the ignominy of siring an illegitimate child in the
village, although his early success raises the less dramatic possibility that
he may merely have been seen as better suited to the greater opportunities
presented by city life. He did have a wealthy relative in York, his greatuncle,
Matthew Bottrill, a gentleman of independent means who lived in Monkgate, not far from the draper's shop, and he may have helped to arrange,
and conceivably finance, the apprenticeship.

While George Hudson was living in Howsham, rural life was relatively
prosperous. In the late eighteenth century farm prices had been depressed
but, during the French Revolutionary and Napoleonic wars of 1792 until
1815, trade embargoes and sea blockades had cut off foreign imports and
raised the price of wheat. This increased the cost of living for consumers
as a whole, but brought 'bountiful profits' to farmers and landowners and
also raised employment levels on the farms.[6]

Trading conditions in York worsened after the end of the French wars,
particularly during the severe slump that began in 1819.[7] York had been
England's second city in Roman and medieval times and, although it had
lost much of its earlier importance, it still had a population of around
twenty thousand people. With its cathedral, assize courts and civic traditions,
it remained an important centre for its wealthy agricultural hinterland and
also enjoyed a good deal of fashionable and aristocratic patronage.[8]

Hudson's own apprenticeship proved a great success. The business had
been founded by William Bell and Hudson was apprenticed to his widow,
Rebecca Bell (née Nicholson). In her efforts to keep the business going she
looked for help to her younger sister, Elizabeth, and her brother Richard
Nicholson, who took over the running of the shop in September 1817. He
took in a partner, who left two years later, leaving him again as sole owner.
An obituary of Richard Nicholson said that he was 'not in business' but
'lived upon his fortune.' It is possible that his wealth and personal inclination
meant that he soon left the running of the shop largely to Hudson, who
had many good qualities as an apprentice, including 'application, good
conduct and perseverance'.[9]

As the end of his apprenticeship approached he was all for starting
out for London but was instead offered a share in the business. By an
indenture dated 17 February 1821, Nicholson and Hudson, who was not yet
twenty-one, agreed to become partners 'for the good opinion they entertain
of each other and for improving their estate by honest endeavours' for
twenty years from the start of that month. The partners in 'Nicholson and
Hudson' agreed to divide profits equally and also put together £6000 in
equal shares. It seems as though Hudson was able to find his share of

the money only with the help of his greatuncle Matthew Bottrill and Elizabeth Nicholson, to whom he had become engaged. The shop premises, at 10–12 College Street, though not large, were very favourably situated, close to the Minster and on the corner of busy Goodramgate.[10]

On 17 July 1821, Hudson married his partner's sister, Elizabeth Nicholson, who was five years his senior, and they set up home above the shop. Their first child, James Richard, was born in April 1822 but he was never very strong and died the following year. Their second child was born in 1824 and was named Richard Nicholson, after Hudson's brother-in-law.[11]

Nicholson and Hudson gradually took their business upmarket, turning it increasingly into a linen drapery and silk mercers that catered for the wealthy. This made good sense. Although York had an unusual number of retail outlets, trading conditions were 'generally pretty brisk' and this owed much to the number of genteel and opulent families in the city and its farming hinterland.[12] It was noted, when Hudson had first come to the business, that he went about with his mouth open in a 'very rustic' fashion, but he soon learnt to cultivate town manners. In fact, it was said that his agreeable personality and manners were a material help to the business as it grew and established its reputation amongst the well-to-do. Ladies of wealth and fashion from the city and county social circles became his customers. Rows of carriages could often be seen outside his establishment and, as the carriages arrived, he would be seen making low bows one after another as he escorted customers to the door. It was even said that he was so attentive to the ladies that 'he would have ransacked the place through before he would allow one to leave unserved, if it was only a purl of silk thread she might want, and bow her to her carriage with as much grace as if she had spent £100 at her visit. By such conduct he won their regard and secured their custom.' Other stories spoke of a sharper eye for trade, however; on one occasion, he apparently effected a sale to one rather difficult customer by calling her attention to the attractions of the 'same goods in their complementary shade'. When his assistant took the material away and immediately brought the same goods back, the lady was won over and bought accordingly.[13]

By a variety of means, the three of them were certainly able to make a comfortable living and, late in life, Hudson was inclined to look back nostalgically on this as the happiest time of his life. It was not this modest, steady success, however, that turned his life in new directions. Matthew Bottrill died on 25 May 1827 and, after various specific bequests to a dozen relatives and friends to a total value of about £4000, bequeathed the bulk of his estate to Hudson, who was also appointed sole executor. The fact that closer relations than Hudson had been largely overlooked in the will, which had been revised as recently as 21 April 1827, led to suggestions that

Hudson had improperly pressed his claims on his greatuncle.[14] There is no real evidence to support this suggestion, although it was still being made as late as 1845 when he fought his first parliamentary election. The generosity of the settlement may well merely reflect the sympathy between the young man and his childless relative. This is a pattern familiar enough to readers of nineteenth-century novels: the young man with 'great expectations' of a wealthy kinsman assiduously attending his death-bed and receiving a handsome bequest. It was a stock situation in fiction and must have been common enough in fact.

The value of the chattels that were left to Hudson has been estimated at around £30,000 and the true value of the inheritance would have been materially higher, once the value of several pieces of freehold land are also taken into account.[15] Whatever the exact figure, Matthew Bottrill's death certainly transformed the lives of the Hudson family. George and Elizabeth left their rooms above the shop in College Street and moved into Bottrill's old house, at 44 Monkgate, York. The house, built in 1723, had three stories and attics and was fronted in brown brick with red dressings. It was spacious and grand, with high ceilings, a wide curved staircase with iron balustrades built around an open well and large windows, in a street that was being 'increasingly used for residential purposes by the wealthier citizens'.[16] Hudson also bought the house next door, 42 Monkgate, initially for the use of his brother-in-law, although later the two houses were knocked through internally to provide more space for the Hudsons. Eventually this provided them with, on the ground floor, an entrance hall, breakfast room, study and rooms for their housekeeper, butler and servants; on the first floor a suite of four drawing rooms, a dining room with adjoining butler's room, two bedrooms and a dressing room; on the second floor, seven bedrooms, three dressing rooms, a bathroom with hot and cold water and two water closets. The attics above also contained further accommodation for the servants, while the large rear garden held three coach-houses that provided stabling for eight horses.[17]

The Hudsons also completed their family in the next few years. Their third child was born in 1827 and named Matthew Bottrill, after their generous great-uncle, but he died within a few months, like their first child, James. After this, they were more fortunate and had four further children, each of whom reached adulthood. George was born in 1829, Ann Elizabeth two years later, John in 1832 and finally William in 1834, although their eldest surviving child, Richard died that same year, aged only nine.

With the improvement in his material circumstances, George Hudson's interests broadened and he soon became active in the public and political life of his adopted city. He was to have a controversial public life and face many criticisms but he could not be accused of 'trimming' or of tailoring his beliefs and values to suit his opportunities; his political convictions did not waver, even when they did nothing to help his material advancement.[18]

Politically, the times were divisive, if not potentially explosive. Britain had emerged from French wars as a world power of almost unchallengeable standing. Steam power was coming to the new manufacturing towns, which were growing at an unprecedented rate. Agriculture suffered considerably from falling prices and did not benefit from the real growth in wealth that took place with the ending of wartime restrictions and taxes, although it was still protected by the 'Corn Laws' which levied heavy tariffs on imported wheat.[19]

Although much wealth was being generated, there was growing disquiet at the way the benefits of Britain's greatness were being shared amongst its populace, particularly among those living in the industrialised urban areas. As a result, the first ten years after Waterloo are best known for a rise in social unrest and popular agitation to levels that had not been known for many years.[20] Rioting over wage levels and food shortages was particularly common in the period 1816–20 and, more generally, there was labour unrest on a frightening scale.[21] This disturbed the confidence of even the ruling elite, who had grown used to presiding over a corrupt and acquiescent political system without the representation of even the middle classes, let alone the newly assertive industrial workers. Demands for reform were met with repression by the authorities, most notoriously in the Peterloo massacre in Manchester in August 1819. Social unrest was moderated by the economic upturn that began in 1820, but returned anew in the later part of the decade.

Reforms, long resisted during the war years, were now agitated for on many fronts. There were demands for factory legislation (particularly on child labour), for the abolition of slavery in the colonies, for the removal of civil disabilities on Catholics, and for the reform of a grotesque political system which gave representation to a depopulated village like Old Sarum, but none to important industrial towns such as Manchester, Birmingham and Leeds.

The Tories, in power almost uninterruptedly since 1783, now began to disintegrate in the face of these pressures. In 1827, as Hudson was receiving his bequest, there were sudden changes at the head of government. Lord Liverpool (Prime Minister since 1812) resigned after a stroke in February. His successor, the Foreign Secretary George Canning, was regarded as too liberal (particularly on catholic emancipation) by Ultra and High Tories such as the Duke of Wellington and Robert Peel, who resigned from the

Cabinet. Canning died in August, his successor Lord Goderich lasted only a few months, and in January 1828 the King turned to Wellington. Ironically, Wellington rapidly became convinced that resistance to catholic emancipation would lead to insurrection in Ireland, and pushed the necessary legislation through Parliament, enraging the Ultras, whose leader he had been.

In June 1830, the death of King George IV precipitated a general election. The timing could hardly have been worse for the Wellington administration; there were deep divisions within the Tory party and the next ten or twelve years were to be among the most politically charged and socially disturbed in British history.[22]

Where elections were contested (and only a minority of seats were) parliamentary reform was the issue on which they were fought. The July Revolution in Paris, which removed the last Bourbon King of France, Charles X just a few days before polling, increased expectations of political change. In the autumn, large-scale unrest in agricultural districts of southern England further undermined the prestige of the régime. There was now a widespread expectation that some measure of parliamentary reform would be introduced, but Wellington, perhaps mindful of his retreat over catholic emancipation, tried to bury the issue in November by announcing that he was opposed to any alteration in the constitution. He miscalculated; within a fortnight his government had resigned and the new King, William IV, turned to the Whig leader Earl Grey, who made a Reform Act a condition of his acceptance of office.

In York, for many years the Whigs had successfully controlled the closed, self-elected corporation, with the aid of considerable patronage from the local Fitzwilliam family.[23] As far as parliamentary elections were concerned, the situation was more complicated; the Whigs had far more political influence but the Tories had more money, which could be translated into political votes through the well-established system of payments to the city's freemen, who had the vote but were not often wealthy. As a result, the city's two seats were normally shared between the Whigs and the Tories.[24]

In York, the Whigs put up Thomas Dundas, who had represented York for the last six years and was linked by marriage to the Fitzwilliams, and Edward Petre, the Roman Catholic Lord Mayor of York and High Sheriff of the County, who came from a leading landed family. On 28 June 1830, the Tories put forward Samuel Bayntun, who was a captain in the Life Guards and closely connected with leading Tory families. He stood as an 'Ultra Tory' candidate opposed to further concessions to Catholics.[25]

George Hudson was one of the group that guided Bayntun's campaign.[26] Whereas the Whigs did not place much emphasis on outward show, the Tories provided a spectacle that was exhilarating and imposing and seemed to have a great effect on the minds of the people. Bayntun's supporters marched about the city with banners and a double band, one of bugles and clarinets and the other fifes and drums. As well as the band and the colours, Bayntun himself headed the procession to the hustings on horseback, dressed in black and wearing an enormous cocked hat. When it came to the efforts of the candidates to bring their voters to the poll, Bayntun's tactics were 'somewhat military', with the *reveille* beaten every morning at eight a.m., but the campaign was widely seen as the most effective York's Tories had ever conducted. Visits were made to every village, canvassing was carried out even on Sundays and the non-resident freemen voters were collected from Leeds, Manchester, Hull and even London.[27]

Bayntun did not attack Petre for being a Catholic, but his supporters certainly did. The degree of hostility they showed towards catholicism may not have been pleasant or tolerant, but it was consistent with the core values of the 'Ultras' and also well suited to the local contest. There were five days of polling and, when the result was declared on 3 August 1830, Bayntun topped the poll with 1928 votes, Dundas took the second seat with 1907 votes, and Petre came only third (with 1793 votes). Hudson was widely seen as the shaping hand behind a Tory campaign conducted with great skill and an astute sense of the dramatic.[28]

The period from late 1830 until the passage of the great Reform Act of 1832 was one of extraordinary turbulence and controversy. The first Reform Bill was introduced by Lord John Russell on 1 March 1831. It passed its second reading by one vote, with Bayntun amongst the majority. Then the government was defeated on 19 April 1831 and a general election called. York was seen as a centre of support for parliamentary reform and both the sitting members, Dundas and Bayntun, put themselves forward as 'strenuous supporters of the reform bill'. Given his voting record, Bayntun was far from popular with Hudson and the other leading Tory 'Ultras' but he was so popular with the electorate that his position was unassailable. The two parties accordingly arrived at a compromise that would save the considerable costs of polling and the two sitting members were returned unopposed, in a 'carnival atmosphere of processions, music, church bells and banners'.[29]

The Whigs now had a majority of over a hundred seats and the Second Reform Bill was expected to pass through Parliament but, on 8 October, the Lords rejected it. At this there were protest meetings everywhere and full-scale riots in some cities; buildings were burned in Bristol and Nottingham and unofficial militia formed in various parts of the north. The Third Reform Bill was introduced in December 1831, incorporating amendments that retained the voting rights of freemen, to the satisfaction of the York Tories. In March 1832, this Bill passed the Commons but was then obstructed by the Lords. Grey demanded an assurance from the King that he would create sufficient new peers to ensure the Bill's passage, and on his refusal, resigned on 9 May 1832.

Everywhere, there were rowdy public meetings and demonstrations. In York, on 16 May a large meeting organised by the Whigs gathered at the Guildhall while, at the same time, the Tories held their own 'hole and corner' meeting at the George Inn. Hudson, now a leading member of the High Tory faction, had organised the meeting at which he also made his first major public speech. Whereas the Guildhall meeting was plain-spoken in the extreme, the speeches of Hudson and other Tories were far more carefully measured, as the party wished to give some appearance of support for reforms that they really hoped to constrain as much as possible. Hudson tried to achieve this by saying that he had no objection to reform, but he thought it should be 'carried and obtained in a constitutional way, and not by inundating the House of Lords with mere delegates'. What he meant by constitutional was not spelt out.

Real reformers were now past caring about such niceties. When the Guildhall meeting ended, around two thousand people went on to the George Inn and tried to storm the Tories' meeting, forcing Hudson and his colleagues to flee from the back of the building by boat. Several days of riots followed, the most violent in the history of York. The house of the archbishop, who was known to oppose the reform movement, was stoned and the crowd dispersed only after the arrival of troops with swords drawn. The homes of several leading Tories also had to be barricaded and protected by special constables for several days.[30]

After Grey's resignation, the King turned to Wellington, who thought, briefly, he might push through a measure of reform more moderate than Grey's but, given the state of public opinion, a Wellington government was impossible. Within a week, Grey was back in office with a pledge from the King to create as many peers as necessary to pass the Bill. Faced with this, about a hundred Tory peers absented themselves from the House of Lords during the third reading of the Third Reform Bill, which became law in June 1832 without the need to create large numbers of Whig peers.

The Reform Act had caused great excitement in York and, just as things were calming down again, the city was visited by an even more serious cause of distress. Warnings about the dangers of cholera had been appearing in the local press since September 1830 and a board of health for the city had been established in November of that year. In York, despite its relative prosperity, standards of sanitation in several of the poorer areas in the old city centre were very bad, even by the standards of the early nineteenth century and the pouring of 'effluvia' into open drains was a common practice that posed the most serious threats to the public health.[31]

On 9 June 1832, the *York Herald* announced that the 'Pestilence of India' had silently entered the city. It had been reported as close by as Hull, Goole and Leeds and was thought to have been brought to the city by 'ragged beggarly gentlefolk' visiting the local races. On 3 June a waterman of 'very irregular habits', living in an area of town known as 'Hagworm's Nest', became the first official cholera victim in York.[32] Quicklime was thrown into the city's drains and people were forbidden to take corpses to church; instead the Board of Health would wrap the bodies in cloth, saturated in pitch and give them a free, open air funeral.

Hudson had been seconded to the Board of Health in April 1832, along with the prominent Quakers Samuel Tuke and Joseph Rowntree. During the cholera attack that ravaged the city until October 1832, killing nearly two hundred people, he was highly active, visiting the sick and dying and helping to distribute food, clothing and blankets to the needy. The disease was rampant in the poorest parts of the city, though the better off were not exempt; among the early victims was the sister-in-law of the editor of the *Yorkshire Gazette*.[33]

Surprisingly, the outbreak became the subject of a major political row that was to greatly advance Hudson's political standing in the city. In June 1832, the corporation had set aside a new burial ground in Thief Lane for the interment of cholera victims and the council's representatives assured the families of those concerned that this was a permanent arrangement. In July, however, the full corporation decided that the land could be so designated for only a twenty-year period and, on 23 July, at a meeting of the board of health, Hudson, with the full support of those present, bitterly attacked the corporation for their meanness and insensitivity to the feelings of the bereaved. After several attempts to evade the issue, at which Hudson clashed with the Dean of York, the corporation gave way a few weeks later. Hudson, who had taken a straightforward and highly moral approach to the issue throughout the dispute, found that his steadfastness had made his name amongst the members of the local Tory party.[34]

There were further Parliamentary elections in York in late 1832 and in 1833. In December 1832, a general election was held under the rules established by the Reform Act. York still returned two MPs, and the voting rights of freemen had given York an unusually broad franchise, so that the broadening of the electorate by the introduction of a standard property qualification was less marked than in many constituencies. Moreover, many among the local electorate were not well off and were as susceptible to bribery as before.

Now that parliamentary reform was settled for the time being, the York Tories could more openly air their concerns over Bayntun, who was too liberal and reformist for their liking. Hudson was among the leading members of the party who met again at the George to see if they could find another candidate.

A committee of six, including Hudson, was deputed to see John Henry Lowther, who was well connected with a number of the leading Tory families. His mother was a daughter of the Earl of Westmorland and his father was Sir John Lowther, Bart, of Swillington Park, near Wakefield. He also had considerable parliamentary experience, having been MP for Wigton and then Cockermouth for nearly twenty years and had a record of opposition to most reformist proposals, particularly concerning Catholicism. He was delighted at being asked to stand and was quickly adopted. There was some expectation on the part of the Tories that Bayntun might not stand again, because of a lack of money, but in fact he did with his credibility as a reformer greatly enhanced by his rejection at the hands of the 'Blue Junta from the George'.

The election was a hostile affair. The Tories attempted to project Lowther as a moderate reformer and made much of his long-standing opposition to slavery and of his support for factory legislation. His speeches now began to sound relatively liberal, although his aristocratic background and track record as an MP suggested to many that he was a 'wolf in sheep's clothing'.[35] Whatever the exact nature of his politics, he was soon accused of bribery and of 'shamelessly intimidating' tradesmen into both voting for him and making sure that their employees did the same.

The Whigs themselves, however, could make no claim to a simple monopoly of political virtue. Lowther was subjected to physical intimidation, his committee rooms were stoned and the members of his committee, including Hudson, were violently attacked even on their way from the George Inn to the hustings. On arrival, Hudson seconded Lowther's formal nomination but most of his speech was drowned by a 'disgraceful uproar'. Polling started on 11 December 1832 and there were further attacks on Lowther's committee rooms and on several Tory public houses. Special constables had to be sworn in and Lowther reluctantly decided that it was simply too dangerous to speak in public again. Not surprisingly, the Tory campaign was not successful. Despite accusations that they had 'spent money like water' to buy votes, Lowther finished a poor third to Petre and Bayntun and only slightly ahead of Dundas.[36]

There was to be an unexpectedly tragic sequel. Bayntun, although only in his twenties, died from scarlet fever in October 1833 and another poll was needed. Lowther, who lacked credibility as a reformer, was still unpopular and at first refused to stand. Finally, he was persuaded to do so by Hudson and his colleagues but to no avail; Dundas won the contest comprehensively by 1337 votes to 846.

In 1833–34 the Tories national position strengthened considerably. They had now accepted the inevitable and ended their resistance to the principles of reform, most notably in Peel's 'Tamworth Manifesto'. The Whigs lost popularity as their great Reform Act became an accepted feature of the political landscape, while their subsequent reforms tended to create enemies. The ability of the 1833 Factory Act to pass the Commons, for example, and overcome the opposition from Whig manufacturers and laissez-faire economists relied upon an unlikely but revealing alliance between radicals and Tory landowners. The Poor Law of 1834 was opposed by many Tories, and hated by the working class.[37]

In November 1834, when the Whig Prime Minister Melbourne resigned, William IV asked Peel to form a minority administration and Parliament was dissolved. In the ensuing election campaign, Lowther, as the only Tory candidate in York, was able to claim that 'we are all reformers now' without much loss of credibility. He was also helped by the disarray in the opposition's ranks. It took the Whigs a long time to realise that Petre's lack of participation in the proceedings at Westminster had seriously damaged his prospects of re-election; he was belatedly withdrawn after earlier initial announcements that he would stand.[38] C. F. Barkley had been put forward to represent the Whig's radical wing and he was eventually joined by John Dundas, the younger brother of Thomas Dundas who had moved on to contest another parliamentary seat. The nominations took place on 5 January 1835 and the poll began the next day. The contest was far more orderly and better tempered than those in the recent past. Hudson was again in charge of Lowther's campaign and the canvass was carried on with 'great spirit', with bands parading the city and an absence of personal rancour. It was soon clear that the Tories had again managed their campaign with great skill, but it was a major surprise and something of a triumph for Lowther when he topped the poll.[39]

Politics in the 1830s was a highly contentious process in which opposition was loudly and uncompromisingly expressed. Poverty was real and a serious problem and political policies often posed threats to the basic wellbeing of the populace at the same time as they raised important issues of principle. Unpopular candidates could expect to be actively heckled and have their

speeches drowned out by those who disagreed. Mob attacks on opponents
were an occasional feature of the political landscape while the bribery and
intimidation of voters was commonplace, particularly since voters were
required to state their preferences out loud.[40] Newspapers were often highly
partisan and inclined to make colourful accusations about the behaviour
and motives of their opponents, while it was not at all unusual for the
supporters of beaten candidates to complain that the victors had resorted
to bribery and the treating of voters.

After Lowther's unexpected victory, the accusations took on a more
serious tone than usual. Several local papers voiced their belief that his
election had only been brought about by organised bribery involving
Hudson, the treasurer of the local Tory party.[41] The pro-Whig *Yorkshireman*
went furthest and claimed that 'never in the annals of electioneering, did
the votaries of drunkenness, bribery and treating hold up their hands and
stalk through our streets with more effrontery and less shame' than they
had in York earlier that month. Both Dundas, who had been elected, and
Barkley, who had not, claimed that large numbers of people who had
promised to support them had instead voted for Lowther, which they could
only attribute to organised bribery by their opponents.[42] Finally, Barkley
and some of his more radical friends were known to be giving serious
thought to petitioning Parliament on the grounds that Lowther's election
had only been gained by Tory corruption, involving bribery, treating and
other illegal practices.

The chairman of the Tories, Thomas Bairstow was not unduly concerned
and responded by pointing out that at least the Tories had not stooped to
the impersonation of the dead. Many establishment Whigs were also uneasy
at the idea of petitioning Parliament; this was an expensive undertaking
which could unseat Dundas. Barkley was eventually persuaded to drop the
idea. At this, the Tories assumed that the threat was passed and settled up
with many of their supporters by sending sovereigns openly through the
post, instead of making the payments in person to their supporters at their
local pubs and inns.[43]

This was too provocative to Barkley and his friends and, on 30 June
1835, a petition was presented to the House of Commons, complaining 'of
the greatest bribery and corruption' by the Tories and of 'vast numbers
of the voters going to the poll in a state of the most disgusting intoxication'.
Omnibuses were said to have run through the town to take voters to the
poll, each receiving 'a sovereign inside the omnibus and sometimes a couple'.
Finally, it was alleged that several hundred letters had been sent through
the post to voters, each containing a sovereign. Parliament decided that
there was some substance in the complaints and decided to investigate

electoral practices at York and in another constituency by means of a select committee.[44]

Hudson and the Tory agent, his close friend and solicitor, James Richardson, were questioned in London several times in July and August 1835. Hudson was unable to produce the party's election accounts when asked, and refused to answer some questions on the grounds that he might incriminate himself. He had been regularly described in some York newspapers as the Tories' 'briber-in-chief' but, when the select committee reported in September 1835, they placed recent events in the city in a broader context that did not cast any particular opprobrium on Hudson. They found that the payment of gratuities by recently returned Members of Parliament to supporters from the 'poorer class of freemen' had been going on for a very long time, perhaps sixty years. The rates of payment had become standardised and, since 1807, two guineas had normally been paid to every freeman who had voted and who wanted to be paid the benefit known as 'the guineas'.[45] Moreover, prior to elections, it had been customary for poorer freemen to be retained as messengers, or runners and paid 5s. a day without prejudice to their receipt of 'the guineas', although this practice was discontinued in 1830, when Lord Althorp's Act forbade people so employed from voting.

Under the exceptional circumstances of 1832, when the reform proposals had so raised the public mood, the freemen had been perfectly willing to vote without payment for two of the candidates, Dundas and Bayntun, even though the other two candidates had made the usual payments.[46] After the 1832 election, Lowther's committee had departed from normal practice and paid not only one sovereign to those who had given their candidate one vote but also three to those who had voted for him alone, spending about a thousand pounds in the process. Petre's principal agent had also made payments to voters. Moreover, the Whigs had resorted to a 'system of intimidation wholly inconsistent with freedom of election', involving forcible entry into Lowther's committee rooms, the display of firearms, serious threats to Lowther's personal safety and an aggravated assault on one of his supporters.[47]

In 1833 no illegal expenditures appeared to have taken place and in 1835 there was no evidence that 'unusual drunkenness' had prevailed, although it was apparent that some voters were conveyed to the polling booths in a state of intoxication. The committee found that several hundred letters had indeed been sent through the post to Lowther's supporters, many containing sovereigns, but the backers of John Dundas were also 'implicated in illegal pecuniary transactions' involving nearly four hundred voters.

While the combined effects were 'highly subversive of the correct expression of public opinion', the select committee were of the view that no further actions were needed. It was also their judgement that, if two equally ambitious candidates presented themselves at York, one of whom made the traditional payments and the other did not, an 'unfair advantage' would accrue to the former, which would probably decide the election.[48] Clearly, given the level of poverty amongst the freemen of York, little would change until the introduction of the secret ballot.

The great Reform Act of 1832 had had relatively little effect on York's parliamentary representation but the seemingly more modest Municipal Corporations Act of 1835 brought major changes to local representation that were to prove important to Hudson's career.

The city had been governed under a charter granted by Henry VIII in 1518, which gave representatives of the crafts of merchants the power to form a common council that would assist the Lord Mayor, aldermen and sheriffs. The charter was modified in 1633, with the members instead elected on a geographical basis, and again in 1663, when the outside election of the common councilmen was abolished. The corporation now became closed in form, with power residing in the hands of the mayor and aldermen, 'chosen out of the wealthier class of citizens, or from the list of those who had served the office of sheriff' by their peers for life.[49]

The Act of 1835 put an end to self-elected or 'closed' corporations, giving voting rights for municipal elections to ratepayers with three years residence. This was a moderately radical measure that enfranchised only about a tenth of the adult male population. Nationally, it benefited the Whigs far more than the Tories but in York it brought competition over the membership of a body that the Whigs had controlled for many years. The new structure extended the four ancient wards to six, each to be represented by six elected councillors, one third of whom were to retire each year, once certain transitional arrangements had been concluded. The council would then consist of thirty-six elected councillors and twelve aldermen, the latter being elected by the councillors themselves to hold office for six years. The Act also abolished the exclusive right of trading by freemen, removing the corporation's power to 'mulct non-freemen for daring to trade in the city' and thereby liberalised trading arrangements within the city.[50]

In York, while 'the distinctions of blue and orange [were] carried ... into every transaction of business and even pleasure', this had not disturbed a longstanding Whig domination of the local municipality.[51] Although the new arrangements were bound to be less predictable, no one really expected a change in power. For the first election under the new procedures, the Whigs showed the grandeur to be expected of a natural governing party and suggested that party loyalties should be forgotten, so that the most able and public-spirited candidates could be voted in as councillors. Publicly, the Tories did not oppose this concordat but, in reality, under Hudson's able management, they worked assiduously at their new opportunity. Although the Whigs duly won the elections in November 1835, it was by only twenty-one seats to fifteen. Hudson was elected with the third highest vote in the Monk ward, which returned both Tories and Whigs.

The Whigs continued to show some magnanimity over the election of aldermen and two of the twelve that were chosen were Tories, including Hudson, who was clearly seen as a man of ability with the city's interests at heart. Some of the aldermen were already councillors and, in the consequent by-elections, the Whigs were entirely relaxed. By contrast, the Tory campaign under Hudson was carefully and efficiently organised and the Tories were able to tie the councillor representation at eighteen apiece.[52]

This gave them good representation on a number of important committees. Hudson was on the all-important finance committee, where he placed great emphasis on reducing expenditure. During the next year it became apparent that municipal politics in York would in future be far more fiercely fought out than before. When further council elections were held as part of the transitional arrangements for the new system in November 1836, fourteen seats were contested. The Tories won eight to obtain a bare (nineteen to seventeen) majority of the elected seats.[53] The Whigs still had a majority of the council seats as a whole, because of the way the aldermen had been chosen, but the Tories were now able to make a great deal of their under representation relative to the popular vote.

Before the next municipal elections, on 20 June 1837 William IV died, precipitating yet another general election. By now a period of good harvests, booming trade and relatively high employment had come to an end and the economy was heading for a five year period of depression that would bring industry, particularly in the nearby West Riding's wool trade, to a standstill and raise unemployment to hitherto unknown levels.[54] The Whig government was on the defensive over their approach to the Poor Laws and disillusionment with them was widespread.

In York, the political temperature was still high. Hudson and Richardson, after their ordeal at the hands of the Select Committee were thoroughly hostile towards Barkley, over his petitioning of Parliament. Barkley, for his part, described James Richardson as ignorant and illiterate and George Hudson as having 'the most elastic conscience of any man in the Empire'![55] The Tories were on the up and decided to contest both the York city seats, although Hudson was known to be unenthusiastic about this. There was a feeling amongst some of the senior political figures in the city that the interests of the York and North Midland Railway would be best served by having an MP from both parties and this was how things turned out in the poll held on 25 July 1837: Lowther again came top, with 1461 votes, with Dundas securing the second seat for the Whigs (with 1276 votes). The Tory barrister, David Atcherley, came only third (on 1180 votes) and felt so poorly supported by the party that he obtained undertakings of better support in the future that were to have a considerable effect on Hudson's own political career.[56]

At the third municipal elections, held in November 1837, the Tories won three seats from the Whigs and obtained a majority on York Council.[57] This precipitated a distinct change in the mood of politics in the city. The Whigs were rancorous over their fall from power and were in no doubt that Hudson was the primary cause of their downfall. The *Yorkshireman*, while making it clear that with Mr Hudson as a private individual they had 'no fault to find [and] had no objection that he should possess the civic honours of York', thought it a 'thing most monstrous' that Hudson and his fellow Tories should have seized control of the municipality. They were equally critical of the 'drowsy Whigs' who had been so easily 'hoodwinked by the Tories and [so] fascinated by their blandness of manner' as to allow the delivery of the 'ancient Whig city of York ... bound hand and foot to the Tories'.[58]

The Tories immediately packed the important committees, particularly finance, with their own members. Their expected nominee as Lord Mayor, the relatively consensual John Wolstenholme, was not put forward when the new council met for the first time but, instead, Hudson was named as the party's unanimous choice, although he was still only thirty-eight.

George Hudson succeeded James Meek, his colleague on the York and North Midland Railway, as Lord Mayor. Meek was a devout Methodist and, despite owning one of the city's largest businesses, practised a very austere public and private life. Hudson was to discharge his office in a very different manner. He and his wife, in that first year of Tory municipal control, entertained on a scale that had no precedent. Politically, Hudson was in favour of 'public parsimony' as far as the council's spending was concerned, but there was no hypocrisy in this attitude; at that time, whereas the council spent municipal money, a Lord Mayor had to use his own funds for hospitality, a major reason why the office was often shunned, rather than sought after.[59]

During his first year as Lord Mayor, Hudson was fully prepared to spend his own money in order to enhance his reputation and prestige. To many he seemed determined almost to 'feast his way into the hearts of his fellow-citizens', as spectacular social events followed one another thick and fast.[60] In December 1837, nearly a thousand guests attended a ball at the Mansion House, although times were bad in the city with building trade workers laid off for several weeks because of the bad weather.[61] In March 1838, a ball for eight hundred at the Mansion House and a banquet at the Guildhall followed, an occasion described by the local press as providing the 'most splendid entertainment' ever seen in the city; the banquet including a brilliant design in gaslight up under the roof in which a large imperial crown was displayed, with the letters 'VR' shown in characters some three feet high. The Mansion House was illuminated by gaslight on the Queen's birthday on 24 May 1838, a spectacle provided by the York Union Gas Light Company which Hudson and others had formed two years before. The coronation in June 1838 was celebrated with a civic procession and a huge feast with free tickets for needy inhabitants and, towards the end of his year, there was a lavish banquet for the Archbishop of York in September 1838 and a ball in October 1838 in honour of the York Hussars. York had seen nothing like it before.

At the council meeting of 9 November 1838, immediately after the next round of municipal elections, Hudson was one of six aldermen whose term of office had ended and who were seeking renomination. This should have been a relatively routine matter (the Tories had increased their majority) but Hudson's vaulting ambitions and desire for public glory made it instead extraordinary. The normal order of proceedings was to elect the Lord Mayor, then the aldermen and then to move on to other business. On this occasion, however, Hudson from the chair announced that the election of the aldermen would *precede* the selection of the new Lord Mayor. When this was questioned, he explained that this was entirely proper procedure as far as the famous lawyer Sir Frederick Pollock was concerned. He also received the support of the Town Clerk, Robert Davies, who, although a Whig appointee was to become one of Hudson's closest business allies.[62] Hudson went on to argue that the council would not be 'complete' until the aldermen had been elected, although other councillors maintained instead that precedent and the wording of the Municipal Reform Act made it quite clear that the first business of the council should be to elect its Lord Mayor.

Despite vehement protests, the Tories used their majority to force through the change in the normal order of procedure. Five of the chosen aldermen were Tories, including Hudson, but the purpose of the manoeuvre had nothing to do with voting powers, as the Tories already had a clear majority. The Liberal solicitor George Leeman was first to understand the reason: Hudson wanted to be Lord Mayor for a second consecutive year, which would not have been possible unless he had first been re-elected as an alderman. Leeman was equally aware that, whatever the arguments, the

Tories would force and win the vote. After the voting in of the new aldermen, George Hudson was indeed elected for a second term as Lord Mayor. He did his best to say the right things, claiming that he was not interested in power and had acted out of 'nothing but a sense of duty', but no one was taken in. The more far-sighted might have even seen that he would then be Lord Mayor and also Chairman of the York and North Midland Railway when their new line opened, a conjunction that would enable him to signal all too clearly his standing as York's most influential and prestigious citizen.

The Liberals (as they were more often now styling themselves) were predictably outraged by these manoeuvres. In January 1839 they went ahead with a challenge in the courts to the legality of Hudson's appointment. They failed to obtain a temporary or restraining order but did win a judgement that the election of George Hudson as Mayor was an 'illegal act', but not until May 1840, six months *after* the end of Hudson's second period of office as Mayor.

Hudson certainly enjoyed the most ostentatious of celebrations when the first section of the York and North Midland's line was opened in May 1839 but, towards the end of his second year in office, the discharge of his duties became so obviously partisan as to cause him some political damage. He took a highly partial and excessive interest in the suitability of candidates for the posts of local schoolmaster and keeper of the city's concert room and also presided over a revision of the voting lists at which the overwhelming majority of Tory objections were upheld and nearly all the Liberal objections rejected.[63]

When his second term of office as Lord Mayor came to an end in November 1839 the Tories proposed a vote of thanks on the grounds that, although Hudson was a 'strong party man', no one had done more for the city. In particular, they thought the munificence and glories witnessed in the previous two years would do much to restore York to its former standing.

Some Liberals fiercely opposed this, however, and objected to the fact that, as a 'thorough party man he could not help considering every political opponent a personal enemy and [that] his rank, influence and money had been generally used to crush those who entertained sentiments contrary to his own'. Several senior Liberals complained that they had never even been invited to the lavish Mansion House parties and Alderman Wilson protested at the way he had been made to suffer throughout the year from Hudson's 'vitriolic tongue', taunts and insulting language. The most bitter attack came from the leading Liberal, George Leeman, who gave full expression to the 'delight of his constituents that Hudson was now leaving office'.[64]

Other councillors, however, were outraged at Leeman's remarks, which they considered quite unjustified and a spiteful response to Hudson's success in having 'conservatized the whole city'. He had clearly been a determined and adversarial leader of his political group and some of the discord was doubtless caused by his difficult personality, yet a good deal of the conflict also stemmed from the failure of the Liberals to come to terms with their own waning influence. Further, criticisms of Hudson for linking the interests of the city and its first railway too closely seemed less convincing from a party that had itself enjoyed the long patronage of the Fitzwilliam family. Hudson listened quietly until the formal vote of thanks was passed by a large majority, but with thirteen votes against, and then delivered a characteristically scornful and indignant response.[65]

Hudson was easily provoked, particularly it seems when he had been drinking and this was becoming an increasing problem. In February 1840, for example, there were 'disgraceful scenes' at a public dinner, when Hudson quarrelled with C. H. Elsley, a prominent Liberal and the Recorder of York, over the right to reply to a toast as the senior alderman present. Elsley was as much to blame and clearly tried to provoke Hudson, making a slighting reference, 'men who get their living by the yard-wand', to his adversary's trade, but the evening's events, in which both men came close to blows and missiles were thrown by their supporters, did nothing to advance the reputation of either. The *York Courant* said that they had rarely if ever seen such scenes, even at electoral hustings. As Hudson became wealthier and more important, the more he resented references to his time in the drapery trade. In fact, a dislike or disdain for retailers appears to have been widespread at the time; Adam Smith, writing in the *Wealth of Nations*, noted the existence of a distinct prejudice among political writers against shopkeepers and tradesmen, which he predictably found 'altogether without foundation'.[66]

The electorate, in contrast, probably regretted the end of the unusually lavish standards of public hospitality and celebration that Hudson had instituted and his successor as Lord Mayor, William Clark, proposed that a public subscription be raised to provide a suitable testimonial. The council was in unanimous agreement with this, despite past differences, and six hundred pounds was soon raised. On 20 July 1840, at a public dinner, a very fine piece of inscribed and ornamented silverware was presented to 'Mr Alderman Hudson, subscribed for by the nobility, gentry, clergy etc. as a testimonial of the subscribers' high sense of the manner in which for two years the worthy alderman discharged' his duties as Lord Mayor. Hudson was very pleased at being honoured in this way.[67]

Politics in York continued to be abrasive and Hudson was involved in several other stormy meetings of the council. The Liberals were increasingly convinced that he had become too self-important. In January 1841, Elsley, during a disagreement about the extent to which prison expenditures could be reduced without prejudice to safety, objected to Hudson's 'un-divided sovereignty and dominion over all ranks and denominations in the city of York'.[68] A month later, Hudson's perfunctory consultations with the council on behalf of the York and North Midland's proposal for a bridge over the Ouse were seen as inadequate and the proposals were sent down.[69]

In June 1841, Peel obtained the barest of majorities in the Commons on a vote of no confidence and a general election was called. In York, John Dundas retired in order to contest another seat and Henry Redhead Yorke stood as an ardent reformer and opponent of the Corn Laws. The Tories kept their promise to put forward both Lowther, whom Hudson formally proposed at the hustings in an excellent speech, and Atcherley, even though this denied Hudson the opportunity of standing.

The voting patterns were complex. Many Chartists and other radicals saw the Anti-Corn Law League slogan of 'cheap bread' as a mechanism used by Liberal manufacturers to lower the price of labour, and this led them into an unlikely alliance with the Protectionist Tories. At the poll on 29 June 1841, Lowther (1625 votes) and Yorke (1552) were elected, with Atcherley a close third (on 1456 votes). This time, it was the Tories turn to complain and Hudson claimed that their opponents had resorted to corruption and bribery 'of the most infamous kind'. The accusations had some credibility. While Yorke was enjoying a celebratory dinner in the White Swan, a large crowd had gathered outside openly demanding that they be 'settled', al-though complaints from Hudson about electoral malpractice could never be taken all that seriously, particularly in the light of counter-claims that the Tories had both bought votes and pressurised corporation tenants into voting for their candidates.[70]

The municipal elections of November 1841 changed little in York. The Tories had a control so secure that they could now afford to be seen as above narrow partisan politics. Accordingly, they took only four of the six available aldermanic seats, accepting the Liberal nominations of James Meek and Sir John Simpson.

Nationally, times were difficult. The trade depression reached its low point in 1842 with very high unemployment, particularly in the north of England.[71] The removal and reductions of a range of tax discouragements on trade in Peel's 1842 budget helped to end the slump but the treatment of landowners and farmers under the reintroduced Income Tax Acts was seen by many as harsh and Peel began to lose the support of some sections of his party.

Municipal politics in York were now quite subdued. Hudson was busy with his business activities although he did help to promote the construction of a new civic building, the De Grey Rooms, by public subscription.[72] The Lord Mayor, Matterson, who had strong Wesleyan sympathies, tried hard to reduce public activity on the Sabbath, closing bake-houses, groceries and other small businesses on that day. At the end of his term of office, he was congratulated primarily for his zealous attempts to promote better observance of the Lord's Day, a far cry from the heady days of Hudson's mayoralty.

Although Hudson was now less heavily involved in local politics (at least until the Corn Laws resurfaced in 1844 as a major electoral issue), he continued to take an active part in most of the important social events in York. He was invited to the annual conference of the British Association for the Advancement of Science, held in York in September 1844. At one of the sessions, Dr Cockburn, the Dean of York, read a paper critical of modern systems of geology, which provoked the response from Professor Adam Sedgwick, on behalf of modern geologists, that the Dean was not qualified to discuss the subject concerned, that he had been allowed to read his paper merely because of his 'rank and intellectual attainments' and that the association's object was the prosecution of science, not 'subjects connected with moral, religious and political truths'! A heated argument broke out again between Sedgwick and the Dean at dinner, which Hudson was hosting, but he stepped in as peacemaker and headed off an embarrassing scene, humorously quietening the disputants by informing them that he had 'talked the thing over with the Corporation and we've decided for Moses and the Dean'![73]

Although Hudson was increasingly preoccupied with his interests elsewhere, he did not retire from the council. When his term of office as an alderman ended in November 1844, he was immediately re-elected. His position on the council still had its uses; as he was aware, there was bound to come a time when it might help to keep the London and York Railway (alias the Great Northern), the greatest threat to his business interests, at bay. When the London and York approached the council in February 1845 with a plan to build a station in the city, he spoke out forcibly against the proposal, claiming that the proposed method of entry into the city, by a tunnel under the walls, would cause 'much wanton destruction' and that there was, in any case, no real need for a new route to London.

No one could have possibly believed that Hudson was really speaking in the dispassionate interests of his city and his position caused a good deal of controversy. Some local Liberals asserted that Tory councillors were merely acting as Hudson's minions and that their position was consistent only with the interests of the York and North Midland railway, not with those of the city. Peacock has argued that this was the point at which 'murmurings about Hudson's overpowering methods' as a municipal politician were first heard, but this probably gives too much credibility to Hudson's opponents, who had their own interests to serve. It is clear that the council as a whole decided to oppose the proposals, arguing that it was incumbent upon them to pay due attention to the fact that the citizens of York had invested more than two hundred and fifty thousand pounds in the York and North Midland and only thirty thousand pounds in the London and York. The vote on the London and York proposals of 25 to 4 also provided a majority that could hardly be attributed to Hudson's political influence, particularly since the four, James Meek, George Leeman, C. H. Elsley and Alderman Swann, were all investors in the London and York and Swann was a Tory.[74]

That year proved to be highly eventful for Hudson. The railway mania was in full swing and he was extremely busy with business promotions. On a related front, he was one of a number of prominent York businessmen who formed the York Stock Exchange, mainly, as with other provincial exchanges, in order to provide a ready market for railway shares. For some time Lowther had been expecting a peerage that would have released one of the parliamentary seats for York, for which Hudson would have been the obvious Tory candidate, but this had not happened by July 1845, when a vacancy occurred at Sunderland and Hudson became its MP. National politics were soon overshadowed by the horrors of the Irish potato famine, which led Peel, with the help of opposition votes, to repeal the Corn Laws and split the Tory Party. Hudson had always been a convinced protectionist, the policy that defended the interests of rural landowners. He also had hopes of high political office and his interest in York politics rapidly waned.

He continued to attend civic functions, however, despite his increasing commitments in London, and in October 1846 he was honoured by the Merchants Company of York at a public breakfast and presented with a 'massive and richly chased' silver box containing a copy of the oath of admission and bearing an inscription on the lid to 'George Hudson, MP as a mark of approval of his public conduct and of great respect for his private character'. In October, he was also guest of honour at Whitby Agricultural Society's annual dinner, where he had been frequently spoken of as a potential parliamentary candidate.

When York Council met in November 1846 after an uneventful round of municipal elections, there was surprise that Hudson was willing to be nominated for a third term as Lord Mayor. Not many people were prepared to take on the office and he was duly elected without great excitement or opposition. It soon became apparent that his reasons for standing related to his railway interests and social ambitions and that he did not always give municipal matters the attention he had in the past.

He proposed that a new road intended to open up the west front of the cathedral should be funded by means of a public subscription, which he offered to initiate with a donation of £500. This would leave the council the better able to pay their share of the cost of a new bridge over the Ouse at Lendal that had been first mooted in 1841. These proposals were sensible enough in themselves but Hudson's refusal properly to define the estimated costs or the proportion of the cost that would fall on the city, and the grandeur of his suggestion, that he would 'take care that the city would not suffer', drew widespread criticism.

It was clear that no council could function in this way. Hudson's position was hopelessly patrician and he soon accepted that not enough thought had been given to the matter, admitted the legitimacy of the objections and gave way. Despite this, Leeman and the other Liberals made every effort to inflict political damage on Hudson. Referring to Hudson's opposition to the London and York proposals the year before, they complained that York was now 'but an appendage of the York and North Midland Railway, including among its councillors not only the chairman and vice-chairman of the company, but also its solicitors, its official agents, its bankers and engineers'. Their accusation that the city was now 'little better than a pocket borough controlled by the "Railway King"' also began to gain some currency.[75]

Shortly before the end of his third year as Lord Mayor of York, in July 1847, Hudson was involved in some of the most controversial electoral procedures the city had ever seen. He had retained his own parliamentary seat at Sunderland and had been pleased to see his friend Robert Stephenson, also a staunch Tory and an ardent protectionist, whom he had recommended to Whitby, elected as their MP.[76] In York, Sir J. H. Lowther had already announced that he would be standing down as one of their MPs, amid widespread speculation that his support for Peel and opposition to Protectionism had alienated Hudson and the other leading York Tories. The *Yorkshireman* had long been extremely critical of Hudson and by now his patience was at an end; he made sure that no adverts for railway companies that he chaired, or for the York Union Bank, would appear in that paper. At a meeting of the Tory election committee, where only the *Yorkshire Gazette* was welcome, Hudson denied that he had pressurised Lowther or had even discussed protectionism and the Corn Laws with him. Instead, he maintained, he had strongly urged Lowther to stand again, until he was told that this was not possible given his state of health.[77]

There were further rumours that Hudson had come to an arrangement with the Liberals to the effect that their sitting member, Henry Redhead Yorke, and the Tories new nominee would both be returned unopposed.

There was nothing necessarily objectionable about this; in the past, the
parties had almost always had one MP each. The arrangement avoided
the substantial costs of polling, although it was highly unpopular with the
freemen who would not receive their 'guineas'. Whether or not any understandings had been reached, by the time of the hustings it seemed clear
that John Smyth of Heath Hall, Wakefield, would be the only Tory candidate
and Yorke the sole Liberal representative, avoiding the need for any poll.

At the hustings, before a crowd of about seven thousand, Hudson personally nominated Smyth, although as Lord Mayor he might have been
expected to appear to remain outside and above the divisive aspects of local
party politics. This was no doubt the straightforward approach to adopt,
as everyone knew Hudson dominated the local Tory party, but it was not
well judged. There was immediate uproar, as it seemed to confirm rumours
that a deal had been struck between the two parties that would deprive
voting freemen of their 'guineas'. Hudson denied 'doing anything to forfeit
the respect which had previously been shown to him', but he was fiercely
jeered and hissed and needed police protection from the crowd, despite the
fact that some three hundred York and North Midland workmen had
'marched en masse to the hustings to support Smyth'.[78]

Events then took a most unexpected turn. Frederick Hopwood, a radical
Chartist and F. E. Williamson, a local schoolmaster, surprised everybody by
putting forward Lowther's name as another candidate, although it was not
clear whether Lowther was prepared to stand. At this there was tremendous
cheering. The Sheriff, G. T. Andrews, asked Lowther's proposers if they
would pay the costs of going to a poll, which they were not able to do.
Hopwood instead offered to guarantee the amount but neither he nor
Williamson were believed to be sufficiently wealthy for this to be a meaning-
ful offer. Significantly, none of Lowther's other friends spoke up at this
point. Smyth and Yorke had each already deposited two hundred pounds
and the Sheriff (who appeared to consult Hudson as Lord Mayor) gave
Hopwood and Williamson short shrift; five minutes to produce the necessary
money. When the time was up, Hudson as the returning officer declared
Yorke and Smyth duly elected, amid scenes of great indignation.[79]

Hudson's and Andrews' parts in this farcical contest were widely condemned and the city's Liberals, including George Leeman and John
Duncan, editor of the *Yorkshireman*, pilloried Hudson for his actions. In
fact, in many ways it was they who were acting out a political charade.
Lowther had consistently denied that he was standing; during and after the
hustings none of his friends announced any change in his position and if
he was planning to stand, he would hardly have arranged being proposed by a radical Chartist. Hudson's view seems to have been that

Hopwood was merely trying to embarrass him over Lowther's absence from the contest and he was probably correct. Throughout, Hudson had been entirely straightforward, although it was not at all prudent to have tried to act in several conflicting capacities at once. The Tories had no doubts and, at a dinner to celebrate Smyth's election, Hudson was described by William Clark, a former Lord Mayor of York, as 'one of the greatest and most noble men England had ever produced'.

Hopwood got together a petition calling on Smyth to resign, which the latter ignored. There was a good deal of discussion about taking things further and some talk of petitioning Parliament about the way Hudson had conducted the election but the radicals received no support from either Lowther or the two official parties and, in the end, their protests were abandoned.

Although the Liberals had not protested at the parliamentary result, they were more than willing to try to make use of the commotion in the municipal elections of November 1847 to erode the Tory majority. One of the Tory candidates was B. T. Wilkinson, City Treasurer and manager of the York Union Bank. He was easily returned, amid allegations of massive bribery.[80] Leeman also protested that a director of the York and North Midland (Davies) was Town Clerk, several directors (Simpson, Barstow, Dodsworth and Hudson) as well as the engineer (Cabry) and their lawyer (Richardson) were on the council and now they were to be joined by their banker. He wondered whether they would be content until they had included their stokers!

Concerted attempts were also made to unseat what were seen as 'Hudson candidates' but the Liberals suffered their heaviest ever defeat in the municipal elections and the twelve more radical candidates who stood in various city wards were all unsuccessful. Even Hopwood, who had been Hudson's main adversary at the parliamentary elections, failed to secure a seat on the council. He blamed this on the way that Richardson had gone round threatening York and North Midland employees with the sack, and tradesmen with loss of patronage if they voted for Hopwood, but these explanations did not adequately explain the substantial margin by which he had failed.[81] Hudson refused a fourth term of office as Lord Mayor and, after Sir John Simpson and James Meek had been nominated and refused, his close friend James Richardson was duly elected.

In May 1848, Henry Redhead Yorke committed suicide in Regent's Park by swallowing prussic acid. This tragedy precipitated a by-election in York that attracted much attention. Economic depression and the overthrow of King Louis Phillippe of France in February 1848 (sparking the 'Year of Revolution' across Europe) had breathed fresh life into the Chartists in Britain. A monster petition had been presented to Parliament in April, supported by large demonstrations, and the York election was seen as a test of public opinion on demands for a widening of the franchise.

In line with their electoral agreement, the York Tories offered no candidate, and the election was fought out between the factions: the (anti-reform) establishment 'Whigs' and the 'advanced radicals'. Hudson's perennial opponent in municipal politics, George Leeman, was considered as a parliamentary candidate but in the end did not stand and William Milner, the candidate of the 'old Whigs' won surprisingly easily against the well-known radical, Henry Vincent.[82]

That same month, May 1848, Hudson's close friend, Robert Davies retired after twenty years as Town Clerk of York, although Hudson's influence over council matters was not greatly diminished as his replacement was Henry Richardson, the brother of James Richardson. Hudson was delighted when his portrait, in his Lord Mayor's robes, was presented to York Corporation and hung in the city's Mansion House in August of that year.[83] He was also doubtless pleased by the unexpected news in September 1848 that his long-standing opponent Frederick Hopwood had been accused of misappropriation and had agreed to pay damages and leave York, in order to avoid being charged.

Hudson was publicly taken to task in the run-up to the municipal elections of November 1848, over the reluctance of the York and North Midland to meet its financial obligations to the Council concerning the Lendal Bridge, but this did not have any major effect.[84] The Radicals captured the seats of two notable Hudson sympathisers and came close to capturing the supposedly impregnable Monk Ward, but still the Tories enjoyed a huge majority, with thirty-three out of the forty-eight available seats. None of the leading Tories had any great desire to be Lord Mayor and the Liberal James Meek was chosen for his second term of office, with George Hudson, three times Lord Mayor of York, now too busy on business matters to have much time for politics in the city of York.

2

Banker and Promoter

The Hudsons' life was transformed by the money that Matthew Bottrill bequeathed in May 1827. They became central to the social affairs of York and George soon became the city's most influential and charismatic politician. The business life of York was beginning to emerge from a period of depression and Hudson was now able to back his opportunistic judgements with substantial amounts of money. He was quick to involve himself in almost every new opportunity that York could offer. His promotion of new textile and municipal gas supply opportunities did not actually amount to much but his enterprising approach to the two major opportunities of the time, provincial banking and the railways, were to make his name and, for a while, his fortune.

After the financial crisis of 1825–26, the government decided to allow the formation of new banks, as long as they were at least sixty-five miles from London. In January 1830, the York City and County Bank was formed and was soon doing so well that Alderman William Cooper and George Hudson decided to follow suit. By February 1833 they had sufficient support to issue a prospectus for the York Banking Company and, on 28 March the first meeting was held at the White Swan Inn. Five directors were appointed. The managing directors, who would take on the active responsibilities of running the business, now to be known as the 'York Union Bank', were Cooper and Hudson. Bartholomew Wilkinson, who remained close to Hudson for much of his working life, was appointed manager. Those present also agreed that the ownership of the bank should not become too concentrated and stipulated a maximum shareholding.[1]

When the bank opened for business, in Coney Street, trade quickly reached an encouraging level and they soon moved to larger premises on Parliament Street. Another branch was opened that summer at Driffield, and others at Bridlington, Thirsk and Malton soon followed. Their London agents were the well-known bankers Glyn's, whose chairman, George Carr Glyn, was heavily involved in the promotion and management of several early railway lines, including the London and Birmingham.

The directors met once a week, with Hudson chairing the meetings when

Cooper could not attend. Both managing directors received £200 for their services and the three assistant directors £50 each.[2] By February 1835, the bank had been successfully established and the members marked this fact by presenting a piece of plate to the managing directors. A year later the proprietors voiced their satisfaction at the 'increasing prosperity' of their business and the dividends soon reached 9 per cent. The directors were also empowered to make transfers to a Guaranteed Fund, where they thought it prudent and desirable, even though this would lower the rate of dividend.[3]

By now Hudson was getting involved in other business promotions in the city. In 1836 a number of prominent local businessmen, including Hudson, floated the York Union Gas Light Company, which set out to provide gas more cheaply than the existing York Gas Light Company. The latter had been formed in 1823 and began to light the streets of York the following year, although its prices caused repeated complaints from both residents and the city authorities.[4] Early competition between the two businesses was unusually fierce (at one point in February 1837, as the new firm was laying in its mains, workmen from the old company arrived and started to shovel earth back into the trenches). Inevitably, there were fights between the rival gangs and the local courts had to be involved before the spirit of competition returned to a more acceptable level.[5] In fact, the new company was not much more efficient than its rival and the two businesses merged in 1844. Also in 1836, Hudson helped to promote the York Flax and Tow Spinning and Weaving Company, whose prospectus spoke of building a mill with ten thousand spindles that would use powered looms and unskilled labour to produce its goods.[6] The company sought £60,000 in capital to make this a reality but the promoters could not attract sufficient support and the initiative came to nothing.

At the bank, business was going well and in 1837 dividends reached 10 per cent, although the underlying returns on capital were closer to 15 per cent. It was now facing increased competition, however, and soon found that further expansion was almost impossible to achieve.[7] Hudson's personal position at the bank gradually strengthened. In 1838, his close friend James Richardson became one of the bank's solicitors and, when William Cooper died in August 1841, Hudson was elected Chairman. In April 1845, his brother-in-law Richard Nicholson joined the five-man board.

The steady growth in profits ended in 1841 and, as trade levels in the economy declined, the bank's returns also fell back. In 1845, however, the onset of the railway mania soon doubled the level of business and in 1846–47 profits were more than £20,000 a year. The collapse of the mania in 1848 brought numerous bad debts in its wake. Even Bartholomew Wilkinson, the manager of the York branch, had joined in the general speculative

free-for-all using bank funds and now owed his employer more than
£20,000. On 19 December 1848, when this could be hidden no longer, he
resigned and returned the horse and gig that the bank had provided for
his use. Although the bank had lost a good deal of money over his speculations, on 5 February 1849 Hudson wrote on behalf of the board to 'express
their regret' at his resignation and to assure him that they would still be
interested to hear of his success in his future undertakings.[8] Wilkinson had
certainly been a successful manager and, as early as February 1838, the
shareholders had voted him an additional hundred pounds as a 'small
acknowledgement of his faithful attention to the interests of the bank'. His
tenure at the York branch had, however, also been personally helpful to
Hudson in ways that were soon to attract a good deal of unwelcome
publicity.

The York Union Bank proved important to the development of Hudson's
business career but, along with other investors, he was well aware that the
best prospects lay with the development of railways, a subject that was
increasingly under discussion in York business circles.

By the 1830s, many of the basic elements of rail transport were already
well established. Wagon-ways had been laid down in Nottinghamshire,
Shropshire and County Durham since the early seventeenth century, often
for the horse-drawn carriage of coal to and from the nearest river. In 1758,
a railway from Middleton colliery to Leeds was constructed under a private
Act of Parliament and other railways were constructed as feeders to the
newly-built canals and then to aid mining work during the French wars.

The early wagon-ways were made of wood, although often plated with
strips of iron to reduce wear, at least until iron rails were made at Coal-
brookdale in the 1760s. The first iron railroad in the north was built by
Thomas Barnes in 1797 from the Walker colliery to the Tyne.[9]

The Surrey Iron Railway, often described as the first public railway,
operated between Croydon and Wandsworth on the Thames from 1805 and
allowed paying members of the public to use the line for their own horse-
drawn traffic.[10] The Swansea and Oystermouth handled passenger traffic
from 1807, as did the Gloucester and Cheltenham, which opened in 1811.
The steam locomotive, invented by Cugnot, developed by Murdock and
put on rails by Richard Trevithick, was first used near Merthyr Tydfil in
1804, but it was not a commercial success until the engine built by Matthew
Murray and John Blenkinsop started work on the Middleton colliery line
near Leeds in 1812.[11]

The earliest railways consisted mostly of short, individual private lines
and were curiously localised; by 1820 there were over two hundred miles
of iron roads on Tyneside and in South Wales but almost none in Lancashire

or the Black Country, where the canals were much better developed. The earliest railways were more of a freight handling system, a way of moving bulky goods over short distances at moderate speeds to and from tidal or navigable water in connection with the operations of coalmines, quarries and docks, rather than a means of moving large numbers of people from place to place.[12]

The early experiments of George Stephenson at Killingworth Colliery, using malleable iron rails from the Bedlington Ironworks, were a great success and in 1821 attracted the attention of William James of the Liverpool and Manchester Railway and of the Pease family, who were promoting the Stockton and Darlington Railway. The latter opened for business in 1825 and was the first line to make use of steam railway techniques on a railway authorised by Act of Parliament as a public line, although most of the traffic was freight.[13]

Outside its immediate locality the Stockton and Darlington aroused limited public interest at the time, although it impressed enough promoters to help bring about the first railway mania in 1824–25. Seventy lines were proposed, forty of which reached the parliamentary stage, including several ambitious schemes for trunk lines from London to Manchester, London to Bristol and South Wales and Bristol to Yorkshire. The boom was ended by a commercial crisis in December 1825 which dampened the enthusiasm of investors, the only major scheme to survive being the Liverpool and Manchester line, designed to meet the dissatisfaction of local traders with the roads and canals that linked their towns.

Even in the late 1820s, it was not clear whether locomotives, horses or stationary engines would provide the best means of propulsion, but a series of tests, notably the Rainhill locomotive trials, established the superiority of locomotives running on wrought-iron edge-rails.[14]

The really decisive change in public recognition came after the opening of the Liverpool and Manchester line on 15 September 1830. Sightseers crowded every building that provided a view of the official opening, although the great day was overshadowed by the death of the Liverpool MP, William Huskisson, who wandered across the track with little idea of the danger posed by the approaching Rocket. The hostile reception by vast numbers of mechanics and artisans in Manchester, dangerously discontented with all things official, also brought a reminder that not everyone was confident that they would be sharing in the benefits of the new technology.

The Treasurer of the Liverpool and Manchester Railway was undeterred and said that the world had received a new impulse: the 'genius of the age, like a mighty river of the new world, flows onwards, full, rapid and irresistible'.[15] From this point, as passengers came to enjoy a regular service provided by company-owned locomotives, there was indeed the sense that a new age had dawned. Far more than any other industry, the railways were to transform the Victorian economy, reducing transport costs and greatly increasing the demand for investment capital.[16]

The successful opening of the Liverpool and Manchester line certainly stimulated railway promotion. By 1832–35, a relatively balanced pattern of railway promotion had emerged with the authorisation of the first major trunk routes from London (providing connections to Birmingham, Southampton and Bristol), lines from Lancashire (including the Grand Junction connection to Birmingham) and a number of short local lines, particularly in Durham.[17]

In many ways, of course, the changes were negative. The newly-constructed railways drove through towns and villages, destroying homes and historic buildings. Their demands for territory cut across the rights of landowners to an extent that would have been unimaginable in earlier times. The railways disfigured the landscape, brought pollution and exposed passengers to new dangers: derailments, explosions and journeys in enclosed compartments with unfamiliar companions. Steam locomotives could terrify both people and their horses, although indictments against their use rarely succeeded, however much legal counsel railed against the great 'snorting, roaring and mighty monsters, vomiting fire in all directions'. Fears like these did not disappear with the 1830s. As late as 1841, a Wiltshire parish clerk found 'the novelty of the sight, the strangeness of the sounds, the marvellous velocity with which engine, tender, carriages and truck disappeared, the dense columns of sulphurous smoke, altogether too much' and he was (temporarily) struck dumb with amazement.[18]

During the eighteenth century, businesses were run either by sole traders or as partnerships, as unincorporated companies or as full corporations. Sole traders and partners were individually liable for all the debts of their business, but companies had a continuity unaffected by changes in their membership. In full corporations, the members' liability was limited to their agreed investment, but the legal right of corporations to exist and the availability of limited liability were both controlled by the state, and permitted only by a Royal Charter of the Crown or by a private Act of Parliament.[19]

In the first half of the nineteenth century the legal position of corporations changed several times. In 1825, the 'Bubble Act' of 1720, expressly designed to make company formation difficult and expensive, was repealed and in 1837 the Board of Trade acquired powers to grant corporate status (with limited liability) on behalf of the Crown although it was not until 1855 that companies could offer limited liability to their members without the specific consent of Crown or Parliament.[20] Earlier, there had been general opposition to the formation of companies to pursue lines of business that were 'within the grasp of private capital and individual management', but not in the case of public works requiring a large capital that would take years to complete, where incorporation was seen as the proper arrangement.[21]

Increasingly, Parliament offered the privilege of limited liability to businesses, notably railways, that were able to meet the necessary criteria. Parliament also allowed authorised companies to purchase land compulsorily, despite the challenge that this provided to the expectations of landowners.[22] The state quickly accepted responsibility for standards of public safety on the railways, investigating accidents and determining whether new lines were safe. From 1840, they also gave more general regulatory powers over the railways to the Board of Trade.[23]

The government's approach to limited liability thus split the market for investment finance into two very different parts. The public utilities, the canals, gas, water and railway companies, were able to attract finance from large numbers of 'arm's length' investors, although the state also required a substantial level of local financial commitment as an essential precondition.[24] On the other hand, manufacturing, commercial and textile businesses, which needed considerably smaller amounts of capital, were left to look for their financial support mainly from their founding families and from wealthier members of their local community who knew and trusted them.[25]

The early railway companies, offering far higher investment returns than the 3 per cent available on government securities, thus held an enormous advantage in the investment markets, at least until 1855. During this period, when they were virtually the only businesses to be financed by the public on a truly large scale, they became the key agents of growth in the British economy.[26] Moreover, although they looked to local investors for much of their support, the railways also greatly broadened the ranks of the shareholding public. Up to this point, shareholding had been almost exclusively a practice of the monied classes. The railways, for the first time, drew enormous numbers of savers, including women and clergymen, into active speculation.

In the early years of the nineteenth century York was a small city with a very limited manufacturing base. Very few factories had been built there, although the city did have active trading links along the Ouse with Hull.[27] Yet even when the Liverpool and Manchester line first showed that railways could be a paying proposition, the level of interest shown among York business circles was relatively modest. Building a railway line was a highly risky proposition, since nearly all the money had to be spent upfront. Most of York's business leaders accepted that York was simply not large enough to justify the potential outlays and risks involved.

On the other hand, a railway line to Leeds would provide access to its nearby collieries and lower the price of coal in York, stimulating further industrial development and reducing the costs facing existing businesses.[28] James Meek, the biggest employer in town, who owned a glass-works burning more than a thousand tons of coal a year, thus stood to gain considerably. He encouraged Henry Newton, a local solicitor, to collect information on the likely costs and benefits of building a line. Newton also shared the results of his early research with two other prominent York businessmen, George Hudson and Samuel Tuke. Hudson was not running a business that used much coal, and he did not yet have any special knowledge of railways, but he was wealthy and took an interest in most important civic matters in York, particularly if they offered commercial prospects. All the same, he was not yet convinced about the benefits of this particular venture.[29]

Meek held meetings with his fellow businessmen to discuss the project and to gauge the likely level of support. Hudson became increasingly involved and was present at an important meeting held on 30 December 1833 at Tomlinson's Hotel, at which the York business elite, with Meek in the chair, considered two main proposals: a direct route from York to Leeds via Tadcaster; and a line to South Milford to join up with the Leeds and Selby line, which was due to open the following autumn.[30] The Leeds to York line had obvious attractions, but the more roundabout route via South Milford would be easier and cheaper to construct and would provide access to several local collieries and quarries.

After the meeting, a committee was formed, drawing heavily on the city corporation for membership. Most of the members were from the ruling Liberal faction, including the Chairman, but Hudson, who became Treasurer, was one of two Tories to join. A prospectus was issued in January 1834 to test the level of support for the two routes. Three weeks later the committee had enough money to make a start and they commissioned a detailed survey of the possible routes by the noted railway engineer, George Rennie. His report in June 1834 suggested that a 15 per cent return, based largely on the transport of coal and minerals, could be achieved, but that locomotive power would not necessarily be more beneficial than the use of horses.[31] The committee was not entirely convinced. Prompted by Hudson and Meek, they decided to wait and see how other schemes fared before they made any firm decisions.[32]

Over the next twelve months, there was continued improvement in the commercial prospects of the railways and the Leeds and Selby line opened in September 1834. It also became apparent, however, that proposals for a direct route from London to York through the thinly populated eastern counties were not going to get enough support, at least for the time being. Far more important, though, was the formation in September 1835 of the North Midland Railway Company, to build a line from Leeds to Derby via Chesterfield that would join the projected Birmingham to Derby and London to Birmingham lines. A line joining York to the North Midland could be built at only modest cost and would provide a link with London via the heavily populated midlands, offering immediate and substantial commercial returns.

After their earlier caution, Hudson and his colleagues realised that a great opportunity had now presented itself and they moved with all possible speed. On 13 October 1835 a public meeting was held in York's Guildhall, at which Robert Davies, the Town Clerk, recommended that they build a line as soon as possible to join and then cross over the Leeds and Selby, so as to link up with the North Midland. Hudson, greatly excited by the prospects, moved eagerly into an active role. He seconded the formal proposals to form a new company, the York and North Midland Railway with a capital of £200,000 and was confirmed as Treasurer of its Provisional Committee. Robert Stephenson, who was heavily involved in the North Midland, was then asked to produce a new survey as a matter of urgency.[33]

The switch in emphasis to passenger traffic and the link-up with George Stephenson, the great railway engineer, and his son Robert had revealed still more exciting possibilities. The potential for the York and North Midland's short line to become part of other long-distance passenger routes, rather than be confined to local mineral traffic as originally contemplated, was further emphasised by a meeting with representatives of the Great North of England Company (then known as the Newcastle and York Railway Company) in November 1835. The Great North of England, whose guiding light was Joseph Pease, suggested that the best way to build a line north to Newcastle would be to link up with the York and North Midland's lines at or near York and then go on through Darlington. Hudson and Meek were highly impressed and immediately made substantial personal investments in the Great North of England.

Robert Stephenson's completed survey for the York and North Midland proposed a route of about thirty miles, crossing the Leeds-Selby line at South Milford before joining the North Midland near Normanton. George Hudson, James Meek and Thomas Backhouse went to London to represent the company when its authorising Bill was considered by a parliamentary committee. As was customary, the committee was chaired by a local MP, in this case J. H. Lowther. These proceedings gave Hudson invaluable first-hand experience of what was involved in railway promotion and his first opportunity to shine in this new area of public life. The York and North Midland party confirmed that they had been able to make 'amicable arrangements' with all the parties concerned' and, as a result, there was little parliamentary opposition to the Bill, which received its royal assent on 21 June 1836.

To all appearances, the various land purchases had gone very well. Virtually all the land needed for the first fifteen miles of track had already been acquired at modest coat and without serious dispute.[34] Behind the scenes though, there had been a serious problem. Lord Howden had objected to the proposed route coming so close to his estate. In May 1836, the York and North Midland decided to 'square' Howden, in order to simplify their stance before the parliamentary committee, despite the considerable cost involved. Hudson, as Treasurer, was authorised by the company to make a (secret) payment to His Lordship of £5000 six months after their Act received its royal assent.

The Act envisaged the raising of £370,000 of share capital. The promoters were reluctant to allow control to move out of the locality but the capital needed for railway construction was enormous.[35] Even the relatively modest York and North Midland line required amounts of capital that were beyond the capacity of local investors. As not much more than half the money could be raised in York, trips to Manchester and London were needed to raise sufficient interest in the share issue.[36] Some local people needed less persuasion. George Hudson was now so convinced of the line's potential that he took up a holding of £10,000, becoming the company's largest shareholder.

The first proper meeting of the new business was held 10 August 1836 when Hudson was elected a director. His fellow directors included James Meek and Hudson's close friends Robert Davies, James Richardson and Richard Nicholson. Although it was Meek who had brought the new company into existence, Hudson was deeply involved and was becoming very well informed about the ways of the new business. Perhaps because he had fewer other commitments than Meek, he was elected chairman, a position that was to launch him on the path to greatness.

The new company built its line without meeting any great setbacks. They were able to shorten their route by arrangement with the Leeds and Selby, and also took powers in the new session of Parliament to reroute their line to avoid disturbing Lord Howden's peace and quiet. Hudson had hoped that the covert payment of £5000 would then be viewed as merely a refundable contingency arrangement, particularly since the YNM was willing

to pay £100 for every acre of Howden's land that it did require, but it soon
became apparent that an aristocrat could act with as little scruple as the
most commercially minded entrepreneur. His Lordship refused to refund
the money, even when faced with a court action embarrassing to both
parties.37

By January 1838, it was already clear to George Stephenson that the section
of line to South Milford would be the cheapest ever executed in England
and that the remaining section of track could also be built at well below
the average cost for railway construction.38 The line was cheap mainly
because the gradients were remarkably easy, with a summit only fifty feet
above the terminus at York. It was not difficult for Hudson, enjoying his
friend's confidence, to realise that these were advantages that the York and
North Midland would never lose and on which its future prosperity could
be based. He promptly doubled his initial shareholding to £21,000, 7 per
cent of the total, the rest of which was dispersed among some three hundred
shareholders, chiefly from York, Bristol, Manchester and Liverpool.39

It is clear that George Hudson knew a good thing when he saw one,
although at the shareholders' meeting on 20 July 1838 he only spoke of
the undertaking's unique contribution to the 'social intercourse of the
city.' The members knew what he meant and the vote of thanks at the end
of the meeting for his conduct in the chair was carried 'by acclamation'.40

Work was now going ahead at full speed, with men employed day and
night building the York and North Midland's line down to South Milford,
where it connected with the Leeds and Selby. This section of line was ready
for business on 29 May 1839.41 A tradition had already developed in the
railway industry of marking line openings with great ceremony and, as Lord
Mayor of York, Hudson had held the most lavish celebrations ever provided
by that office. It was therefore, not all that surprising that the festivities on
this occasion were the most elaborate 'ever planned to celebrate the opening
of no more than fourteen miles of railway'.42 A sumptuous breakfast was
served at eleven o'clock in the Guildhall. Hudson, being both Chairman of
the York and North Midland and Lord Mayor of York, made a brief speech
of welcome to the very 'numerous and respectable' audience, there to
celebrate a new era in the history of the city of York. The assembly of some
four hundred included the directors of the York and North Midland and
of the Great North of England Railway, the officers of the Seventh Hussars,
the members of the York Corporation and the local magistrates, clergy and
gentry. After breakfast was over, at a little after one o'clock, a train of two
engines and eighteen carriages carried the party out of York, saluted by
flags, the Minster bells and cannon fire. Although the day was not an official
holiday, many employees had taken the day off. Huge crowds, many of

them from areas outside the city, paraded the streets in their holiday clothes and, when it was time for the mighty new 'fire-horses' to leave for South Milford, every rise within sight of the line was crowded with groups of spectators eager to see the train pass.

Shortly after three o'clock, the train returned, 'without the slightest inconvenience or accident' and a banquet for four hundred guests followed at the Guildhall, at which George Stephenson was the official guest of honour and, along with Hudson, the general focus of attention. A grand ball followed in York's Mansion House, at which Elizabeth Hudson led off the company in the first dance. The ball carried on through the night, so that it was not until four in the morning that all the revellers had finally gone home.[43]

By mid 1839, Hudson must have been feeling more than pleased with progress since he had come into his inheritance. Mayor of his adopted city, he was on good terms with both the local aristocracy and the York business elite, he had founded a successful local bank and had become chairman and largest shareholder in his city's first railway. His new position provided excellent insights into the modus operandi of the new industry and he soon realised that the York and North Midland, although of modest size, would provide a sufficient base for involvement in the biggest prize of all, the route from London to Scotland. This was a heady prospect indeed, although it would take some achieving in the face of determined competition.

The first part of the general meeting of the York and North Midland in July 1839, so soon after the triumphant opening of the first section of line, was devoted to elaborate Victorian courtesies, with Hudson reassuring those present that no body of men could have been more anxious to make the York and North Midland a prosperous and lucrative concern than the board had been.

The next item on the agenda was more substantive and was to present Hudson with the chance to exercise even closer control over the policies of the company. The proposal that the York and North Midland should not run trains on Sundays for the 'ordinary conveyance of passengers' was based upon a petition originating in the offices of the Lord's Day Society, signed by nine hundred people. It had naturally aroused strong feelings but, more importantly, it was seconded by James Meek. A former Mayor and a leading Liberal in the city, well known for his strongly Methodist principles and demonstrably austere lifestyle, Meek had genuine concerns at the propriety of the York and North Midland's position and had decided to commit himself publicly to the proposal.

In 1839 religious sensibilities were important to the respectable middle

classes and the demarcations between commerce and religion were poorly
defined.[44] As in many a principled disagreement, personal hostilities and
resentments quickly surfaced. Those of religious persuasion stressed the
importance of a seventh day free of toil in a base world of commerce. Meek
argued strongly that the Sabbath was a sacred institution and that other
considerations should not be weighed against this. Other members, however,
detected the whiff of hypocrisy and assumed with ostensible civility that the
proposer of the motion, Samuel Tuke (a prominent Liberal, Quaker and
owner of the rival gas works) and James Meek (the glass-manufacturer)
would of course be coming to court 'with clean hands', in which case, there
would presumably be 'a disconnection with the Gas Company and a cessation
of light to the city' and the letting out of the glass-blowers' fires on Sundays.

It was Hudson who cleverly sharpened the edge on the issues submerged
within the proposal when he confessed to his own concerns at seeing 'his
friend Mr Meek connected with a company whose servants labour on the
Sabbath to keep up the fires', and his unease that proposals which 'were for
closing up all communication to the poor man' came most easily from those
with carriages and horses and grooms to take them to church or chapel.
There was a comfortable majority (350 to 233) against the proposed restriction
on Sunday operations but many of the defeated felt unhappy at the outcome.
Meek, who had chosen to be personally involved in the disagreements and
had suffered from Hudson's populist demagogy, immediately resigned from
the board of directors.[45]

Hudson's criticisms of Meek were so sharply personal as to suggest that
they had been intended to make the latter's position on the board untenable.
The business of the meeting had removed Hudson's main rival from the
board and provided some commercial benefits to the company but he was
acute enough to realise that it was important to recover lost ground among
the local religious community. Accordingly, in October 1839, George Hudson
and his fellow directors entertained a 'fashionable party' to lunch at the
Mansion House. Amongst such important guests as Lord and Lady Radstock,
Lady Norreys and Lord Melbourne's private secretary, who was himself a
director of the London and Birmingham Railway, were the Archbishop of
York, the Dean of York, and several other members of the clergy. The meal
was 'of the most sumptuous description' and afterwards the guests were
taken for a short journey. The company's best engine, the *Lowther*, took
them down the line at about forty miles an hour, four times the speed of
a fast stage coach, and the guests were highly gratified to discover that 'not
the least uncomfortable motion was experienced, or the slightest accident
occurred'. The day had been a great success.[46]

Although the York and North Midland was a small railway line, it was large enough to provide Hudson with plenty of opportunities to demonstrate his talent for generating favourable publicity. The excellent progress the line had made was used to boost his reputation for competence and its strategic position in the rail network northwards also offered potential as a springboard to larger ventures. Hudson announced a 21s. dividend at the half-yearly meeting early in 1840, even before the second half of their line had been opened. He was thus able to describe the company's progress (and, by implication, his own) as an 'unabated success', but the comments of a representative of the North Midland Railway who attended the meeting were more revealing. He thought the York and North Midland Railway was being 'conducted upon principles which their neighbours would be glad to imitate', a comment which was widely quoted to evidence Hudson's growing reputation. The North Midland representative was keen that the two lines should open together and, in an exchange that must have been prearranged, Hudson, from the chair, said that he had information that 'the great railway from north to south would run by way of York'. At this point the North Midland representative suggested that the most important factor in determining this question would be the completion of the line between York and Newcastle. These remarks were duly reported in the *Railway Times*.[47]

The planned simultaneous opening of the North Midland and the remaining southern section of the York and North Midland, from South Milford to Altofts near Normanton, took place on 30 June 1840. Since the Midland Counties Railway also opened the final section of its route on that same day, the York and North Midland could now offer its passengers an immediate and uninterrupted link with London, 217 miles away, via the midlands. Four trains a day would run each way and those leaving York at 7.30 a.m. could expect to be in London at 6.45 p.m., after stopping for refreshments at Derby. Although the joint opening provided an obvious excuse for more celebration, Hudson and his fellow directors were more restrained this time and contented themselves with a special train pulled by the locomotive, *Hudson*, which travelled from York to Oakenshaw where the formal opening of the line from Derby to Leeds took place.

In July 1840, although the second half of the line had only just opened, Hudson was still able to announce an increased dividend of 24s. He explained that the dividends to date had come out of capital but that in future they would be paid out of operating receipts. The distinction between capital and revenue has generally been cited as the great problem area in early railway accounting and Hudson has been seen as its prime manipulator, but at this point in the York and North Midland's history there was no attempt at misrepresentation nor was there scope for confusion. It was entirely legitimate for the shareholders to pay themselves a dividend as if it were interest on loan capital, although they gained nothing from so doing. In effect they were paying themselves some of their own money while they awaited the profits anticipated on the actual operation of the trains. Hudson favoured this measure as a demonstrable sign of confidence, one that was to be entirely vindicated by the company's forthcoming financial results.

Once Meek had left the board, Hudson took almost total control of the company's affairs. Although his dominant position gave some grounds for concern, he was able to claim much of the credit while things were going well and he retained his popularity with the York and North Midland's members largely because the company continued to be a highly profitable investment.

It was clear that the York and North Midland had got off to an excellent start and Hudson's thoughts turned towards expansion. He now advocated an enterprising change of direction that provided the scope for higher personal rewards for himself but also contained the seeds of an eventual downturn in the company's fortunes. He had been introduced to George Stephenson in 1834 or 1835 in Whitby, where the Hudsons liked to take their holidays. Stephenson was building a modest horse-drawn line to Pickering and had been considering the construction of lines to the coast for some time.[48]

The great engineer George Stephenson came to the York and North Midland shareholders' meeting in July 1840 to lend his personal support to the proposed line from York to Scarborough, and the related branch line to Pickering, which would link up with the existing line to Whitby. Scarborough and Whitby were coastal towns with great developmental potential, particularly if they were on the railway network. Indeed, according to Hudson, Scarborough, a popular spa town with a population of about ten thousand, could become the 'Brighton of the north'. Stephenson, for his part, was so convinced by the proposals that he offered to act unpaid, until the relevant company or lines were formed. Faced with such enthusiastic expertise, the shareholders had no hesitation in authorising the necessary expenditure to survey the areas concerned.[49]

That summer, while the feasibility of these lines was being explored, Hudson gave further evidence of the impressive way his abilities had developed in his adopted industry. The railways were already beginning to change. Rival companies and even new promoters were actively looking for new routes that would pay, so that established companies were vulnerable to new projects and link-ups that could offer shorter journeys to the paying customer and thereby sabotage the appeal of their own railways. Railway promoters were having to develop an increasingly sharp eye for the possibilities presented by local geography and terrain. In his own area,

Hudson had been aware for some time of the potential complications posed by the Leeds and Selby and Hull and Selby lines.

The opening of the Hull and Selby in July 1840 brought an immediate threat to the York and North Midland's traffic. The Leeds and Selby intersected the York and North Midland's own main line, midway between York and Leeds, providing a level of competition helpful to neither company. The decision of the North Midland in October 1840 to switch its traffic from the Leeds and Selby onto the YNM, while helpful in the short term, also carried its own veiled warning of what could happen to the YNM in the future, under different circumstances. In particular, the takeover of the L&S by a rival company would seriously threaten the basis of the York and North Midland's east-west traffic whereas, in the hands of the York and North Midland it would bring control of a strategic crossroad, with access to east-west traffic from Liverpool to supplement the north-south traffic they already enjoyed.

Hudson quickly consulted both Robert Stephenson and James Meek, who was still a major shareholder and a figure of considerable importance and, with that prompt tactical judgement which distinguished him, immediately approached the directors of the Leeds and Selby with an offer to lease the line at a rate that would effectively guarantee their members a permanent dividend of 5 per cent. He also sought an option to buy the line outright at some future time, effectively on the same terms. In this situation, Hudson showed how shrewd he could be, being aware of possibilities before his rivals and flexible enough to think of new financial arrangements in the pursuit of important strategic gains. Moreover, Hudson behaved intelligently rather than aggressively in offering a price that was entirely reasonable to take over the business of a company that was only just beginning to pay its way and had so far been able to pay only small dividends to its shareholders; returns in the railway industry had already begun to fall, so that 5 per cent in perpetuity was a tempting offer. The real gain for Hudson was, of course, to achieve a quick result and so avoid a bidding war with a rival company that might have raised the offer price.[50]

The proposed arrangements were promptly ratified by the York and North Midland's shareholders in October 1840. They were well aware of the commercial logic of the deal: the use of an initial leasing or rental arrangement would avoid further calls on the proprietors' share capital, while control of the Leeds and Selby's track would also enable the York and North Midland to simplify its own routes and close down some sections of line to passenger traffic, thereby reducing its running and maintenance costs.[51]

Hudson's good sense in consulting Meek, despite their past differences, paid off handsomely when Meek, towards the close of the meeting, thanked the Chairman for his 'assiduous attention to their interests', adding that they were indebted to him personally, for he was the first person to have suggested that a lease should be taken. This was, politically, highly valuable praise, coming as it did from an unimpeachable source.[52]

Things were going very well for Hudson, whose cleverness was now clear to all. He was rarely consistent, however, and he was certainly never at his best when crossed or frustrated in his designs. In that same month, November 1840, the less palatable side of Hudson's managerial approach was demonstrated. Hull was the principal port for the Baltic trade and its shipments, notably of Lancashire cottons, woollen goods from the West Riding and lace from Nottingham, amounted to a fifth of UK exports, so that the opening of the Hull and Selby Railway was marked with due ceremony, with Hudson one of the speakers at the grand dinner. The York and North Midland had already made an attempt to buy out the strategically important Hull and Selby, even before its traffic potential had really been demonstrated, but had been rebuffed. Undeterred, Hudson simply bought up and operated the steam tugs that the Leeds and Selby had previously run on the Ouse and Humber between Selby and Hull, before the Hull and Selby Railway had opened. The Hull and Selby found this a 'peculiarly objectionable' form of competition, as the Leeds and Selby had promised to discontinue the use of the tugs once the railway line was open through to Hull. They indicated that Hudson's manoeuvre would interfere with the cordial cooperation which should obtain between closely connected railway companies. Hudson's spoiling tactics thoroughly alienated the Hull and Selby and also failed to generate enough business to exert any real pressure. Belatedly, Hudson decided to be more reasonable and phase out the boats, but by then much political damage had been done for no perceptible gain.[53]

To complete an eventful month, there was a serious collision at the junction of the York and North Midland and the Leeds and Selby. Two carriages were smashed to pieces, two passengers killed on the spot and several more were badly mutilated. The new, more economical, running arrangements were blamed and the highly negative publicity took much of the shine off Hudson's initiative with the Leeds and Selby.[54]

By January, however, matters were improved greatly by the opening of the new York terminus. The York and North Midland had been using a temporary terminus just outside the walls, which Robert Stephenson thought the best site for the permanent station, but Hudson relished the prestige value of bringing the railway into the heart of the city and insisted on taking it through the medieval walls. The most suitable site for development, in the Toft Green area, was the site of the city's House of Correction but this did not present undue problems, given Hudson's position on the council. The intended breaching of the city's historic walls aroused far more anxiety and opposition but, fortunately, the plans for a graceful Tudor arch proposed by G. T. Andrews found general favour, even with the York Philosophical Society, making it much easier for the council to give its formal approval.[55]

George Townsend Andrews (1804–55) was a close friend of Hudson, had been on the York and North Midland Provisional Committee and had been instrumental in drawing up the company's first prospectus. He was also an excellent architect and was in charge of designing the new station, aided by the engineer Thomas Cabry.[56] It was not an overly expensive construction but was generally seen as a fine and elegant building. Much of it was brick but the colonnaded entrance and the sixty-yard front were built of polished stone in the Italian style. The train shed had a cast iron and glass roof that provided shelter for facilities arranged in a horseshoe fashion around the platforms, including first and second-class refreshment rooms, a bar and large tearoom, a general waiting room and separate waiting rooms for first-class ladies, first-class gentlemen and second-class ladies. The terminus was operated jointly with the Great North of England company, which paid rather less than half the overall cost of the project, and a wharf was built just outside the walls for handling coal. A new street, Hudson Street, was later added to improve public access to the station.[57]

George Hudson was now feeling more than pleased at the York and North Midland's progress. At the regular meeting with the shareholders that same month, January 1841, he made the ebullient statement that they would soon receive 'such a dividend that no company in the kingdom would excel it'. He was, accordingly, the more discomforted when some shareholders were so ungrateful as to press him instead on matters of accountability.

Thomas Laycock, a mildly eccentric shareholder whom Hudson knew quite well, complained that the latest accounts (for the half-year to December 1840) included 'a number of items jumbled together which men like himself could not understand', pointing out that several cost items had been aggregated. He suggested that in future the revenue accounts should be more detailed. The York and North Midland was a genuinely profitable business, the accounts were reasonably detailed and the cost items concerned were small, although the way they had been presented was a little casual. Laycock's request for better information was entirely proper and carried no threat to Hudson as it only related to the minutiae of the accounts.

Hudson's reply, however, was unnecessarily lofty and his observation that the books were open to every shareholder to inspect provoked a second and rightly famous incident. Another shareholder, Amos Coates, was well aware that, though Hudson's suggestion sounded very fine, it was far from practical. His suggestion was therefore that they should consider including a clause in their next Bill 'providing for the appointment of auditors'. If this was intended to provoke Hudson in retaliation for his rudeness, it was more than successful and he overreacted to what he saw as a slur on his management of the company:

> It was the first time he had ever heard such a suggestion in a meeting of railway proprietors. The accounts were always audited by the directors and every book was open for the inspection of the proprietary. If Mr Coates doubted the competency of the directors he had better move a resolution to that effect. If he was dissatisfied he had it in his power to move the appointment of auditors without an Act of Parliament and he [the Chairman] should be happy to put such a resolution to the meeting.

Hudson's comments on auditors have rightly attracted notoriety, although they have often been taken out of context. Very few railway companies appointed auditors at that time and, where they existed, they were simply shareholders elected by their fellow proprietors, not professional accountants. There was a widely-held and entirely sincere belief that the shareholders' interests in all areas of corporate activity were best served by their own active involvement, rather than by looking to the state or other outsiders. Even the influential Joseph Rowntree, who was no particular friend of Hudson, thought auditors 'perfectly useless' and preferred that the York and North Midland's shareholders 'accept their responsibilities, rather than interpose a third party between themselves and the directors'. Alderman Hotham, on grounds of effectiveness, preferred the weekly examination of the accounts by the directors to 'two or three individuals coming once a year'. He thought that the shareholders should simply chose directors in whom they had confidence and, if not, turn them out.

While Coates's not unreasonable view was that insurance firms and banks used auditors and could be considered a more businesslike practice, he had to suffer an unnecessarily confrontational challenge from another director, Sir John Simpson, who asked whether he would persevere with such opinions if he had any confidence in the directors. Thomas Backhouse, who actually checked the books each week, joined in the altercation and said what Hudson should have said at the outset, that the 'greatest regularity prevailed in keeping their accounts', but if they needed to be a little more classified in future then that would be done. After this, matters were soon resolved, with the shareholders expressing some support for the preservation of their right to inspect the books, when they were 'in any way dissatisfied'.[58]

Both incidents have been widely quoted but not always in their proper context. They have nothing to do with the accounting manipulations

Hudson practised much later in his career but they do point up his inability to defuse situations when he felt he was being slighted, which he was quick to do.

Where this was not the case, problems were often dealt with very easily. A letter of complaint to the *Times*, for example, from a group of travellers who claimed that the directors of the York and North Midland at York had cheated them and 'deliberately sent [them] on to Normanton, knowing that (they) should have to stay at one of their own hotels', a repeated trick of the 'insolent monopolising railway company', was met by a reply of considerable restraint and courtesy from Hudson as Chairman in which he pointed out that the company actually had 'no interest whatever in the hotel at Normanton'.[59]

Despite these minor difficulties Hudson was beginning to receive fulsome praise for the way he was managing the York and North Midland. In the north- east, financial returns at the York and North Midland were second only to those at the pioneering Stockton and Darlington. At the end of March 1841, the company's prospects were also boosted by the opening to passenger traffic of the Great North of England line from Darlington to York. The history of the York and North Midland, according to an editorial in the *Railway Times* on 21 August 1841, presented a 'very cheering lesson to the shareholders in unfinished lines'. Before the line opened, the York and North Midland shares stood at a low value on the Stock Exchange, but once it began to carry traffic the company's stock was eagerly sought after, and it now held a proud position among railway company shares that traded at a premium. From all that the editors could see, the public had 'in this instance judged wisely at last'.[60]

Effusive tributes to the chairman became a regular feature of York and North Midland meetings. In August 1841, for example, one shareholder praised his energy and talent as 'equal if not superior to any other man'. Alderman Meek, who was certainly not in Hudson's pocket, also commented on the unusual amount of time devoted to their interests by the chairman and proposed, in the light of the extra burden of managing the Leeds and Selby and the prosperous state of the business, that the directors' remuneration be doubled to £1000 a year. The proposal was carried unanimously and Hudson thanked those present on behalf of the directors for their kindness and their confidence, which 'enabled them to go forward boldly'. Six months later, when Thomas Barstow proposed Hudson's re-election to the board, he suggested that the success of the company was due to Hudson alone and was the real proof of his efficiency.

All other tributes were eclipsed, however, in October 1842, when the Chairman of the Northern and Eastern Railway, taking into account the dividend record of the York and North Midland, described Hudson as the 'best railway manager in the kingdom'.[61] This was high praise indeed. W. W. Tomlinson, the official historian of the North Eastern Railway, writing more than fifty years later, concluded that Hudson's success at this point was in fact no accident. While the fortunes of many companies managed from a distance were a disappointment, the closer attentions paid by the chairmen of some lines, such as the Stockton and Darlington, the Newcastle and Carlisle and the York and North Midland, paid off. Thus, it was the 'zeal and energy' that Hudson put into the promotion and management of the York and North Midland and the extension of his supervision to the smallest details of railway work that was decisive; if the authority he wielded was close to that of a dictator, the railway nonetheless flourished under his rule.[62]

The excellent progress of the York and North Midland had been widely attributed, rightly or wrongly, to Hudson's managerial skills. The favourable publicity helped him to expand the scale of his own business activities beyond the York and North Midland. He now formed a Newcastle and Darlington Junction Railway that would eventually provide a route to the north and he had been appointed to a Committee of Inquiry at the North Midland that would in time provide him with an entrée to their board of directors.[63]

He also pressed on with the venture that would so materially change both the York and North Midland as a company and his own public position. This was the new line from York to Scarborough and Pickering, which was to run close to Howsham, his birthplace. The proposals were fully discussed on 18 November 1843 at a special meeting of the company, which proved to be a notable one for both Hudson and the York and North Midland. The estimated cost of the new line was £260,000, which George Stephenson had carefully checked. Based on the estimated revenues and running costs of the new venture, Hudson was able to announce 'every expectation' of a 10 per cent return on the investment, which would have made it one of the more profitable ventures in the railway industry of that time.[64] These predictions were to prove easier to make than to achieve.

In order to go ahead with the line to Scarborough, the York and North Midland needed to raise substantial amounts of additional share capital. Hudson proposed offering the new shares initially to the existing shareholders. While the line was being constructed, the shareholders would receive nothing on their new shares but, from around July 1845, the two types of shares would be amalgamated and dividends would then be paid. None of this was at all unusual as an arrangement. What made the meeting 'truly memorable', as far as the *Railway Times* was concerned, was the proposal by the company that Hudson would receive a bonus. This was because the number of new shares to be issued exceeded the amounts required, leaving a surplus of three hundred and fifty shares to be put 'at the disposal of the Chairman'. If Hudson bought these shares, he would then stand to benefit from the premium at which they were standing in the market, worth around £8000 in total.[65]

Two of the more active shareholders of the York and North Midland, Joseph Rowntree and Thomas Laycock, objected to the payment of any bonus before the enabling Act had been obtained and 'before the services of the Chairman were completed'. In the case of a genuinely new undertaking, the profit or loss would be apparent and would be borne by those concerned, but with an extension, once the stocks were amalgamated, any profits or losses would be pooled and lost to sight. They were also concerned that the bonus would be paid to Hudson personally, rather than to the directors as a whole, although four of the board (Barstow, Davies, Richardson and Backhouse) waived any claim to these shares on the grounds that the Chairman had taken such an infinite amount of trouble in promoting the undertaking that he was due 'a compliment'. They also recognised that Hudson could have formed a separate company to promote the line and doubtless would still do so if the shareholders were not in favour of the scheme.

This left Rowntree and Laycock very much in the minority. The other shareholders thought they should

> instead acknowledge the stupendous efforts and ability of one who might be aptly termed the Colossus of Railways, whatever might be said by some as to the punctilios of principle ... when the ability of that individual was recognised in every direction, far and wide ... when Providence not only blessed him with an intellect of which the cleverest of people might be proud, but also with a constitution which enabled him to go through as much work as would have killed half-a-score men ... such an individual was especially deserving of such a compliment.

Some shareholders were roundly abusive of the dissidents and, in one heated exchange, Laycock was told that he was never satisfied and would not be quiet until he was 'put under the sod'!

As the meeting warmed up, Hudson raised matters of some substance that illustrate the lack of incentives to managerial initiatives in early Victorian England. He laced his words with some hostile remarks towards the two who had dared to oppose him. He found it difficult to speak of himself and 'had hoped that he should have been spared that painful duty'. He considered himself entitled to the bonus, having worked for them for seven years during which he had devoted 'all the energies of his mind' to their welfare. He had performed many additional duties that would have been costly for them to buy in, yet he had received only a pound a week for his services. What, he finished, could then be 'the meaning of this miserable drivelling, which must disgust any public man in the execution of his duties'? When the original proposals were finally put to the meeting, Rowntree and Laycock were the only members prepared to signal their opposition.[66]

The trade press was far less impressed with Hudson's position than the majority of the York and North Midland shareholders. According to the *Railway Times*, the proposal itself was deceptively worded. They saw the placing of surplus shares 'at the disposal of the Chairman' as an official construct that required the recipient to use them only for the company's advantage, given the fundamental obligation on all chairmen to 'act as the agent and steward of the company'. Since the sum involved was substantial, the fact that the shares were to be disposed of by the Chairman for his own 'private and personal use and emolument' should have been far more explicitly stated. The editorial sheds further light on the attitudes of Victorian commerce towards managerial incentives, for it saw nothing different in Hudson's efforts to the 'host of chairmen of railway companies who labour as zealously as he has ever done.' Above all, it deplored his 'vain-glorious boasts, conceived and uttered in a spirit of inflated pride' and greed:

> If offices which heretofore have been valued mainly for the honour they may confer upon worthy occupants are to be held now under the mere pretence of being in a great degree honorary and in fact with an earnest eye only to the arrival of a seasonal period for requiring munificent payments for the tenure of them, then indeed farewell to the thirst for office, or rather the willingness to take it when requested, amongst high-minded men! It will cease to be an object of ambition, because no longer unconnected with the suspicion at least of sordid and unworthy motives.

The new lines to the coast were to prove a watershed for both Hudson and the York and North Midland. Hudson's horizons had expanded well beyond the York and North Midland; the Newcastle and Darlington Junction had bought the Durham Junction line and he had formed a company to handle the construction of an iron bridge over the Tyne, now that the route to the north was rapidly moving ahead. The movement to merge three companies into the Midland was also well in hand.

Public perception of Hudson's character was also changing. Earlier admiration was now tempered by the recognition that he had a self-seeking side. Hudson may have seen this change as hypocritical of course, and was well aware that admiration was not a bankable commodity in itself, but things had changed. He was still a man to be reckoned with but his self-control was loosening, perhaps because of vainglory, perhaps also because of his weakness for drink. He was now being spoken of in the railway press as the 'Railway Napoleon' as much for the dictatorial nature of his tone as for the grandeur of his new ideas.[67]

Parliament had accepted the principle of branch lines and was making it easier for existing companies to construct them, rather than sanction the formation of separate competing companies and lines. This may have encouraged Hudson to go ahead with his plan to turn the York and North Midland into a much bigger company.[68] The proposed extensions were critical to this development. In November 1843 the York and North Midland was a small but successful local railway with less than fifty miles of line and share and loan capital under £700,000. Five years later, the extensions that had begun with the lines to Scarborough and Whitby raised the capital invested in the company to nearly £4,500,000 and added a further 215 miles of track,* but at the cost of an irrevocable weakening in the profitability of the York and North Midland's operations.[69]

Although the question of 'Hudson's bonus' excited much comment, no one at the meeting seemed to doubt Hudson's judgements on the commercial prospects of the line to Scarborough, although a letter to the *Railway Times* questioned the logic of a 'scheme by which the comfortable 10 per cent dividends of the York and North Midland will henceforth depend on the success of a line forty miles long to a town of 10,000 inhabitants'.[70] On the other hand, at the time the railways were under quite considerable political pressure over allegedly excessive profits. A witness to the 1844 Select Committee on Railways commented that the York and North Midland was actually capable of paying dividends of nearer 20 per cent, but looked upon that as 'rather dangerous' and, therefore preferred to build a line to Scarborough and appear to make 10 per cent on it, 'which of itself might not pay two per cent'. This turned out to be the most acute of observations.[71]

Hudson's aggressive use of competing steam tugs on the waterways between Hull and Selby had only antagonised the directors of the Hull and Selby without inflicting any real damage on their commercial position. It was no great surprise when the Manchester and Leeds, a company entirely hostile to Hudson's overall plans, announced that they were close to amalgamation with the Hull and Selby in the autumn of 1843. This carried the serious threat of excluding the York and North Midland from cross-country traffic between Liverpool and Hull. Hudson immediately held talks with

* See Appendix 2.

the board of the Hull and Selby and, in November 1843, made a reasonable offer which guaranteed Hull and Selby shareholders 6 per cent on their capital. This was rejected. Hudson, belatedly, tried to improve the tenor of their dealings by wishing his rival chairmen well with their merger, a courtesy which cannot have been entirely convincing to those involved. Although the merger was approved in principle in February 1844, its actual implementation was in fact deferred several times and Hudson began to realise that the Hull and Selby were much less committed to the Manchester and Leeds than they wished to appear.[72]

Throughout 1844, George Hudson continued to actively expand the scale of his various activities. In February, he told the York and North Midland's shareholders that he had every expectation that the Newcastle and Darlington Junction railway would be 'open in July next' and recommended on behalf of the board that the company purchase £50,000 of the shares in the North British, to help towards and also share in the proceeds from their construction of a line from Edinburgh to Berwick. The proposal was carried unanimously.[73]

As Hudson had predicted, the Scarborough Bill had an easy ride through Parliament and received its royal assent in June 1844.[74] The new line required, however, that changes be made to the terminus at York. Another platform was needed, to the north west of the main concourse and the consent of the city council was sought both for another crossing over the Ouse and for a second breach in the medieval walls. Even after these changes, the arrangements were very awkward. The station was a terminus that could be approached only from the west; trains to and from the east coast had to stop and then reverse in order to enter and leave.[75]

Hudson was able to tie together his business, political and personal interests on the east coast when he negotiated the York and North Midland's purchase of the Whitby and Pickering Railway in September 1844. Whitby, a remote and beautifully situated town twenty miles north of Scarborough, had a long tradition of fishing and whaling. It had also begun to attract a modest amount of holiday trade. Some miles inland, at Grosmont, there were deposits of an excellent stone suitable for building work as well as ironstone and lime, but transport had always been a major problem.[76] Until the 1830s, the only land route to Whitby was a rough moorland track. George Stephenson's basic, horse-drawn line, built in 1836, promised to improve matters but it turned out to be unequal to the terrain and steadily lost money.[77]

The York and North Midland paid only £80,000 for the line, well below the original cost of £105,000, but the entire twenty-four miles of track had to be relaid with stronger rails suitable for the planned introduction of locomotives. The new owners also built a more elegant station far more conveniently sited in the centre of Whitby. Given the limited market that Whitby provided, this represented a considerable investment, but it was consistent with Hudson's publicly-stated view that Whitby would become 'as flourishing a place as any in England'.[78]

The Hudsons were undoubtedly fond of the area, where they spent many of their holidays. George was so convinced that the railway would boost the town's prospects that he formed the Whitby Building Company in order to develop parts of the town, particularly the popular West Cliff area. His fellow shareholders in this venture all had close connections with the York and North Midland and with Hudson personally. They were James Richardson, the solicitor who handled most of his legal business, Robert Davies, his close business ally, Richard Nicholson, his brother-in-law, John Close, a manager of another of Hudson's railway companies, and George Andrews, his close friend and the architect who designed many of the York and North Midland's buildings.[79] Hudson had, however, another important reason for taking a central role in a project that had been discussed locally since the late 1820s. The benefits to the town from his drive and initiative would surely establish him as a candidate for election to Parliament as MP for Whitby.[80]

Behind the scenes, Hudson was still negotiating with the board of the Hull and Selby, trying to stave off the threatening prospect of their proposed merger with the Manchester and Leeds. The need for action was all the greater as the Hull and Selby was now projecting a branch line to Bridlington. The Hull and Selby was well aware of the strategic value of their line to both the rival companies and wanted a commensurately generous price. This was one of the problems with early railway development. Some lines carried excellent prospects, but existing companies were always under the threat of being outflanked by a rival. They could easily find themselves having to pay prices for acquisitions that would bear little relationship to the additional traffic revenues these acquisitions could actually generate. In March 1845, matters came to a head when a merger was proposed between the Manchester and Leeds, the Hull and Selby and two other smaller companies. Many of the Hull and Selby shareholders were apparently uneasy about this proposal and Sir William Lowthrop visited Hudson in York on their behalf to see on what terms the York and North Midland might be willing to offer. Hudson now decided to improve his terms to a most impressive 10 per cent on the shareholders' capital, with an associated option to buy H&S shares at twice their face value. A series of meetings were held until, on 2 May, the shareholders finally rejected the advice of their directors and resolved that the line be offered to the York and North Midland, if the latter were prepared to increase somewhat the share purchase option price. Towards the end of the proceedings, George Baker, Secretary to the York and North Midland, rose to speak to the meeting, saying that 'Mr Hudson and the directors of the York and North Midland were prepared to accede to and fully carry out the resolution [they had] so triumphantly carried'.

The members then separated, evidently in 'high spirits at the result', which was not surprising. They had used the Manchester and Leeds 'merger' like a shotgun to the head of the York and North Midland and persuaded Hudson to pay a very high price for their shares. The most striking thing is that, perhaps because of Hudson's personal unpopularity, almost a fifth of the votes were still against the revised proposal.[81] The prices that Hudson paid, on behalf of the York and North Midland, for the Hull and Selby (and also for the Whitby and Pickering) lines also led to the remark that some of those who had the all-important inside information were able on one or two days to 'sit down to dinner £20,000 richer than they breakfasted'.[82]

Despite these successful outcomes, Hudson, as Chairman of the York and North Midland, continued inexhaustibly. He was, after all, nothing if not energetic. The previous October, he had recommended four new lines to the York and North Midland shareholders: one to Doncaster, one to Bridlington, one to Harrogate and another from Pontefract to Castleford. In early July 1845, the complete set of extensions, in the form of draft Parliamentary Bills, were formally approved by the York and North Midland's shareholders without any dissent or doubt being expressed. This was rapid expansion indeed; the York and North Midland would soon hold nearly two hundred miles of line, an enormous increase on the company's thirty-mile core track from York to Leeds.[83]

There soon followed another of Hudson's truly triumphal days. On 7 July 1845, the York to Scarborough line was opened with much celebration. A 'sumptuous breakfast' was held in York's Guildhall after which an enormous train of thirty-five carriages, drawn by the engines *Hudson* and *Lion*, pulled the dignitaries out of York. A crowd of thousands watched their departure. The train arrived in Scarborough on what had been declared a local public holiday, to be met by the Mayor, the corporation and 'an immense multitude who had assembled in the cliff and height'. A magnificent luncheon followed, laid out in the temporary station, at which were present 'the young and beautiful Lady Mayoress of York and a large party of ladies'. After this, headed by a band, they all proceeded round the town, at the entrance to which a magnificent triumphal arch had been erected. Following the return journey, about seven hundred gentlemen sat down to an elegant dinner, served in the Town Hall, York. Guests included Lord Morpeth, the Lord Mayor of York, Sir John Lowther, the Dean of York and George Stephenson, who declared that the line was 'one of the first railway works which he had conceived'. He added, to great cheers, that it had been 'upon this subject that he had first met Mr Hudson and a fortunate meeting for all England it was'.[84]

George Stephenson, born in 1781, had been engineer to some of the most important lines yet built, the Stockton and Darlington, the Liverpool and Manchester (which he successfully built across the notorious Chat Moss), the Birmingham and Derby Junction, and the Manchester and Leeds.[85] He also engineered the North Midland, which was central to a vision he shared with Hudson of the railways as a 'great nation-wide system'. It was his involvement in the North Midland that had convinced Hudson and Meek to go ahead with their line from York to Leeds. Hudson clearly had plenty of reasons to be grateful to George Stephenson.[86]

Not surprisingly, the two Georges were the best of friends and, at the meeting of the York and North Midland in August 1845, Hudson proposed to the shareholders that they contribute £2000 towards Stephenson's testimonial. Hudson reminded those present of their debt to the 'fostering care and kindness' that had enabled the York and North Midland to surmount its original difficulties. At a time when many people were uncertain about buying their shares, 'his friend Mr Stephenson came forward – such was his confidence in the undertaking – and not only induced others to buy into it, but purchased a large number of shares himself, saying he would take all that came to him'.

Hudson was also capable of hospitality to humbler servants of the York and North Midland. In mid October 1845, on arriving at York he gave a substantial dinner to nearly three hundred engine drivers, stokers, mechanics, porters and other employees who all assembled in the early evening in one of the large workshops at York station and gave Hudson 'the most deafening cheers, renewed for several minutes'. The rest of the evening's entertainment passed off in the most agreeable manner and the party broke up at about eleven o'clock.[87]

At the same time he managed to broker a high-level alliance that would defend the York and North Midland's interests against strategic damage. On 25 October 1845, the York and North Midland and the Manchester and Leeds announced the settlement of their long-standing rivalry. Their accommodation meant that the Manchester and Leeds would become a joint lessee of the Hull and Selby line, would avoid any acts of competition against the York and North Midland's business in the East Riding, would not oppose a York and North Midland line from Selby to Goole, and would also withdraw from its alliance with the London and York Company.[88] This was a politically astute way for Hudson to damp down one of the major threats to his extensive empire. He had come a long way from the narrowly hostile tactics used against the Hull and Selby five years earlier.

Hudson was now living at a hectic pace. On the same day in January 1846, for example, that he addressed meetings of the Newcastle and Darlington Junction and the Newcastle and Berwick on their prospective merger, he also addressed a meeting of the York and North Midland, where he obtained support for lines from York to Hull, York to Leeds, an extension to Goole and the doubling of the track from York to South Milford. This was a regular occurrence and, although the meetings were usually held in York, for his convenience as much as that of the various groups of shareholders, they still required him to master a great many intricate matters to a standard sufficient to deal with a range of unexpected questions.

Confidence was still everything. In October 1846, the branch line to Bridlington was opened and a wealthy East Riding landowner, Sir T. D. Legard, wrote that 'when railways and railway shares were dark as night, men said that Hudson ruled and all was right'. That same month, Hudson told the members of the York and North Midland that they were

> richly entitled to their 10 per cent dividend, for they had made railways when no one else would embark in them. We embarked our money in the Scarborough line when almost every person thought it would be unprofitable ... I need not say to you that the Scarborough is one of the best paying lines in the kingdom.

Most, but not all investors were convinced of future prosperity under Hudson's management. Charlotte Brontë wrote to a friend in early 1846 that, although

> the York and North Midland is, as you say, a very good line yet I confess to you I should wish for my part to be wise in time. I cannot think that even the best lines will continue for many years at their present premiums and I have been most anxious for us to sell our shares ere it be too late and to secure the proceeds in some safer, if for the present less profitable, investment.[89]

This was a most perspicacious view. The Scarborough line in particular, although built efficiently and cheaply, was not a paying proposition, even though a sufficient number of the York and North Midland lines did go on earning well over 10 per cent to disguise the fact.[90]

The York and North Midland maintained its dividend in 1847 at the impressive rate of 10 per cent amid clear signs that the major programme of line extensions was coming to an end. On 4 June 1847, the improvements to the Whitby to Pickering line were complete and the first train drawn by a steam locomotive made its way into Whitby. This event prompted Hudson and his partners in the Whitby Building Company to acquire the entire West Cliff fields site as a speculation in 1848.[91] The branches to Seamer, Bridlington and Spofforth opened that summer and a number of smaller lines were also expected to open in the autumn.[92] Royal assents had been obtained for a number of other extensions that would take their total route mileage above two hundred and fifty. This included a line from Harrogate to Boroughbridge, which Hudson surprisingly saw as 'the most important line they had ever obtained from Parliament. It gave ... a direct communication from the north of England, as well as having a direct line to the south; so that it was now impossible for any other company to come in and rob them of their traffic.'

Also included in these authorisations was a short curve of line from Burton Salmon to Knottingley. Its ostensible purpose, to provide access to lime deposits at Knottingley and enable the residents of that town to travel to Leeds and Hull, was in reality secondary to longer-term considerations. Hudson's commitment to the two York-based companies he had helped to build from nothing was almost absolute and much deeper than his loyalties to the Midland and Eastern Counties. Parliamentary approval of the Great Northern's direct route from London to York through the eastern counties had changed his long-term objectives. Even in 1847, he was sufficiently farsighted to see that the Knottingley curve would offer the Great Northern a far easier route into York and would save them the construction of twenty-five miles of new line. Edmund Denison, MP for Doncaster and the driving force behind the Great Northern, at last realised this himself and towards the end of 1848 swallowed his pride and approached Hudson to seek a deal. An agreement was reached on 28 November 1848, whereby the Great Northern abandoned its proposed line from Askern to York but was granted running rights from Knottingley into York. This deal was to earn the YNM £1000 a year plus 60 per cent of Great Northern's earnings on all traffic on this section of line but, once this was known, the Midland shareholders denounced Hudson for acting against their interests.[93]

Behind the scenes, in 1848 the York and North Midland was in some financial difficulty and Hudson tried to cut expenditures in a number of ways. He was even prepared to ask a long-standing colleague, G. T. Andrews, to reduce his architectural fees, but the latter was quite offended and refused. Hudson instead looked to John Dobson, who had designed Newcastle Central to great acclaim.[94]

It now became clear to those inside the York and North Midland that new developments had almost run their course. Hudson, though, put the most constructive face on matters in public. He did not think that they would need to go to Parliament at all in the next session, since the York and North Midland had now 'got all that it could get; there was no prospect of any further profitable outlets for its capital and all that it had to do was to sit down and enjoy that which Parliament had committed to its charge, without fighting any more battles in Parliament'.

This state of affairs left Hudson free to concentrate on other things, for his attention had been steadily moving away from the York and North Midland. Since 1845 he had been active in Parliament as MP for Sunderland and as Chairman of the Eastern Counties Railway. His family moved to London early in 1846. It is probable that he was now glad to avoid the 'harassing anxiety' caused by regular attendance at committees of the House of Commons. He also had good hopes that, with the 'exception of some little temporary diminution' the following year, dividends would be maintained at their usual high level, since other lines could not easily interfere with their traffic. Their policy had been to resist any reduction of fares before Parliament and keep to the same fares as when they first incorporated. They had 'already filled up the country; there was no town in the north which they did not meet and they had only, therefore, to wait for the development of their traffic and enjoy the dividends'.[95]

This comforting view of the future was not to be borne out by events. Instead, the aftermath of the mania would prove more severe than the shareholders of the York and North Midland Railway had anticipated. It would also bring consequences for their chairman that no one could have foreseen.

3

The Way North

George Hudson had promoted the York and North Midland line during the period in which the commercial potential of locomotive passenger railways first became apparent, the five years following the opening of the Liverpool and Manchester Railway in 1830. During this time, a relatively balanced pattern of railway promotion began to emerge, with Parliament authorising major trunk routes from London as well as shorter lines to meet more local needs.

The period 1835–49 was the key time for railway construction in Britain: far more people were employed in building than running the railways, and far more money was invested in the railways than they took in revenue.[1] By 1849 most of the trunk lines of the English railway system had been built, in a construction boom that absorbed unprecedented amounts of labour and capital.[2] Hudson played an important part in this as he pursued the most glittering prize the railways could offer, control of the 'way north' from London to Scotland.[3]

In the early 1830s, the price of railway shares rose fairly steadily but railway speculation then reached fever pitch; in the single year from June 1835 to May 1836, the price of railway shares more than doubled.[4] This boom proved to be short-lived. Collapsing by the end of 1837, it was followed by a severe depression across the whole British economy that lasted for six or seven years.[5] Business confidence was generally low. Some railway schemes failed and others, including the Eastern Counties and the Manchester and Birmingham, were cut back in scope. Many of the companies that had already been formed had to raise more capital because they had over-run their construction budgets and there was 'alarm and disgust' at their hopelessly optimistic estimates and at the 'gross and glaring mistakes of Engineers'.[6]

Despite this, in the years 1837–43 there was a steady growth in the route mileage open to traffic, as lines promoted in the boom were constructed. The railways were also becoming a reliable, trustworthy part of daily life and in 1842 Queen Victoria herself made her first journey by steam train. The rate of progress had been very rapid and some now believed that the railways were getting close to their ultimate form. It was possible to travel

from London to Newcastle in seventeen hours, by rail to Darlington and
then by coach. 'What more', asked the *Railway Times*, 'can any reasonable
man want'?[7] In the 1840s, there were further improvements in locomotive
design, so that engines were able to haul heavier goods trains, and by 1850
freight was providing greater revenues to the railway companies than their
passenger trade.[8]

The sums of money needed to build a railway were enormous and could
run into millions of pounds at a time when the cost of a steam-driven mill,
for example, might be measured only in tens of thousands. Investors were,
nonetheless, waiting for favourable opportunities in such numbers that the
coffers of the Bank of England were said to be 'choked with bullion'. The
national press was well aware of the underlying situation and in 1844 one
newspaper wrote that 'capital clamours for profitable investment; confidence
has become eager, and may shortly become blind'. A public which 'but the
other day buttoned up its pockets is now becoming eager to embark in any
scheme'.[9]

By 1844 railways had regained their reputation as a secure and profitable
investment. The surge in railway speculations that built up in this and the
following year was far greater than during the railway boom of 1835–37 and
also on a much greater scale than the boom in other trades.[10] The speculative
peak of the mania was reached in the autumn of 1845; on 30 November
1845, the deadline for railway plans to be deposited with the Board of Trade
for consideration in the next parliamentary session, there were extraordinary
scenes. Roads and railway lines to London were blocked by the coaches
and special trains of several hundred rival promoters:

> As promoters elbowed each other in the pursuit of incorporation from Parliament,
> investors tumbled over one another in a mad scramble to secure a share in the
> golden harvest. In every street of every town, persons were to be found who were
> holders of railway shares. Elderly men and women of small fortunes, tradesmen
> of every order, pensioners, public functionaries, professional men, merchants,
> country gentlemen – the mania affected all.[11]

The end of the mania reduced the levels of investment in new railway lines
to very low levels, but the railway system had still grown considerably, from
only 700 miles in 1838 to 5000 miles of railway open to traffic by 1849. The
cumulative capital raised by the railways had risen from £65 million in
January 1844 to over £200 million by 1849.[12]

The arrival of the railways affected society in many ways, including
speed of news distribution, conceptions of time and the development of
the capital markets. Before the railways, printed news was distributed by

the mail-coaches and privately owned stagecoaches; only in places as close as Brighton or Oxford was it possible to put a London morning paper on sale by the afternoon of the day of publication. By 1851 the London morning papers were arriving on the train by 11 a.m. in cities as far away as Bristol or Birmingham.[13]

The notion of a 'gigantic, nation-wide, complex and exact interlocking routine symbolized by the railway time-table ... revealed the possibilities of technical progress as nothing else had done' and brought standard time to Britain. The natural difference of about half an hour between the east and west coasts had never mattered in a more leisurely age but in 1840, in order to keep time consistent across the networks, the South Western and Great Western railways decided to keep London time at all their stations. Greenwich mean time was gradually adopted throughout the country. The Dean of Exeter was persuaded to move his cathedral clock by fourteen minutes on 2 November 1852, after which symbolic surrender there was little further opposition to the notion of standard time.[14]

The railway construction era had major effects on patterns of saving, as shares in railway companies became a popular investment for the first time, bringing provincial stock exchanges into existence. The successful operation of the Liverpool and Manchester line led to the setting up of stock markets in both cities during the mini-boom of 1835–36. The later mania of 1845–47 led to the establishment of provincial markets in Leeds, Birmingham, Bradford, Bristol, Halifax, Huddersfield, Hull, Leicester, Newcastle, Nottingham and Sheffield. The number of stock-broking firms increased similarly, in Liverpool and Manchester from six in 1830 to more than eighty in 1837–38 and nearly three hundred in 1847. In York the increase was from three in 1837–38 to twenty in 1847. In the mania of 1845, partly-paid shares could be bought cheaply and then realised at a premium before further calls were due. 'Everybody is in the stocks now' said the *Economist*, 'needy clerks, poor tradesmen's apprentices, discarded serving men and bankrupts – all have entered the ranks of the great monied interest'.[15]

Until the formation of the York and North Midland, all the railways in County Durham and North Yorkshire ran east to west, their primary function being to carry coals from mines to seaports. The potential benefits of north-south travel soon became obvious and Joseph Pease, the leader of the Quaker businessmen who controlled the Stockton and Darlington Railway, saw that a line from York to Newcastle would occupy a highly strategic position in the developing main line network.

The line from York to Newcastle was projected in 1835. It was a meeting with representatives of the newly projected company, at first called the

Newcastle and York, then the Great North of England, in November 1835
that really brought home to Hudson the possibilities of the route and the
importance of its links with the York and North Midland. At this point
Hudson and Meek both made large investments in the Great North of
England.

The Great North of England's promoters obtained parliamentary acts in
1836 and 1837 enabling them to raise £1,000,000 in share capital, but by
August 1837 their difficulties had already become apparent. Although the
original intention had been to build the northern section of line first, the
projectors decided to start work on the easier section south from Darlington,
amid rumours that the money they were authorised to raise would be
nowhere near enough. The York to Darlington section of the line opened
in 1841 but the promoters were worried about their position; despite the
easy terrain, the first section of line had used up virtually all the capital
that should have taken them to Newcastle. The *Railway Times* called it 'one
of the worst-managed undertakings in the Kingdom'.[16]

On the face of it, the Great North of England's poor progress was a
serious setback to the directors of the York and North Midland. They had
anticipated a major boost to their revenues from the opening of a line to
Newcastle. In contrast, Hudson had been aware from the outset that the
Great North of England's failure would give him the opportunity to seize
personal control of a strategically important rail route. Towards this end
he encouraged close working relationships between the two boards although,
behind the scenes, the Pease family and other representatives of the Stockton
and Darlington were trying to weaken Hudson's position whenever possible,
to prevent their own overthrow.[17]

When the public opening of the York-Darlington line was celebrated by
a grand dinner for more than a hundred at the King's Head, Darlington,
the York and North Midland was almost as central to the proceedings as
the Great North of England and a toast to the 'Chairman and directors of
the York and North Midland' was greeted with great applause. Alderman
Hudson returned thanks on behalf of the York and North Midland and
gave the clearest possible signal to investors about the shape of the future
by expressing his hope that the 'unanimity which had been witnessed that
day, would last as long as they were connected together', a sentiment greeted
with warm applause.

Hudson was no expert in the technicalities of railway construction. What
he had above all was the ability to realise visionary schemes through a
combination of intense practicality and a gift for organisation. He was
expert, too, at persuading other people of the rightness of his vision.

The construction of the further sections of a line from York to Scotland, although fraught with major construction problems and unprecedented financial risk, would bring about a through route from London to Edinburgh and Glasgow; a rich prize, but Hudson would have to act fast. In March 1841, a parliamentary commission reporting on the question of railway communication between England and Scotland had favoured a west coast line from Lancaster to Glasgow via Carlisle, but only on the assumption that the line from Lancaster to Carlisle would be ready by the time the Carlisle-Glasgow section was built. If not, the better prospects lay with an east coast route.

The section of line from Darlington to Newcastle was now a matter of enormous strategic importance and on 30 April 1841 Hudson called a meeting of senior representatives from eight railway companies with a potential interest in it. The first meeting took place in Newcastle. When Hudson was called to the chair, he identified two reasons for holding the meeting: first to consider how they might be able to encourage traffic levels on the present railway line between Rugby and Darlington, and secondly to consider the best means of continuing the line northwards from Darlington to Newcastle. He pointed out that a route through Derby, York, Darlington and Newcastle would offer the shortest route to Edinburgh and eastern Scotland for passengers from the south and west of England. It would then be possible to travel from London to Newcastle in a day, which would greatly increase traffic levels. The Great North of England had an Act for the line to Newcastle, but the route from Thrislington, twelve miles north of Darlington, would be very expensive to construct.

His proposal was for a line to follow a more circuitous route than had been planned by the Great North of England, to make use of the existing lines of the Durham Junction, Clarence, Stanhope and Tyne, and Brandling Junction Railways. This route, which had been surveyed by Robert Stephenson, was seven miles longer than the original, but required the construction of only twenty-five miles of new track, nine less than planned.

The idea of using the patchwork of existing lines in the north east on a cooperative basis was not new, and had already been addressed in earlier, unsuccessful initiatives, but Hudson now put forward an ingenious solution based upon enlightened cooperation. The vehicle would be a newly formed company, eventually the Newcastle and Darlington Junction, with a share capital of £500,000. Hudson was well aware that investors would be reluctant to finance this venture, given the Great North of England's difficulties and the generally depressed state of the money markets. His brilliant suggestion was that the eight lines whose revenues would be considerably enhanced by the opening of the proposed line should collectively lease the new company for ten years from its opening, so as to provide shareholders in the proposed undertaking with guaranteed annual dividends of 6 per cent.

Hudson's proposals caused great excitement and found immediate favour. The 'greatest cordiality and good feeling' prevailed and John Clarke, Town Clerk of Newcastle upon Tyne, later recalled that when Hudson put his ideas forward, 'the light seemed suddenly to have broken upon us. We saw that the thing would be achieved and achieved soon and we returned to our homes comfortable and happy'.[18]

Robert Stephenson had helped Hudson to identify the issues relevant to the exact route and the Tory MP for York, J. H. Lowther had lobbied the government in support of his proposed route to Scotland: in September 1841, the Board of Trade confirmed the proposal as a 'fair subject for an application to Parliament'.

Although the proposal relied on a high degree of cooperation by the participants, it was politically well conceived. The railways whose lines he planned to use were small and financially weak. His plan did not include any of the Stockton and Darlington's track, although its lines ran parallel to the suggested route for the first five miles out of Darlington and could easily have been used. The Stockton and Darlington was a powerful and prosperous company and the Pease family a potential threat to Hudson's control of the 'way north'; he deliberately cut them out.

Hudson's scheme had a further advantage. It would cement his already cordial relations with the highly influential Stephensons, by offering Robert Stephenson a means of escaping his ruinous involvement in one of the small lines in the north east. Robert (1803–1859), like his father George, was one of the great names of the early railways. He was particularly noted as an engine builder and had, since 1823, been in charge of Robert Stephenson and Co., Newcastle, the first purpose-built locomotive works in the world. In 1829, he built the famous 'Rocket'. He was also heavily involved in line construction and planning, having carried out surveys for the Stockton and Darlington and for the Liverpool and Manchester lines, having been engineer to the Canterbury and Whitstable and the London and Birmingham companies. Despite his wide experience, he had accepted shares in the Stanhope and Tyne in lieu of fees owed to him as consulting engineer, without realising that the railway had not obtained an Act of Incorporation. He was thus liable for an unlimited amount of the quite extraordinary debts that the railway built up, sums far beyond his ability to pay, despite a highly successful career. Hudson's scheme had the potential to rescue him, by using the line as part of the route to Scotland.[19]

By September 1841, there was broad agreement with Hudson's plan and the representatives from the meeting went back to their respective companies to seek the support of shareholders. At least two other companies were actively considering the possibilities of a west coast line, so speed was vital.[20]

At a special meeting of the York and North Midland, Hudson outlined the various proposals that had so far been made in private. He confirmed that the board of directors of the York and North Midland were fully in favour of buying into the great connecting link between north and south and revealed that his ambitions were not only to provide a link to Newcastle but also to complete a route to Edinburgh. They would need to build about one hundred and twenty miles of new railway to achieve this, far less than would be needed for the west coast route. He held out the very real hope that they could achieve in two years on the east coast line 'what the western people could not accomplish in seven'. Moreover, although the York and North Midland was being asked to make a substantial contribution to the cost of leasing the Darlington to Newcastle line, the traffic from Hull to the north, all the traffic from south of Normanton, from Lancashire and from Leeds to Scotland would then have to pass over their line. The necessary resolutions were passed unanimously and long-standing shareholder Thomas Laycock spoke for all when he paid his 'high compliments to Mr Hudson for the energy and talent that he displayed in managing the affairs of the company, which were equal if not superior to [those of] any other man'.[21] The North Midland also met in November 1841, under the chairmanship of William Newton. The members were generally supportive, although one of the leading Liverpool investors, P. W. Brancker asked for the decision to be deferred for six months so that shareholders could be more fully informed about the proposals. These were carried, however, with only seven members against.[22]

The proposed scheme went through its various meetings without serious opposition, although the Stockton and Darlington were less than delighted at the way that Hudson had treated them. Captain Watts of Darlington, a shareholder in both the Stockton and Darlington and the North Midland, wrote an extraordinary series of letters about the plan to the *Railway Times*. His chief complaint was that the scheme was *ultra vires*, as it lay outside the original, stated intentions of the North Midland, but he also complained, in a letter published on 10 December 1841, that the editor had 'mutilated' his earlier letter by removing from it epithets seen as unnecessarily offensive. The editor must have been trying to reduce the risk of action for libel but Watts objected to even this, on the grounds that he was 'sufficiently tangible' to be responsible for his own acts.

He claimed that Hudson had hailed him at a station 'in the voice of a Stentor and with the publicity of a common crier' and had 'exulted' at carrying his point against Watts at the North Midland meeting. Apparently

Hudson had also met Watts's arguments about the principle involved with the dismissive rejoinder, 'pooh, pooh, we don't mind principle in matters of business'. The *Railway Times* regretted that a respectable individual (Hudson) should be charged with 'bluster and bullying and inflated and self-important notions', described as 'crowing like a cock upon his own dung-heap in the full plenitude of his tumultuary and noisy powers', as well as to be accused of 'seeking by threats and intimidation to cover his own insidious and selfish ends'. Such language, it believed, 'should not to be used by one gentleman to another'.[23]

The intemperate comments of Captain Watts on Hudson's impetuous manner, 'more nearly resembling a tornado than a common storm' and on his acumen, 'an abortion [of a scheme] conceived in cupidity and begotten in fraud', have been widely quoted as if they were revealing of Hudson's character and personal manner yet even Watts later tried to pass them off as only 'serio-comic remarks'.[24] He often acted as a spokesman for the Stockton and Darlington Railway and a careful reading of the full text of the correspondence suggests that Watts was a highly eccentric individual out to embarrass and discredit Hudson. The *Railway Times*, often critical of Hudson, concluded by openly doubting that Hudson's words or meaning had been 'rightly understood by Captain Watts'. Although the letters were clearly offensive and may well have caused some distress, Hudson seemed to decide that business was sometimes a rough trade and had the good sense not to be drawn into a response.[25]

Parliamentary authorisation was given in 1842 to incorporate the Newcastle and Darlington Junction Company and transfer to it the Great North of England's powers to build the line from Darlington to Newcastle.[26] Hudson was the inevitable choice as Chairman of the new company and the closeness of the links between the Newcastle and Darlington Junction and the York and North Midland was revealed by the composition of the new management team: John Close as Secretary; Richard Nicholson, Hudson's brother-in-law as Treasurer; Robert Davies, York's Town Clerk as Deputy Chairman and James Richardson, Hudson's solicitor, as one of the directors. The York and North Midland directors George Dodsworth and Sir John Simpson were appointed auditors and Hudson's close friend and architect to the York and North Midland, G. T. Andrews, was taken on as architect to the Newcastle and Darlington Junction as well.[27]

At this point, Hudson must have been delighted with his progress. He was now effectively in single-handed control of the creation of the east coast route to Scotland. He had had to use all his skill to get things to this stage; if others before him had thought of making use of the patchwork of existing lines in the north east, no one had managed to produce a workable scheme. It was Hudson, demonstrating classical entrepreneurial abilities, who had first persuaded his colleagues that such a desirable objective was within reach and then created the necessary cooperative mechanisms to make it happen. At the first meeting of the new Newcastle and Darlington Junction in October 1842, the shareholders offered fulsome praise to their chairman. He in his turn assured them that he had a very large interest in the undertaking and he had never been so confident about the success of any speculation into which he had entered.[28]

Six months later, in February 1843, Hudson announced that the Newcastle and Darlington Junction would be 'found quite as competent to pay 10 per cent as the York and North Midland' and, at the end of the meeting, his political adversary, the Recorder of York, C. H. Elsley, proposed a cordial vote of thanks to the chairman for the 'talent and zeal' he had always brought to bear on their railway interests. Other shareholders expressed the hope that their wholehearted support would be seen to contradict the 'calumnies which had been put forth against their respected friend and chairman'. The declaration that 'no man had been more abused [and] no man was more deserving of their confidence' drew loud applause.[29]

Hudson had been for a time on the Provisional Committee of the Great North British, later the North British; he had persuaded them that their original idea of a line from Edinburgh to Dunbar should be extended to Berwick. His ability to concentrate on 'the big picture' was emphasised in the summer of 1843, when the planned line from Edinburgh to Berwick drew favourable comment all round. The *Railway Times* had little doubt the proposals would be carried 'because the undertaking is in the hands of some of the most skilful, experienced and energetic gentlemen' connected with the railways. The position of the west coast route to Scotland was almost hopeless, 'now that the cause of the line to Berwick has been taken up by men who are able and ready to execute it'.[30]

Hudson rarely allowed the grass to grow under his feet. By the late autumn of 1843, having got to grips with the exorbitant demands of the Dean and Chapter of Durham over necessary land purchases, he had bought the Durham Junction line, which was in financial difficulties and unable to pay for the heavier track needed for the Darlington to Newcastle trains. He had also gained the support of the Newcastle and Darlington Junction shareholders for applications to Parliament to build a station at Gateshead and a high-level bridge across the Tyne.[31]

By February 1844, work on the Darlington to Newcastle route was well advanced. Capital of nearly £300,000 had been raised and much of it had been spent on construction work, with most of the contracts for building the stations also placed. The line was due to open on 1 July 1844. The Newcastle and Darlington Junction was now strong enough to cancel the original agreement for a lease of the line, at a guaranteed 6 per cent on the capital involved. The North British was seeking parliamentary permission to build the sixty-five miles from Edinburgh to Berwick and the Newcastle and Darlington Junction directors now sought the support of their shareholders for construction of the line from Newcastle to Berwick, so that no time would be lost in completing the east coast route to Scotland.

On 18 June 1844, despite all this activity, Hudson was able to enjoy the ceremonial opening of the thirty-nine mile route of the Newcastle and Darlington Junction from Darlington to Gateshead, on the south bank of the Tyne, where G. T. Andrews had been in charge of the design of the station. A special train, carrying Mr Carr Glyn, Chairman of the London and Birmingham and a small party of friends, left Euston at five o'clock in the morning so as to dine with his 'brother chairman', George Hudson, in Newcastle later that same day. Glyn's three hundred mile journey made apparent the integration that Hudson had already been able to achieve with his far-sighted plans; the train ran over more than eighty miles of the London and Birmingham (to Rugby), fifty miles of the Midland Counties (to Derby), sixty miles of the North Midland (to Normanton) and shorter sections of the York and North Midland (to York), the Great North of England (to Darlington) and the Newcastle, Darlington and Durham Junction, Pontop and South Shields and Brandling Junction Railways on its way into Gateshead at 2.25 p.m. George Stephenson's dream of linking the Tyne and the Thames had been realised at last, although for this first journey the average speed of thirty-seven miles an hour was artificially enhanced by running a very light train carrying only nine passengers.

The arrival was memorable. Glyn, George and Robert Stephenson and Hudson alighted to a wonderful reception from thousands of spectators, the greetings of the Mayor of Newcastle, the flying of flags, the firing of cannon and the ringing of church bells. At 5.30 p.m., the usual lavish dinner was provided in the Assembly Rooms for five hundred dignitaries and shareholders. The guest of honour was George Stephenson, who had long looked forward to the day when 'the mails would be carried by steam power from London to his native Newcastle' and many people expressed wonderment that some of their guests had been in London earlier that day and that they were able to read speeches in the newspapers that had been made in the House of Commons not much more than twelve hours before.[32]

Robert Stephenson was probably even happier. Hudson may have made plenty of enemies but he never forgot his friends; the arrangements between the Newcastle and Darlington Junction and the Pontop and South Shields

Railway (formerly the Stanhope and Tyne) had put an end to Stephenson's
acute financial anxieties.

This was a particularly successful period in Hudson's life. His touch and
judgement seemed utterly assured, despite the huge pressure of affairs. The
Brandling Junction's working of the line into Gateshead had been causing
concern. Hudson decided that the Newcastle and Darlington Junction would
be better off if the Brandling Junction were bought out completely, even
though the sum involved would be substantial. When the directors of the
Brandling would not see reason on the price, Hudson announced that the
Newcastle and Darlington Junction would build its own competing line
from Durham Junction to Newcastle. In August 1844, shortly before the
Newcastle and Darlington Junction shareholders were asked to adopt the
scheme, the Brandling directors approached Hudson again and a more
acceptable price was agreed. The deal allowed the Newcastle and Darlington
Junction to rationalise and shorten the route to Newcastle and to relay it
with heavier rails, better suited to the fast trains they were now running
from Darlington.[33]

With the line to Gateshead secured, Hudson's attention now turned to
matters north of Newcastle. He had already decided that the £700,000 capital
for the Newcastle to Berwick would be offered in the first instance to the
shareholders of the Newcastle and Darlington, in proportion to their holdings in that company. Before an Act could be sought from Parliament,
however, the route had to be determined and the major land acquisitions
agreed. The main problem concerned the objections of Lord Howick, MP
for Sunderland and eldest son of Earl Grey, the former Prime Minister, to
the proposed route. This ran close to, but not through, his grounds, land-
scaped by 'Capability' Brown and also passed between Howick's 'Long Walk'
and the sea. Lord Howick wanted the line moved inland where the gradients
were steeper and the costs of construction much higher. Hudson believed
the objection to be largely counterfeit, as the proposed line did not cross
any part of Howick's land nor interfere with it in any objectionable way.

His Lordship took a rather different view. He decided to put his weight
and influence behind the promotion of the Northumberland Railway, a
rival line from Newcastle to Berwick, to be built on the atmospheric system.
Brunel was to be retained as engineer. The legislature would only support
one of the rival bids, so Howick's intentions represented a very real threat
to Hudson's overall ambitions. He accordingly called for further survey
work and, at the end of July 1844, was told that an alternative route was
possible, although more difficult and much more expensive. He wrote
immediately to Lord Howick to say that his company would after all reroute
the line to the west of his grounds. Howick had by now resolved to pursue

the alternative line, regardless of the intentions of the Newcastle and Berwick Company. Howick's prospectus indicated that he would be seeking a capital of one million pounds for his sixty-mile line. He seems to have been quite convinced by the atmospheric system and promised an 'entire absence of noise, smoke, chance of damage from fire and other annoyances inseparable from the use of the locomotive engine'. Based on the experiences of the Croydon to Epsom Railway, the promoters hoped to 'convey trains more economically, at greater velocity and with more safety and comfort to the passenger' than on the orthodox locomotive system.[34]

Although Hudson had, both politically and socially, some sympathies with landowners, he was not easily outfaced or discouraged. Since his days at the York and North Midland he had grown used to intransigence and mendacity from even the most respectable of landowners and he was by now a very sound judge of the prospects of railway promotions. He told a meeting of the Newcastle and Darlington Junction Railway that 'he looked upon the competing line with perfect indifference', and argued that the scheme was 'trifling with the gullibility of the public' and was not one that anyone of 'practical mind would ever have thought of suggesting'.[35]

His down to earth approach was welcomed by the shareholders and, on 22 October 1844, he followed with an open letter to the 'Landowners of the County of Northumberland' on the subject of Lord Howick's projected line. His letter judiciously combined resilience and courtesy:

I trust I may be permitted, without disrespect to his Lordship, to offer you an explanation of one or two circumstances which his Lordship has, I am sure inadvertently, misrepresented ... Had the Newcastle and Berwick line, as proposed by Messrs Stephenson, been laid down in any other direction ... Lord Howick's scheme would never have seen the light. His Lordship with much ingenuousness says, that when he found the Newcastle and Berwick Railway was to pass between Howick and the sea, he apprised us that he must oppose it to the utmost, but as he knew that his objection would not form a parliamentary ground of opposition, his only mode of defeating the objectionable line was to get up a rival scheme ... which has not originated in a desire to promote the public convenience, or even to offer an advantageous investment for Capital, but solely and exclusively for the purpose of accomplishing a private and personal object. Lord Howick is pleased to say he believes that my concession to his wishes was only made when I learnt that his Lordship's determination to bring forward a competing line was no idle boast. This imputation I entirely disavow. I repeat that, as soon as Lord Howick had apprised me of his objection to the original route, I felt the utmost anxiety to conciliate him, and that when Messrs Stephenson acquainted me with the change that had taken place in their plan (which I communicated to Lord Howick on 1 August) he had not published any prospectus for the formation of a new company ... On the part of the Company with which I am connected, I can state with great sincerity that ... we have pursued an open and straight-forward course ... At the proper time we announced our intention to embark in this project; the country was carefully surveyed, the most eminent engineering skill and experience were applied to the selection of an eligible route. When that route was proposed it proved to be objectionable at one point to a single landowner – we were anxious to meet the wishes of that individual, but we were bound not to decide upon an alteration without due caution and circumspection; our deliberation, it seems was unfortunately protracted too long, the dissatisfied party could not wait and we have been rewarded for our caution, or in other words, punished for our tardiness by the appearance of a rival scheme.

Hudson ended by saying, on behalf of the Newcastle and Berwick, that they were happy to 'leave the merits of the two projects to the judgement of Parliament' as the Newcastle and Darlington Junction Railway had shown what they were capable of accomplishing, both as regards construction costs and speed of execution.[36]

As Hudson was well aware, most schemes would be bound to infringe somebody's aristocratic privilege and Howick's proposal duly provoked its own set of objections. Sir Matthew Ridley wrote to say that

the line to be adopted by Mr Brunel is so extremely objectionable to me as affecting the quiet of my residence and so much at variance with my views as regards the public interest that I must give it all the opposition in my power.

He particularly objected to the fact that the intended line

passes immediately contiguous to my steward's house and the main entrance to my seat ... the immediate contiguity of the line to any gentleman's country lodge is to most people a most serious objection [and] after it passes my steward's house it crosses and interstices into my private carriage and horse ride to the Down Hill.

Interference with his rights would reduce the time he spent in the area, with consequent effects on local employment.[37]

Lord Howick's proposal was materially weakened by his obvious self-interest; he was clearly putting his own convenience above all else and Hudson was not slow to point this out. When the Board of Trade reported in February 1845 on the rival plans, it was clear that Hudson's judgement had been much sounder than Howick's; the Board found that the Newcastle and Berwick was a 'decidedly better line than the Northumberland' in terms of the established nature of the method of propulsion, the accommodation it gave to local towns, and its 'connections with the other railways forming the eastern line of communication'.[38] When Lord Howick offered to drop his opposition in the House of Lords to the Newcastle to Berwick line 'for a mere £11,000', Hudson apparently retorted that he would pay 'not a

farthing, my Lord'.[39] Whether or not this is true, the fact remains that
Hudson had fought a difficult adversary with exemplary judgement.

Although Hudson could appear hard-nosed, he was actually a flexible player
of the game and often prepared to make generous concessions in the short
term as a way of achieving strategic gains. When these gains did not go on
to produce sufficient revenues, the deals could look far less attractive.

The Newcastle and Darlington Junction had always had a difficult relationship with the Great North of England, on which it depended for the
working of the York to Darlington line. The Great North of England had
overpaid for the construction of the line and its dividend record was poor,
with payments of less than 2 per cent as recently as August 1844, in spite
of the extra traffic from the new Darlington to Gateshead line. Hudson had
been publicly critical of many of the Great North of England's recent plans,
although his real difficulty was strategic rather than operational: the Great
North of England directors welcomed the progress of the direct line from
London to York, since it would greatly increase revenues on their own line.
For Hudson, the reverse was true; the arrival of the direct route in York
would be ruinous to the York and North Midland and would also frustrate
his own ambition to control the route from London to Scotland via the
east coast.[40] These inescapable differences came to a head in 1844 when the
York and North Midland projected a branch line to Harrogate and was
met by a counter-proposal from the Great North of England for a Harrogate
Junction scheme that would extend their own proposed Harrogate and
Knaresborough line to Leeds. Hudson noted his vulnerability to a deal
between the London to York line and the Great North of England and, on
18 February 1845, made a written offer on behalf of the York and North
Midland to the Great North of England shareholders. The offer of a guaranteed 8 per cent seemed generous, but was still not acceptable to the Great
North of England shareholders, who were well aware of the situation and
thought they could get 10 per cent.[41]

Hudson then learnt that the London and York had also offered 8 per
cent for the Great North of England. This was a real threat to his interests
and on 19 May he made an improved bid by letter to the Great North of
England board, on behalf of the Midland, the Newcastle and Darlington
Junction and the York and North Midland, which were now willing jointly
to lease the Great North of England's lines from 1 July 1845, given an
associated option to purchase. Their offer provided Great North of England
shareholders with the guaranteed dividend of 10 per cent in perpetuity that
they had been seeking, terms that immediately and sharply raised the price
of their shares on the open market. Wilkinson, the chairman, thought it

would be 'absolute madness' to refuse the offer and his shareholders agreed on 27 May 1845. Hudson described the arrangement, somewhat ruefully, as the 'hardest bargain he ever drove'.

He then immediately withdrew the Great North of England's proposal for the Harrogate Junction line, even though it was part way through its parliamentary hearing. This was one railway projection that had got a little too close for comfort.[42]

With Lord Howick vanquished, the process of seeking parliamentary approval now went ahead quickly and the Newcastle and Berwick Bill received its Royal Assent on 31 July 1845. It had always been likely that the Newcastle and Berwick would be a satellite of the Newcastle and Darlington Junction; this was confirmed with the announcement that the managing committee would consist of Hudson as chairman, Robert Davies and James Richardson, both of whom were to be directors, Richard Nicholson, who was to be the treasurer and John Close, who was appointed secretary.[43] The new company had a proposed capital of £1,400,000, the bulk of which would come from Newcastle and Darlington shareholders, already encouraged no doubt by the dividend they had received in February at the rate of 8 per cent per annum, based on the results of the first half-year's operations. The board intimated that the dividend should soon rise to 10 per cent. Their confidence was manifest in their personal shareholdings: Hudson took up £200,000 worth of shares, Davies £100,000 and Nicholson £50,000.

In the late summer of 1845 Hudson's career continued to flourish with almost extravagant energy. At the half-yearly meeting of the Newcastle and Darlington Junction in August 1845 he was able both to declare another dividend of 8 per cent per annum and to note that the company's £25 shares were now worth £85, making it 'one of the most fortunate companies in the kingdom'.[44] In that month, he was elected as MP for Sunderland, a matter of great importance to him. With the setting up of the Newcastle and Berwick he would also have personal control of a continuous railway route running from Bristol to Berwick.

When he took the chair at the first general meeting of the Newcastle and Berwick in September 1845, the triumphant nature of his progress was brought home to him by a 'loud burst of cheering from all parts of the room'. The *Railway Times* had 'never seen so much enthusiasm' at any railway meeting. This was one of the peaks in Hudson's career; he must have felt that his great efforts had been thoroughly worthwhile. He was able to confirm that the company had obtained its Bill against Lord Howick 'without any compromise', but he also hinted at the strain he had been under, by adding that he would always remember the 'weeks of great mental anxiety' and the gratification he felt when 'right succeeded against wrong'.

A shareholder who had been present throughout the six or eight weeks the Bill was passing through the Committee of the House of Commons gave thanks for 'the great exertions, the incessant attention and the more than human efforts of [their] excellent chairman'.

Their chairman could now look forward to the time when the line from York to Berwick would be controlled by only one company, instead of being shared between two or three, and hinted at the mutual trust of the committee in the discussion on the annual salary of John Close, the company secretary, which was fixed at £300. Hudson praised his many fine qualities and said he could entrust anything to Close as he had ever found him 'zealously devoted to those whose interests are committed to his charge'. Finally, said Hudson, he was looking forward to the opening of the line in perhaps a year's time (aside from the construction of the two major bridges). The meeting, a triumphant one for George Hudson and George Stephenson, ended with the approval of testimonials to both of them.

However excellent Hudson's progress, the issue of entry into Newcastle could no longer be postponed. In autumn 1843, Hudson had obtained the approval of the Newcastle and Darlington Junction shareholders, who were concerned only with the approach to Newcastle from the south, for applications to Parliament for a station at Gateshead, on the south bank of the Tyne, and a high-level bridge across the river. A proper entry into Newcastle would require both the bridge and a terminus in Newcastle rather than Gateshead, but the costs of each were daunting. Hudson avoided confronting the issue for some time, although he was well aware that when Newcastle became merely part of the through route from the south to Scotland the case for a bridge and a central station in Newcastle would be irresistible.

While he waited for the proposals for the Newcastle to Berwick line to become firmer, Hudson manoeuvred for a better position over Newcastle's bridge and station. When the line from the south reached Gateshead in June 1844, his position still seemed to be that passengers alighting there for the north should travel two miles to the nearest bridge before crossing the Tyne. In August 1844 he attempted to fudge matters by claiming that the cost of the bridge was too great to be covered by the Newcastle and Darlington Junction and Newcastle and Berwick companies alone and would have to be borne by the various businesses that operated between Rugby and Edinburgh. The bizarre logic of this proposal convinced no one and the problem remained unresolved.[45]

George Stephenson, along with the directors of the Newcastle and Carlisle and Newcastle Town Council, pressed Hudson to reconsider his position. Stephenson's opinion had always been that the credibility of an east coast through route to Scotland would depend on their commitment to an effective high-level bridge over the Tyne gorge. The directors of the Newcastle and Carlisle Railway were also understandably keen to see a prestigious station in the centre of Newcastle. They were known to be prepared in principle to pay some of the costs of a station south of Neville Street, although Hudson was concerned to establish the precise level of their contribution. Newcastle Council was hugely supportive of both projects for two main reasons: first, the city's position on the through line would transform its importance on the national map, and, secondly, they had already embarked upon the ambitious development of the city centre, in which a new station would be crucial.

The all-important breakthrough came towards the end of 1844. Hudson met the Newcastle Town Improvement Committee on 30 December 1844 and guaranteed that the high-level bridge would be constructed within five years of completing the formalities. He agreed that the bridge would carry horses, carriages and foot passengers as well as the railway and that a suitable station would be constructed in the centre of Newcastle. A few days later, the council gave their full support to the Newcastle and Berwick Bill, which was to go to Parliament later that year.

By the time of the first meeting of the new Newcastle and Berwick Railway Company, in September 1845, the directors were clearly well aware, whatever the cost considerations, that the crossing of the town of Newcastle was a 'great national work'. Hudson also gratefully acknowledged the 'almost unanimous support of the Corporation and town of Newcastle' and said that it would be most ungrateful of the railway company if they did not 'erect such a station and such a bridge as will prove an ornament to that town and the latter, as a work of art, an object of admiration for the kingdom at large'.[46] This was to be no mere hyperbole.

In the same year Hudson obtained the Acts of Parliament for the bridge and station. Work progressed on Stephenson's design for a bridge to carry a railway above the public road, the roadway to be suspended 22 feet below the rails and 90 feet above high water mark. The bridge was to be 1300 feet long with arches of a span of 125 feet, resting on relatively light piers and wrought-iron tension chains taking most of the lateral thrust.

Although very little happened about the station for almost a year, the die was cast. Hudson, pressed again by the Newcastle and Carlisle, appointed John Dobson as architect on 23 February 1846. It was an excellent choice. Dobson was already involved in Richard Grainger's major redevelopments in the centre of Newcastle and would eventually be recognised as the north east's 'most eminent architect'.[47]

Dobson worked closely on the plans for the station with Hudson, with

whom he got on well.[48] His first design for the building was quite magnificent. Although his brief had been complicated by the fact that Newcastle
would be a through station, rather than a terminus, and by the gentle curve
of the tracks, Dobson's scheme was splendidly cohesive. It was also on an
enormous scale, with the train shed covered by an iron and glass roof built
across three enormous arches that each spanned sixty feet. The façade was
nearly six hundred feet long, featuring numerous pairs of Roman Doric
columns set on raised plinths. In the opinion of the architect, the most
striking feature of his design was the central portico. Two hundred feet
long and seventy feet wide, it was flanked on each side by an arcade that
allowed plenty of room for carriages to drive in from either end, turn and
go out again, a feature of great convenience, given the Newcastle weather,
as well as grandeur. The overall scheme for the station was approved by
the Newcastle and Carlisle, who were to pay about a third of the cost, in
June 1846 and by the Newcastle and Darlington Junction that August.[49]

Hudson's election as MP for Sunderland was probably his most important
achievement in 1845 and led to his involvement in a number of other railway
ventures in the north east. Hudson's selection by Sunderland did not rest
primarily upon the appeal of his political ideology, although the protectionist
case was a perfectly respectable one, but far more on the benefits he was
able to bring to Sunderland's local economy, principally the construction
of a new dock and related improvement of the town's rail connections.

Hudson's plan was for the Newcastle and Darlington Junction to buy up
virtually all the small lines in the northern part of County Durham and,
by linking them closely with the development of the north-south main line,
to be able to offer the great colliery owners, the Marquess of Londonderry,
the Earl of Durham and the Hetton Coal Company, a much cheaper and
more efficient means of transport than their own piecemeal network of
local lines.[50] The plan would bring trade to the Newcastle and Darlington
Junction and would also enhance Hudson's own reputation as a major
benefactor of the town he represented. The support of the coal masters and
a grateful electorate would confirm his position as an MP and enable him
to make his mark on national politics and London society.

There had been wagonways in the town since the 1790s and, in 1822, the
first complete line to be engineered by George Stephenson opened, running
from the colliery at Hetton Lyons to the coal staithes at Sunderland and
worked by locomotives for part of its length. Until the 1830s, all the railways
on Wearside were private lines constructed by the owners of collieries and
quarries. The first public railway in the area, the Stanhope and Tyne, opened
in 1834 to run lime and coal to South Shields. It was soon followed by the

Durham and Sunderland, promoted by the town's civic leaders, which began to carry coal and passengers in 1836 from a basic wooden station on the town moor in Sunderland to Hetton and Haswell. It was not, however, a very well constructed railway; its curves and gradients were so bad that the line could only be worked by fixed engines. More lines were soon built, the Durham Junction and the Brandling Junction from Monkwearmouth on the north bank of the Wear to South Shields and Gateshead. The latter carried both coal and passengers, but its priorities were clear from the fact that the terminus at Monkwearmouth, when it was built in 1839, was little more than a wooden shed.

The various lines all struggled financially, perhaps because the coal masters were too powerful to tolerate proper tariffs, and those that were relevant to the construction of the main line towards Newcastle, such as the Durham Junction and the Brandling Junction, were taken over by the Newcastle and Darlington Junction. The other lines continued to struggle and travel east-west was invariably slow; on the Durham and Sunderland line, for example, it could take more than two hours to travel thirteen miles.[51]

In January 1846, the members of the Newcastle and Darlington Junction were asked to approve a whole raft of acquisitions in the north east that were proposed as ways of generating good business for the company. They actually made more sense in the context of the pledges Hudson had given to the local constituency party and electors of Sunderland. Here was the inescapable question of whether acquisitions that best met the demands of Hudson's position as a local MP were necessarily in the commercial interests of the shareholders of the Newcastle and Darlington Junction. Few were prepared to challenge Hudson's judgement on this matter, given the dividends he had always been able to generate for the members. They merely noted his comment that 'they had got possession of nearly the entire district ... and he did not think there was anything left for any other party to take up', approved the proposed acquisitions and agreed that the money would be sought by the offer of new shares to the existing shareholders.[52]

In the summer of 1846, Hudson's position began to look less secure. The Great Northern had obtained the royal assent to its Act on 26 June 1846 for a direct line from London to York, although this did not threaten his interests north of York, now that the Great North of England had been so expensively purchased. The line from Newcastle to Berwick was not finished, although completion was expected by the following February. Hudson said repeatedly that the line 'would pay, very soon, as good a dividend as any line over which he had the honour to preside', because it had been constructed so cheaply, but his calculations of the average construction costs per mile were rubbished in the railway press.[53] There was also a good deal of negative publicity about high fares on Hudson lines, particularly in the *Times*. He responded by trying to focus attention on sections of line where the fares charged were low and by accusing the *Times* of hypocrisy in charging more for advertisements than some other newspapers, but his counter-attack was unconvincing.

During the summer, the Newcastle and Darlington Junction, without the help of the York and North Midland or the Midland railways, decided to exercise its right to buy out the Great North of England, which operated the line from York to Darlington. As a result, the Newcastle and Darlington Junction changed its name to the York and Newcastle Railway, which better described its area of activity. In September 1846, the new company's Richmond branch was opened, most unusually, without pomp or ceremony. At the company's half-yearly meeting, Hudson also drew attention to allegations against him of share misdealing. These he denied, stating for the record that he had 'not purchased a single share either in the Great North of England or the Hull and Selby lines and consequently he had not made a single sixpence by either of the purchases'. He added, in spirited fashion, that he 'had no interest in the lines except as a trustee over the interests of the shareholders and as a joint shareholder with them', but his protests had a hollow ring. It was beginning to look as if he could be rattled by relatively minor difficulties.54

There were no further problems for the time being and Hudson attended the festivities for the opening of the Clarence and Hartlepool Junction railway in October 1846. The line was not strategically important but it was a great day for the port of Hartlepool, which was now linked to the main line. Hudson, both as Chairman of the York and Newcastle Railway and as MP for Sunderland, embarked with several directors, the Lord Mayor of York and a 'numerous party of friends' on a special train from York. This met another special train from Hartlepool containing the mayor and corporation of that town, along with directors of the Hartlepool Dock Company and of the Clarence and Hartlepool Junction Railway. The two trains went on together to Hartlepool to inspect the docks, now owned by the York and Newcastle Railway. The weather was less than kind, the rain 'poured in torrents, while the wind blew a perfect hurricane', but the other aspects of the day were entirely enjoyable. After inspecting the docks, the party adjourned to the Town Hall for a 'highly congratulatory address' by the local council, which Mr Hudson 'acknowledged in suitable terms'. Later that evening, at six o'clock, about 'sixty gentlemen sat down to a truly splendid dinner', with Mr Hudson presiding. The mayor was particularly proud that, only fourteen years ago, Hartlepool had been but a poor, insignificant fishing village but had now become a port of considerable importance. The final toast was to Mr Hudson, drunk three times three to cheers and applause. The dinner finished at 10.30 p.m. and special trains then took the visitors back to York and Newcastle.[55]

The York and Newcastle Company got off to a good start when Hudson was able to announce a highly impressive dividend of 9 per cent per annum for the second half of 1846. They also looked forward to the opening of a number of branch lines, while the shareholders in the line north of Newcastle were encouraged by the opening of the section of line from Newcastle to Morpeth, despite delays due to bad weather.[56]

In Newcastle itself, delays continued to postpone the start date for the station. Legal problems over the transfer of land from Newcastle Council to the railway company were resolved in January 1847 and the Newcastle and Carlisle line then opened a temporary station, near to the proposed site in March 1847. Work on the foundations of the station building finally began in March 1848.[57]

The frenetic promotions and exaggerated expectations of the railway mania were now rapidly coming to an end, as can be seen from the dealings between Hudson and the North British, who were building the line from Edinburgh to Berwick. In February 1847, there was some prospect of a takeover by one of Hudson's companies and an offer of a guaranteed return of 8 per cent on capital was made. The shareholders in the North British held out against this, no doubt because Hudson had paid 10 per cent to other lines in the past, but Hudson refused to raise his offer. The North British eventually decided that they had been wrong to turn him down and sent round a deputation to seek an offer of only 6 per cent, but this met with no success.[58] Clearly, the times were beginning to change.

Work on the Tyne bridge did, however, continue at a satisfactory rate. By early August 1847, one of the six arches had been completed and Hudson 'dropped in' on his way to Sunderland to see how things were going. He was given an excellent reception; 'guns at the works were immediately fired as a welcome and St Mary's bells set a-ringing'. For his part, he examined the arch with great care and interest, expressed his utmost satisfaction with the work and, as he left, 'bestowed a gratuity of £20 on the workmen, without any injunction to keep their powder dry'.[59]

The York and Newcastle Company also appeared to be making good progress. Hudson announced that they were going to build several small branch lines in Durham and a new dock at Jarrow Slake on the Tyne, although the project to build a line from Gateshead to Durham via the Team valley had been opposed in committee and was to be delayed by a year. This apart, Hudson said, they would not have to go to Parliament for any Bill in the next session. He proposed an impressive 9 per cent dividend, adding that, 'when their branch lines were finished, he did not know a railway that had better prospects before them'.

An amalgamation of the York and Newcastle (formerly the Newcastle and Darlington Junction) and the Newcastle and Berwick railways had been approved in principle as early as January 1846 and, in August 1847, it was duly approved by the two groups of shareholders. The line had opened on 1 July 1847 and the members were excited by Hudson's announcement that temporary bridges over the Tyne and the Tweed were expected to be ready by June 1848, to provide 'uninterrupted transit from London to Edinburgh', although half the claim was totally unrealistic, as work on the Berwick-Tweedmouth bridge did not start until May 1847 and would not be finished until three years thereafter.[60]

The two companies were duly amalgamated into the York Newcastle and Berwick Railway as from 9 August 1847, with Hudson once again the Chairman, Robert Davies, the Town Clerk of York, the Deputy Chairman and John Close the Company Secretary. The members met in February 1848 and Hudson was pleased to be able to propose a dividend of 9 per cent per annum and to confirm that their traffic levels were most encouraging. They had carried the astonishing quantity of more than a million tons of coal in the last six months and their trains could now travel the 394 miles from Rugby to Glasgow in eight hours twenty minutes. Moreover, increased traffic levels and even shorter journey times were in prospect when the Tyne and the Tweed were both successfully bridged.

In 1848, the replacement for Monkwearmouth station was completed, the starting point for northbound traffic from the north bank of the Wear. Monkwearmouth was the deepest colliery in the world and a trip down its shaft was a formidable experience

there was no sense of descent but the little round hole of light seems to be flying faster and faster over your head upward, as if it were going to the skies and at length – in a couple of minutes perhaps – the orifice of the shaft has apparently turned itself into a daystar which shines far, far above you in the firmament, some fifteen hundred feet away.

The previous station had been little more than a wooden hut, though curiously suited to the working locality. Hudson had determined on a replacement that would celebrate his election as MP for Sunderland. On behalf of the railway, he commissioned Thomas Moore (1796–1869), the leading architect in Victorian Sunderland, to design it and the new buildings were unusually grand for what was essentially quite a small station. It drew its inspiration from the architecture of ancient Greece, with a classical portico and Ionic columns that were clearly meant to impress. The train shed was covered with an iron and glass roof, the glass supplied by Hartley's glass works, which was close by. At that time, there was no railway bridge over the river, so passengers wanting to go to Sunderland, on the south side of the precipitous Wear river valley, had to walk or take a horse-drawn cab over the road bridge into town.[61]

In the summer of 1848, work on the Tyne high-level bridge was well advanced and the bridge from Tweedmouth to Berwick was expected to open in about a year. The 'unsettled state of the continent' had seriously reduced the levels of coal exports and trade levels were generally low. This was in the nature of things; Hudson was far more concerned to hear of the interest the Caledonian Railway was taking in the Newcastle and Carlisle and the Maryport and Carlisle Railways. The Newcastle and Carlisle had been completed first, in May 1839 and the Maryport and Carlisle was formed to continue the line thirty miles to the west, so as to develop the northern part of the west Cumberland coalfield and to 'unite the German Ocean and the Irish Sea'.[62]

There was some commercial logic in the York Newcastle and Berwick establishing closer links with cross-country routes in northern England, but the interest of the Caledonian raised a strategic threat that Hudson was anxious to avoid. Prompt and decisive action was needed and, with insufficient time to consult the members of the York Newcastle and Berwick, Hudson entered into personal contracts to lease the two lines at guaranteed rates of 4 and 6 per cent, leaving the contracts to be adopted in due course by the shareholders of the York Newcastle and Berwick. Although these guaranteed rates were much lower than Hudson had been offering to other companies, the offers were perfectly reasonable in the context of the substantial fall in the market value of railway company shares generally. By now, many were thinking that 'so rapid and fearful a decline' was the result of many of the large companies overestimating their strength and making improvident purchases and guarantees; thus it was said that 'branch lines may be turning out dear, preference shares may interfere with the dividends upon old shares; and 10 per cent guarantees are inconvenient things'.[63]

George Hudson had come a long way from his modest entry into railway promotion with the York and North Midland Railway. In 1842, the plans of the Great North British to build a line from Edinburgh to Berwick had given him the opportunity to pursue the most coveted prize in the railway world, a through route from London to Scotland, if suitable relations could be established with the Great North British and if a line from Newcastle to Berwick could be constructed quickly enough to head off developments on the west coast. The various companies that were formed to achieve the different parts of his grand design acted in close harmony because, with each new formation, he looked to fill the senior positions with trusted colleagues from his early years in York.

The shape of the great railway system Hudson intended to create had now become clear. The routes stretched from Edinburgh to Doncaster, from Maryport to Sunderland and from Hull to Leeds; only one company, the Leeds and Thirsk, had broken through the cordon. Posterity, in the person of the North Eastern Railway's official historian, W. W. Tomlinson, has judged this grand design well, arguing that the concentration of power in the hands of a 'great railway tactician secured unity of policy and management from Rugby to Berwick and resulted in the rapid consolidation of railway interests throughout the three northern counties'.[64]

By the end of 1848, Hudson was close to achieving his ambitions. A new company, the York Newcastle and Berwick, had consolidated the various separate ventures, he and his close friends controlled the company, and the various sections of line had been built despite the difficulties presented by the collapse of confidence in railway promotions in 1847. In 1848, the 9.30 a.m. express from Euston, for first-class passengers only, reached York by 3.40 p.m. and, after calling at Newcastle and Berwick, arrived at Edinburgh at 10.35 p.m. The major bridges over the Tyne and Tweed and Newcastle Central were scheduled for completion in 1849–50, to then bring 'uninterrupted transit from London to Edinburgh'. The various companies had all paid high dividends once their routes had opened.

There is also some evidence that the management committee of the Stockton and Darlington invited Hudson, in late 1848, to bid for the lease of their lines and guarantee their shareholders 15 per cent a year on the face value of their shares, in recognition of the line's unusually strong profit record. The board of the York Newcastle and Berwick gave this serious consideration, but did not go ahead because other events overtook them, arising out of an apparently innocuous meeting of the shareholders to ratify the contracts made by Hudson with the Newcastle and Carlisle and the Maryport and Carlisle Railways and to discuss the proposed reduction in the dividend for the second half of 1848 to 6 per cent a year.[65]

4

The Great Amalgamator

The three railway companies that later formed the Midland Railway were all authorised during the first railway investment boom of 1836–37. They formed a network centring on Derby, where a single station provided the terminus for all three lines. Each opened in 1839–40 but none was very profitable, a fact that must have been particularly galling to their share-holders, placed as they were between the highly profitable London and Birmingham to the south and the small but lucrative York and North Midland to the north.

The North Midland Railway ran the seventy-three miles to Leeds via Chesterfield and Normanton, rather than through Sheffield and Barnsley, in deference to the 'easy gradients' philosophy of its engineer, George Stephenson.[1] At Leeds, the North Midland fed traffic onto the York and North Midland that ran the thirty-mile route to York.

The Birmingham and Derby Junction Railway lines ran for nearly forty miles to Hampton, about ten miles south east of Birmingham, where it made a junction with the London and Birmingham line. Opened in August 1839, it provided a continuous rail link between London and Derby. The situation was complicated by the existence of the third line, the Midland Counties Railway, whose line covered the fifty miles from Derby through Loughborough and Leicester to Rugby, where it also joined the existing London-Birmingham line. When the Midland Counties opened, in July 1840, the choice of routes for through traffic from London to Derby led to bitter and damaging competition between the Midland Counties and the Birmingham and Derby Junction.

The first section of North Midland line between Derby and Masborough opened on 11 May 1840 without formal ceremony, although George and Robert Stephenson and George Hudson all travelled on the first train to run on the track.[2] George Stephenson lived nearby at Tapton House, on a hill overlooking the tracks. He and Hudson were partners in an enormous lime-works at Crich and in the Clay Cross coalmines and ironworks, both of which looked to the new line to move their goods.

It was the North Midland's connections to London that encouraged Meek and Hudson in York to build the York and North Midland and Hudson soon became a major investor in the North Midland. Stephenson thought the North Midland the 'finest piece of railway engineering associated with his name', but to investors it was a constant disappointment. At a cost of nearly three million pounds, it had proved unexpectedly expensive to build. There was no dividend in 1840 and only a very small one for the first half of 1841, by which time North Midland one hundred pound shares were trading at less than seventy pounds.[3]

A Committee of Inquiry recommended a whole series of economies, including reductions in the rates of pay for many staff from 19s. to 18s. a week. The *Railway Times*, although an investor's journal, did not think much of measures that would turn every employee into a 'discontented spirit'; an hour's inattention on the part of a policeman, a signalman, or a switchman might cause a crash that would swallow up ten years' worth of the supposed savings. Such 'cheese-paring, candle-end' savings were unworthy of a company like the North Midland and suggested that, if satisfactory dividends could not be provided 'without cutting off the shillings of policemen and porters, they may as well shut up the line at once, or dispose of it to the best bidder'.[4]

Despite the economies, the dividend for the second half of 1841 was only 3 per cent per annum. George Hudson attended the shareholders' meeting at which this was announced but contributed little, apart from opposing a motion that Peter Brancker, a leading figure amongst the Liverpool investors, be elected in place of one of the retiring directors. Hudson was one of a number of shareholders who opposed this, on the grounds that directors should be local and, after a 'long and somewhat warm discussion', the proposal was rejected. In time, this opposition to Liverpool interests was to rebound on Hudson.[5]

The situation deteriorated over the next six months, with the dividend down to 2 per cent per annum and the share price to less than £60. The shareholders gave vent to their frustrations at a marathon five hour meeting. They complained in particular about past extravagance; the erection of unnecessary premises, and of station refreshment and waiting rooms furnished 'more like drawing-rooms in palaces than places of comfortable accommodation'. The members then voted almost unanimously to set up another Committee of Inquiry, composed of leading shareholders who were not on the board, to 'investigate minutely the causes why the concern had so long been unprofitable'.

Hudson had again taken only a modest role in the proceedings, but he was a large shareholder as well as chairman of a neighbouring, and highly profitable, line and was voted onto the Committee of Inquiry, to be chaired by Brancker.[6] The group worked quickly, and issued its report on

20 September 1842. Its main recommendation was to reduce staff numbers and wages, and so drastically cut the bill for wages and salaries from £40,600 a year to £22,800.

The board studied the report and supported some of the proposals, but opposed the overall level of cuts proposed by the committee as 'risking the welfare of the establishment and endangering the safety of the passengers'. Instead they put forward a less severe round of economies, which they hoped would save two-thirds of the amounts suggested by the committee, but without the same damaging consequences.[7]

The *Railway Times* adopted a tone of sceptical neutrality and thought the committee's proposed savings 'startling' and probably impractical. However, the board's response constituted, in their opinion, 'the severest censure that that could be cast upon the past management of the company's affairs' and, when the shareholders assembled for an extraordinary meeting on 16 November, it was clear that they had lost confidence in their directors. A resolution accepting the report was carried almost unanimously and loud applause greeted calls for the board to be replaced.

Hudson spoke once, confirming that wages on his line were lower than on the North Midland. He explained that, when the York and North Midland found that the Great North of England was paying engine drivers 5s. a day against their 6s. they thought it right to make some reductions; he did not see why the North Midland Company should not learn the same lesson, a sentiment that was well received by the members. Hudson had taken a moderate and relatively dispassionate position, but there was a good deal of further argument between the shareholders and the directors as the meeting threatened to get out of hand.

The board were clearly unhappy at the contents of the committee's report and the Chairman, William Newton, was so outraged by the threat to safety standards that he considered reporting his own company to the Board of Trade. They did not convince the members, however, and within weeks six directors had resigned, to be replaced by members of the Committee of Inquiry, including Brancker and Hudson.

Although Newton remained as chairman and the new directors constituted only half the board, they had the upper hand and set about implementing the drastic measures they had proposed. Hudson now emerged as the leader of the new group of directors and effectively took charge of the company although, as he was not chairman, he did not have any real platform for public comment.

In December 1842, the North Midland brought in significant cuts in the wages and numbers of drivers and firemen, and drastically intensified conditions of work. Workers who protested were dismissed and replaced with less experienced men willing to accept the company's terms. A group of drivers and firemen who sent a petition to the board, protesting at the changes that had been made, were dismissed without notice on Christmas Eve.[8] While the remaining employees were outraged at the way they were being treated, the managers had no intention of abandoning their new policies and, for a while, the company was in a state of near chaos as the two sides struggled for ascendancy.

The North Midland's treatment of its employees was most unusual, even in those days. It divided the opinions of their investors and led to bad publicity that did nothing to help customer confidence. A scathing attack was launched in a letter published in the *Railway Times* on 26 December 1842 from 'Veritas Vincit'.[9] The writer was unusually well informed and persistent; this was the first of a series of letters written over a period of five years in which he attacked the abuses of railway management.[10] His early letters singled out the new North Midland management and he pointed to Hudson and Cabry as the real architects of the new policies. Hudson had certainly brought Thomas Cabry, Engineer of the York and North Midland, to the North Midland to act as a troubleshooter and to oversee the reorganisation of the locomotive department as well as Peter Clarke of the York and North Midland as Company Secretary.[11]

'Vincit' alleged that many of the North Midland's new drivers were inexperienced and that others had been dismissed from other lines for incompetence or drunkenness. He predicted serious, even fatal consequences. Ominously, within three weeks, there were two accidents on the company's lines: a luggage train crashed into a passenger train at Cudworth, near Barnsley, killing a traveller, and two North Midland freight trains collided at Derby.

The company protested that the new men had all come with good references and were perfectly competent, but there was public outrage when it became known that the driver of the luggage train, Edward Jenkins, had only been driving trains for three weeks. 'Vincit' claimed he had been employed on Cabry's recommendation, even though he had previously been dismissed from his job as a fireman at the York and North Midland.

The inquest jury sent the unfortunate Jenkins for trial and publicly blamed the directors for employing unsuitable staff. The Railway Department of the Board of Trade found the accident to have been partly due to the combination of low wages and long hours. They wrote to the company on 7 February 1843 to voice their regret that 'the directors should have adopted measures ... calculated to compromise, and have in fact compromised, the safety of the public travelling by that line'. They objected to a requirement that every engine-man drive nearly one hundred and fifty miles on thirteen days in every fortnight as 'too harassing for the men and calculated to lead to accidents' and called upon the company to change these arrangements so as to provide reasonable intervals of rest.[12]

Brought thus 'under the lash of the Board of Trade', the company agreed to provide additional rest periods and to use more experienced drivers. The Board of Trade also sought an undertaking from Hudson on behalf of the company that there would be no further cuts in wages but, while he denied any *intention* of seeking further cuts, he refused to give any undertaking to this effect, as this 'might then appear a victory for the workmen'. He was also sufficiently brazen as to claim that the changes in engine-drivers, to which the Board of Trade attributed the whole melancholy event, was forced upon the directors by the 'refusal of the men to submit to a reasonable and proper reduction' in their wages, which left the company 'no alternative but to take the course adopted, lest they make the engine-drivers masters of the line, thus compromising the safety of the public by the absence of discipline and sub-ordination'. This was the heady stuff of class politics although, in more reasonable vein, Hudson did also claim that the engine-men had made 'no complaint of over-exertion, and express themselves perfectly satisfied with the present arrangements'.[13]

The case was notable in public policy terms for three reasons. The accident was the first to be attributed by the Railway Department to low wages and long hours. The initial refusal of the company to provide the information requested by the Railway Department of the Board of Trade also provoked the threat that any withholding of reasonable requests for information would induce Parliament to arm the Railway Department with greater powers. Finally, the judgement marked the acceptance by an agency of the state that 'if wages fell below a reasonable minimum, or if hours of work exceeded a reasonable maximum, evils would ensue whose cost would be borne, not by the employers, but by society itself'.[14]

The accident and its aftermath defined the political aspect of Hudson's stance towards working men. Hudson had not been a prime mover in the initial disputes between the directors and shareholders at the North Midland but, now that he had become involved, he had no qualms about taking a thoroughly uncompromising position. It was not entirely wise to alienate the Board of Trade or to let himself be seen in so unsympathetic a light by the general travelling public, but Hudson was aware that his brand of overt class politics would appeal greatly to the shareholders of both the North Midland and the York and North Midland Railways.

As he was not chairman of the North Midland, he started to use the meetings of the York and North Midland as a platform for presenting his side of the dispute. At the half-yearly meeting of the York and North

Midland, in February 1843, Hudson referred quite openly to the problems
at the North Midland, where he alleged there was a 'conspiracy among the
servants of [that] company [whereby] oatmeal had been put into the engines
to spoil them and other tricks played'. This was absurd: as 'Veritas Vincit'
was quick to point out, oatmeal was commonly used to *stop* leaks in
boilers and had been routinely issued to drivers for this purpose. Cabry
was at the meeting and must have known better, but wisely refrained from
contradicting his master.

Whatever the technical merits of his case, Hudson was clearly determined
to spread the dispute beyond the North Midland. He saw it as a question
of 'whether a combination of men should dictate to the directors of the
company ... it was not a question of money, but it was a question of
whether the engine-men should become masters of that line and through
that become masters of every one in the kingdom'. His stance was entirely
consistent with his political beliefs and was warmly applauded by the members of the York and North Midland. As he had hoped, many of the
shareholders present saw Hudson in an almost heroic light and one expressed
the general consensus that the engine-men who had been dismissed had
'no reason to complain and their Chairman, in resisting their exorbitant
demands, had shown a degree of firmness highly advantageous to the North
Midland Company in particular and to railway companies in general'.[15]

At the North Midland itself, Hudson was far more circumspect and
properly allowed Newton, as chairman, to take the shareholders' plaudits.
Newton explained that lower spending had improved the company's results
before the recommendations of the Committee of Inquiry had been acted
upon and also described the directors' stand against engine drivers and
firemen, when the latter 'combined to resist a reduction of their numbers.
This emergency was met by the prompt substitution of a new set of men
who, with few exceptions, proved themselves to be able and expert, as the
present [unprecedented] regularity of the trains testifies'.[16] Newton had
retained his position as Chairman despite major changes to the composition
of the board and judged his approach to the shareholders with some
shrewdness, even though his about face was hard to defend. The *Railway
Times* took him severely to task, for he had 'denounced further reductions
as dangerous, and now turns round to defend those very reductions, even
after his own predictions of danger have been sadly fulfilled'![17]

William Newton continued as the public voice of North Midland policy,
but few doubted that the real driving force behind the scenes was Hudson.
This was certainly the view of the *Railway Times*, and very critical it was
of the way in which he was changing the company's practices. An editorial
in February spoke darkly of 'mushroom management', of 'office after office

abolished, check after check abandoned, accounts voted useless and a rapid concentration of all offices, including the directorial functions, taking place in the person of one individual'. Two months later its tone was even sharper

old servants [of the company], too honest and too high-spirited to lend themselves to trickery, are daily being removed to make room for the unscrupulous tools of the dominant faction. A great authority at the board – greater far than the poor puppet who sits in the Chair – boasts that he will have no statistics, no comparative returns, no 'useless' classification of receipts and expenditure, and verily he appears to be in a fair way of accomplishing his ends. We confess that we are strongly prepossessed in favour of a clear and minute system of account keeping. It may sound strangely to the reformers of the North Midland Railway, but our firm belief is, that without such accounts (which they are doing their best to abolish), deception, fraud, and robbery must inevitably ensue.

Supporters of the new regime agreed with the critics' assertion that Hudson was the dominant influence behind the scenes, although they saw this as a matter for congratulation. One correspondent to the *Railway Times* fulsomely supported the new directors, pointed to the rise in the North Midland share price and added that 'the exertions and abilities of one of them, whose name it is unnecessary to mention, are above all praise'. He did not need to name Hudson, and neither did the editor, who had only to refer to the 'great authority' or 'Mr Peter Clarke's patron' for readers to know who was meant. The *Railway Times* also attacked Peter Clarke as an 'apt instrument in the hands of his patrons' and hinted that there was something crooked about him. Although widely cited, such a suggestion was not entirely fair; by August 1843 Brancker, who was certainly not close to Hudson and his circle of friends, described the appointment of Peter Clarke as Secretary as 'one of the best that could possibly have been made'.[18]

Hudson may have been callous in his treatment of the employees of the North Midland, and cavalier with the safety of its passengers, but he had promised that the upheaval he had helped to instigate would produce improved returns for the shareholders. 'Vincit', however, constantly reiterated his claim that the policy of wage and job cuts never actually achieved any real savings. The accident at Cudworth, for example, besides leading to the death of a passenger also caused damage to rolling stock of more than a thousand pounds. The havoc created by the introduction of so many new drivers meant that the number of men who needed to carry out repairs had to be increased from two to twelve.[19] Moreover the wage bill, even before the cuts, of all the drivers and firemen on the North Midland payroll was less than four thousand pounds a year and even genuine economies could not have saved amounts of any great magnitude.

At the same time, the board was taking other measures to improve their financial situation which attracted far less attention and controversy; fares were raised and services cut, with some of the rolling stock being sold off as surplus to requirements, and several stations were closed. Reported profits were also increased by quietly dropping the depreciation charge on rolling stock.[20]

When the shareholders met in August 1843, they were informed that operating expenses for the first half of the year were £11,500 below their level a year previously, and the dividend was slightly increased from 2 to 3 per cent per annum. The share price had been rising steadily but had still only reached £80, well below its value when the shares were issued. This represented the most meagre returns on intensive, divisive management activity, especially given the rise in economic activity from the depression year of 1842, but in reality the directors were in an impossible position. The real problem they faced was the excessive cost of construction; only a major increase in traffic levels would have much effect on this. Cost reduction could in fact achieve very little: even if the North Midland had incurred no operating costs whatsoever, it would still have been able to pay a dividend in 1842 of only 7 per cent. Hudson claimed that the North Midland would soon be paying dividends of 5 per cent, but the fare increases had reduced the volume of traffic so that revenues in 1843 were only 3 per cent above those of the previous year.[21]

Hudson was in effect operating a dead-end policy; cost reductions and a confrontational approach towards those who worked on the railway were going to provide only small savings. Despite the heat generated and a great deal of publicity, the policies were going to do little to address the real problems of the North Midland. Nevertheless, Sir John Simpson proposed that the shareholders vote £600 to the members of the Committee of Inquiry 'as a testimony of their appreciation', but Hudson took a very proper position and thought they should 'take nothing from the proprietors, being contented in earning ... their confidence and sympathy', a perspective well received by the meeting. He did, however, confess that the position had been of a 'most harassing and difficult description – a position which neither the £600 nor the whole of the company's capital should place him in again'. The Chairman of the committee, Brancker, took a similar view and the shareholders voiced their sincere thanks for the 'honourable and disinterested spirit' the members of the committee had displayed'.[22]

The system whereby Parliament licensed the schemes of private sector companies to construct particular railway lines enabled the UK government to develop an early railway network without the need for public subsidy.

This may have been a political necessity but it was also physically wasteful; far too many lines were built for the traffic that could be generated. Profit expectations were high in the early days, but it soon became apparent that more economical arrangements would be necessary if shareholder expectations were to be met. In some cases, as at the North Midland, this led to reduced operating expenses, but in many others companies sought to lower the average cost of their capital. This could be achieved in a number of ways: by buying out closely competing lines owned by smaller rival companies; by making arrangements with other companies where lines merged, so that track and other facilities could be shared; or by amalgamating with other companies so as to create a more coherent system out of a number of disparate elements. This last, which helped the railways towards a more mature structure and was often used as a means of ending a 'ruinous competition', was now to be pioneered by George Hudson in an imaginative attempt to reshape the railways running into Derby.[23]

When the Birmingham and Derby Junction opened in 1839, it provided the only through route from Derby to London, but the construction of the Midland Counties produced a shorter competing route via Rugby. Attempts were made to reach agreement on a division of traffic, but these came to nothing, and the Birmingham and Derby Junction directors decided on drastic action to retain their company's position. On 2 July 1840, the very day after the Midland Counties had opened to the public, the Birmingham and Derby Junction made the most severe cuts in its fares, facing the new company with a level of competition that would quickly threaten its ability to survive. The scale of the cuts was quite startling: the price of a first class ticket between Derby and Hampton was reduced from 8s. to 1s. 6d., but for through passengers only. The Midland Counties took legal action to try to force the Birmingham and Derby Junction to charge the same fares for through and local passengers but failed, and then decided to match its rival's prices. A lengthy and mutually destructive war began with both companies charging uneconomic and often identical fares.[24]

A number of plans were put forward by the two companies in an attempt to end excessive competition; the Midland Counties, for example proposed that they should take all the through traffic and pay the Birmingham and Derby Junction an agreed compensation. In January 1843 the Birmingham and Derby Junction proposed that the two companies amalgamate and, although negotiations broke down over the valuations to be placed on the respective shares, amalgamation had been placed firmly on the agenda. There were numerous letters in the *Railway Times* urging the companies to merge and, in some cases, suggesting the inclusion of the North Midland as well, although several shareholders opposed this on the grounds that North Midland shareholders would thereby reap the benefits of the ending of competition between the other two companies.[25] Amalgamation was an idea whose time, it seemed, had come; another proposal popular with correspondents at this time was a merger of the London to Brighton and the London to Dover lines.

Hudson's espousal of amalgamation may, on his part, have been the classic trick of the 'moving target', whereby he could change the rules of the game before North Midland shareholders became disillusioned with his lack of success, but the idea had clear business logic and Hudson was to manage the process expertly.[26] Foreseeing opposition from the Midland Counties directors to an amalgamation that included the North Midland, he opened negotiations with the Birmingham and Derby Junction. Once these were satisfactorily concluded, he met the Midland Counties directors at Derby on 1 August 1843, together with William Newton and John Waddingham, a fellow director of the North Midland who was also a large Midland Counties shareholder. Hudson presented the Midland Counties directors with an ultimatum: if they refused to accept the amalgamation, the North Midland would lease the Birmingham and Derby and book all its trains down that line.

Despite the weakness of their position, the directors of the Midland Counties would still not agree and, their Chairman, Thomas Dicey, attacked the proposals as effectively a ramp by the North Midland, which would be the principal beneficiary. The Midland Counties and the Birmingham and Derby Junction, he said, would be in the position of 'the two foolish animals that quarrelled about the division of the oyster, and appealed to the monkey, which ate the whole oyster, and gravely returned to the disputants the shells'.[27] Given that the share capital of the North Midland was greater than that of the other two companies combined, Dicey had a point, but he was unable to convince his shareholders. Share prices in all three companies rose strongly in July and August in anticipation of a positive outcome to the negotiations.

The basic idea of the amalgamation was very straightforward. Shareholders would receive shares in the new undertaking equal in value to the nominal value of their existing shares, with no adjustment for any discount at which their shares might have been issued.[28] Special meetings of the companies involved were scheduled on consecutive days in September 1843. The North Midland carried the proposals 'by acclamation', while a moderately attended meeting of the Birmingham and Derby passed the proposals without excitement, but at the Midland Counties meeting on 21 September 1843 things were not so straightforward.[29]

In the context of the prior arrangement that had been made between the other two companies, the terms offered to the Midland Counties were generous. Indeed, as a means of bringing about a highly innovative procedure, the process was intelligently calculated to achieve the overall objective without driving so hard a bargain as to excite undue opposition. On the other hand, if the Midland Counties chose not to cooperate, the North Midland would have every excuse to go ahead with leasing the Birmingham and Derby, a cheaper approach that would immediately ruin the Midland Counties.

Some of the Midland Counties shareholders felt aggrieved at the manoeuvre used by the North Midland. Their concerns were shared by their Chairman, Dicey, who was clearly unwilling to accept the logic of Hudson's scheme, which he described as a 'blind bargain'. He preferred an agreed division of earnings south of Derby, an extraordinarily obtuse position to take, as that possibility had been specifically excluded under the agreement reached between the North Midland and the Birmingham and Derby Junction. This was apparent to most people and Dicey was taken to task for his intransigence by several of the larger investors. Another director, Mr Wyld, spoke at length against the amalgamation and then suggested that the North Midland could be outflanked by means of a line up the Vale of Burwash.

Hudson, at the meeting as a shareholder of the Midland Counties, was in fine form and seemed to enjoy the situation no end. With much warmth of manner and expression he said

> he had never before today had the honour of attending a meeting where so many poetic and oratorical flourishes had escaped from the lips of a proprietor. That gentleman had introduced a novelty into railway discussion, which must be heard to be fully felt and appreciated; and though he [Mr Hudson] was entirely of the opinion that poets might afford them the highest delight in their moments of retirement and study, he thought that they were not the very best authorities in matters of simple business.

In more sober vein, he then settled to a masterly dissection of the substantive issues, criticising in some detail the misleading comparisons Wyld had drawn between the traffic figures of the various companies. He also complained at the unfairness of Dicey's earlier references to 'plunder', as the proposition was entirely fair and equitable. He accepted that the Midland Counties line was cheaper to run but, with the Birmingham and Derby to contend with, 'if they did not by some means get rid of the opposition, they would go on until the period arrived when the shareholders would find their pockets entirely emptied and then exclaim, what fools we have been'. He promised annual savings of £25,000 and dividends of 5 per cent and, to prolonged applause, finished by warning the proprietors not to reject an opportunity they might not have again. The vote was 115 to 11 in favour of the amalgamation.

Dicey, who was clearly upset by the whole business and possibly concerned about his loss of position after the amalgamation, then astonished everyone by saying that he 'felt it his duty to demand a poll'. To call for a poll, in which numbers of shares rather than shareholders present would be counted, was really clutching at straws given the size of the majority and the extent to which his opponents were major shareholders. Dicey's stance caused immediate 'uproar, disapprobation and cries of shame' and several shareholders spoke loudly and indignantly amidst a scene of 'excessive confusion'. One of the leading Liverpool investors, Mr Heyworth, agreed that Dicey was within his rights but then described him as the 'most disorderly of all disorderly gentlemen' and thought his conduct had disgraced the chair. For good measure, he added that the Midland Counties would have amalgamated with the Birmingham and Derby long ago 'had it not been for the interference of their Chairman', an accusation that caused tumult. The resulting poll count, of 1752 to 498, then confirmed the amalgamation.

Some accounts of Hudson's life suggest that he was always involved in controversy and imply that he was often the cause of the disputes that took place. Reports of meetings like the Midland Counties in September 1843 are useful because they remind us that railway company meetings at this time were often rumbustious and outspoken, and could be marked by insults bordering on the florid as well as by gracious courtesies. Dicey was clearly upset by the level of criticism he had faced, and Hudson, who was not the direct cause of the contentious scenes, had the good sense, in his moment of triumph, to do the decent thing; on moving the usual vote of thanks to the chairman he added that Dicey's strong feelings were 'actuated, he believed, by the most honest convictions'.[30]

However generous the pleasantries, the realities of the situation were apparent and Hudson now became famous in the railway world. Some descriptions of him in the press, such as 'the Railway Napoleon' effectively acknowledge his strategic grasp, although others were more obviously critical and accused him of an 'intolerable egotism' and of recently assuming a 'dictatorial tone', as if fame had suddenly gone to his head.[31] Hudson's achievement was, however, truly astonishing; less than ten months after becoming a director of the North Midland he had pushed through the first major amalgamation of UK railway companies, the real beginning of the process of consolidation in the industry which was to lead to the 'big four' companies of the 1920s. In the process, he had created the largest railway company in Britain.[32]

While Hudson was waiting for the amalgamation he had organised with such panache to receive the necessary parliamentary approval, a promotion that he had been involved in some time before came to public attention and severely damaged his reputation. The construction of a line between the two major cities in the West Riding, Bradford and Leeds, had first been suggested by a group of Bradford businessmen when the North Midland was being set up. The promoters of the North Midland did not, however, want to include it in their scheme; their own plan was as much as they could handle, though George Stephenson was willing to offer his services as engineer, if an independent company was promoted. There was then some expectation that the line would be built by the Manchester and Leeds Company, but these hopes were similarly disappointed. Interested parties in Bradford then approached George Stephenson, who in turn discussed it with Hudson. In August 1843, William Newton, the Chairman of the North Midland, told his shareholders that the directors were interested in extending the North Midland to Bradford and asked them to approve expenditure on the necessary surveys and estimates, before the submission of a formal proposal to a special meeting of the proprietors. Through this entirely normal process, the shareholders were given the clear understanding that the North Midland would apply to Parliament for authorisation to build the line and that they would have first refusal of the shares to be issued to finance it.[33]

Instead, a separate company, the Leeds and Bradford, was formed by a group of five promoters, including Hudson and two other directors of the North Midland, John Waddingham of Leeds and William Murgatroyd of Bradford. Peter Clarke became the Secretary and George Stephenson was appointed engineer. The directors' report to the North Midland members in February 1844 explained this step as necessary 'in deference to the wishes of the Midland Counties and Birmingham and Derby boards', who did not wish to get involved in any new projects before the amalgamation took effect. There was, nonetheless, a plan to link the new line to the North Midland and manage the two lines jointly, so that all the benefits of an extension to Bradford would accrue to the North Midland, consistent with decisions taken at the earlier meeting.[34]

Despite these attempts to smooth things over, many North Midland shareholders were very unhappy, not at the setting up of an independent company as such, but at the fact that they had not been able to subscribe for shares in the Leeds and Bradford. The Provisional Committee claimed

the distribution of the shares was a 'difficult, delicate job' and that they
had paid due attention to 'the local position, commercial standing and
influence' of the people that applied for shares, but most people saw it as
a simple fix. The company's share capital was to be £400,000, in £50 shares.
Investor demand had been very high, yet the largest allocations had been
made to Waddingham and Hudson, while many applicants received no
shares at all. The shares quickly moved to a premium of about £10 a share,
even though only 5 of each £50 had so far been paid.

The *Railway Times* asked, rhetorically, why the directors had not ensured
that all had been served alike in the distribution and gave their own
immediate answer that:

> Hudson was not a Railway Reformer for nought. He does not make and unmake
> boards of direction for nothing. Oh no! He is much too far north for that. He
> has the more sensible object in view of putting money in his purse ... Who after
> this, will venture to assert that railway tinkering is not a good trade – better, far
> than toiling behind a counter, or sweating for the lieges beneath the capacious
> folds of an aldermanic gown.[35]

Many saw the directors' statement as a cover-up and objected to the
fact that, despite the material changes to the resolution passed on 9 August
1843, they had received no circulars or statements nor been called to any
special meeting. When one speaker pointed out that they had not been
given any opportunity to take up shares in the Leeds and Bradford, and
that they had not been placed on a 'fair footing with the directors on the
matter', this was greeted with loud applause. The atmosphere became
very tense when another speaker argued that shareholders in the North
Midland Company had not been able to get shares in the Leeds and Bradford
line primarily because two of the directors of the North Midland had
received six hundred and eight hundred shares respectively in the Leeds
and Bradford, a pointed and accurate reference to the holdings of Hudson
and Waddingham.

When he rose to reply, Hudson was visibly discomfited by the continuing
commotion and his sense of pique quickly became apparent. He said he
had attended many railway meetings and 'had always previously received
due attention when he rose to address them'. He had hoped on this occasion
to 'receive that courtesy and attention which he had, at all events a right to
expect at the hands of the North Midland Company', but was now 'indifferent
to remaining in the directory and ... willing to place his resignation in the
hands of the Chairman'.

His position was that there had been little interest in Leeds and Bradford
until he became involved in it, and that the rapid rise in the share price

on allotment that had caused so much bad feeling amongst North Midland shareholders was merely the consequence of market knowledge that he and Mr Waddingham had made such large investments.[36] He pointed out that the share price had fallen considerably since then, added sardonically that they would therefore soon have the opportunity of 'buying plenty of them', expressed his 'conviction that he had acted with the strictest propriety in the affair', and ended by saying that, had he thought there would have been 'all this outcry about the Leeds and Bradford shares, he would not have had one in the concern'.

Hudson was usually very good at judging the mood of meetings but on this occasion the hostility of his reception had angered him to the point where his judgement failed. His vanity was badly exposed and one shareholder, with plenty of verbal support from his fellows, 'hoped Mr Hudson would be a little pleasanter than he had been and not be so pettish. They might be glad if Mr Hudson remained a director, but they would not beg and pray of him to remain one'. Hudson, more intelligently, then suggested that the shareholders pass a resolution indemnifying himself and Mr Waddingham and refunding the money they had paid out, in which case the railway shares they had taken could be placed at their disposal, but his offer was not taken up and discussion moved onto other matters.

His investment in the Leeds and Bradford had earned Hudson a lot of money but the controversy undoubtedly damaged his public image. At the shareholders' meeting he rode out the objections, but only at some loss of personal credibility and dignity. He also received his first real warning that, however grand his reputation, too great a display of pique was as likely to stiffen as to soften shareholder opposition.[37]

The highly influential *Railway Times* was now convinced that Hudson had 'puffed' the Leeds-Bradford scheme and was not to be trusted. In March 1844, they announced that henceforth 'our opposition to Mr Hudson and his schemes takes a far wider range. We regard him, and such as him, as the worst enemies of the railway system. He is the Prince of Premium-hunters [and] as such we shall continue, in season and out of season, to expose him'.[38]

The Act for the Leeds and Bradford line received its Royal Assent in July 1844 and Hudson wrote to the landowners whose property might be affected to give them early notice of the company's detailed intentions. He also assured them that

all damage done to growing crops will be amply compensated for ... that it will always be their wish to prevent all unnecessary annoyance or damage to adjoining property, to consult whenever it is in their power the convenience of the landowner

and his tenant [and to] hope to be met by a continuance of that same friendly
spirit that had previously been shown to the company.

Hudson had always had a good understanding of the concerns of landowners
but this letter was highly intelligent and did much to restore his reputation
in the eyes of the railway press. The *Railway Times* was so impressed that
it drew the attention of their readers to the letter's 'liberal and enlightened
spirit', a quality often absent in the early days of the railway companies,
who could be very aggressive in the exercise of their new powers, while
landowners often seemed to see railway promoters as people 'seeking to lay
violent hands upon the rights and property of others'. The paper noted the
importance of the better understandings that were now beginning to develop
and hoped that all promoters would act in the spirit that 'so eminently
pervaded' Hudson's letter on behalf of the Leeds and Bradford.[39] Hudson
could afford to be liberal; by September 1844 Leeds and Bradford shares,
on which only £5 had been paid, were trading at over £20, giving him a
paper profit of nearly £10,000.

The Midland Railway Act received the Royal Assent on 10 May 1844. The
new concern had fifteen directors, drawn from the boards of the three
constituent companies: six from the North Midland, five from the Midland
Counties and four from the Birmingham and Derby. Hudson's colleagues
on the Leeds and Bradford, Waddingham and Murgatroyd, had places on
the new board, as did William Newton, the great survivor, although neither
Dicey nor Brancker were included, despite the latter's role as spokesman
for the influential 'Liverpool Party'. Hudson's protégé Peter Clarke became
the superintendent of the Midland, whilst J. F. Bell of the Midland Counties
was the new company secretary.[40]

The new board met for the first time on 24 May 1844, in the station
offices at Derby, and Hudson was inevitably, and unanimously, elected
Chairman. He claimed to accept his elevation with reluctance, but it was
a proud moment for him; he was now in charge of the largest railway,
indeed the largest company, in Britain, with one hundred and eighty miles
of line and a share capital of more than five million pounds. This alone
made him one of the leading figures in the industry; with his other interests he was indeed the 'Railway King'. He soon struck a buoyant note,
promising those present that he would 'develop the traffic, reduce the
expenditure, increase the dividends and satisfy the public'. He also anticipated annual savings of at least £20,000 from the consolidation of the three
lines.[41]

John Ellis (1789–1862), a Quaker farmer and corn merchant from Leicestershire, and MP for Leicester in 1848–52, was elected Deputy Chairman.

He had been a director of the Midland Counties Railway and was a man of unquestionable integrity.[42]

On 16 July 1844, Hudson presided over the first general meeting of the Midland shareholders. The final accounts of the three merging companies, which showed significantly higher profits, partly through better economic conditions, allowed commensurate improvements in the final dividends payable to the shareholders of the old companies. Some expansion of their network had also been initiated, with powers taken to build new lines in the area between Swinton, Lincoln and Nottingham. Hudson was optimistic that there would be a 'handsome increase' in next year's dividend.[43]

Although the Midland had only just been formed, it was already facing a challenge that was to involve Hudson in his biggest railway battle. The prosperity of the Midland depended largely on its control of all London traffic to the north east and to eastern Scotland, which had to pass through Rugby and Derby on its way to York and points further north. A direct London-York line would siphon off much of the Midland's traffic, and in 1844 the threat became tangible when several schemes were promoted. The most serious was the London and York, whose moving spirit was Edmund Denison, MP for Doncaster, which had been launched on 3 May, just a week before the Midland's amalgamation Bill became law. Their plans involved the construction of a London-York line via Huntingdon, Peterborough, Newark and Doncaster, which, with various branches and the absorption of several other schemes, would amount to building 325 miles of track at a total cost of £6,500,000.

The Direct Northern also published a prospectus, in September 1844, which proposed a line from London to York via Huntingdon, Stamford, Lincoln, Gainsborough and Selby. At about the same time, some Lincolnshire supporters of the London and York, disgruntled that Lincoln was only to be served by a branch line, seceded to promote a Cambridge and Lincoln scheme, to connect the two via St Ives, Ramsey and Peterborough.[44]

Hudson's riposte was laid out at a special meeting of the Midland on 8 October 1844. He began by warning the members that the London and York, now moving towards an alliance with the Manchester and Leeds Railway, posed a threat that would have 'serious consequences' for the interests of the Midland and required their 'anxious solicitude'. Hudson's remedy was simple. The Midland shareholders had 'nothing to fear if they placed their confidence in the board and gave them the powers necessary to carry out the plans they had in contemplation', and he asked them to approve a number of projects to be put before the next session of Parliament. The largest was a line of more than 120 miles from Swinton (just north of Rotherham) through Doncaster and Lincoln to March.

The Eastern Counties was also planning to promote a Bill to build between Cambridge and March and, a few weeks later, on 28 October 1844, the York and North Midland put forward plans for its own extension line from Burton Salmon to connect with the Midland at Doncaster. Jointly, these schemes would provide an alternative London-York link, much of it over Midland lines. The Midland board were also in favour of several other extensions, one of which, the Cambridge and Lincoln scheme, was meant only as a contingency measure, to wreck the London and York proposal should the Midland's own scheme be rejected.[45] Hudson pointed out that

> in asking the proprietary today for certain powers, the Board of Directors did not bind themselves to the whole or any of the routes now presented to them ... the Board thought it far wiser that the question should be left open until 30 November, when the proprietary would learn the whole of their schemes. He had, therefore, to invite their confidence to a great extent and the only answer he could give was that, to the best of his ability, it should not be misplaced.[46]

His real pitch followed, a request that they authorise the directors to 'apply for Acts of Parliament for such extension lines as they may deem advisable'! Although such discretionary powers had never previously been sought in the brief history of the commercial railways, the resolutions were 'carried unanimously, not a single dissentient voice being raised'. Thus, the members of the Midland, at Hudson's request agreed to support the directors to the tune of two and a half million pounds 'without a single question as to where it was going, or the slightest murmur of doubt'![47]

This was exciting stuff indeed and presaged a period of considerable expansion at the Midland; in January 1845, through the personal initiative of Hudson's vice-chairman, John Ellis, the Birmingham to Gloucester and Gloucester to Bristol lines were leased, bringing major increases in the geographical coverage of the Midland, as well as keeping the Great Western Railway, which was also attempting to acquire the lines and encroach on what the Midland regarded as its territory, out of Birmingham. Hudson later told shareholders that he could take none of the credit. 'His friend Mr Ellis ... suggested to the board this bold course and I candidly confess that at first I shrank from incurring further liabilities on the part of the Midland Company'. At the Midland, responsibilities were shared amongst members of the board and Hudson was not the autocrat that he had become at the York and North Midland, where such an initiative by anyone other than himself would have been out of the question.[48]

Although the members were called upon in May 1845 to approve a large number of proposed extensions that were to be the subject of Bills before Parliament, it was the battle with the London and York, to be decided in the 1845 session of Parliament, that was now the main issue facing the Midland.[49]

In January 1845, Hudson announced a 6 per cent per annum dividend for the first six months of the amalgamated company's life, delivering on his earlier promise of a 'handsome increase'. He then laid out his plans to combat the London and York in more detail, and mocked its 'juvenile promoters', who would, even if their scheme was approved, run out of money by the time they reached Grantham.

Immediately after this meeting, Hudson had an argument at Derby Station with Edmund Denison, the main London and York promoter. Although the various eyewitnesses are not entirely consistent, the main problem appears to have been the failure of Denison's sense of humour. After a friendly initial encounter, Hudson apparently leaned in at the window of Denison's carriage and declared that the capital for the London and York line had been obtained dishonestly, knowing full well that Denison was the person primarily responsible for obtaining that capital. Although Denison's friends protested that he had shown 'great forbearance under provocation' and that Hudson was 'lamentably lacking in discretion', others were most surprised when Mr Denison took such offence at remarks 'evidently used in joke' as to call Hudson a 'blackguard' to his face. As his train pulled out, Denison shouted 'Hudson, I've done with you; go, go away'! His fellow passengers continued to advise Denison that he had completely misunderstood the situation and that Hudson had meant no personal offence, pointing to Hudson's repeated attempts, 'in the most courteous manner' to effect a reconciliation with Denison before the train started on its journey. If it was only a joke, it was an ill judged one, which cast Hudson in a rather negative light.[50]

In line with established procedure, the various railway bills were allocated to a committee for detailed consideration. Committee X was to hear the case for the various lines from London to York and Denison's scheme's hearing began on 28 April 1845. Excitement was intense as huge interests were at stake. The proceedings, it was rumoured, were costing the various promoters more than £3000 a day, while no expense was spared by its opponents. Hudson was lampooned in the House of Lords by the former Lord Chancellor, Lord Brougham for 'working with a twelve-counsel power … the object of Mr Hudson was delay, in order that a report might not be made in the present session, and of course counsel would talk just as long as Mr Hudson was disposed to spend money'. Dragging out the proceedings so that the rival scheme would not receive parliamentary approval in that session would of course have suited Hudson very well and give him more time to put together alternative promotions.

It would be a mistake, however, to conclude that it was only Hudson who was prepared to sail close to the wind or that his opponents were, by definition, determinedly ethical. Towards the end of their deliberations, the committee created uproar by refusing permission for representatives of the lines competing with the proposed direct route to state their case and by not even appearing to know that the Milford to Doncaster line had been referred to them for consideration as part of their overall brief. With perfect justification, Hudson, who had arranged a great deal of legal support, asked if it was right that the opponents of the London and York, representing thirty million pounds of people's money, should be told summarily that they were not allowed a hearing to prove their case before the Committee, a decision he found 'monstrous'. Although the confusion over the Milford to Doncaster line smacked of simple incompetence, the view of many was that Hudson's business rivals, Denison, Yorke, Elsley and Lord Howick, had fixed the committee and that the decision on the direct route was now a foregone conclusion. It was, therefore, no great surprise when the committee chairman announced their decision on 23 July in favour of the direct London and York scheme, although even this decision was dependent upon his own casting vote.

The half-yearly meeting of Midland shareholders took place on 25 July, just two days later, at which Hudson made a bravura speech attacking the decision and pledging that the fight would go on. He concluded by saying

> Gentlemen, on the principle that we have not been heard, we take our stand; and it is the anxious wish of my colleagues and myself to fortify our position ... by any means [available]. It may be that I have expressed myself somewhat too strongly (at which there were loud cries of 'no, no', from the entire meeting), but I feel that we have been hardly dealt with. I feel that we have done nothing to forfeit our rights as Englishmen, and I trust that some means may yet be devised of not deciding against us unheard.

He then sat down amid a 'hurricane of applause'.[51]

Even the *Railway Times*, generally critical of Hudson's dealings, felt that Hudson had taken his stand on 'proper ground' and fully supported his criticisms of Committee X. The Midland appealed to the House of Commons, but to no avail. This was bad news for the Midland shareholders and a shattering blow to Hudson's personal ambitions. His career never entirely recovered from it and it was probably small consolation that his reasonable objections to the direct line had been negated by the same trickery that had brought him such renown.[52]

After the decision reached by Committee X, the London and York Railway was in a strong position, although there was little time to complete the passage of their Bill through Parliament in the 1845 session. But Hudson now demonstrated that his earlier promise to 'fortify our position ... by any means' was no rhetorical flourish. He opened up a new front against the London and York, turning to its subscription list, the listing of people who had said they would invest in the new company. Agents had for some time been making inquiries about the names on the list from London and other cities, whilst others, with 'cool audacity' sent official-looking circulars to rural postmasters asking for information about subscribers in their districts. They compiled a list of subscribers, accounting for over £500,000 of the London and York's capital, who were, they alleged, simply fictitious or without the means to pay future calls. This claim was then duly documented in a petition by the Cambridge and Lincoln promoters to Parliament.

Both Houses set up a committee to investigate the allegations. They quickly confirmed that some of the subscriptions were unsound, but only to the extent of about £75,000, less than 2 per cent of the London and York's share capital. The House of Lords committee did, however, have sufficient concerns about the subscription list to require a further investigation, which meant that the London and York Bill would not be able to pass through Parliament in the 1845 session. Both committees were, however, highly critical of the cavalier manner in which the allegations had been made and saw the whole process as an abuse of the right of petition, a mere device to obstruct the London and York.[53]

The London and York promoters were not deterred and announced that they would reintroduce their Bill in the 1846 session. Hudson's victory had lifted his and the Midland shareholders' morale but it had only provided a temporary respite. He was well aware that some other means would be needed if the London and York was to be stopped. The latter's plans had stood up very well from an engineering point of view and parliamentary sanction was plainly available for a direct London-York line. His only remaining hope lay in the fact that Parliament tended to favour the schemes of existing companies over new ones, at least within their area of operation. This meant that the only company that could now block the London and York Company was the Eastern Counties, if it was quick to put forward an alternative scheme. Hudson accordingly became Chairman of the Eastern Counties in October 1845 and it was from this vantage point that he conducted the last phase of the battle with Denison.

It was common for meetings of railway proprietors to consider important issues of accounting principle and, in January 1846, the same Captain Watts of Darlington who had made highly public attacks on Hudson in late 1841 queried the inclusion of both £18,000 spent on 'new wagons etc' and £14,000 spent on 'works of road and stations' in capital rather than revenue.

Hudson handled the situation ably. He defended the practice on the grounds that 'the trade of the company was doubling itself, and that increased means of conveyance were necessary for the two new lines [as] the want of wagons was daily felt [since] when the receipts were increasing at the rate of £200,000 per annum, it was necessary to increase not only the station accommodation, but the means of conveying the traffic'. He personally would 'readily concur' in any resolution to move the £18,000 from the capital to the revenue account, but pointed out that, if this was done, the shareholders would have to accept a considerable reduction in their dividend. The Vice-Chairman, Ellis, added, to cheers, that the directors had proposed an 'honest dividend' and hoped that Captain Watts would give them credit for their 'common honesty', at which point Watts said he was satisfied. Expansion was continuing, and the meeting approved schemes to build a series of lines, including those from Chesterfield to Newark and from Burton to Nuneaton. It also approved investment in several companies, including the Manchester and Southampton (which in fact, failed), the Warwickshire and London and the South Midland.[54] In May, a special meeting approved no fewer than twenty-six Bills, involving the expenditure of nearly seven million pounds, mainly on new constructions.[55]

In July 1846, Hudson, as chairman, was able to announce another good dividend, to confirm that Acts had been obtained for branch lines from Pye Bridge and Newark to Clay Cross and to announce the successful conclusion of arrangements to lease the Sheffield and Rotherham line. The other matters he had to discuss, however, the taking over of the South Midland and the Leeds and Bradford railways were to cause him a good deal of discomfort and difficulty.

The affair of the South Midland had a tortuous history. In 1845 a company called the Leicester and Bedford had been floated; although nominally independent it had links with the London and York with which it planned to connect at Hitchin. Hudson was naturally determined to oppose this encroachment into Midland territory by allies of Denison. A rival scheme, the South Midland, was formed to build lines from Market Harborough to Bedford and from Kettering to Huntingdon. Hudson was keen to support this, so the Midland agreed to take up 40,000 of the £20 shares (just under half the total capital) and to nominate six of the twelve directors. Their nominations included Ellis and Hudson, with the latter becoming Chairman. The agreement also stipulated that 10,000 of the shares were to be made available to the directors of the Midland personally and each of the fifteen directors subscribed for 500 shares, with the remainder being distributed to landowners along the route as 'sweeteners'. The Midland directors naturally paid for their shares, which reduced the amount that the Midland had to pay as a company, but each director stood to benefit personally by the premium of seven to eight pounds to which South Midland shares soon rose in the market. In the event, both rival schemes were defeated in Parliament. Hudson now proposed to the meeting that they buy out the South Midland shareholders and present the scheme to Parliament in the 1847 session as a purely Midland venture. There was little opposition at the meeting, although Hudson and his fellow directors had already been publicly accused of 'pocketing' £50,000 of premiums on the South Midland shares, and in October, when Hudson agreed to buy out the Leicester and Bedford for another £40,000, he was roundly criticised by the prominent Liverpool investor, J. H. Brancker, for spending so much of the Midland shareholders' money to so little apparent effect.[56]

The need to discuss the take-over of the Leeds and Bradford meant returning to a subject that had caused Hudson a great deal of embarrassment in early 1844. In January 1846 the members of the Leeds and Bradford had formally approved a merger with the Manchester and Leeds but, in July 1846, their directors withdrew the Parliamentary Bill necessary to sanction the arrangement. At a meeting later that month Waddingham, deputising for the absent Hudson, proposed that they accept a Midland offer to lease the line and its extensions, on terms that gave them a guaranteed 10 per cent on capital in perpetuity, a suggestion approved unanimously 'amidst loud cheers'.[57]

The offer was certainly an extremely generous one. The main Leeds to Bradford line had opened on 1 July, just a few weeks previously, and the company was now constructing a much longer extension to Colne. The high price to be paid by the Midland was supported not by any evidence of potential traffic levels or profitability, but by Hudson's own belief that it would prove to be a source of great benefit to the Midland. It also included dark warnings of the imminent dangers, should it fall into the hands of Denison, via the Manchester and Leeds.

It is possible to construe the Leeds and Bradford's manoeuvres as little more than a device to coax a better offer from the Midland, although there is some evidence to the contrary. An amalgamation between the Leeds and Bradford and the Manchester and Leeds made good sense geographically and the latter's offer was not a bad one. However, the Manchester and Leeds's offer, whilst generous (in January 1846 Hudson calculated it would probably give the Leeds and Bradford shareholders a return of slightly more than 10 per cent) was in the form of its own shares, and the value of those shares fell considerably in the following months before the legislation necessary to effect the merger had been passed. This made the offer much less tempting to the Leeds and Bradford shareholders and provided every reason for Hudson to repudiate it and seek something better on behalf of his members.[58]

Although Hudson said he was 'particularly anxious' to carry out the preferences of the Midland shareholders, there were a number of obvious and legitimate concerns. He faced a major conflict of interest, being Chairman and a major shareholder in both companies. There was also undoubted cause for concern over due notice, as the special meeting had been advertised only at the last minute and then only in local newspapers, though this apparently satisfied parliamentary requirements.

It had been expected by almost everyone, given these misgivings, that Hudson would absent himself from the meeting, as he had done at the Leeds and Bradford the previous day, or at least avoid any active role in the proceedings. Instead, he not only attended the meeting and took the chair but also rose to move the resolution to lease the Leeds and Bradford. This was an extraordinary thing to do that pointed to a persistent weakness in Hudson's strategy for dealing with difficult situations: unwillingness to stay out of discussions about matters in which he had a large financial stake, where his motives were bound to be questioned.

Hudson began with a whole series of disclaimers. He had no wish to press the matter unfairly and no wish as a Leeds and Bradford shareholder to induce the Midland to take the line over, as their interests were best served by remaining independent. He had not bought or sold a single share in the Leeds and Bradford since it came under consideration by the Midland. He had 'never made an unsuccessful bargain'. He had never made a single penny through the purchase of any of the Bristol and Birmingham, Brandling Junction, Leicester and Swannington, Hull and Selby, Great North of England or Newcastle and Darlington lines. These were surprising claims and Hudson was interrupted several times. He was challenged about never making an unsuccessful bargain by a reference to the Great North of England line. The *Railway Times* detected a 'strange want of courtesy' by the members towards their Chairman.

Hudson must have noticed this too because he lost his temper, bursting out that 'all this has been concocted in Liverpool'. The leading member of the 'Liverpool party', J. H. Brancker, certainly expressed his concerns at the way that important decisions were being rushed through. He moved an amendment to Hudson's resolution, to delay the proceedings by two months to enable the proposal to be properly considered. Brancker had judged this cleverly; the objection could be seen as perfectly reasonable, but he also knew that the delay would cause considerable complications and threaten the whole scheme, given the interest of the Manchester and Leeds. This provoked Hudson into outright opposition. He said he would 'feel himself aggrieved if they did not receive with fair liberality and kindness ... any proposals which he might think it advisable to submit to them', particularly if they were to reject proposals without giving him a reason. He also asked whether they thought they would be acting fairly towards the Leeds and Bradford proprietors, having already induced them to withdraw from alternative arrangements with the Manchester and Leeds. John Rand, another of the directors of the Leeds and Bradford who was present, said flatly that they would not wait that long; they would sell either to the Manchester and Leeds or to the East Lancashire.

Finally, Hudson abandoned all pretence at neutrality by asking Brancker to withdraw his amendment, which he refused to do. Hudson's approach did succeed in the short term, since the meeting approved the leasing of the Leeds and Bradford with 'only six hands held up against it', but only at the cost of openly joining battle with an influential member of the caucus of major Liverpool investors, which was eventually to have the most momentous consequences.[59]

Brancker immediately wrote an open letter to Hudson, published in the *Railway Times*, to air a number of obviously important issues: the generosity of the offer for a line that had not even been completed and where the 'traffic had never been ascertained', the hurried nature of the process; and the inadvisability of being asked to simply rely on the directors (he clearly meant Hudson) whose judgements had not always been correct. The major Liverpool investors had always kept in close contact with one another and they now became increasingly critical and distrustful of Hudson. They let it be known that they did not like his 'gigantic creations', and they also began to use professional accountants to examine more carefully the published accounts of Hudson companies.[60]

Brancker also continued his feud with Hudson at the next meeting of the Midland in late October 1846, raising the issue of the disparity between passenger fares, which were 'higher on the Midland than on any other line', and the rates for coal, which he had heard were 'lower even than on the London and North-Western'. From this starting-point, he went on to ask whether any of the directors had interests in collieries served by the Midland's lines that would bring their private interests into conflict with their public duty to represent the shareholders. This was probably intended to signal the continuing displeasure and distrust of the Liverpool investors towards Hudson and perhaps to try him out or just to nettle him. Hudson was never one to duck out of a challenge and he responded to this one, although the exchanges show that both parties were wholly capable of observing the civilities of the time.

Hudson started by addressing some of the cutting points in Brancker's statement. He was more than willing to go along with the wishes of the Midland proprietors, if they wished to recommend a reduction of passenger fares and would be content with lower dividends, although he denied that fares on the Midland were all that high, once allowance was made for the accommodation they provided to third-class passengers.

As far as coal rates were concerned, Hudson said he 'hated mystery' and declared that his colliery interests (with George Stephenson at Clay Cross) were known to every proprietor at the time he was appointed Chairman. He then confronted the moral challenge by asking the other directors whether they ever saw in him the 'slightest inclination to deviate from the strict path of my duties – whether I have not always looked to the interests of the shareholders – or whether I have ever appeared to be influenced in my conduct by my private interests'? He denied that he had ever received a shilling from the colliery, despite his large investment in it. In response to a further question, he then issued his own warning to the Liverpool faction not to toy with him, expressing his sorrow that the honourable gentleman should 'think so ill of human nature as to believe that public men are swayed by their private interest, in the discharge of their duty'. Finally, he offered to 'leave the management of your affairs to any party whom you may please to honour with your confidence'.

Hudson sat down at this point to loud cheers and, after some further discussion, Brancker said he was

> exceedingly sorry the honourable Chairman or Mr Ellis should suppose he meant anything personal towards them [but] rumours on the subject were very current out of doors and he had thought it only justice to the directors that they should have the opportunity of contradicting them before the shareholders.

One shareholder suggested, amid laughter, that the least Brancker should do was to move a vote of confidence in the directors, but Brancker thought it would be insulting to the board to suppose there 'had been any want of confidence in the directors, which he felt sure there had not'. Indeed he seconded the vote of thanks to the Chairman and directors, giving Hudson the opportunity to offer the meeting the kind of ringing assurances he delivered so ably:

> there is no object to which we aspire more, or which gives us more unmixed satisfaction, than the assurance that we continue to enjoy your confidence ... at the present time, directors hold no very enviable position as they are liable to be constantly held up to public opprobrium but ... so long as we have your

confidence – so long as we are supported by an impartial Press – so long as we in our judgement can be useful to the public, we shall not be deterred by attacks upon the system, from giving our best attention to carry out the interests of the company.[61]

Although the exchanges had been ostensibly polite, the antagonism was real enough. At another meeting of the Midland, in February 1847, Hudson reminded the members that the Midland had succeeded in carrying two million people on their lines during the previous six months without injury, avoiding those dangerous accidents which were 'so distressing to the directors and proprietors'. Brancker expressed his concerns about the number of contracts the company had entered into and called upon them to publish the gross receipts on every line that they had guaranteed. In reply to requests for further details regarding the Leeds and Bradford line, Hudson said that it was not yet possible to provide these but, when the directors thought it advisable to do so, he had 'no doubt it would be found highly satisfactory'. One shareholder responded to this lordly evasiveness by saying that he would like to be informed what Hudson meant by 'highly satisfactory'. When other shareholders laughed and cried out 'hear, hear', Hudson was quickly annoyed and responded hotly, adding for good measure that he would take the line off their hands, if they were not satisfied with the bargain.[62]

The shareholders raised one or two other minor points, but Hudson's anger or anxiety was now almost out of control and he added, testily and unnecessarily, that

he could not come a long distance from home to attend their meetings and to pay attention to their business, to be treated as he had been. It was true he received eighty-six or ninety pounds a year as their Chairman, but he could not devote his time and attention to the advancement of their interests and then come there to be ... baited and his time wasted by gentlemen asking questions which had previously been answered ... He and the directors had done everything in their power to forward the interests of the company. If, however, their proceedings did not meet the approbation of the proprietors, for his own part he would with the greatest alacrity withdraw [as] he was not ambitious of continuing and would willingly have more time to devote to looking after his own affairs.[63]

The Midland continued to grow rapidly. In March, no less than thirteen proposed Bills were approved, involving the construction of a further 250 miles of track at a cost of over £4,500,000, more than the Midland had possessed at the time of the amalgamation by which it was formed.[64] By the summer, Hudson and the Midland had both consolidated their positions.

He was again able to take some satisfaction from the company's safety record, but he was also sensible enough to offer his critics an olive branch by reducing the company's fares at a time that they were doing so well that the dividend did not need to be cut.[65] In August 1847, he was 'proud to say that the company never stood in a higher position than it did at the present moment', a sentiment endorsed even by Brancker, who thought the accounts for the first half of that year provided a 'very good report' on the company's progress and rose to second their adoption without further inquiry. A considerable amount of work had been done in the meantime to improve the more important stations, notably Nottingham, Leeds and Leicester, and most of the Bills intended to strengthen the Midland's position against its competitors had completed the parliamentary process. Hudson was now in the unusual position of stating that he would rejoice if the name of the Midland Railway were 'not heard within the walls of the House of Commons during the next session'. Indeed only three very minor Acts were obtained in 1848.[66]

At the meeting of the Midland in February 1848, Hudson was well received, partly because he had spoken up successfully for railway interests in Parliament and partly because the dividend, at 7 per cent, was surprisingly high considering the generally distressed state of the country. In his speech as chairman, he referred to recent suggestions that Midland dividends were paid out of capital and gave the most specific assurances that this was not the case. He also indicated that rumours of a merger with the London and North-Western Company were ill-founded, partly because the Midland was now reaching the effective limits of its growth; as he said, the 'proprietors of the Midland had as much under their hands as one department could well manage and he did not think it likely that any further amalgamation would take place with any other company. There was a point beyond which it would not be prudent to push amalgamations and he believed they had now arrived at it'.[67]

The railway press was still sceptical about the realities behind his confident utterances. Trading conditions were now more difficult and, in May 1848, the *Railway Times* wrote in sarcastic tones of his talent for inspiring confidence among shareholders:

> the plain and emphatic declaration of his hopeful convictions is usually contagious ... increased dividends are prognosticated, traffic, expanding and expandable, glides in prophetic streams before their rapt vision: a bold comparison with the position of other companies dazzles and exhilarates and men depart rejoicing as the Ephesians in their great Diana.[68]

Later that year, Hudson announced that the Midland's intention was now to weather the generally difficult trading conditions by a 'steady determination to economise the expenses of the company'. The company had opened only twenty-five miles of track in the last six months, including the line from Nottingham to Mansfield, and would open a further forty miles in the next half year, but thereafter they had no intention of entering into any fresh engagements until they could more clearly see their way. The dividend was reduced slightly to 6 per cent, but this was still a good return for the times and Hudson hoped that they would soon be offered as satisfactory a dividend as they could reasonably desire. He was also asked about newspaper reports of his impending resignation and replied that he had 'no intention whatever of leaving the company'. To considerable applause he added that, 'until he felt he could no longer preside over their affairs to the advantage of the company, nothing on earth should induce him to leave the company'. Even on the highly political issue of the relations between the directors and the enginemen, Hudson was rather more moderate than he had been in the past and said 'he was not aware but that the best feelings existed between the directors and the men in their employ ... He knew the engine-men on their line to be a most respectable body of men and as long as they conducted themselves as servants, and not as masters, they would receive the kind consideration of the directors'. He ended on a genuinely solemn note, expressing his sorrow at the death of his close friend George Stephenson and offering the deepest sympathy to all friends and relatives. Stephenson had died on 12 August 1848, at the age of sixty-seven. The great engineer had been in retirement for some time in Chesterfield and his death ended a long and close friendship that had been important to Hudson.[69]

The 'Liverpool Party' now decided to launch a further offensive against Hudson. A meeting of Liverpool shareholders was held in October, at which the Midland management was severely criticised. Early in 1849, Brancker wrote a detailed letter to the *Railway Times*, accusing Hudson of deliberately holding down mineral traffic rates, by implication for his own personal benefit. There was nothing new in these accusations and Hudson was able to assure the Midland shareholders in February 1849 that Brancker's claims were ill founded. Another of the Liverpool shareholders, A. H. Wylie, then continued the attack by complaining that the current dividend on the Midlands, at 5 per cent, was less than the rates they were paying on many of their leased lines, and only half the rate they were paying to the Leeds and Bradford, and that their accounts were one of the most 'meagre, bald statements ever issued by any Board of Directors'. It was time to 'declare boldly that the results of their management were not such as the shareholders were entitled to look for'. He then announced, 'without the slightest personal feeling of hostility to the directors and without any factious motives', his intention to propose the appointment of a Committee of Inquiry', at which there were shouts of 'Liverpool again' and 'that was concocted in Liverpool'.

After the proposal had been seconded, Ellis, the Deputy-Chairman, spoke at length in support of the directors' record and described the proposal as effectively a vote of censure on them; were it to be adopted he would then certainly 'use his own discretion as to the length of time he should retain his seat at the Board'. Another shareholder disputed this construction, however, and said that he did not see by what 'ingenuity it could be twisted into a vote of want of confidence. As public men they had a right to call for such an inquiry', particularly since their shares were now down to little more than £60 in the market.

Hudson had wisely kept out of the discussion until he thought it could be won, but he now joined the debate. He also saw the proposal to set up a Committee of Inquiry as a clear vote of censure and suggested to the seconder of the proposal, a Dr O'Brien, that it would have been far more honourable for him to put forward his own preferred list of directors. O'Brien was taken off guard by this challenge; he wavered and then withdrew his support. Hudson swiftly moved on to castigate the foolish expectations that dividends could be fully maintained during the trade depression they were in. When the vote was taken, only a handful of the five hundred shareholders present supported the proposal for a Committee of Inquiry.[70]

Whatever he liked to claim, Hudson's commitment to the Midland was undoubtedly weaker than his loyalty to the two York-based companies. Later that February, the directors of the Great Northern, formerly the London and York, were able to tell their shareholders that the York and North Midland had agreed to allow their trains to run on its tracks into York, and that Hudson had given an assurance that the new Knottingley curve would be completed without delay.[71] This arrangement would bring additional business to the York and North Midland and to the York Newcastle and Berwick, confirming their position as essential elements in the new, direct east coast route. It would also reduce the capital commitments of the hard-pressed Great Northern, although the new arrangements would be largely at the expense of the Midland, whose route via Rugby would then be almost thirty miles longer than the Great Northern route to Scotland.

Hudson had handled the call for a Committee of Inquiry at the Midland well, but it was now apparent that the shareholders were no longer as convinced by his record as they had once been, while some, including the Liverpool caucus, were clearly looking for a showdown. This would not be long in coming.

5

High Stakes

The Eastern Counties was without doubt an exceptionally bad railway. The prospectus, issued in November 1835, envisaged building from London to Ipswich, Norwich and Yarmouth, a distance of about a hundred and twenty miles. Construction was expected to take two years and to require a capital of one and a half million pounds.[1] The authorising Act was obtained in July 1836 and the first meeting of the shareholders looked confidently to the future. The directors predicted a possible return of 22 per cent, a heady prospect, although the Chairman, Henry Bosanquet, reassured his members that the Board would always act with due deliberation. He declared their motto would be 'festina lente' ('make haste slowly'), which unfortunately proved all too prophetic; the period of construction turned out to be extraordinarily prolonged and expensive, despite the easy terrain.[2]

The company took seven years to reach Colchester and then gave up after only fifty-one miles and an outlay of nearly £2,800,000.[3] After this, the line was bound to be a poor investment and paid only meagre dividends to its increasingly unhappy shareholders.[4] Passengers fared no better; the Eastern Counties was notoriously slow, unreliable and accident-prone. It was soon known as the 'scapegoat of companies, the pariah of railways' and became the butt of innumerable jokes and cartoons.[5]

The directors tried to rescue the company's fortunes by extension, encouraging other companies to build connecting lines, buying or leasing connecting lines and by promoting their own new routes.[6] The Northern and Eastern Railway had been established in 1836 to build a line from London to Cambridge and made slow progress on its construction. Nonetheless, by May 1842 the line had reached Bishop's Stortford, with a branch from Broxbourne to Hertford added in October 1843. For some time the trains of the Northern and Eastern had run on Eastern Counties tracks from Stratford into the latter's terminus at Shoreditch. The collaboration deepened when the Eastern Counties took over the management of Northern and Eastern freight traffic in 1843. It was soon agreed that they would lease the Northern and Eastern operation as a whole from 1 January 1844, which provided scope for the new concern to push north from Bishop's Stortford through Cambridge and Ely to Brandon, where they would eventually meet the Norfolk Railway, building from Norwich. When this happened in July 1845, the Eastern Counties had finally acquired a continuous line from London to Norwich, albeit by a completely different and much longer route than originally planned.[7]

Denison's London and York scheme, launched in 1844, was naturally seen by the Eastern Counties directors as a major threat, so they entered into an alliance with Hudson and the Midland, putting forward an alternative route to York that used Eastern Counties lines from London to March via Cambridge and Ely. As further encouragement, Hudson offered the Eastern Counties a half share in the through traffic to York and points north of that city.[8]

Though the London and York Bill failed to get through Parliament in 1845, it was due to go forward again in 1846. Parliament was disposed to authorise a more direct route between the two cities, so the London and York was going to be difficult to stop. The best hope lay with an alternative scheme put forward by a single company rather than a piecemeal arrangement organised by three separate companies. This being so, the only eligible company was the Eastern Counties and Hudson began to devise ways and means to bring it under his control.[9]

In spite of its dreadful reputation, there were by early 1845 some grounds for believing that the Eastern Counties was about to turn the corner. The directors insisted that, once their traffic was fully developed, they would prosper and they were not alone in their belief. The *Railway Times* was optimistic about the Eastern Counties' prospects and by January 1845 discerned a 'full tide of prosperity' that had set in at the Eastern Counties, despite its earlier troubles and adversities. One correspondent also predicted that 'the time is not far distant when this line will be sought after as a safe investment'.[10]

At a meeting on 28 August 1845, the directors reminded the members of the new lines that were being built, including the line from Colchester to Ipswich that was under construction by an independent company. The Eastern Counties, they predicted, would soon 'be one of the most flourishing [railways] in the kingdom'. Its shares would pay dividends of 10 per cent and be worth £50 each, two and a half times their then market value.

Despite these hopes, the directors were still only able to announce a dividend of 2 per cent per annum for the first half of 1845 and one shareholder referred to the company as 'an insolvent concern'. Another, James Scott, angrily complained that the shareholders 'were now assembled after nine years' operations, to receive less than any other company in existence'. There was much truth in his assertion. Over the previous eighteen months every one of the other major railway companies had paid dividends at least twice as high as those at the Eastern Counties, where the going rate was less than a third of the average dividend of other large companies of the time. Scott bitterly attacked the mismanagement of the directors, pointing out that five of them lived two hundred miles away in Liverpool and could not possibly manage the company from such a distance.[11] At first he called for a Committee of Inquiry, a procedure that had produced benefits at other companies such as the North Midland. Then he changed tack, and after declaring that the company could not be in a worse state ('any change must be for the better') urged that Hudson be invited to join the Board

> Let them look to what Mr Hudson had done. They wanted Mr Hudson amongst them, who had displayed so much energy in the North Midland Railway. Never was there a man who was so much entitled to the gratitude of the country as Mr Hudson. He was sure that Mr Hudson could not be insensible to an appeal from them ...

One of the directors revealed that the Board had previously and unsuccessfully invited Hudson to join them. No formal resolutions were passed but it was clear that most of the shareholders were in favour of asking him again.[12] A committee of shareholders was formed, chaired by Scott, which set about gathering signatures for an appeal to Hudson. The directors got involved in further negotiations behind the scenes and, in October, John Duncan, the Eastern Counties' solicitor, and a Cambridge shareholder named Fisher went to York, at the behest of the directors, with an offer not merely of a seat on the Board, but the Chair itself. There 'quite an effective little scene was played out ... Hudson was summoned from a festive gathering ... and was apparently so unprepared for their offer that he had to ask for a night's sleep upon it before giving a final answer'.

In fact, it was Hudson who had engineered the invitation in the first place; the deputation's declared willingness to promote a 'direct northern communication on continuation of the present Cambridge line of the Eastern Counties Company' provided him with confirmation of their acceptance of an important condition he had already identified.[13]

He formally accepted the offer to become Chairman of the Eastern Counties on 13 October 1845 and promptly signed a notice summoning shareholders to a special meeting 'to sanction extensions or new lines from Cambridge to York, and from Tottenham to Farringdon Street'.[14] The meeting was a great triumph for Hudson, as the *Railway Times* confirmed

> upon his entrance into the room the hon. gentleman was received with a loud and long-continued burst of cheering from one of the most densely crowded meetings we have attended. The large room at the top of the tavern shook again with the violence of the applause with which the hon. Chairman was greeted.

Shouts of 'bravo Hudson, Hudson for ever, and Hip, hip, hip, hurrah!' were continued for some minutes after he was seated, and it was some time before silence was restored and the business of the meeting commenced.

When Hudson addressed the shareholders, he began with the remarkable statement that he was already

> sufficiently acquainted with the position of this company to feel confident in assuring [them] that there is no line in the kingdom that should yield a better dividend than the Eastern Counties Railway. It wants only energy and exertion in its management, by which confidence will be given to the public.

The members found this very uplifting. His plan was to use the existing Eastern Counties line from London to Cambridge and Ely, and the branch from Ely to March, and then build from March through Spalding, Lincoln and Doncaster to meet the York and North Midland at South Milford. The line would be longer than that proposed by the London and York but it would be cheaper and quicker because of the easier gradients. It would also pass through such major towns as Cambridge, Lincoln, Grantham and Newark.[15] The cost would be met by an issue of £4,500,000 worth of 'York Extension Stock', in £20 shares. Many of these shares were to be used to buy the cooperation of competitors; ten thousand would go to the shareholders of the York and North Midland if they agreed to abandon their planned line from South Milford to Doncaster, seventy-five thousand to the Cambridge and Lincoln shareholders and, most importantly, a hundred thousand for shareholders in the London and York. When the expected opposition came at Board level, Hudson was fully prepared to appeal over the London and York director's heads to their shareholders, confident that they would recognise the superior nature of the propositions they were being offered.

Hudson then sat down 'amidst loud and long-continued cheering, with waving of hats, handkerchiefs, etc. In fact, the whole proceedings were accompanied with such enthusiastic applause, that they appeared more like those of a meeting of the friends of some successful candidate for parliamentary honours than the business proceedings of a railway meeting'. The resolution was carried with 'unanimous approbation' and more loud cheering. In moving the vote of thanks, Scott went on to deliver one of those fulsome tributes that in those days seemed to accompany so many of Hudson's doings; 'when times were dark with them ... they had appealed to Mr Hudson ... he was the pilot under whose guidance they were to weather the storm. He it was who opened to them a brilliant prospect for the future'.[16]

Some observers were impressed by what had happened at the meeting.

The *Railway Times* reminded their readers that they had 'frequently expressed [their] conviction of the excellence' of investment in Eastern
Counties shares and were gratified to have their opinion confirmed by
Hudson's 'oracular words'. Given his unbroken record of success, they were
confident that dividends of 10 per cent would materialise and that the
shareholders in the London and York would exchange 'their doubtful line
and hazardous stock for a safe and profitable investment in Eastern Counties
shares and sweep their directors away, or force them into obedience'.[17] But
the London and York directors were made of sterner stuff than this and
Hudson knew it well. Two days after the Eastern Counties meeting they
issued a circular making it abundantly clear that they would be proceeding
with their Bill, which had only to secure its passage through the House of
Lords in the 1846 session. They also intended to put forward an entirely
new list of subscribers and vet it carefully to forestall any repeat of Hudson's
earlier blocking tactics in Parliament.

Hudson made no formal approach to the London and York until he
represented the Eastern Counties at a public meeting in Cambridge called
by the local council on 19 November 1845. At this, he asked the London
and York representative to arrange a conference of directors from the two
companies to discuss amalgamation. He followed this up with an offer of
a share exchange.[18] The London and York were in no hurry to provide
Hudson with a response; they went ahead with a request to their own
subscribers to sign the new papers at one of their offices.

A series of advertisements began to appear in the railway press, the *Times*
and some provincial papers, signed 'One of You', urging subscribers to the
London and York not to comply with their directors' request. The first, in
late November, claimed that the need for a new subscription deed would
mean that the company's Bill would have to go through the Commons
procedures all over again, swallowing what remained of their deposits, and
argued that the House of Lords would, in any case, inevitably reject their
Bill to the ultimate benefit of none but the lawyers. Alarmist, and almost
hysterical in tone, the advert concluded 'you shall hear from me frequently.
The film must be withdrawn from your eyes. You are rushing to destruction
in consequence of your blindness'.[19]

The second advert gave the game away, as the anonymous correspondent
declared

> I repeat solemnly that I shall resist signing the new deeds. If we are forced to do
> so, it would be preferable to accept Mr Hudson's offer, which, if I understand
> rightly, is to grant an Eastern Counties share of £20 for each London and York
> share. Such an Eastern Counties share would be worth £10 premium per share
> upon the London and York line being withdrawn and, should Mr Hudson

continue Chairman of the Eastern Counties Railway and its York extensions, and throw upon the line the metropolitan traffic from his York and North Midland and Midland lines – what a brilliant prospect!

The writer also thought it sensible to respond to accusations that

> I am not one of yourselves, but one of the enemy. This I totally deny. I hold many more London and York shares than I like; and which, if Mr Hudson's offer be not accepted, shall be sold at whatever price they will fetch.[20]

It required no great penetration to see that these advertisements came from the Hudson camp and were inspired by him personally (even if they were actually placed by John Duncan, solicitor to the Eastern Counties).[21] The 'mania' of spring and summer 1845 had been temporarily checked by panic in October, with many investors anxious to unload their investments; Hudson may have thought he was pushing at an open door. The London and York investors were not, however, so easily alarmed into 'sweeping away' their directors and, by the time the latter met on 16 December to consider the offer, there was a healthy list of signatures to the new subscription deed.

As expected, the London and York directors rejected the proposal and, in an open letter to Hudson, denounced his 'bold effort to raise the value of Eastern Counties stock, and, as Chairman of the Midland, to get rid of a rival'. They also pointedly asked why, 'in your new position as Chairman to the Eastern Counties, you should be so jealous of a line passing through Hertfordshire and Bedfordshire, while you proclaim that the Eastern Counties Railway, with its present lines and branches, may be made to pay 10 per cent'. They accused him of using the Eastern Counties as a mere pawn in the Midland's battle.[22]

Hudson had demanded 'the entire control and management of the affairs of the Company' as a condition of joining the Eastern Counties and knew that he had the unquestioning support of the shareholders. He was perfectly willing to threaten resignation whenever his intentions were opposed by other members of the Board. This placed him in an almost invincible position as the other directors were all too aware that his departure 'would not be agreeable to the proprietors'.[23] He soon drafted in experienced men from his other companies to bolster the Eastern Counties management team. By the end of October the locomotive superintendent, Fernihough, had been replaced by a Hudson protégé, Thomas Scott, superintendent of the Midland's locomotive depot at Leeds, and a former apprentice of Thomas Cabry, who was again called in. Hudson also appointed Cusack P. Roney as Company Secretary.[24]

On 7 January 1846 the directors issued a notice, signed by Hudson and Roney, announcing a dividend of nine shillings a share, a rate of 6 per cent per annum for the second half of 1845, three times the level of the previous dividend. This was a remarkable achievement, especially since the accounting period had only ended three days previously. Yet here was tangible proof of the improvement that the directors had predicted and, when the shareholders met for their regular meeting in February, they were naturally enthusiastic.[25] Hudson referred to the imminent opening of two new lines, from Ely to Peterborough and from Colchester to Ipswich, and expressed confidence that traffic levels would soon bring in ten thousand pounds a week. The growth in traffic had even outstripped locomotive capacity although, with the company giving orders 'in all directions', this would soon be put right.[26] One shareholder, Mr Love, asked why the accounts no longer included any charge for depreciation, but most of the members were simply delighted at their progress. Scott said that 'no railway had undergone so much improvement, both for the benefit of the public and of the shareholders' and proudly pointed out the absence of any fatal accident on their lines in the last six months.[27]

Progress in the important battle over the London to York line was less satisfactory. The Direct Northern still had an interest in the new route but it had yet to take its Bill through all the stages in the Commons. The London and York Company Bill, on the other hand, was nodded through the House of Commons on 13 March and on 8 April came before the Standing Orders Committee of the House of Lords.

The Hudson party roused itself for a last effort and on 14 April 1846 a circular appeared from the 'Committee of Shareholders of the London and York'. This self-constituted body was chaired by Joseph LaMert but had actually been set up by John Duncan on behalf of the Eastern Counties and included other prominent Eastern Counties shareholders such as William Cash. The committee worked from the offices of LaMert's solicitor, Henry Philippson, at 4 Size Lane in the City of London, and all expenses were clandestinely reimbursed by the Eastern Counties.

The circular maintained that, given 'the state of the money market, and the increased price of railway works', passage of the London and York Bill would 'be the greatest misfortune that [could] happen to the shareholders, as calls must then be made and the share become valueless'. The members of the committee claimed to hold nearly five thousand London and York shares between them and to have the support of the holders 'of upwards of thirty thousand' altogether. They also ostensibly opened negotiations with the Eastern Counties Board, claiming that their appeal had already been responded to, to an extent which left no doubt in the mind of the committee that they could obtain the agreement of the majority of the shareholders to an amalgamation. An elegant charade took place: an exchange of letters between the committee and Hudson appeared in the press, with the former demanding better terms and the latter graciously obliging.

The London and York joined in and not unreasonably denounced the committee as having been 'got up for the purpose of serving the Eastern Counties interests'. They were aware of LaMert's involvement, knew him as a prominent Eastern Counties shareholder and quoted press reports of Eastern Counties meetings at which he had referred to the London and York as 'the common enemy' and talked of sending it 'to the devil'. They also added sardonically that 'whether Mr LaMert has become the chairman of the Size Lane committee in order to accomplish this benevolent mission, or from a real anxiety for the interests of the London and York shareholders, must be a matter of inference'.[28]

The Direct Northern remained very much on the sidelines and they decided to accept this position and try to join up with the London and York in order to obtain something for their shareholders. A deal was done and formally signed by the respective directors on 5 May.

'One of Yourselves' mounted a last gasp campaign against this amalgamation and the climax of the battle for the shareholders' loyalties came at meeting in London on 30 May. A Major Richardson proposed acceptance of the Eastern Counties' offer on the grounds that, if they did not accept, Hudson would still manage to destroy their Bill 'by fair means or foul!' This admission of the nature of Hudson's approach, by someone who was prepared to support it, was seized on by Denison in a forceful (but not entirely truthful) speech in which he said that 'our opponents are very cute ... they adopt tricks and devices that which never would have occurred to us [who] are unskilled and untutored in railway world'. Richardson withdrew his proposal and the directors' resolution to proceed with their Bill was approved unanimously. The meeting also decided to amalgamate with the Direct Northern and to call the new company the Great Northern.

The Size Lane committee turned out, therefore, to be an expensive failure, costing the Eastern Counties more than £7500. It held, it transpired, proxies on fewer than six thousand shares, less than a tenth of those held by the London and York board and was thus unable to wield any real influence on the London and York's affairs. It could not influence the parliamentary battle either; on 8 June 1846, the Lords' committee, chaired by the Earl of Lovelace, pronounced unanimously in favour of the London and York's bill, which became law on 26 June.[29]

The passing of the London and York Bill was a heavy blow to Hudson's ambitions, but he was not willing to admit defeat. In a speech to Eastern Counties shareholders, he denied using any underhand tactics against what was now the Great Northern and promised both that he would not be a party to any arrangement with that company and that the Eastern Counties would persevere in its attempts to build its own line to York.[30]

In the meantime, his problems as Chairman of the Eastern Counties had begun to mount. That summer he faced severe criticism on three aspects of more routine Eastern Counties policy, relating to accidents, punctuality and fares. The Eastern Counties record on accidents had generally been very poor. On 18 July 1846, despite a recent improvement, an accident at Romford killed several people and injured many others. The inquest jury censured the company for failing to observe safety regulations and added its own considerable weight to widely voiced concerns about Hudson's willingness to cut corners in order to increase dividends. A month later, the *Times* joined the growing chorus; according to Board of Trade returns, one quarter of all railway casualties in the first half of 1846 had occurred in the fifteen accidents that had taken place on the Eastern Counties lines. *Punch*, for its part, suggested that travellers, before boarding their Eastern Counties Railway carriage, 'might with justice salute the engine' with the words addressed by gladiators to the Roman Emperor 'morituri te salutant' ('those about to die salute you'). They also suggested that criminals awaiting execution should have their sentences commuted to journeys on Eastern Counties trains.[31] The unpunctuality and slowness of the Eastern Counties was also legendary: in one current joke a boy boarded an Eastern Counties train having paid a child's fare, only to have an adult fare demanded when he reached his destination.

In the summer of 1846 there were renewed criticisms, which Hudson unwisely decided to contest. His claim that the company had run more than four thousand trains in the last three months, on which the average delay had been 'three-quarters of a minute per train' prompted a deluge of contrary letters to the press. It was becoming obvious that Hudson was prepared to manipulate the facts in none too subtle a manner. The *Times* offered the sarcastic hope that those who suffered delays might be able to draw some consolation from his 'admirable' approach to averaging.[32]

A *Times* editorial of the same period suggested that the Eastern Counties shareholders had 'got a king of their own choosing – a monarch of vast pretensions and singular renown – but it still remains to be seen whether the acquisition be not more brilliant than beneficial'. The editorial went on to give readers a comparison of the fares on the various railways, which showed that 'a very considerable duty is levied on the public for the privilege of travelling by lines under royal management'. Other correspondents claimed that 'Hudson lines' were often twice as expensive as other lines and that this was a deliberate policy (since it never occurred against close competition) necessitated by the need to recoup the excessive price that Hudson had paid to expand his empire. In similar vein, a letter to the railway press suggested that the name of Hudson 'seems to scare away both judgement and discretion' and urged his supporters to 'compare the fares and accommodation of the Hudson line with any other in the kingdom and see if the one be not higher and the other worse than any of his contemporaries'.[33]

Life went on, of course. At Christmas the company entertained their 'numerous workmen' at a splendid dinner and ball at Stratford. Fifteen hundred people were invited to the dinner and twice that number to the ball. 'Few Christmas parties', said the *Railway Times*, 'whether on a small or a large scale, presented a scene of more unalloyed enjoyment'. The dinner was held in the new repairing workshop, 'tastefully decorated' for the occasion and complete with a band and 'a most effective corps of vocalists'. Hudson himself could not be present, being otherwise engaged, but he had not forgotten them; he sent from his estate in Yorkshire a 'plentiful supply of game, besides many other presents calculated to cheer the inner man'. The dinner began at five o'clock and, after that, the dancing 'was kept up until a late hour with an unflagging spirit that was highly pleasing'. Those who could not attend because of their official duties received an extra day's pay.[34]

Hudson was still highly popular with the Eastern Counties shareholders. The *Railway Times* carried a report of the half-yearly meeting in February 1847, one of the largest they had ever attended. 'As the Chairman entered the room, the entire body of proprietors rose to receive him – a compliment we have never yet seen paid at any railway meeting'.[35] Hudson had failed to stop the London to York Bill and the formation of the Great Northern Railway but he still refused to admit defeat. The Eastern Counties would now pursue two strategies; to try to cripple the Great Northern Railway wherever possible and to expand the Eastern Counties, both through new construction and by dominating its smaller neighbours. In his pursuit of the latter objective Hudson used 'blackmail, obstructionism, rate wars and sheer dishonesty', but it was the expansion schemes that he chose to bring to the attention of the shareholders on this occasion.[36] Some progress was being made: a branch from Ely to Peterborough had recently opened, lines from St Ives to Cambridge and from March to Wisbech were under construction; and traffic levels would require more lines running in from Mile End to their Bishopsgate terminus. In the last six months, the company's stock of locomotives had increased from seventy-one to ninety, the locomotive works at Stratford was nearing completion and electric telegraph lines had been laid along all the company's tracks.[37] An increased dividend of 10s. per share, well over 6 per cent per annum, was also proposed.

This, however, was only the prelude. Hudson then created a sensation by laying before the shareholders fourteen Parliamentary Bills, for two hundred miles of new lines requiring five million pounds of capital. Despite the sums involved, all the schemes were approved, virtually unanimously, apart from a proposed line from Tottenham to Guildford Street in central London, six miles that would have cost one and a half million pounds. Curiously, at the first sign of opposition from the shareholders, Hudson backed off, saying that it was originally planned to give the Eastern Counties a West End terminus for their northern traffic in opposition to the London and York and that he was not, in any case, 'very much in favour of the Bill'.[38]

Hudson, as chairman of both companies, was also able to ensure that the Eastern Counties and the Midland pursued consistent policies towards the Great Northern Railway; some limited cooperation, accompanied by concerted attempts to limit its room for manoeuvre. This complicated strategy was due to the fact that there were challenges other than the Great Northern to contend with. The Midland had no direct access to London: traffic for the capital travelled via Rugby over the tracks of the London and Birmingham, the company that had recently amalgamated with the Manchester and Birmingham and the Grand Junction to form the London and North-Western, the largest railway in the country. Once the west coast main line to the north was completed, the London and North-Western would inevitably route all through traffic along it, a serious loss to the Midland. An alternative route to London was therefore needed, and in October 1846 Hudson came to an agreement with the Great Northern that the Midland would construct a line from Leicester, through Bedford, to connect with the Great Northern at Hitchin, with clear benefits for both companies. Hudson had also included in the Eastern Counties' expansion plans, new lines from Hertford to Hitchin, Cambridge to Bedford and from Wisbech to Newark, all of which would link directly to the Midland as well as a line from Peterborough that would join the independent Ambergate, Nottingham and Boston Railway to provide a Midland link. These lines would connect up the Eastern Counties with the Midland and cut across the Great Northern's route, a plan consistent with Hudson's overall intention to strangle future Great Northern Railway traffic wherever possible.

Towards the end of the meeting, he paid a generous tribute to the Deputy Chairman, David Waddington, who had devoted 'so much of his time, so much of his ability' to promoting the interests of the company. One of the shareholders asked Hudson about persistent rumours aired in the *Times* of his imminent resignation from the Chair. Hudson said he was 'much surprised when he heard the rumour [as] he had never entertained a notion of vacating his seat [and] he was more thoroughly convinced than ever of the value of the line'. His final hope that he would pass many years in the service of the company led to resounding cheers.[39]

One of the social peaks of Hudson's life came that summer. At 11.24 a.m. on 5 July 1847 Queen Victoria and Prince Albert arrived at the Eastern Counties station at Tottenham, *en route* for Cambridge and the Prince's investiture as Chancellor of the University. It was to be the first royal journey on the Eastern Counties railway and no effort was spared to make the occasion memorable. Two hundred yards in front of the station, a lofty triumphal arch had been raised, decorated with flags, flowers and evergreens and the company coat of arms. The route to the station itself was lined with flag-staves trimmed with wreaths and led to a Swiss-style pavilion, designed by the railway's resident engineer. On each side of the reception room, in white and scarlet, retiring rooms had been provided for the comfort of the royal party. A colonnaded, wreath-trimmed corridor, with niches filled with the 'choicest exotics', led from the pavilion to the departure platform, all of which gave the place the appearance of a conservatory. The galleries that had been prepared on either side of the corridor and to one side of the platform entrance were occupied by elegantly dressed ladies who had been able to listen, while they were waiting, to a succession of inspirational marches played by the Queen's guard of honour.

When the royal coach, attended by a troupe of Lancers, drew up outside the pavilion, a crowd of about three thousand had gathered to greet them. 'Hudson and his co-directors advanced to meet the Queen who, upon alighting, addressed the worthy chairman very affably'. With Hudson as her escort, she immediately passed through the pavilion towards the royal carriage, beautifully decorated in white and gold on the outside and lined in figured French grey satin and handsomely furnished. The royal standard floated over the Queen's carriage. An elegantly bound and beautifully drawn map and plan of the Eastern Counties Railway route was presented to Her Majesty by Mr Hudson. The Queen appeared 'greatly pleased with the evident care which had been taken to promote her comfort' and the Prince Consort was equally delighted. He 'complimented Mr Hudson in good terms on the taste displayed in the erection of the pavilion'. The royal train set off at 11.28 a.m., four minutes after the Queen had arrived at the station, with a hand-picked driver at the controls. The four carriages contained the royal party and a 'fine posse of princes, noblemen and ladies', including Mrs Hudson. Every station the train passed had its own complement of employees and passers-by to cheer the royal party on and, when the train stopped at Bishop's Stortford, a detachment of the West Essex Yeomanry was drawn up along the platform and a 'rustic band' played the National

Anthem while the train took on water. On reaching Cambridge, shortly before one o'clock, Hudson sprang out and opened the door to the Royal carriage, offering Her Majesty his arm, which she was graciously pleased to take before she passed into the pavilions erected on the station, where the representatives of the city and university of Cambridge were waiting.[40]

All had gone splendidly and two days later Hudson received 'Her Majesty's gracious acknowledgement of her entire satisfaction at the transit to and from Cambridge and at the arrangements for her accommodation'. The press also approved. Everything was in keeping and Hudson and his colleagues had not entered into the arrangements as 'mere official matters; there was a care, a finish, a judicial comprehensiveness about the preparations ... and a pervading spirit in all that was done upon the line throughout the day, speaking plainly to the observer that the company were proud of their illustrious visitors, and had made all their preparations in a truly loyal *con amore* spirit'. A few days later, a whole week's banqueting and entertaining began at the Mansion House, York.[41]

At the half-yearly Eastern Counties meeting in August 1847, Hudson was still exuding confidence. He made a point of reminding the members that over a million passengers had been carried in first half of the year without a single accident. The dividend was reduced to 5 per cent per annum, but Hudson was confident it could soon be increased, because traffic levels were now increasing quickly. Several of the company's new lines had recently opened and more were to follow. Moreover, when the Midland's line from Leicester to Peterborough was complete, the Eastern Counties would then be 'in communication with the whole of the north of England' and much of the freight traffic to London would be passing along their line. He was evidently feeling buoyant enough to take a sideswipe at the Great Northern, which would, he predicted, soon find itself 'stuck fast in the mud ... or the London clay', whose treacherous character was well known. At the same time, he did seem very touchy about recent press criticisms. When the Eastern Counties receipts reached £15,000 a week, as they soon would, he declared, then they could treat with contempt 'whatever pamphlets may state or papers publish' and he urged the shareholders to hold fast to their shares, regardless of the attacks any 'hired scribbler' might make on the company from 'mercenary or other unworthy motives'.[42]

One of the 'scribblers' to whom Hudson referred was Arthur Smith, whose lively and argumentative pamphlet, *The Eastern Counties Viewed as an Investment*, published in 1847, caused quite a stir. It raised a whole series of doubts about whether the Eastern Counties was sufficiently viable as an investment ever to pay reasonable dividends. It also made a sustained attack on the company's accounting practices, pointing out by way of example that there was a major discrepancy between the working expenses for the first half of 1845 as shown in the company's parliamentary returns (£145,856) and in the accounts laid before shareholders (£126,432).

The increase in receipts in the second half of 1847 was slightly less than Hudson had hoped for, and the dividend had to be reduced to 4 per cent, a situation not entirely remote from Arthur Smith's main argument. That was not how Hudson saw matters when addressing shareholders in February 1848. The Midland's line from Leicester to Peterborough, which would join Norwich to the Midlands and also provide access to the coalfields of Lancashire and Yorkshire, was still not open for traffic although an engine had 'gone over the line without stopping'. It would open properly in March, as would the St Ives branch, two months ahead of the Maldon, Witham and Braintree. After expressing his disappointment at the dividend, Hudson said they had done their best and appealed 'with confidence to you for a continuance of your approbation and support. But if you think any other person, or any other body of men, can manage your affairs better than we have conducted them, I am perfectly ready to resign my trust to other hands', an offer met with the expected cries of 'no, no'.

One Dr Riley thought the dividend was better than might have been expected, 'considering the cloud that has for some time hung over the monetary world', although he also complained about one of the darker sides of Hudson's operations, the persistent interruption at the last meeting of any views that differed from those of the chairman. Other shareholders were critical of the way the company had spent its money and wanted more spent on the permanent way and less on 'securing the public from the wind and weather at stations'. Another popular target was the size of the legal costs, which had reached £35,000. The comment by one member that the proposed new branch lines and stations were mainly 'feeding the solicitors and engineers' provoked tremendous support. Hudson tried to sidestep by saying how little he liked the amount of their legal costs and by claiming that their 'parliamentary expenses were less per mile than any other railway of equal extent', but he was met with cries of 'no more lines'.

The meeting was becoming difficult for Hudson. A further proposal was made from the floor that auditors be appointed with 'full authority to examine every voucher and document relative to the accounts of the company'. This proposal went to a formal resolution that was lost by a large majority, yet Hudson was still uneasy at the shareholders' attitude. He complained that the proposals represented 'nothing more or less than an expression that the accounts which the directors had produced were false', but conceded that the directors would consider the matter and would probably 'invite two or three of the largest proprietors to join them in the examination of the accounts [which] he had gone through several times'.[43]

Despite the calls for no more lines, Hudson summoned the shareholders to a special meeting on 2 May 1848 and laid before them yet another proposal, to amalgamate with the Norfolk Railway and the very small Newmarket line. He argued that this would bring about a considerable saving in expenses: the locomotive department alone would save £12–14,000 a year as, 'instead of blowing off the steam at Brandon, we can run on to Norwich, and the saving of expense will be enormous'. The proposals were supported by most members, although some dissent was expressed.[44] The leasing of the Norfolk Railway had, however, disastrous consequences for both its workers and its passengers; within a week of that meeting, all the Norfolk employees had been dismissed and the service soon deteriorated, with higher fares, slower trains and more accidents.[45]

If Hudson thought he had taken the sting out of shareholder concerns, he was quickly disabused at the next meeting, on 17 August 1848. Few of the shareholders were willing to take the generally depressed state of trade into account as far as the dividends were concerned and some expressed their dissatisfactions quite bluntly; Hudson had told them some time ago they were to 'have 10 per cent [but] last year it was only 4 per cent and it is the same this year'. The most serious challenge to Hudson's position came when several shareholders returned to the subject of auditors. When he was asked whether the accounts had been audited, Hudson said that they had indeed been audited by the directors and that he also had a resolution for their approval, appointing two gentlemen as auditors. The loud cheers greeting this assertion did nothing to inhibit those who thought it 'desirable that the auditors should chosen by the shareholders and that the nomination ought not to emanate from the directors'. Hudson was then asked for further details about the auditors he was putting forward. The shareholders were not prepared to go 'immediately into the appointment without some preliminary examination or inquiry. Without they had full confidence in the auditors, it was a farce to appoint them'. Another member openly raised the issue of how much they could or should trust their directors. The only guarantee they could have regarding the accuracy of the accounts was their confidence in the auditors and he once again asserted the need for the nominations to come from the meeting and not the directors.

At this, the directors closed ranks. Waddington challenged the proposal on the grounds that it was the duty of the Board to ensure that any nominee auditors were 'responsible men and fit for the office'. He was strongly supported by Hudson and the other directors and their original proposal was then carried without further challenge. William Cash, a former member of the Size Lane committee, supported Hudson on the grounds that he personally knew both the nominated auditors and 'was sure the meeting could not make a better choice'. He fulsomely seconded the vote of thanks to the chairman.[46]

Hudson had not been long at the Eastern Counties but, by 1848, it was clear that the gap between the grand forecasts he had made when appointed as chairman and the modest level of dividends that had actually been paid had sapped the confidence of the shareholders. There were also ominous signs that some members no longer really trusted the Board. Most disturbing of all, it was now obvious that Hudson had used the Eastern Counties Railway as a pawn, to 'play a considerable part in thwarting the ambitions of the Great Northern, Hudson's chief enemy, in matters that hardly concerned it at all'. The strains of this were now becoming apparent to all.[47]

6

The Heights

Hudson's ever-expanding railway activities, in particular the creation of the Midland Railway, for a time the largest in the country, made him a leading figure in the railway industry. This position was cemented by his role in shaping and responding to attempts by the government to regulate the industry.

In February 1844 William Gladstone, President of the Board of Trade, set up a Select Committee to consider how the railways could best be regulated in the public interest. As natural monopolies, the railways had the potential to abuse their position at the expense of the public. Some thought that the success of the leading lines, and the fact that their shares were trading at more than twice their face value

> disclose[d] a state of matters constituting a monopoly of the very worst kind. The directors of the leading railway companies ... act towards the public as they think proper. They make their own terms because they know the public have no remedy [and] are completely at their mercy. And hence, the exorbitance of their charges ... The public are grossly and grievously wronged in this matter. And they have a right to look to the Legislature for redress ... Passengers ought to be travelling in the leading lines at from 50 to 75 per cent cheaper than they are at present. Extravagant prices, as the result of monopolies in corn, and in all other commodities, are now everywhere denounced; and why not the exorbitant prices consequent on the monopoly in the conveyance from one part of the country to another, which is enjoyed by most of the railroad companies? ... The [Select] committee lately appointed ... have had large powers conferred upon them by Parliament ... We trust ... that one of the results ... will be the extinction of railway monopolies, by fixing a moderate scale of charges.[1]

Some of the leading companies were very profitable; the London and Birmingham and the Grand Junction, for example, were paying dividends of 10 per cent a year in 1844. The obvious 'free-trade' solution, competition, was not easily practicable and Gladstone was interested in establishing a regulatory regime for the railway industry that would provide a middle way between monopoly and competition, before the onset of a new phase of railway promotion, which was clearly on its way.[2]

The latter worried some railway directors. The prominent railway director

George Carr Glyn, chairman of the London and Birmingham, thought that railway property, as property, would be dangerously threatened by the unchecked promotion of new lines. Without some systematic form of regulation 'the property of many of the existing railways must become very seriously depreciated' as a result of competition, although without concomitant benefit to the public. But he also forsaw that it might be difficult to persuade shareholders of the advantages of regulation.[3]

Gladstone's hope was that existing railway companies would accept regulation in return for protection from competition. This was made explicit in a paper drafted for him by the Board of Trade official Samuel Laing, expressively entitled 'Hypothetical Outline of Considerations which May be Given to, and Asked from, Railway Companies as Equivalents in an Amicable Settlement'. This formed the basis of the Select Committee's deliberations. Laing was the first witness, and was questioned about it at great length for six days. He suggested two ways in which the railways could give 'valuable consideration to the public': improved accommodation for poorer passengers and reduced fares where companies were making excessive profits.[4]

The early railways had concentrated on high-priced first–class passenger traffic. Third-class accommodation, where railways bothered to provide it, usually consisted of open wagons whose passengers were 'hardly better treated, or more rapidly conveyed, than the cattle which were sent by train to farmstead or to market'.[5] Laing proposed that railway companies be required to provide some reasonable third-class trains, at low charges, even if this was in itself uneconomic.[6]

Laing also suggested that maximum passenger fares, laid down in each line's authorising Act, be subject to periodic revision (perhaps every twenty years) if the company's return on capital exceeded a certain limit. This provoked more discussion than any other issue and Laing was questioned about the practicability of his plan.[7] As security against its evasion, he also proposed that the government effectively take out an option to purchase railways at the end of the twenty-year period, on agreed terms. This excited little controversy and was discussed only briefly.[8] Gladstone had discussed the proposals with representatives of railway companies and Laing's view was that that part of the scheme had been 'rather favourably received by them'.[9]

Gladstone wanted an amicable settlement with the railway companies and the proceedings of the Select Committee gave good reason for believing he could reach one. Two of its members were railway directors, others were known to be sympathetic to the industry, most of the witnesses were railway company directors or officials and there was general acceptance of Gladstone's plan.

When Hudson gave evidence on 18 March, he was not supportive of Gladstone's proposals. Instead, he made it clear that he was with the 'high fare' party. He did not think that profits were to be made from third-class traffic. The York and North Midland did not carry third-class passengers, although he was willing to accept a requirement that they be catered for, within limits. He rejected Gladstone's suggestion that the introduction of closed carriages for third-class passengers would be 'a great boon to the public' with the distinctly implausible assertion that third-class passengers did not like second-class carriages and 'preferred theirs being completely open'.[10] He flatly rejected the idea that reductions in fares would lead to a substantial increase in traffic, described the suggestion that traffic might double were fares to be halved as 'preposterous', and thought low fares a 'dangerous experiment for railway companies to try, as regards their revenue'.

Hudson was also convinced that it would be in the best interests both of railway shareholders and the public if Parliament refused to sanction any line whose 'primary object was to compete with an existing line'. He thought, as a railway proprietor, that it was worth giving up something for that: 'if you could give me a protection against competition, I should very seriously consider whether it would not be advisable for the railway companies to agree to a fair consideration of their case at the end of twenty years'. His real difficulty with the plan was that he did not see how such protection could be assured since Parliament could not guarantee that a future Parliament would not allow a competing line.[11]

In his evidence, Hudson emerged as deeply conservative rather than visionary as far as the railway industry was concerned. He was unconvinced that major increases in traffic could be achieved, even by the completion of a route north to Edinburgh. Increased profits would come from reducing costs and increasing fares, not from increasing volume. And he was no evangelist for the benefits of travel:

> Gladstone: I understand you to say that you have considerable doubt whether it would improve the state of society, people travelling more?
>
> Hudson: I think it is a very good thing in its way, but like everything carried to an extreme, it is not good.[12]

He also allowed his self-interest to show through in a rather obvious, even naive, way during a discussion of national policy. As an example of the evils of new lines that competed with existing lines, he referred to the Cambridge and York scheme, then being promoted, which was intended to give a more direct route between London and York and compete with his own lines. He denounced it in no uncertain terms: the line would develop no traffic of its own, merely abstract it from other lines. Lincoln (through which the line would pass) needed communication with the Midlands and Manchester (the Nottingham-Lincoln branch of the Midland), it had no need of communication with London and it would not pay. The self-serving nature of his argument was painfully apparent. (He did not foresee that he would, within eighteen months, be promoting a very similar scheme himself, and arguing that one of the distinct merits of his scheme, as opposed to that of the London and York, was that it provided direct communication with London to towns such as Lincoln). He also piously (and gratuitously) said he 'would not be connected with any line which was competing with an existing line', but later referred to the York and North Midland's acquisition of the Leeds and Selby, and how most of the latter had then been closed to passenger traffic. This led one of the committee to observe that, in that case, the York and North Midland must have been a competing line, to which he could only reply, rather lamely, that it 'turned out to be a competing line'.[13]

On 20 June 1844 Gladstone introduced his Railway Regulation Bill in the House of Commons. It was largely based on the reports of the Select Committee and, amongst other things, provided, at the end of a fifteen-year period, for the revision of fares on any new railway whose annual profits reached 10 per cent of share capital, or the purchase of such a railway by the state.[14] At once a storm of protest broke out over the fare revision and purchase clauses of the Bill. The *Railway Times* named it the 'Railway Plunder Bill' and called for it to be 'resisted and defeated *in toto* as a breach of faith', prompting an almost hysterical campaign to defeat the 'imminent danger which threatens the whole railway property of the country'.[15]

Hudson moved very quickly to assume the leadership of the campaign. He summoned and presided over a meeting of representatives of seventeen railway companies in London, on 26 June 1844, which drafted a petition or 'memorial' to the Prime Minister, Sir Robert Peel, with his own signature first. This did not address specific features of the Bill but argued only that it proposed 'a most inexpedient change in the system on which railways have been hitherto promoted and maintained'. It also attacked the processes of the Select Committee, particularly the taking of evidence 'with closed doors, and without affording your Memorialists an opportunity of hearing and rebutting it'. It had been 'an *ex parte* inquiry', whose Reports and evidence had only been made public 'within the last few days', and it would be wrong for such a Bill to be 'hurried through Parliament' late in the session when it was impossible for it to be maturely considered.

The stance taken by Hudson and the other railway company chairmen is puzzling. The most likely explanation is that Glyn's apprehensions about obtaining the consent of shareholders had been borne out and the chairmen who had negotiated with Gladstone were taken aback by the degree of opposition to the Bill and felt that they had no choice but to put themselves at the head of the campaign. On 1 July Hudson and Glyn, now representing thirty railway companies, led a deputation to Downing Street to appeal to both Peel and Gladstone. Privately Gladstone expressed his anger at the attitude of the railway directors and his 'perfect amazement' at the position of Glyn.[16]

During the debate on the Bill's second reading in the Commons, on 8 July 1844, Gladstone robustly rejected the criticisms that had been made. Opposition to the Bill was being promoted through the 'grossest misrepresentations as to its objects and provisions' and by exaggerating the powers that the government were really seeking. It was absurd to say that the Select Committee had conducted an '*ex parte* inquiry'; he had originally proposed four railway directors as members of the committee but withdrew two names after accusations of having packed the committee in favour of the railway companies. The option to purchase only applied to new railways and would in any case require parliamentary approval: the executive had no independent power to effect a purchase under the Bill. The purchase and revision proposals were based on the third report of the Select Committee, which had been available since early April and the object of the Bill was 'not to close the question of purchase, but to open it, and place Parliament in a position to entertain and decide that question'.[17]

Hudson replied with an open letter to Gladstone, written from the King's Arms Hotel, Westminster, and printed in most newspapers on 11 July 1844. Hudson denied that the representatives of the railway companies were 'so ignorant as to have utterly misconstrued the meaning of the Bill now before the House, or so dishonest as to have misrepresented its provisions to their co-proprietors or to the public'. Their major objection was to the one-sided inquiry process whereby

> Mr Laing, an officer of the Board of Trade, presented a paper to the committee, was seven days under examination and was subsequently present during the whole of the inquiry, listening to, marshalling and bringing forward the whole of the evidence on which the Bill was founded, whilst the railway companies were refused even an inspection of that evidence.

Further, various witnesses were 'examined on matters of detail according to the manner in which the government officer found it desirable to support his case and none were ... examined with reference to the whole scope and objects of the Bill now before the house'. They also objected in particular to the seventh clause, which gave the government the 'absolute power of purchasing compulsorily any new railway after a period of fifteen years from the passing of the Act authorising its construction'. They did not believe the built-in safeguard, that individual companies could not be bought out without the government having to apply to Parliament for the necessary funds, would afford sufficient security to the railway industry, once the principle had been previously sanctioned by the legislature. The railway companies had remained passive during the proceedings of the committee and had patiently awaited its report before taking any steps that 'might be considered premature or disrespectful to the government', but this should not be construed as tacit acceptance of the government's intentions. He ended with two final points, both of which were framed with conspicuous courtesy. First, 'if there be defects in the system of management of railways, the companies will cordially unite with the government in their correction and in framing any Bill which, on full inquiry and after a fair hearing of both sides, shall be considered necessary for the correction of every such abuse proved to exist or likely to arise; but they humbly yet strongly protest against the present measure of the government'. Secondly, he hoped 'that in addressing you this letter I shall not be considered as having stepped beyond the strict line of propriety and that I have not, in the observations I have made, expressed myself in terms which can be considered in the remotest degree uncourteous or disrespectful [for] certainly nothing can be farther from my intentions'.[18] Gladstone and Hudson then conducted some private negotiations; on the day that Hudson wrote his open letter, Gladstone sent him some revised proposals, and by 17 July had noted in his diary that he had 'settled as I hope the railway enactment in a long conference'.[19]

It has been argued that Gladstone overreached himself, and that Peel regarded the objectives of the Bill as 'too sweeping' and intervened to produce a final outcome more acceptable to the railway companies, so that Hudson was able to exploit the differences between them.[20] Others have seen Peel as simply alarmed by the strength of the opposition generated by the railway lobby; however misconceived it might have been, there was no point in alienating so powerful an interest. He certainly acted to conciliate the railway companies, letting it be known that he did not think Parliament would ever agree to nationalisation.

Certainly, Gladstone was compelled to retreat and announced a considerable revision to his Bill on 22 July. When the Regulation of Railways Act became law in August, the terms under which railways could be nationalised, or their fares revised, were much more favourable to the companies and existing railways were *specifically* excluded from any threat of acquisition by the state, even though Gladstone thought this was clear enough in the original Bill. The Act was to be best known for its continued support for poorer travellers: its requirement that railways provide at least one third-class train per day, each way, on all lines, with covered coaches, charging no more than one penny per mile. These 'parliamentary trains' pushed the companies into the development of third-class traffic, to their own benefit as well as that of their passengers.[21]

This was all seen as a great success for the railway interest and Glyn generously attributed the favourable outcome 'entirely to the exertions of Mr Hudson'.[22] In fact, it was a hollow victory for the railway industry; no Parliament in the nineteenth century would have seriously entertained the nationalisation of the railways and Glyn's perception that the multiplication of lines would damage profitability was not appreciated by investors. The frenzied promotion of lines during the Mania of 1845–47 soon led to a collapse of profitability that made the dividends of 1844 no more than a happy memory and rendered nugatory the provisions for a revision of fares.

Nevertheless, the episode was a considerable triumph for Hudson personally. The *Railway Times* had been very critical of Hudson since his excessive economising at the North Midland. In January 1844 it had attacked the 'Northern Napoleon' over his allotment of six hundred shares in the Leeds and Bradford and his 'bare-faced appropriation' of a large number of Scarborough railway shares. In March, a few days after he had given evidence to the Select Committee it described him as one of the 'worst enemies of the railway system [and] the Prince of Premium-Hunters' and declared that, as such, it would 'continue, in season and out of season, to expose him'.[23] By 13 July 1844, however, when it printed his open letter, it was described as being 'from the pen of Mr Hudson, the intelligent and spirited Chairman of the Midland Railway Company. The statements in it are so conclusive, that we feel called on to give it a most prominent place in our columns'. Two weeks later it was 'anxious to call particular attention' to Hudson's letter to landowners on the route of the Leeds and Bradford line, praising its 'liberal and enlightened spirit'.[24]

He had been given several nicknames in the papers, including the 'Yorkshire Balloon', the 'Railway Napoleon' (sometimes derisively) and 'King George of York' by the railway investors' paper, *Herapath's Journal*, from late 1843. Now he was the hero who had challenged the government and won, and the soubriquet 'The Railway King', was first attached to him about this tme. It was often said that this title was first applied to him by the Reverend Sydney Smith, the famous wit and rector of Foston-le-Clay, near Howsham, as a compliment; whereas conventional monarchs achieved their titles through bloodshed and misery, Hudson had come to his by 'his own peaceful exertions and by a course of probity and enterprise'.[25] Whatever its origins, it was soon universally applied, and as the 'railway mania' got under way in 1845, pushing railways to the centre of public attention, the

Railway King became a national figure and a household name, a favourite target of newspaper cartoonists. Hudson has been described as the 'first Englishman from the middle-class commercial world who was made by the caricaturists into a familiar image', recognisable to all.[26]

Hudson's public position, and the considerable personal fortune he had amassed from railway speculation by 1845, were the basis of his social and political ambitions. When he first became involved in politics in York, he had quickly been accepted by the members of the leading land-owning families, who were also typically Anglican, protectionist Tory Ultras. The Hudsons had certainly been introduced into London society by 1834, when he was in his mid thirties. As he became more important in York, he entertained more and more himself, and, when he was Lord Mayor, spectacular social events, balls, banquets, processions and feasts followed one another thick and fast. He was now in a position to acquire land and the social cachet that went with it, and to play a leading role in London Society. Politically, he had been the dominant figure in York for nearly a decade; now it was time to enter the national political stage. For this he needed a seat in the House of Commons and beyond that he might aim at ministerial office. Social and political ambitions reinforced each other; social contacts would aid a successful political career, which in turn might help him to a title, and full integration into the upper classes.

At first, Hudson had plans to stand for Parliament in Whitby. Instead, in the summer of 1845 another opportunity presented itself. Earl Grey, who had been Whig Prime Minister at the time of the Reform Act of 1832, died in July 1845 after a lengthy illness. His son Lord Howick, an MP for Sunderland, 'only a few weeks after tilting so hotly with Mr Hudson in the cause of the Northumberland Railway', was then elevated to the Upper House, creating a vacancy.[27]

Both the local Members, Lord Howick and David Barclay, were Liberals, but they owed their selection to local factors as much as to political sympathies. As the veteran Liberal agent Joseph Parkes put it

[in] English borough constituencies [the impact of] '*political* principle and particular Cabinet policies [was] much overrated [results were] much more influenced by particular *local* circumstances than generally imagined and greatly influenced by the *sufficiency and purse weight of candidates.*[28]

From 1833–41, one of the Sunderland seats had been held by the Conservative William Thompson, 'the friend of the shipowners', and a leading figure in the City. He had known Hudson since the mid 1830s and it is likely that it was he who introduced Hudson to leading local Tories in Sunderland during Earl Grey's illness, when it was clear that a by-election would not be long delayed.[29]

By the mid 1840s, there were serious problems in the Sunderland shipping industry. The town's prosperity was based on the export of coal from the Durham coalfields, a trade that dated from the late sixteenth century, and on shipbuilding, which had developed in the second half of the eighteenth century. According to Lloyd's Register, it had become the 'most important shipbuilding centre in the country nearly equalling, as regards number and tonnage of ships built, all other ports together'. But coal shipments were facing increasing difficulties. Most coal was loaded from staithes built on the banks of the River Wear and, with the inexorable rise in the size of ships, Sunderland was facing growing competition from other ports. There was a widespread recognition that the town needed proper docks if the industry was to have a future.[30]

A company had been promoted in the early 1830s to construct a dock on the south side of the Wear, a logical plan since nearly all the coal shipped from Sunderland came from collieries on that side of the river, but its private Bill was defeated in the Commons through the opposition of Sir Hedworth Williamson, an influential local landowner and MP for North Durham. Instead, Williamson sponsored a rival scheme for a dock at Monkwearmouth, on the north bank of the Wear, on his own property and also put a good deal of money into a proposed Monkwearmouth to South Shields Railway.

The dock venture turned into a fiasco. The anticipated cost quadrupled to £120,000 and Sir Hedworth suffered considerable financial embarrassment; he was forced to retire from Parliament and even give up his carriage. When the dock opened in 1837, it proved hopelessly inadequate. At only nine acres, it was far too small, could only cope with small ships of less than two hundred tons and was impossible to access in rough weather. The planned suspension bridge over the Wear was never built and very little coal was ever shipped through the north dock, which was viewed as a 'baronial folly' and popularly known as 'Sir Hedworth's bathtub'. It was generally agreed, even by David Barclay, that a new dock on the south side of the Wear was essential to Sunderland's prosperity, but potential investors were understandably hard to find.[31]

Railway communication was also a problem. The south side of the Wear was served by the Durham and Sunderland Railway, built as a coal line and operated by stationary engines. Improvements were badly needed, but in 1845 its shareholders (mostly from Sunderland) had not received a dividend for several years and shares were trading at less than half their £50 nominal value. There was hardly any provision for passengers and trains took over two hours to cover the thirteen miles from Durham to the wooden

shed that served as Sunderland's railway station. By the early 1840s, despite
a rise in output, coal shipments from Sunderland were falling in the face
of competition from ports with superior facilities and local businessmen
desperately needed a boost.[32]

Colonel Perronet Thompson had been 'nursing' the constituency since
1843 when Earl Grey had become seriously ill. He was a veteran free trader
and a leading spokesman for the Anti-Corn Law League, which was cam-
paigning for the abolition of protective tariffs on imported corn, and had
pushed the issue of the Corn Laws to the top of the political agenda. This
was not entirely to the taste of the powerful shipping interest in Sunderland.[33] They had their own protection in the form of the Navigation Laws,
and were concerned that if the Corn Laws were repealed, the Navigation
Laws would soon follow, a fear that turned out to be entirely justified. The
wealthier and more moderate section of the Liberals, the Whigs (as they
were often termed), also objected to the Colonel's advanced democratic
views; he supported Chartist demands for manhood suffrage and the secret
ballot. They had an alternative candidate; John Bagshaw of London, a free
trader and eminent merchant with interests in shipping and railways. Clearly
Liberal disunity might work to the advantage of the Tories.[34]

Colonel Thompson gained a tactical advantage by being first to declare
his candidacy. The Earl died on the evening of Thursday 17 July and
Thompson's prepared election address was published on the Saturday morning. He arrived in Sunderland the following Tuesday accompanied by George
Wilson, the chairman of the Anti-Corn Law League, and 'a host of League
agents, who in a short time were spread over the borough'. Bagshaw met
with his supporters the same morning, issued an address and began an
active canvass.

That same morning, 22 July, more than a hundred local Tories met in a
Sunderland hotel. They had no candidate in waiting and Chairman Robert
Scurfield, a director of the Durham and Sunderland Railway, reminded
everyone of the importance of new investment in the docks and railways
and of any candidate's ability to promote these interests. A smaller group
of leading Tories decided to go round the town to test the water for a
possible nomination of George Hudson. It is highly likely that there had
already been some contact between them, possibly initiated by Hudson and
probably previous to Earl Grey's death. He would not want to be seen
advancing his own candidacy; instead he would have to be invited, even
implored, to stand in Sunderland and he would need solid evidence that
he could win a previously Liberal constituency.

The canvass was 'highly satisfactory' and a deputation went to see Hudson
in London with the pledges of support they had gathered. Hudson, while

expressing interest, asked for more evidence of his support. A further canvas was undertaken and another deputation travelled to York on Friday with the results. Hudson was now convinced and issued an address ('To the Worthy and Independent Electors of the Borough of Sunderland') the following day which stated that he was largely in accord with the Peel government, would endeavour to maintain unimpaired their 'glorious constitution', and that, if elected, he would watch over their interests and promote the prosperity of the town and port of Sunderland.[35]

Rumours that Hudson might come forward as a candidate alarmed the leaders of the Anti-Corn Law League, who realised what an impact he could have. Richard Cobden, the effective leader of the League, wrote to George Wilson on 24 July that Thompson had

> no chance unless the Bagshaw party assist and even if they do, and he is opposed by Hudson he will be beaten. A more formidable opponent he could not have than this Railway King. He would go into the constituency with an intangible bribe for every class. The capitalists would hope for premiums. The smaller fry would look for situations for their sons in the vast railway undertakings over which he rules absolutely and the rope, iron, coal and timber merchants will all bid for his patronage. His undetectable powers of corruption at this moment are greater than the Prime Minister's ... All the eloquence of Moore or Bright will be like dust in the balance [and] if we are beaten [in a straight fight] it will be a terrible blow.[36]

The Liberals were now in great disarray. It was apparent that, with two candidates, they would lose to the Tories now 'as one man united' behind Hudson. The League wanted to find a way to withdraw Thompson and Bagshaw suggested a preliminary ballot amongst Liberal voters, but the Radicals would not hear of it. There were attempts to withdraw both in favour of a compromise candidate, but Thompson was determined to stand and remained convinced, almost to polling day, that he would win. Finally, Bagshaw withdrew but without urging his audience to support the Colonel. The call of the Liberal Chairman and prominent Whig, Walker Featherstonhaugh, for electors to 'assert their independence' was widely interpreted as advice to shun the League's candidate and vote for Hudson.[37]

On 28 July Hudson made a triumphal entry by special train into Sunderland. When his party reached the George Inn they presented themselves at the window of one of the upper rooms, 'amidst loud and most enthusiastic cheering'. Joseph Wright introduced Hudson and made clear the basis of the Conservative campaign: the commercial interest of Sunderland

> whose port [is] retrograding, her commerce diminished, her property depreciated, her trade taken away to other places ... unless some decided and vigorous step

be taken for its improvement, it will be impossible to preserve even its present position. To what is this to be attributed? Every child in the borough will say it is for want of capacious docks and extended railway communication. Then, if that be the case … select that person to represent you who is most likely to change this aspect of affairs.

He finished by describing Hudson as the man in the kingdom who most possessed the influence and power to effect these improvements and said that, if Hudson had one characteristic above all others, it was a 'most dextrous skill in uniting conflicting interests and differing parties', a quality well suited to the needs of the locality. He attached little importance to Hudson's politics and said it would not matter to him if Hudson were a Whig, or the 'fiercest Radical in the ranks of democracy'; what was important was that he advanced local interests.

When Hudson spoke, he described himself as 'the friend of improvement'. He pleaded 'guilty' to being a railway speculator and left it to his audience, which included hecklers from Thompson's camp, to 'decide whether the formation of a thousand miles of railway, giving employment to the in-habitants and developing the resources of the district through which it passes, is or is not beneficial to the country'. To loud cheers, he said his opponents talked about the poor, which was all very well, but he preferred to *act* for the poor. He had been a benefactor to his country, he would not shrink from giving his opinions upon the great questions of the day, and would give his votes more especially for the poor, from whom he had himself sprung. He supported the Corn Laws because he believed them to be 'beneficial to all classes', objected to the manufacturers' claim that they could not compete with continental manufacturers because of the effect of the Corn Laws on the cost of labour and opposed their repeal.

> A great portion of the land of this country would be thrown out of cultivation … The best cultivated country in the world would become a desert. Those mansions which have been the residences of our aristocracy for centuries would be destroyed and the return for all this would be the supposed advancement of some great manufacturing interest.

He finished by saying that he had 'no private purpose to serve' and promised that, if elected, he would do everything in his power to further the interests of Sunderland. In particular he would support plans for a new coal dock for the output from the Durham field.

After his address, Hudson's friends carried out an 'active canvas, which was prosecuted throughout the day with most signal success'. The *Times* reporter concluded that 'the public enthusiasm was altogether in Mr Hudson's favour, and a more brilliant reception was perhaps never given to any candidate in any part of England'.[38] Hudson's later statements were in a similar vein; he talked of Church and Queen and of upholding the 'glorious constitution', but he said little about political questions beyond attacking the 'wild, visionary cotton lords of Manchester' who wanted to ruin the country through free trade. Instead he emphasised his intention to do great things for Sunderland. Hudson's speeches were well received by sympathetic audiences and were punctuated with laughter and loud cheering but even the *Times*, which was broadly supportive, complained that he said little about politics beyond expressing general support for the government and commenting in detail on the effects of the Corn Laws.

The Anti-Corn Law League, on the other hand, had to treat the election as an unwanted trial of strength. Its best speakers, Richard Cobden, John Bright and Robert Moore, came to Sunderland, but as Cobden had foreseen this was mere 'dust in the balance'.[39] A radical paper subsequently gave a sardonic account of how the Whigs were won over

> Mr Hudson came down ... He declared his principles. They were – it was not very clear what – but conservative, of course. But what he should mainly attend to ... was the local interest of the town. He saw many ways of promoting their interests. He really thought that the Sunderland and Durham Railway, for example, might be very advantageously made a branch line of the York, Newcastle and Berwick (loud cheering). And of course the original promoters ought to be dealt with upon liberal principles (renewed and very protracted cheering) ... the old scheme of the South Dock ... must be revived [and] together [they] would become a most paying concern (here the enthusiasm of the audience knew no bounds, and many an insolvent scrip-holder was observed shedding tears of joy) ... The Whigs ... speedily discovered that Colonel Thompson had 'used poor Mr Bagshaw very ill'. So they pledged themselves without difficulty to his opponent.[40]

Concern for the town's interests was an important factor for many voters. Colonel Thompson's radically democratic views and belief that repeal of the Corn Laws would reduce the price of bread appealed more to the poorer classes, who did not have the vote, and did little to increase his popularity amongst a total electorate of about fifteen hundred, drawn from the most affluent of a population of perhaps sixty thousand. The Tory *Newcastle Journal* found 'scarcely a respectable inhabitant on Colonel Thompson's committee' and the *Times* thought his meetings were 'attended by the mere rabble'.[41]

The argument over the Corn Laws had overt class overtones. The League believed that the laws simply transferred wealth from the pockets of the poor into those of an idle and greedy landed aristocracy, and argued that the benefit of the higher price of grain resulting from protection accrued neither to the farmer nor the farm worker but solely to the landowner, in the form of higher rents and land values. The result of *falling* prices would merely be lower rents. Hudson and fellow Tories argued instead that the manufacturers who supported the League simply wanted to be able to reduce wages, or, as a by-election campaign song put it, 'To pull yer wages down to nought'. This doggerel attacked the manufacturers on other grounds as well

> There's Johnny Bright, that modest man,
> Just like a buke can talk
> He maks the bairns work every day
> Before they weel can walk.[42]

As the campaign warmed up, Colonel Thompson was denounced as a republican, a socialist and an atheist intent on the desecration of the Sabbath. Hudson was then attacked by the Thompson camp over his inheritance from Matthew Bottrill: an election poster pictured the ghost of 'old Botterill' appearing to Hudson and referring to 'the tin thou so "adventitiously" got'.[43] His supporters took no notice and sympathetic local papers shamelessly eulogised their candidate

> Mr Hudson is the author of his own fame. He has created the position he occupies. The magic of his touch has revolutionized the world. Civilization has been rendered a work of years, not of centuries ... Such men are formed to rule and direct the energies of others ... In sending Mr Hudson, for the first time to Parliament, the borough of Sunderland will not only achieve a just appreciation of his abilities, but achieve for itself an immortality of fame, while the immediate local advantages it will derive from such association must be immense.[44]

On 13 August 1845, Hudson arrived for the hustings with his wife, daughter and two sons, while the crowd made 'tumultuous demonstrations' in favour of the two candidates. After his nomination, Hudson emphasised his desire to serve the interests of Sunderland and his vigorous support for the Corn Laws, repeal of which would throw 'immense tracts of land out of cultivation', to the benefit of the wealthy 'cotton lords' but not their 'poor labourers' whose wages would not be raised and who would consequently be forced 'to combine for the purpose of raising the price of their labour'. He added

> Gentlemen, is it for these men [the 'cotton lords'] that you are prepared to see the ruddy population of your agricultural districts homeless and unemployed, your beautiful villages deserted and desolate, the mansions of your landed gentry closed, and consequently the many dependent upon them indigent. In short, are you prepared for these men for the promotion of their selfish interests to have the agricultural interest entirely swept away, to have England be 'happy England'

no more, to have this country no longer the pride of the world and the envy of surrounding nations?

The speech was greeted with 'immense applause' from his supporters. After the candidates had been nominated, the Mayor called for a show of hands by the assembled crowd, many of whom would not have had the vote. Far more were raised for Colonel Thompson. Under normal process, Hudson's proposer, Joseph Wright, demanded a poll. This took place the following day and from the beginning Hudson was clearly in the lead (voting being open). By the time the poll closed at four o'clock, Hudson had won by 627 votes to 497 and ugly scenes followed; 'the mob in front of the hustings became very turbulent and stones and brickbats were thrown in all directions'. The Mayor was injured by a flying stone and the Riot Act was read.[45]

Hudson had planned a spectacular, public recognition of his victory that would demonstrate his place in modern life. As soon as the poll had closed, James Allport, manager of the Newcastle and Darlington, left Hudson's committee room for the station, where a special train left at 4.24 p.m. Travelling at speeds of up to an 'incredible' seventy-five miles an hour, via Darlington, York, Leicester and Rugby, the train reached Euston just after 1 a.m. and Allport arrived at the offices of the *Times* at 1.25 a.m. When he left Euston again at 3.05 a.m., he had with him several hundred copies of that day's *Times*, containing a report of the poll. He reached Sunderland just before 11 a.m., while the Mayor was making the official declaration and Hudson, during his acceptance speech, was able to throw copies to the crowd; 'here is *The Times* newspaper of this morning just put into my hands ... see the march of intellect'.

This was wonderful publicity, that emphasised both Hudson's success and his importance in the new world. The *Times* was most impressed; an editorial thought

> the unexampled rapidity with which the news of the result of the Sunderland election was brought to the metropolis is worthy of the great achievements of the successful candidate [and] will give a fresh assurance to his electors that, whatever his theoretical opinions on some points may happen to be, he is at least a public benefactor.

The editor thought him, as one of the practical and businesslike men of the age, a member of a class which 'ought to be the staple of the British Legislature'. The writer's imagination was much taken by the traversing of England 'almost from north to south within eighteen hours, two of which were spent in the metropolis', which made him realise that the whole of the island was now, to all intents and purposes, as near the metropolis as

Sussex or Buckinghamshire were two centuries ago and that 'with the space and resources of an empire we enjoy the compactness of a city'.[46]

Hudson did not neglect more orthodox means of earning political good-will. The Mayor of Sunderland had described Hudson as someone who possessed great power to construct works of public utility and who would 'as he has promised ... do what he can to promote the interest of the borough'. He was also able to note that Hudson had left 'the munificent sum of three hundred pounds' to the charitable institutions of the town. The money, entrusted to Joseph Wright and Richard Spoor, his election proposer and seconder, was distributed to eighteen local charities including the Sunderland and Bishop Wearmouth Infirmary, which received one hundred pounds.

Hudson was always generous to charitable and other good causes. In Darlington for example, where railway development had greatly expanded the population of the area east of the River Skerne, a new parish was established that lacked a church. A public subscription was opened in September 1845 and Hudson joined the building committee and donated a hundred pounds towards the eventual fund of £2500. George Hudson was able to lay the foundation stone of the new church of St John the Evangelist at a ceremony in February 1847, while Mrs Hudson donated a peal of bells and a stained glass window depicting the Ascension.[47]

There were great celebrations when Hudson returned with his family to York after his election victory. They were met with the ringing of the cathedral bells, a salute of cannon, the playing of a brass band and a display of flags over the whole city, after which a procession escorted Hudson to the De Grey Rooms for a triumphant and prolonged dinner.[48]

There were mixed reactions to Hudson's success. The Conservative and Protectionist *Standard* saw it as a decisive 'defeat and disgrace' of the League, although the greatest value of the Sunderland victory, was, undoubtedly, the 'bringing into the House of Commons of such a man as Mr Hudson'. They also thought his campaign speeches 'among the most able and manly we have ever read ... they evade no topic [and] are the plain and eloquent declaration of his principles and convictions'. The *Railway Times* thought there was 'not one man in the railway world who will not rejoice at the event' and wished there were 'half a dozen others like him in the House of Commons'. The *Times* was moved to 'congratulate the House on its acquisition of Mr Hudson', particularly given the volume of railway business that it faced. The free-trade *Manchester Guardian*, mouthpiece of the cotton lords, preferred a Parliament of Hudsons to one of (Radical) Colonel Thompsons, but was nevertheless dismissive of the contribution Hudson could make to the national legislature, arguing he knew no more of 'the political economy of the country' than if he had recently 'dropped from the moon'. The *Yorkshireman*, which had always opposed Hudson, thought he would be out of his depth in Parliament: 'out of Parliament he was a great man and wielded great influence. In Parliament he will be nobody and destitute of all influence ... It is quite a different thing to address a meeting of railway speculators panting for 10 per cent and the congregated intellect, learning and gentlemanly accomplishments such as the British Parliament contains'. The similarly anti-Hudson *Sunderland Herald* suggested that he could retain his influence in the country only by being 'a *silent* member of the House', while the *English Gentleman* asserted roundly that in 'the House of Commons he will be nobody, excepting on Railway Committees ... the character of his oratory will only excite the impatience, if not something worse, of the House'.[49]

More than three hundred and fifty gentlemen attended a celebratory dinner at the Polytechnic Hall of the Sunderland Athenaeum on 21 October 1845. The walls were covered with election banners and a portrait of Hudson placed opposite the chair, which was taken by Joseph Wright. Guests included Lord Adolphus Vane, son of the great coal-owner Lord Londonderry, Lord Seaham, Sir John Lowther, and the Rev. Dr Townsend, prebendary of Durham, whose speech on behalf of the clergy and bishop of the diocese reveals the extent to which organised religion had adapted to the new technology of the age and its commercial prospects

> he for one was not afraid to say that he rejoiced in the full development of the railway system ... at a time when the funds were paying only 3 per cent, were those who lived in retirement on such property to be blamed for coming forward and embarking on projects which, while they increased their own incomes, diffused capital and employment throughout the entire country? ... He had admired his zeal, energy and common sense and he had never seen anything calculated to cast the slightest stain on his fair fame and character.

Joseph Wright lauded Hudson for his great works, which had become 'matters of European wonder' and noted that

> he wields at command and presides over an amount of pecuniary capital exceeding that of any other man in the empire ... He might be said to be a sort of national Chancellor of the Exchequer in railway matters (cheers and laughter) with this difference, however, that he not only founded a national stock, providing safe investments, but he returned it tenfold to his paymasters ... he had provided business for the citizen, employment for labour ... trade for the shopkeeper, markets for our manufacturers, channels of industry and oceans of business unequalled in the annals of the world. As a politician, Mr Hudson upheld Conservative principles and was unsurpassed for his attachment to the Throne and to the principles of our unrivalled constitution ... of Mr Hudson, in his capacity

of a private gentleman ... he believed their distinguished guest had as large and attached a circle of friends as had ever fallen to the lot of any man. It might be said that Mr Hudson had accumulated riches in profusion, but he had also dispensed them with liberality; in fact, in his opinion, Mr Hudson was exactly the sort of man that ought to be rich.

When he proposed a toast to Hudson, the entire company rose and remained standing and cheering for several minutes. In reply, Hudson said he could 'hardly find words to do justice to the feelings now crowding round' his heart, but he went on to deliver a most conciliatory speech, in which he called for a victory that

> did not sound a triumph over our conscientious local opponent; but on the contrary, let us use it to the advantage, local and general of this town and county ... there is, after all, nothing like peaceful times ... let us, then, as Conservatives, set a bright example ... let us show that we are no political demagogues, but having obtained our victory, let us use it moderately for the benefit alike of friends and opponents.[50]

The parliamentary session of 1845 had ended a few days before the Sunderland by-election, so Hudson was unable to take his seat until the start of the next session, early the following year. In the meantime, alongside a mass of railway business, he acted quickly to cement his position in Sunderland, and to make preparations for his new political and social role.

Within days of the election, John Murray, Engineer of the River Wear Commission, who had already drawn up several plans for new docks, resigned to work on a new plan, with Robert Stephenson as a consultant at Hudson's behest. By the time Hudson visited Sunderland in October to attend his celebratory dinner, he was able to approve an ambitious scheme for a forty-seven acre dock basin capable of accommodating 350 vessels 'in every state of the wind and weather', an advantage not possessed by any of its neighbouring ports. The prospectus of the Sunderland Dock Company, which Hudson promoted to construct the dock, forecast dividends of 10 percent on a capital of £225,000.[51]

At the same time Hudson acquired the Durham and Sunderland Railway, paying a modest premium over market value for its shares, and also paid a reasonably generous price to buy up 'that crumbling concern, the North Dock, to save the pockets' of Sir Hedworth Williamson, who had control of a large number of Sunderland votes. In both cases the new owner was actually the Newcastle and Darlington Railway, which Hudson also committed to subscribing for £75,000 of the share capital of the Sunderland Dock Company.[52]

In this same post-election period, Hudson became a large landed proprietor.

In 1844 he had purchased Octon Grange, near Bridlington, and the splendid estate of Baldersby, near Ripon in the North Riding; the latter at a cost of £100,000. Then in September 1845, he made his most spectacular purchase; the 12,000 acres of Londesborough Park, near Market Weighton in the East Riding, from the Duke of Devonshire for £475,000. The estate had only a hunting lodge, as Londesborough Hall had been demolished in 1818 and Hudson's intention was to build a new mansion in the four hundred acre home park. He became 'fond of taking visitors there to sketch out the magnificence not yet called into being'.53 When the York to Market Weighton branch of the York and North Midland was constructed in 1846–47 it ran across the estate and a station was sited in convenient proximity. The station, designed by G. T. Andrews, was styled as a neat Italian villa and was far superior to others on the line. This, and a carriage track and avenue leading towards the intended site of the new house, reinforced the critics' view that this had been built purely for Hudson's future personal convenience.54

Building at Londesborough was for the future and, a few weeks after acquiring Londesborough, Hudson purchased Newby Park. A park of some two hundred acres at Rainton, close to Thirsk on the River Swale, contained a beautiful mansion built in 1721 by Colen Campbell. It was a very grand building, one of the earliest examples of the Palladian revival in England and was constructed from local stone with a magnificent double staircase and many other fine features. It was also adjacent to Baldersby, which had no mansion, and so formed 'a most desirable *appanage*'. The house in Monkgate was sold and Newby Park then became the Hudsons' Yorkshire home.55

Hudson also needed a London house, not merely as accommodation when Parliament was sitting (usually from late January to early August) but also as a base for inclusion in London society, whose 'Season' ran from about Easter to mid July.

The famous builder Thomas Cubitt had constructed two five-storey Italianate mansions on either side of Albert Gate, at the entrance to Hyde Park. These *palazzi* were the largest speculative houses ever built and for a long time remained unsold; they were nicknamed 'the two Gibraltars' on the basis that they would never be taken. They were, however, ideally suited to George Hudson's social ambitions and in the autumn of 1845 he purchased the eastern 'Gibraltar' for £15,000. A similar sum was also spent on furnishings and decoration, under the direction of Mrs Hudson. This then became the largest private house in London and was so large that *Punch* declared it 'uninhabitable', except by the 'Railway King' who could overcome the difficulties of internal communication by installing a railway network in the house; servants would be taken to their places of work by a third-class train from the attic station and so forth.[56]

A nearby stable and coach-house were also rented, and the family moved into No. 1, Albert Gate, Knightsbridge on 21 January 1846, the day before Hudson took his seat at the beginning of the parliamentary session. Now he had to attend the House, run four railway companies and carry out his municipal duties in York, which increased late in 1846 when he was elected for a third term as Lord Mayor. The residence at Albert Gate enabled the Hudsons to play an active role in the Season and it was said that, after he moved to London, Hudson would be at a large dinner whether as visitor or host every two or three days. Active socialising continued out of season at Newby Park.[57]

The *Railway Times* in May 1846 gave Hudson's itinerary for a day

> On Friday week this gentleman left the House of Commons at two o'clock in the morning, and proceeded to his home to sleep. He rose between seven and eight, took a walk in the Park, returned to breakfast, then attended four consult-ations, passed three Bills before Mr Greene's committee, gave evidence before the commission on the metropolitan termini, attended Mr Morrison's committee, was in his place in the House at four, dined with the Duke of Buckingham in the evening and afterwards attended the Sheriff's ball in the city, which he did not leave until two o'clock in the morning.[58]

Thomas Carlyle recorded a more jaundiced view of the Railway King's lifestyle, as described to him by a friend

> overwhelmed with business, yet superadding to it ostentatious and high-flown amusements, balls at great country houses fifty miles off, etc., etc. With early morning he was gone from Newby Park ... returned weary on the edge of dinner, then first met his guests, drank largely, with other wines, ate nothing at all, hardly an ounce of solid food, then tumbled into bed, worn out with business and madness ... Oh, Mammon! Art thou not a hard god!

His only exercise, it appears, were morning walks in Hyde Park and to Billingsgate fish market to choose his fish for the day.[59] Hudson's frame was 'naturally broad and massive, with a tendency to develop every way but upwards' and he became noticeably more corpulent over the years. He also aged rapidly; the well-known actress, Helena Faucit, when travelling from Derby to Edinburgh for an engagement in January 1848, met Hudson who was in her carriage for part of the journey. He got her a change of tickets at York and took great care of her and she was 'quite sorry to part with the old gentleman'. Helena Faucit was thirty and George Hudson forty-seven.[60] He was blessed, however, with a robust constitution and his health remained good, despite his excesses, although he did suffer at various

times in his life from gout and angina pectoris. His first real illness seems
to have been severe digestive problems that seized him while on a visit to
Whitehaven Castle as the guest of the Earl of Lonsdale in October 1848,
but he recovered fully after being laid low for several days.[61]

Hudson was now at the zenith of his fame and influence. His doings and
movements were chronicled like 'veritable royal progresses' and it was said
that you 'could not take up any newspaper, whether Tory, Whig, or Radical,
whether local or metropolitan, nay whether English or continental, without
finding some article in his praise'. The *Railway Express* headed its collections
of such items 'Hudsoniana', although in their case the commentaries were
not always favourable.[62] Whether or not he actually enjoyed this sort of
publicity, it was nevertheless essential; he could not have been so successful
in his business activities, given their reliance on money attracted from
people in all parts of the country, unless he lived by the press.

Hudson's fame undoubtedly brought a good deal of money to his personal
business transactions, particularly during the railway expansion of the period
immediately before and during the 'Railway Mania'. By this time, his name
was so synonymous with success that the mere use of it in conjunction with
a new railway project would provide the credibility that promoters needed.
This in turn often led on to early increases in the company's share price, a
rich source of profit to speculators engaging in what was already known as
'stagging'. In 1844, for example, Hudson was a director of the Manchester
and Birmingham line, which was known to be thinking of leasing the Sheffield
and Manchester jointly with the Midland. Hudson's name and his position
at the Midland provided credibility, the terms that were to be offered were
apparently generous, and the share price of the Sheffield and Manchester
in late 1844 rose quickly from £30 to £100. Those who knew what was going
on could have made substantial capital gains from their inside knowledge,
although the gains were short-lived as the proposals were then turned down
by the Sheffield and Manchester shareholders.[63]

Hudson's involvement in September 1845 with the newly-formed Liverpool, Manchester and Newcastle Junction Railway also proved lucrative,
even if the publicity it brought him was rather damaging. This recently
formed company was intended to provide a line that would connect the
Great North of England Railway with the Leeds and Bradford. Hudson was
not involved at the outset but joined the provisional list of directors and,
it was reported in the *Cumberland Pacquet*, the business 'was for a time
most favourably viewed in the market and shares reached the high premium
of £6 10s. each', even though only a small deposit and first instalment had
been paid on the £25 shares. The company later set up a Committee of
Inquiry in February 1847, with George Leeman as one of the members, to

look into what had been going on. They discovered that Hudson had only agreed to become a director if he were provided with *gratis* shares. A wealthy investor connected with the formation, Christian Allhusen, duly paid the deposit on one thousand of the £25 shares on his behalf. The share price rose quickly, partly because Hudson was known to be connected with the company, and a considerable amount of business was then done, buyers being unaware that three-quarters of the shares had been placed with directors and officials and that only a relatively small number had been released to the public. Hudson then sold out and was quickly able to realise very large profits without ever risking any of his own money. The *Yorkshireman* reported the whole manoeuvre under the heading, 'A Royal Railway Stag!' [64]

Hudson was also the first major railway entrepreneur really to appreciate what the newspapers could do to promote the expansion schemes of the companies he represented. During his working life he had an active interest in three newspapers, the *Yorkshire Gazette*, the *Railway Chronicle* and the *Sunderland Times*, each of which related closely to his areas of activity. He was also widely believed, it seems wrongly, to have helped to establish a fourth, the *Daily News*.[65] Reporting in the Yorkshire press at this time was highly partisan. The main ownership interest in the *Yorkshire Gazette* was held by Henry Bellerby who, along with the editor, J. L. Foster, was a close friend of Hudson. The *Yorkshireman*, on the other hand, was edited by a prominent Liberal, John Duncan, a staunch opponent of Hudson, and was consistently hostile towards him. The *Yorkshire Gazette* was even more useful as a means of propagating perspectives favourable to Hudson than it appears at first sight, as the *Times* regularly took extracts from the *Gazette* as a regional news source. Hudson's financial interest in the *Railway Chronicle* may have helped to fuel the relative hostility of the *Railway Times*, although even the generally well-disposed *Herapath's Journal* voiced its concerns about a major railway entrepreneur using the railway trade press to publicise and advance his own interests.[66]

In the autumn of 1845, it was rumoured that Hudson had agreed to join with Joseph Paxton in supporting a new radical newspaper, the *Daily News*, to be edited by Charles Dickens; Hudson had supposedly agreed to provide both financial support and reliable information about the railways. It was never the most plausible of rumours as Dickens strongly disliked Hudson, who stated in September 1846 that he had never had anything to do with the paper 'for he so differed with its principles that he should be the last man in the world to be a supporter of it'.[67]

The editorial slant of the press, other than railway papers, was of course

1. George Hudson addressing a shareholders' meeting.

2. Railway Mania. Promoters hurrying to get their schemes to the Board of Trade.

FANCY PORTRAIT.

THE RAILWAY KING.

3. Cartoon of 'The Railway King'.

4. Central Station, Newcastle upon Tyne, begun in 1847.

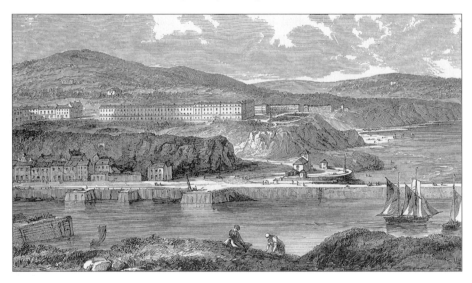

5. West Cliff, Whitby, seen across the harbour, 1852. (*Illustrated London News*)

6. The Railway King's Levee, 1845. (*Punch*)

7. George Hudson welcoming Queen Victoria, 5 July 1847. (*Punch*)

8. A Victorian shareholders' meeting, caricature by Richard Doyle, 1849. (*Punch*)

9. The Railway Clown and the Indignant Shareholders, 1849. (*Punch*)

10. 'The Modern Dick Turpin: or Highwayman and Railwayman', by John Tenniel, 1868. (*Punch*)

OFF THE RAIL.

11. Off the Rail. Hudson's fall, 1849. (*Punch*)

usually a party political one; Tory-Protectionist papers such as the *Standard*, which supported Hudson's political stance, naturally tended to support and praise Hudson's business dealings as well. Liberal or Radical papers on the other hand, including the *Manchester Guardian* and the *Yorkshireman*, tended, equally naturally, to be more critical. Some papers also fell out with Hudson because he responded to their criticisms by ensuring that the railway companies he was connected with did not place adverts with them.

In March 1847 the *Gateshead Observer* told its readers that if the railway announcements of George Hudson, previously advertised in their paper, were missing from its pages, 'let there be no surprise' as all advertisements relating to his railway companies had been withdrawn, after it had favoured a Manchester and Leeds scheme to construct a railway in the Team valley over a rival plan from the York and Newcastle. 'Mr Hudson', it declared, 'imagines that the monies of the companies which he governs, when ex-pended at a newspaper office, should ... yield him ... editorial support and servility', as well as publicity. The *Sunderland Herald* reported that a similarly 'dastardly display of personal spleen' had been shown towards themselves and other papers, including the *Newcastle Advertizer* and the *Yorkshireman*. The latter – Hudson's sternest critic in the press – attacked him with typical mid-century journalistic invective, claiming that

> because we ... will not fall down and worship the Dagon of Railways, swear, for his selfish purposes, that black is white, and white is black, blow the hollow trumpet of his fame, and do violence to all principle and all integrity, we come within the boundaries of his advertising power, and the thunders of the railway Vatican. Since you will not puff me and flatter me, but own other gods than me, he shrieks in impotent wrath, why, Sir, *withdraw my advertisements!*

They drew a further conclusion about Hudson's relationship with the press:

> What reliance can newspaper readers place upon the laudatory essays, past and to come, on Mr Hudson's infinite worth and unbounded wisdom? ... they are the outpourings of swelling hearts, grateful for any crumb which may fall from the table of the Royal Dogberry of Railways. Let all men, therefore, accept, with becoming caution, all paragraph-Hudsonian-panegyrics appearing in such organs as are specially patronized by His Majesty. *These are paid for*, directly or indirectly – by money or by advertisements. *This* is confessed.

These were the (rather overblown) sentiments of only a small minority of the press, but their comments must have damaged his reputation.[68]

He was further harmed by the publicity given to the almost feudal approach he had towards his railway companies: he seemed to regard them as his own fiefdoms and their employees as personal retainers. Not only did Hudson travel to Sunderland for the by-election in a special train but salaried officers of the lines over which he had control were on board, impressed as canvassers in their master's cause. Train schedules were altered to suit his personal convenience: in January 1847, an outraged correspondent to the *Times* related how the night mail train had been held at Gateshead station to wait for Hudson, who was attending a dinner in Newcastle. A large number of passengers, including several MPs, were materially inconvenienced 'for the sole accommodation of Mr Hudson … his Iron Majesty [might] at least refrain from thus openly showing his arrogance and his contempt for his unfortunate subjects'. Similarly, a correspondent to the *Yorkshireman* told how his train to York had been delayed for nearly half an hour because 'the Lady Mayoress (Mrs Hudson) had sent by telegraph for a pineapple and … we were waiting for its arrival, that her ladyship might not be disappointed'. The 'Railway Queen' (as she was sometimes styled) also thought nothing of ordering a special train if she missed the scheduled service.[69]

Poor publicity also resulted from an accident on the York Newcastle and Berwick in February 1848. One of the axles fractured on an express train, tearing up the rails for some ninety yards. Hudson, who was travelling on the train with the Duke of Northumberland, was 'most energetic … in giving directions'. When the accident report by the Commissioners of Railways was published, however, it criticised the fact that the train had started late from York because it was waiting for 'Mr Hudson, the chairman of the company and a party of gentlemen', a frequent occurrence that put pressure on the driver to regain the time lost. Fortunately, on that occasion although the carriages were thrown on their sides, no passengers were hurt.[70]

The Hudson Testimonial was another trigger for criticism. At meetings of his companies in the summer of 1845 Hudson proposed a testimonial to George Stephenson, to pay for a presentation of plate and a statue on the proposed Tyne bridge. The idea was eagerly taken up, but 'testimonial bred testimonial' and Hudson's supporters immediately suggested one for him; it was widely believed that he had in fact inspired it, and that the testimonial for 'old George' (which was completely overshadowed) was merely an icebreaker for his own. A committee was set up, with John Close acting as secretary, and donations invited from the public; by Christmas 1845 over £16,000 had been raised. Such public generosity towards so rich a man was frequently contrasted with the fate of other, less wealthy benefactors of mankind, and excited much comment of the 'worship of Mammon' variety.

There was much speculation over what Hudson would do with the money. It was widely assumed that he would devote it to some charitable purpose; a widely touted suggestion was almshouses, perhaps for former railway workers and their widows (or, suggested some wags, for those ruined by failed speculation in railway shares). 'Of course, he can never think of putting it in his pocket' wrote one paper. But although the sum raised was tiny in comparison with his existing wealth, that is exactly what he did.[71]

Resentment over the matter of the testimonials may also go some way to explain George Stephenson's expressed hostility towards Hudson at this time. In a letter to a friend he confided that Hudson had 'become too great a man for me now. I am not at all satisfied at the way the Newcastle and Berwick has been carried on and I do not intend to take any more active part in it. I have made Hudson a rich man, but he will very soon care for nobody except he can get money by them. I make these observations in confidence to you'.[72] But panegyrics were far more common. In December 1846 the *Standard* commented

> Mr Hudson gave a dinner on Thursday to some happy hundreds in the Guildhall of York, but was that all? No; Mr Hudson was yesterday giving and has for months and years of yesterdays been giving, dinners to HUNDREDS OF THOUSANDS ... who, but for him must have gone without dinners ... Two hundred thousand well paid labourers, representing as heads of families, nearly one million men, women and children, all feast through the bold enterprise of one man. Let us hear what man or class of man ever before did so much for the population of a country?[73]

At about this time, Francis Grant executed a portrait of Hudson, for a fee of three hundred guineas, which was exhibited at the Royal Academy in 1847 and in York. An engraving of this was later made, and published in June 1848, for admirers of Hudson to purchase. But the most extraordinary symptom of the Hudson cult was probably the production by Mitchells of Stonegate, York, of miniature statues of the great man, 'full-length ... executed from a model ... pronounced by competent judges as a most faithful likeness', seventeen inches tall and available at three shillings and sixpence each.[74]

From Albert Gate, Hudson promoted his social career. In January 1846 he was elected to membership of the Carlton Club, one of his sponsors being Sir John Lowther. In February he dined with the Lord Mayor of London and in March scored a considerable social success by being introduced to Prince Albert. This meeting was at a grand reception, or *conversazione*, given by the Marquess of Northampton, in his capacity as President of the Royal Society, at his mansion in Piccadilly. Distinguished guests included the Prince Consort and the Duke of Cambridge (the Queen's uncle). More than eighty people were listed by the *Times* in order of social rank before they arrived at a 'Mr G. Hudson MP'. Nonetheless, a report in the (pro-Hudson) *Sunderland Times* stated that

> many who had not previously had an opportunity of scanning his burly form and fine manly countenance appeared almost as much interested in the honourable member as in the more legitimate objects for which they were assembled. The Prince was indebted to Viscount Morpeth for the opportunity of making Mr Hudson's acquaintance. His Royal Highness shook hands very heartily with the honourable member, and remained in conversation with him for some time.[75]

Almost simultaneously, at a 'drawing room' in St James' Palace a 'number of ladies were presented to her Majesty, including Mrs George Hudson, by the Countess De Grey'. This was in fact an extremely grand affair at which over eighty ladies were honoured. The listings (again in order of rank) showed Mrs Hudson about half way down, after five countesses and numerous ladies and honourables but no doubt she was far more an object of attention than this implies.[76]

In turn, the Hudsons entertained lavishly at Albert Gate, their guests including Benjamin Disraeli, William Gladstone, Lord and Lady George Bentinck, the Duke of Buckingham, the Earl of Lonsdale and many others. Perhaps the most glittering occasion was the 'Grand Concert' hosted by Mrs Hudson in May 1847, which proved to be 'one of the most numerously attended and fashionable *réunions* of the season'. This was partly due to the entertainment, for which 'all the leading Italian vocalists were engaged' but also because this provided the 'opportunity ... of inspecting the saloons of the hon. member's superb mansion ... equal to any ... in London and which were thrown open on Monday evening for the first time to receive company'. Guests included the Dukes of Wellington and Cleveland, six earls, three marquesses, and innumerable countesses, viscounts, lords and ladies.

Elizabeth Bancroft, the wife of the American Ambassador, wrote of this event with pardonable exaggeration, 'there was the Duke of Wellington and all the world'. In a letter, she explained the 'curious way' it was arranged. A *nouveau riche* who is 'desirous to get into society [will get] several ladies of fashion to patronise their entertainment and invite all the guests. Our invitation was from Lady Parke [who] stood at the entrance of the splendid suite of rooms to receive the guests and introduce them to their host and hostess'.[77]

The Hudsons were, however, still outsiders. Lady Dorothy Nevill later remembered that

> there were rumours of Hudson, the 'Railway King', and his wife, but they were never in Society, which, however, was amused by the reports of their doings

which reached it. [The 1840s and 1850s] were aristocratic days ... London Society [was] like a large family [and newcomers could not enter] until credentials had been carefully examined and discussed. Mere wealth was no passport.[78]

The fact that the Hudsons were *arrivistes* has to be taken into account when scrutinising the opinions of their contemporaries. When the artist Haydon, unable to pay his debts, committed suicide in June 1846, Sir William Gregory wrote in his journal:

What a miserable gang of tradesmen we are! We give testimonials amounting to thousands of pounds to a successful and bloated speculator ... Hudson ... the haberdasher of York, a vulgar brute; but he who adorns his country by the creation of his genius is left to die by his own hand, crushed to the earth by shame and penury.[79]

Gregory mentions no particular incident and does not appear to have ever met Hudson, but he was a tradesman, a haberdasher; that was enough.

Many memoirs of the period describe him as arrogant and rude; 'a tremendous bump of self-esteem', says one; 'a pronounced air of "bounce"', says another. 'He is singularly abrupt – we may say, indeed, insolent' declares a contemporary (hostile) account although the portrait in *Fraser's* is more balanced; saying 'so proud is he ... of having been the architect of his own fortune, that he occasionally allows his independence to degenerate into something approaching rudeness and arrogance'.[80]

His reputation for brusqueness was no doubt also accentuated by the sheer pressure of business that Hudson was dealing with. As the *Fraser's* portrait put it, going to see Hudson at his offices 'for no adequate cause were worse than to enter a lion's den at feeding time, without food'. If you were shown in

you found him immersed in a multitudinous sea of papers – estimates, evidence, correspondence – surrounded by clerks, giving audience to deputations, or members of parliament, or engineers. He affected ... a lofty economy of time. Your business must be ready cut and dried. He listened, not always patiently or politely, but with sundry fidgetings and gruntings, to your story, gave you your answer in a few monosyllables, turned his back, took up the affair that came next, and – you were shewn out.[81]

Another account noted his 'vulgar affectation of ease and equality in aristocratic society'; he treated his aristocratic friends as equals, or even something less. When sitting down to coffee after dinner at the Duke of Richmond's, he noticed that the Dukes of Buckingham and Newcastle were at the same table and remarked "Three live dukes! Well, I never before sat down with three live dukes." On another occasion he told Lord Campbell 'the old nobility, Sir, are all paupers ... I am going tomorrow to Clumber [the Nottinghamshire seat of the Duke of Newcastle] where a large party of nobles is invited to meet me, but I could buy them all'.[82]

Hudson also offended – or amused – people with the (to some) rather tasteless ostentation with which he displayed his newfound wealth. During his third term as Lord Mayor of York it was noted that the 'dinners of his Lordship rival, if they do not eclipse, the civic entertainments of London'; indeed the 'Lord Mayor of London must look to his laurels'. On 17 December 1846, as Lord Mayor, he hosted a civic banquet at the Guildhall and welcomed four hundred guests, including the Archbishop of York, the Duke of Leeds, the High Sheriff of Yorkshire, J. H. Lowther, Lord George Bentinck, George Stephenson and several admirals, archdeacons, Members of Parliament and mayors. Each was received by the Lord Mayor in his brilliantly lit stateroom. An hour later, a flourish of trumpets announced that dinner was served and the Lord Mayor, in his official robes and preceded by the sword and mace, led his guests from the reception-room to the Guildhall. On entering, the city band played his favourite air, 'The Roast Beef of Old England' and Hudson went to the central chair and his close friends occupied the other chairs nearby.

The banquet was indisputably of the 'most sumptuous description, the dishes were excellent and of luxurious variety and everything was served up in the best style'. The Archdeacon of York described Hudson as a most regular attendant at church and as a 'munificent supporter' of church charities. The Duke of Leeds said how much he esteemed the friendship of the Lord Mayor and enjoyed his hospitality. He also thought that 'not only this but also succeeding generations would feel the liveliest gratitude for his exertions ... in the facility of communication and the consequent increase of prosperity'. Lord George Bentinck, who said they had 'come from all parts of the country to enjoy this splendid banquet ... that we may show to the country at large that we look upon Mr Hudson as no common man', suggested that the railway, next to printing, was the most powerful instrument known for civilising the world and that Hudson, 'can claim more than any other man in the world, that he has carried that invention into practice'. Although the occasion was florid in the extreme, Hudson had the good judgement to speak only briefly in reply and say merely that 'it had ever been his first object to look to the public good and if thereby he had promoted his own private benefit he was proud to feel that at the same time he had secured their good opinion'.

The *Times* was fascinated in an amused sort of way with the proceedings and thought the great dinner at York a 'very grand affair ... a banquet on the Brobdingnagian scale'. In an editorial, it suggested that, 'since the *chorus gigantum* was turned to stone on Salisbury Plain, there has not been so august, so titanic an assembly', although it was not entirely clear what 'unity of design, what gravity of purpose, what glory of achievement there was in Mr Hudson and a dozen other Yorkshire mayors and railway gentlemen meeting the Duke of Leeds, Lord George Bentinck and other Protectionist gentlemen [who] in a succession of well-weighed and carefully worded eulogies ... declared [Hudson] to be the saviour and regenerator of his country!'

They also noted that 'His Lordship, to do him justice, showed himself every inch a King and took it meekly enough'. Finally they took some sardonic pleasure in the fact that the new telegraphic system should be used by the Mayor of Newcastle, who could not be present, and by Hudson to inform the Mayor that his toast had been reciprocated and concluded that 'no other monarch ever conveyed his behests and received recognition and obedience with such marvellous celerity', although they did hope rather waspishly that 'the next time electric shocks traverse the railway world, they will announce an event of more general importance'.[83]

All accounts of Hudson, however snobbish or hostile, had to own the ability by which he had climbed to his pre-eminent position. No such allowance was necessary for Mrs Hudson and she appears in many memoirs as not only vulgarly ostentatious and gauche, but also rather stupid. She was not physically attractive; several years her husband's senior, she was fifty when they moved into Albert Gate and apparently looked older. 'A homely old lady', according to one memoir, and 'a homely lady on a large scale' according to another.

Despite her homeliness, she, like her husband, was rather prone to (allegedly tasteless) display. When out for a drive, she could be seen, according to one newspaper report, 'dazzling Hyde Park in a chariot, whose gaudy hues could be *heard* from Knightsbridge to Notting Hill'. She was noted for her 'gorgeous apparel', and Lady Charlotte Guest, who sat opposite her at a dinner in 1834, wrote in her journal of her 'horror' at the sight of the 'fat woman ... opposite ... in a *yellow* gown and an *amber* cap with *red* flowers'. In 1838 Elizabeth Hudson sat for the painter William Etty. The result was greeted with 'derision' from the press, when exhibited; in particular, her millinery was 'much excepted to'. One newspaper described the subject as a 'devil incarnate, *with such a cap!*'[84]

The memoirs which mention Mrs Hudson contain many stories of her *faux pas*, mostly dubious in provenance, although often amusing. In one she orders a cake from a French confectioner, who asks, "de quel grandeur le voulez-vous?" Mrs Hudson, wanting one the same size as her last order, answers "aussi grand que mon derrière". When in Paris, she instructs her maid to call on Messrs Droit et Gauche who 'must be the most fashionable cordonniers in Paris, for she saw their names in every pair of French shoes'. Such stories are legion, but are patently untrue. According to Lord William Pitt Lennox, who sat opposite her at a dinner, anxious to see whether the stories he had heard about her were true, she had a good command of French, albeit spoken 'with a pure Yorkshire accent'.[85]

Other stories about Mrs Hudson seem to be similarly apocryphal and are the kind of thing that would be told about the *nouveau riche* ignoramus Mrs Hudson was presumed to be. In one that exists in several variations she asks about a bust in a house where she is a guest, and being told it is Marcus Aurelius, says, 'Would that be the present Markis?' Her interlocutor is variously said to be Lord Westminster, Lord Lansdowne or Prince Albert. Other stories are simply silly; she sends to the fishmonger 'for gutta-percha soles'; 'on being asked if she would take port or sherry, "a little of both" was her reply'. Lady Dorothy Neville dubbed her 'the Mrs Malaprop of her day', but admitted that she never met her. On the other hand, Lady Dorothy also said she was 'somewhat shrewd in her own peculiar way, and had a trenchant manner of hitting off people's characteristics. Speaking of an individual of unreliable disposition, she said 'He is like a pat of butter on a hot plate – you never know when you have got him'![86]

Outside London, the Hudsons entertained on a considerable scale at Newby Park and were invited to many other country houses, including those of Lord Londonderry, the Duke of Devonshire and the Duke of Newcastle. One gathering at the house of the last-named was described as a 'large and distinguished party of Conservative Peers and Commons', including Lord George Bentinck and Lord Edward Stanley, although there was not always a political dimension; in July 1847 Hudson stayed with Lord Morpeth, a leading Liberal, who had introduced the Health of Towns Bill in the recent session of Parliament. Like most people, Hudson got on better with some acquaintances than others; he was 'taken up by the Duke of Devonshire' and was very popular with Lord Londonderry. Castlereagh, on the other hand, found he had had nothing in common with Hudson and in early 1847 marvelled at Londonderry's hospitality and civility towards him.[87]

A local newspaper recorded the activities of the Hudsons over the previous week in October 1847. They had entertained for several days 'a distinguished party' that included the Dowager Countess of Essex, Lady Wallace, and Baron and Lady Parke, then gone to Scrutton Hall to be the guests of Mr and Mrs Gore, and attended the Northallerton Races, where Hudson officiated as a steward. From Northallerton they went to Duncombe Park as the guests of Lord and Lady Feversham and then travelled back to Newby Park to welcome back their son George, 'on his return from the continent'. The paper added that the Hudsons intended to stay at Newby Park 'until the Lady Mayoress leaves for Paris', while 'the Lord Mayor visits Sunderland next week to preside at the Soirée and Ball of the Literary and Philosophical society'.[88]

The Royal Agricultural Society's annual meeting and show was held in July 1848 in York and Prince Albert was to officially open it. Hudson invited a number of guests to stay with him at Newby Park during the show and its attendant social events. Elizabeth Bancroft was one and she gave a detailed itinerary in a family letter. Her party travelled to York on Saturday 8 July, where they were met by Hudson and conducted to a special train that would take them to Newby Park. Other guests there included the Duke of Richmond, the Earl of Lonsdale, Lord George Bentinck, Lord Ingestrie, Lord John Beresford and Lady Webster.

On Tuesday 11 July, the Bancrofts and Lady Webster travelled to Castle Howard, to see Lady Carlisle, on a special train by courtesy of Hudson and the following day they went to York to watch the arrival of the Prince Consort. Hudson, as Chairman of the Midland and York and North Midland Railways, had travelled to Rugby and then accompanied the Prince to York. On Thursday the Prince was guest of honour at a formal (and all-male) dinner, Hudson and Mr Bancroft being present together with the above-mentioned guests (apart from Lord George Bentinck and Lady Webster), which was followed by a ball given by the Lord Mayor. Most other guests (including the Duke of Richmond) left Newby Park the following morning and Hudson travelled with Prince Albert to London, but he returned that evening. On Saturday the Bancrofts went with him to see the Londesborough estate before returning to London on the Monday.[89]

The Hudsons had, it seems, been generally accepted by the local gentry, and in turn had adopted an appropriate lifestyle. After his election as MP for Sunderland, Hudson was made Deputy Lord-Lieutenant of County Durham. His sons went to Harrow and Christ Church, Oxford and an important motive behind his acquisition of landed estates in 1844 and 1845 was his desire to see them properly qualified for membership of that society.

In the autumn of 1848 there were rumours of an impending engagement between Hudson's daughter Ann, then barely eighteen and George Dundas, MP for Linlithgow and Deputy Lord-Lieutenant of that county and a scion of an old Scottish aristocratic family; 'rumour speaks strongly of the beauty, amiability and highly cultivated mind of Miss Hudson', but no engagement seems to have been announced.

Hudson had acquired, with his estates, the patronage of two church 'livings' (the appointment of the vicar or rector was in his gift). He had a large private pew, 'upholstered in rich crimson', in the church of the local village of Topcliffe, where the family worshipped when at Newby, complete with a reading desk at which Hudson could attend to paperwork during the sermon. There, the story goes, 'he used to stand up with his portly back turned on the vicar and, if the sun shone on the occupants of the pew, Mrs Hudson would put up her fine parasol'.[90]

George Hudson made his maiden speech on 26 January 1846. Appropriately it was a defence of the railway industry. The 'Railway Mania' had reached its peak in the summer of 1845 and in the autumn there had been a reaction, and something of a crisis of confidence. The Bank of England had raised interest rates and share prices had fallen. Nevertheless, Parliament had been presented with a record number of Railway Bills and the 1846 session was to enact more Railway Acts than any other before or since.

The Prime Minister, Sir Robert Peel, had proposed a Select Committee to consider how the unprecedented volume of Railway Bills could be dealt with. He pointed out that 815 plans had been deposited with the Board of Trade for consideration that session, involving the construction of over 20,000 miles of line at a cost of £350,000,000. Many Bills would not be passed, but even so it was impossible that there could be 'any such application of capital in this country without the most material derangement of the money-markets'. In spite of his generally *laissez-faire* principles, he thought some curb on the speculation might be necessary.

Hudson responded to this, arguing that since the capital raised was spent in the country and went to landowners, ironmasters and other employers it could not be economically damaging. It would be a different matter, he suggested, if large quantities of capital flowed out of the country, to buy South American bonds or imported corn; indeed, it was the prospect of 'large importations of foreign grain' that was causing 'some alarm at the derangement of the currency'.[91]

Hudson's first speech seems to have been a perfectly competent effort, although hardly a noteworthy oration. The following day, a leader in the *Times* enthusiastically reported and endorsed Peel's comments, which were in accord with the warnings that paper had been issuing of the dangers of excessive railway speculation. Hudson's reply was mentioned only in passing and his arguments were obviously not considered worthy of comment.

In newspapers sympathetic to the Tory-protectionist cause, on the other hand, quite extraordinary praise was showered on him. An editorial in the *Standard* said he had 'exposed the fallacy of the railway alarmists, that the money required [for calls on railway shares] would not be forthcoming when wanted ... These opinions, from a gentleman having so great a practical knowledge of the subject, cannot fail to allay the absurd apprehensions ... which have led to so serious a deterioration of railway property'. The *Yorkshire Gazette* went completely overboard at this first effort by its hero

> in no instance have we witnessed a more successful debut that that of the member for Sunderland ... All eyes were fixed upon him the moment he stood up, and the house was instantly hushed into silence. With wonderful self-possession – yet without the slightest appearance of forwardness ... he rushed at once into the very thick of his subject, and refuted, in a most clear and conclusive manner, the erroneous views that had been advanced by the Premier. Every sentence was to the point. And told with marked affect on the House ... his maiden speech occupied ... about ten minutes ... We confidently predict that he is destined to acquire an enviable status in the senate, as well as in the railway world.[92]

As the acknowledged leader of the railway industry Hudson may have felt that it was incumbent on him to defend it, and it was certainly bold – or arrogant – to contradict the Prime Minister, his party leader, in his maiden speech. A general support for the Peel government was one of the few political principles he had voiced during his election campaign the previous August, and in the autumn he had been the Prime Minister's guest at Drayton.

Peel, whose policies had been generally in favour of free trade, had become intellectually convinced of the case for repeal of the Corn Laws and that same autumn he had been impelled by the beginning of the potato famine in Ireland and a declaration in favour of repeal by the Liberal leader, Lord John Russell, to propose repeal of the Corn Laws to the Cabinet, and then to Parliament when it met in January. This change of position had caused some of the strongest feelings of shock and betrayal in British political history and led to bitter divisions within the Tory party.[93]

Hudson had always been ideologically committed to protectionism and unhesitatingly turned against Peel, even though he fell out with J. H. Lowther as a result. All of Peel's Cabinet had supported him over the Corn Laws, with the exception of Lord Edward Stanley, the Colonial Secretary, who became the leader of the Protectionists. He was in the Lords; in the Commons a leadership emerged around Benjamin Disraeli and Lord George Bentinck. The former provided the brains and the oratorical talent, the latter, who was the younger son of the fourth Duke of Portland, the necessary social cachet. Bentinck had been MP for King's Lynn since 1828, but had taken little part in the Commons, and was better known as a successful racehorse owner.[94] 'The Jockey and the Jew' as they were sometimes called, welcomed Hudson to the front opposition bench as a 'successful man of business [who] supported the agricultural interest'. He soon became a friend and adviser of Bentinck and, given the dearth of ministerial experience amongst the Protectionists his political prospects looked good, when they should be returned to power.[95]

The debate on the Corn Laws dominated the 1846 session of Parliament, and Hudson made his first major speech on the question on 17 February. It was far more sophisticated than his speeches on the subject in Sunderland six months earlier. He argued that farm labourers in Britain earning twelve or fourteen shillings per week could not compete with those in Russia and Poland on less than half that amount. Farmers had to pay taxes not borne by overseas competitors and land in general was charged with impositions, such as county rates, not suffered by other forms of property. 'What we want is justice', he declared (the 'we' meaning the 'agriculturists' amongst whom he now counted himself). He repeated his assertion that large tracts of land would go out of cultivation if the Corn Laws were repealed. He also added a couple of unfortunate observations. He rejected the argument that the famine in Ireland necessitated free trade in corn; rather it should be 'met by public subscription or parliamentary grants, not by repealing the Corn Laws'. Secondly, to underline the threat from foreign imports, he explained that he had had dealings in corn himself, and said that in 1837 he had been able to import corn, all charges paid, at twenty-five shillings a quarter.[96]

Both statements were seized on by his opponents. Hudson was 'a man of iron nerves; he was not to be easily frightened', mocked Viscount Duncan two days later. 'To be sure, four million unfortunate persons in Ireland were starving; that is nothing'. It could be cured by a public subscription. A week later, C. P. Villiers, who had for some years been a leading parliamentary advocate of Repeal, inquired into Hudson's corn imports of 1837. After saying that it 'was impossible to doubt the truth of that which any gentleman says he did himself; and quite impossible to doubt anything which the Member of Sunderland says', he quoted the monthly prices of grain at Danzig in 1837 and demonstrated that the price of good quality wheat had never been less than twenty-nine shillings a quarter, exclusive of freight and other charges which would add another eight or nine shillings.

Hudson intervened to say that his supplies had come from Odessa, but made no further attempt to justify his figures. Whatever the merits of Protection, he had been made to look rather foolish. Nevertheless he continued to participate in the debates, with apparent confidence; he had, after all, 'met the body of the [Anti-Corn Law] League in Sunderland, and he thought he might fairly say he had routed it'. He continued to predict dire consequences that would follow the repeal of the Corn Laws. On 6 March he

> assured the House that, in his own neighbourhood, numbers of small proprietors [with] one hundred acres of land and upwards, found it very difficult, under all the advantages which the present law afforded, to maintain their position ... If [repeal passed] it was his firm conviction, and the conviction of the landed interest in his county (Yorkshire), whether Whig or Tory, that certain ruin would be the result.[97]

He made a much better effort the same month in defence of the railway industry. He restated the burden of his maiden speech, but in a far more considered manner, referring to figures from official returns and specific companies to support his argument. Responding to those who said the railways' capital requirements could not be met, he pointed to the equivalent sums that had been raised to pay for the French Wars. Answering suggestions that the profits of railway companies were excessive, he quoted the actual dividends being paid, pointed out that of thirty-nine railways in operation, only seven were paying 9 or 10 percent, while twelve paid less than 5 per cent and concluded 'this is surely no rich field for enterprise'. He made some nice debating points and expressed his surprise that, although the profits of the railways were nothing compared with those that had been earned by some canals, there had never been attempts 'to interfere with canal charges and canal property'.[98]

Hudson made only one more major contribution to Commons debate that session, in May, and once more it was on the Corn Laws. His argument was similar to that of his speech in February but with the additional statement that he had let some farms on his own estates since the Repeal Bill had been introduced and had 'felt it only right' to promise his tenants that, if the Bill passed and was followed by the 'disastrous results which he anticipated', he would make a corresponding reduction in their rents. The Radical J. A. Roebuck interjected 'that must generally be done', underlining the fact that Hudson was effectively conceding the position of the League, which had always argued that the only result of falling grain prices would be lower rents.

This speech was made on May 15 during the debate on the third reading of the Repeal Bill in the Commons. The Bill moved to the Lords, and completed its passage on 25 June 1846. That same night Bentinck and Disraeli led dissentient Tories (including Hudson) into the opposition lobbies to defeat the government's Irish Coercion Bill, whereupon Peel resigned. Thus 'the battle was won; the victor was in the dust'. This was an act of revenge on the part of the Protectionists and the practical result was a minority

Liberal government under Lord John Russell, with relations between the two wings of the Tory Party embittered. Lord Edward Stanley was anxious not to further alienate the Peelites, but he could not control Bentinck and his followers in the Commons.[99]

At a party at Albert Gate a few days later Hudson 'proceeded to assail Sir Robert Peel with abuse so vulgar that it is said to have come through his lips as through a familiar channel'. The one non-Protectionist present, Lord Arthur Lennox (who had served under Peel) was so affronted at this 'marked insult, conveyed in the gross attack on the head of the government of which he was a member' that he walked out. Lord George Bentinck's attacks on Peel were also so intemperate that the latter had to be restrained from challenging his tormentor to a duel.[100]

The current Parliament had been elected in 1841, and although Peel had advised the Queen against a dissolution when he resigned, a general election could not be far away. Hudson's political prospects, newcomer to Parliament though he was, looked very bright. Most of the members of Peel's government had effectively seceded and he was close to Bentinck, the Protectionist leader in the Commons. A place in the Cabinet would surely be within his reach, if the Protectionists came back into office. A contemporary portrait of him noted that, although he had been scarcely two years in Parliament, 'yet he occupies ... a position, side by side with Lord George Bentinck ... on the front bench of the Opposition [and is] recognised as one of the chiefs of that large majority of the Conservative party who seceded from Sir Robert Peel'.[101]

On the 4 February 1847 Bentinck introduced an Irish Railways Bill to the House of Commons. Its basic idea was to use government assistance to promote railway construction in Ireland, which would function as a form public works and relieve distress (Bentinck estimated that up to 110,000 might be employed) as well as providing long-term economic benefits. Much of the preparatory work in the autumn of 1846 had been done by Hudson, in collaboration with Robert Stephenson and, ironically, Samuel Laing, the author of the 1844 Railway Bill. These were men, said Bentinck, 'whose time might be measured in minutes and valued by gold' yet they had 'given freely of their time'.[102]

Hudson also spoke well in support of the measure. It had been attacked on *laissez-faire* grounds, but it was clear

> that there was little chance of capital [for railway construction] being found in Ireland, unless the aid of government were given; and their object was merely to obtain the assistance of government to private enterprise. Let them look abroad; did not France lend her money for the execution of such work? And although some might find fault with the principle, were not their advantages evident? Let

the plan be adopted, and people would be found to subscribe willingly, knowing that for every pound they paid to forward the undertaking, the Government would pay two. He repeated that it was no new principle; the only thing novel about it was its application to the construction of railways ...

Bentinck's plan was bold and imaginative, but despite his protestations that it was not a partisan measure, Russell made the Bill an issue of confidence, ensuring its defeat, only to be forced to bring forward his own scheme of government assistance for Irish railways. Bentinck and Hudson were subject to some virulent criticism; J. A. Roebuck declared that Bentinck knew perfectly well that the measure would never pass and simply wanted the 'gratification and glorification [of having] brought forward [a] great comprehensive plan for the relief of distress in Ireland', and the *Yorkshireman* questioned whether Hudson and his leader intended, in the event of their 'stupid project passing [to] indulge, by deputy in a *leetle* speculation, the one enhancing his already overgrown wealth, the other redeeming his losses on the turf?' [103]

In February Hudson again led the opposition to proposed regulation of the railway industry, in the form of a Bill proposed by Edward Strutt, Chief Commissioner for Railways and MP for Derby. Hudson convened a meeting of railway directors and officials in London on 3 March and about eighty attended, including Glyn (now Chairman of the London and North-Western, the largest railway company in the country), Charles Russell, Chairman of the Great Western and W. J. Chaplin of the London and South-Western.

Hudson chaired the meeting and gave an account of discussions that had already taken place between himself and Sir Charles Wood, the Chancellor of the Exchequer. He reported that the minister had expressed a desire 'not to interfere unduly with the interests of railway companies, while every means would be taken to protect those of the public'. After discussing their objections to the Bill, the members deputed Hudson to call on the Chancellor again to explain their position.

When he reported back, Hudson was able to state that he had been assured that every effort would be made to see that regulation did not press 'unnecessarily on the interests of the railway companies'. He expressed his own confidence that the government was favourably inclined towards the railway companies and did not think that any party political issues were involved. The Bill was eventually abandoned and Hudson's pre-eminence within the railway world became strikingly apparent, especially when it is considered that, unlike many directors, he was not a supporter of the government. [104]

In May 1847 the government introduced a 'Health of Towns Bill', that tried to tackle the very serious problems of sanitation in the towns and cities by creating a Board of Health and Public Works to investigate the state of health in urban areas and supervise improvements. Hudson opposed the measure strenuously on traditional Tory lines. He said that 'the country was sick of centralization, of commissions, of preliminary inquiries', claimed that the people wanted to be left to manage their own affairs and cited York as a city whose local government managed such matters perfectly well.

His opponents accordingly inquired into conditions in York and quoted a report prepared in 1844 by a local doctor, Thomas Laycock, which had painted a grim picture of the state of health of the poorer citizens of York and indicated that, in some areas, life expectancy was less than twenty years. Hudson dismissed Laycock's report as exaggerated and false, whereupon a Radical MP, Thomas Wakley, read out a letter from Laycock in the House, in which he flatly rejected Hudson's claim that 'eminent medical men' had impugned his report. He had been made Secretary of the Sanitary Committee in York 'at the instance of Mr Hudson', the Committee had unanimously adopted his report and Hudson had moved a vote of thanks at York Council for an 'able report on the sanitary condition of the city'.

Rather intemperately, Laycock went on to suggest that Hudson had 'no knowledge of the sanitary condition of the city [and had] probably never visited a poor sick person in his life, unless it was at the earliest period of his career'. Hudson's response was restrained and dignified. He referred to his activity during the cholera outbreak of 1832, when he had been one of the few dignitaries who had visited the sufferers in their homes as well as in hospital. He had also gone round York six times in the last fifteen years to canvass voters, when he had visited 'all the lanes and alleys'. Moreover, he had only moved a vote of thanks in 1844 at Laycock's own suggestion, as a means of helping him to advance in his profession; he was not ashamed of this 'as he really believed Dr Laycock to be a deserving person, though he had not succeeded in obtaining as great a share of public patronage as perhaps his merits entitled'. He did not, however, provide any evidence of the 'eminent medical men' who had supposedly criticised Laycock, he did not properly explain why he had publicly endorsed a report he actually thought a travesty and he ended by sneering at Wakley's own professional competence as a doctor.[105]

The *Times*, which strongly supported the Health Bill, excoriated his opposition to it as 'positive nonsense' and added:

> The honourable member for Sunderland, to do him justice, is a perfectly consistent legislator. From one simple rule he has never deviated. He denounces everything whatever except railways. Health and strength, sufficiency of food, and purity of air, are with him very trifling affairs. Railways are everything. Ireland is famished

– feed it with railways. England is distempered – railways will set it right. Railways are both medicine and meat.[106]

The attack in the *Times* was not entirely without foundation; Hudson was at his best when railways were the subject under discussion, and less impressive otherwise. A more sympathetic, although still critical portrait published in *Fraser's Magazine* at about this time, asserted that

> upon railway subjects he is listened to by all parties with respect ... His decision, *pro* or *con*, on a measure connected with railway management, is almost law. But on questions of a political or more general nature ... so many members ... are far better qualified to speak or to take the lead [that he should] avoid ... the higher walks of politics ...[107]

Hudson could not be considered a great parliamentary speaker. Even the *Yorkshire Gazette*, in eulogising his maiden speech agreed that

> there was no attempt at rhetorical flourishes ... It was a plain, practical, businesslike address ... Mr Hudson speaks with great ease and fluency ... though not having any pretensions to the graces of oratory ... His voice, without being musical, is agreeable to the ear. His articulation is distinct, and his utterance, though rather rapid, is not unpleasantly so.[108]

His opponents delighted in finding linguistic lapses in Hudson's speeches and holding him up to ridicule; the *Yorkshireman*, for example, cited a number of grammatical errors apparently made during his first major Commons speech on the Corn Laws in February 1846; 'surely', it commented, 'the honourable gentleman will not again venture to address an assembly of educated gentlemen'. The portrait in *Fraser's Magazine* is perhaps more to the point

> He speaks in volleys, with a thick utterance ... His words are just those that come first, and chiefly monosyllabic, and not always marshalled by the best grammatical discipline; but although he seems to speak with difficulty, and almost to blunder, yet he succeeds in making himself thoroughly understood.

In print, the speech criticised by the *Yorkshireman* reads reasonably well, both in *Hansard* and as reported in the *Times*. The grammar is not always correct, but it is, after all, a speech, and a perfectly competent one, whatever one thinks of the ideas expressed, although it does suffer in comparison with that of really able speakers, such as John Bright, who preceded him in the debate.[109]

Hudson was also prone to misjudge the mood of the Commons, failing to realise that actions or statements that would have been accepted without question in more sympathetic surroundings would simply expose him to attack or ridicule in the sceptical and partisan atmosphere of the House. In

the summer of 1846, for example, stung by attacks on the Eastern Counties
Railway's accident record, he 'moved for a return, from 31 October to the
present time, of all accidents which had caused deaths' on that line. At once
his opponents were upon him. Joseph Hume did not oppose the return,
but wanted to make it more comprehensive by covering 'all accidents which
have caused death or injuries to the person'. Sir James Graham, a close
associate of Peel, and Home Secretary in his government, suggested instead
(to cheers) a complete return of all accidents since the opening of the line.

Hudson explained, amid laughter, that he had chosen 31 October because
that was the time he took over the management of the line; 'charges had
been made that once or twice a-week deaths had occurred on this railway
and ... he had therefore moved for those returns which would ... show
that the statement was not founded in fact', at which his manner and state
of excitement caused considerable and renewed laughter. After further 'helpful' comments on the shape of the return, Hudson withdrew the motion.

The *Gateshead Observer* gleefully reported the episode, under the heading
'Mr Hudson and the Eastern Counties catastrophes'

> Mr Hudson is more at home in the De Grey Rooms than in the House of
> Commons. Among smiling shareholders, rejoicing in '10 per cent' he is 'monarch
> of all he surveys' ... but in the Senate, the Yorkshire dictator is pecked at on all
> sides, and stands alone. His 'return', however convenient to the honourable
> member, is refused.[110]

In February 1847, after unsubstantiated insinuations that he had some
personal motive in supporting Bentinck's Irish Railway Bill, he protested
not only his disinterest in this case, but also that that he had never entered
into a railway scheme 'for private gain or selfish purpose' and that 'his sole
object was to benefit his country'. The claim was treated with much mirth
and scepticism, particularly since it came only two weeks after the story
about his 'stagging' activities at the Liverpool, Manchester and Newcastle
Junction Railway had appeared in the *Yorkshireman*.[111]

Parliament was dissolved on 23 July 1847 and Hudson had to face his
first general election. He was expected, from the outset, to 'be very high at
the head of the poll' and quite possibly to achieve 'as great a triumph as
any in the kingdom'. His position in the constituency was so strong because
he could fairly say that the docks question was well on the way to resolution.
Even the *Sunderland Herald* tacitly conceded defeat, and admitted to seeing
him as having

> one master talisman ... He is money personified, Mammon's representative here
> on earth ... This makes him more formidable than would the eloquence of a
> Canning, the foresight of a Burke, and sagacity of a Peel, all united.[112]

On 29 July Hudson addressed a large meeting of his supporters at Hunter's Hotel and took up two political questions in particular. First he attacked Peel's Bank Charter Act of 1844, which restricted note issuance by the Bank of England. This was a new venture for him but, taking his cue from Bentinck, who felt his supporters lacked interest in such questions, he described it as a 'fair weather scheme' that might work well in good times; but, as soon as confidence was shaken and 'alarms gets possession', its rigidity would lead to unnecessary difficulty and panic.

Next Hudson moved on to a more familiar subject, the Navigation Laws. Their repeal was now clearly on the agenda, but Hudson vociferously denounced the idea, using familiar arguments from the Corn Laws debate: foreign sailors and artisans were paid far less than their British counterparts and, if the Navigation Laws were abolished, British shipping and shipbuilding would be in jeopardy. Nicely linking this issue with another he asked

> when you see these docks rising up (loud and protracted cheering), a monument of the enterprise, ability, and determination of the people of Sunderland ... when you see these docks completed, would you like to walk round and see them full of nothing but Swedish ships (thunders of applause; shouts of 'never') and see there also those shipbuilding yards ... no longer busy with the building of the lofty vessel by the English artisan (reiterated cheers).

The printed record of Hudson's speech gives the impression of an orator completely at ease with his audience, telling them only what they wanted to hear. He was frequently interrupted by applause and sat down 'amidst deafening plaudits'.[113]

It was left to one of his backers, James Hartley, to deal with a more ticklish question; although Sunderland elected two MPs, Hudson was the sole Tory candidate. The Liberals had two, the other sitting MP, David Barclay, a Whig who was generally a free trader but who made an exception of the Navigation Laws in deference to local interests, and William Wilkinson, a Radical who supported their abolition. Although Hartley said all the right things about it being his bounden duty to record a 'plumper for Mr Hudson' (to cast only one vote when having the right to two), he pointed out that Barclay, although in favour of the repeal of the Corn Laws, did support the Navigation Laws and so was 'entitled to receive the support of all those who believe that those Laws are of any advantage to the port'.

Similarly, when Hudson was formally proposed at the hustings on 2 August, his backers reminded their audience of what he was doing to improve the position of the port but also declared that it would be the 'height of insanity' to elect a candidate opposed to the Navigation Laws, which could only refer to Wilkinson. Barclay denied the existence of any coalition (between the Tories and Whigs) but went on to praise Hudson for conferring 'great benefit upon this borough'. In case any of the voters had not got the point, he even said that he did not 'hesitate to tell you that I think he ought to be one of your representatives'. After the result had been announced, with Hudson and Barclay returned, Wilkinson complained at his defeat by an 'unprincipled coalition' and proceeded to read out the names of leading supporters of Hudson who had split votes with Barclay, and *vice-versa*. Analysis of the voting pattern confirms that the Whig and Radical factions had operated as distinct parties and that the former had functioned in alliance with Hudson.[114]

Nationally, the outcome of the general election was less happy for Hudson. Although the Liberals were still a minority, the Tories were hopelessly divided between about two hundred and twenty-five Protectionists and a hundred Peelites, with the latter in only nominal opposition to the minority government of Lord John Russell.

Parliament met on 22 November 1847 to consider the severe commercial crisis. The restrictions of the Bank Charter Act had intensified the credit squeeze that developed in the autumn, until the government was forced to suspend the Act on 25 October, whereupon the credit crisis instantly evaporated. Hudson was made a member of the Select Committee set up to inquire into commercial distress and the role of the Bank Charter Act. Although attending the committee assiduously, and voting with Bentinck and Disraeli, he was almost a 'silent member', asking few questions and tabling no amendments. Similarly, when included on Bouverie's committee on railway labourers in April 1847, he attended only the first eight sessions and made little contribution to its report.[115]

On 16 December the Prime Minister, Lord John Russell, threw a grenade into the Protectionist ranks. Russell represented the City of London, which returned two MPs, and in the general election the second successful candidate had been another Liberal, Baron Lionel de Rothschild, of the famous banking dynasty. But, as a Jew, Rothschild could not take the oath of allegiance, as this contained the phrase 'on the true faith of a Christian'. Russell now introduced a proposal that this disability be removed. The majority of the Protectionists (including Stanley) opposed this, although Bentinck and Disraeli both voted in favour. It is difficult to guess at Hudson's view on the question, although Lionel de Rothschild had been a guest at Albert Gate, but not joining the outcry against the proposed Bill must have weakened him within his own party. Hudson did not even vote in the division, and took no part in the debates on the Jewish Disabilities Bill when it was introduced in 1848.

Bentinck resigned and this seriously damaged Hudson's position. He was not close to Disraeli, who eventually emerged as the Protectionist leader in the Commons, although he did help him financially and invited him to Albert Gate on number of occasions. The prospect of high office receded even further.[116]

In Sunderland itself, however, his position was still unassailable, as the construction of the docks continued. On 4 February 1848, he laid the foundation stone of the half-tide basin before a 'vast concourse of spectators'. A local paper described the scene

> the day was generally a holiday: the bells of the Parish Church – 'the poor man's only music', pealed forth during the morning; the vessels in the harbour were decorated with flags and banners were displayed at all the principal works and public establishments in the town [and] the streets and the windows of the houses were crowded with spectators.

In the company of a group of dignitaries that included the Mayor, the Duke of Cleveland and Robert Stephenson, as well as directors of the Dock Company, Hudson placed a sealed bottle 'containing the various coins of the realm, and a copy of the local newspapers' into a cavity of the foundation stone, together with an engraved zinc plate recording the occasion.

The south dock was a considerable engineering feat; some had thought it would be impossible to construct. A huge coffer dam had been built and thirteen thousand men, twelve hundred wagons and ten steam engines had been needed to excavate the main basin. George Hudson stood on the foundation stone and delivered a brief oration, reminding his audience that the docks would supply a great need, a southern outlet for their coal output, and would avoid the recent blocking up of the Tyne and the Wear 'for the want of the very accommodation that we are now about to give'. He also waxed lyrical over the protective groynes placed to form a sand bank and 'triumph, as it were, over Neptune himself by the force of genius'. In the evening there was a grand ball at the Athenaeum, attended by more than a 'thousand of the *élite* of the community'.[117]

Despite the disappointment of his ambitions for high office, Hudson remained active in Parliament in 1848. His longest speech of the session was in June, in opposition to the repeal of the Navigation Laws. Not only was he ideologically committed to Protection, he also sat for 'one of the largest shipping ports in this country'. It was his conviction that, as soon as the Bill was passed, 'twenty thousand of the labouring people of Sunderland would be thrown out of employ' as the government sacrificed the shipping interest to 'some fanciful principle of political economy'.

Earlier he had demanded the repeal of the Bank Charter Act, and opposed the reduction of import tariffs. In February, he had claimed to see the free trade mania, which 'raged' a few months previously, beginning to subside, although this was mere fancy on his part. Some of his interventions now had a curiously querulous, even eccentric tone. The House, he declared on one occasion, 'was fond of meddling with everything – there was no subject too trifling or too minute to engage its attention'.

The Borough Elections Bill, designed to combat electoral corruption, had, he thought, 'the symptoms of a job', for the 'purpose of assisting the lawyers, and if it passed into law there would be lots of pettifoggers receiving the five guineas a day ... The government appeared exceedingly anxious to find fault with a few poor men for getting a breakfast for half-a-crown [and] inquire whether the present of a new hat was intended to influence a vote'. He referred to the 1835 inquiry, which had cost £7000 and achieved nothing, at which he had himself been interrogated for three days and answered twelve hundred questions while 'every lawyer employed had five guineas a day'. He added sardonically that he had not been 'so wide awake then as he was now, and he only got a guinea for three days, and outside coach expenses'. Perhaps two or three hundred poor freemen in a constituency of four or five thousand might have received 'what some people call a bribe', although the same thing was done by both parties and the recipients of these sums did not look upon them as bribes. Besides, bribery did not merely consist of making payments to electors; making extravagant promises to electors could also be considered a form of bribery and he gave, as an example, the fine promises given to the constituency of Sunderland by the Anti-Corn Law League of the advantages they would derive from abolition, all of them 'great promises which they must have known were perfectly fallacious'. This is a statement of such extraordinary effrontery that one can only assume that Hudson actually believed it.[118]

A few days after this speech Hudson was involved in what one paper called a 'scene'. He had apparently taunted and cat-called Radical members while they were speaking, in the case of Joseph Hume referring to old, and baseless charges of corruption ('the Greek loan') dating back to the 1820s. Hume then rose to protest at Hudson's practice of 'making constant personal allusions' to himself and Richard Cobden

> after thirty years' experience, he must say that he had never known another honourable member come down after dinner, night after night, flushed – he would not say with champagne – (great laughter, and cries of 'order') ... night after night [Cobden] and himself were called upon by name as often as twenty times in the course of a speech ... It was breaking through the rules of the House ...

Unwisely Hudson rose to answer this attack, and he was not in the best of conditions, as Hume had suggested. He questioned whether Hume

> was speaking to the question when he told them about the champagne that had been drunk (great laughter). He had not been forty minutes away from the house the whole evening (laughter) ... The honourable member seemed to have drawn some inference from the dress in which he appeared [here Hudson, with a good-humoured smile, pointed, amid much laughter, to his white waistcoat], but the truth was that he had gone home to accompany his family to another party (roars of laughter). Whether he wore a white waistcoat or a waistcoat of any other colour had nothing to do with the present debate ... he had never attacked the honourable member for Montrose on account of his wearing a white waistcoat or attempting to look a little gay. Whenever he attacked the honourable member for Montrose – or rather when he attacked the speeches of that honourable gentleman – he did so upon public grounds ... and at all events, he should never charge the honourable member for Montrose with having dined out or with ever having given a dinner to a friend ('hear, hear' and laughter).

No report, said one newspaper, can give anything like a vivid idea of the incident

> if Hudson had had twice the champagne, that would only have aggravated the meanness and malignity of his revival of the ten-times-refuted calumny against Hume about the Greek loan, and for the non-chastisement of which the House deserves all the ignominy the disgraceful proceeding is calculated to throw upon it.

Immediately after Hudson's response, the press gallery was cleared for a division, but the debate continued, and Cobden, Hudson's other victim, delivered a rebuke 'of the severest character'. The white waistcoat was something of a Hudsonian trademark; the Irish nationalist Daniel O'Connell had once pointed to his rotund figure on the Commons benches 'and likened him to a 'turbot ... sitting on its tail with its belly outwards'.[119]

Hudson's drinking had been alluded to on previous occasions. The *Times* reference to Hudson's 'excitement' in reporting the incident of the Eastern Counties return probably hints at this. During the debate on the Health of Towns Bill on 5 July 1847, Wakley (a coroner himself) had said that 'medically, he would strongly advise the right hon. gentleman [Hudson] to moderate his excitement; for if he did not, the coroner of London would, perhaps, have to perform the duties of his office upon the Lord Mayor of York'. Again the word 'excitement' probably hints at excessive drinking. More obviously, when he had derisively referred at the hustings in York in August 1847 to Frederick Hopwood as 'an itinerant teetotal lecturer', the *Yorkshireman* had responded that Hudson himself would have done better had *he* become 'a disciple of the pump'. A few days before the incident with Hume another MP had suggested that proceedings in the House would be improved if Hudson were to join a temperance society.[120]

Nonetheless, it was the considerable publicity over the row with Hume that finally gave Hudson a reputation for drinking that he could not shake off. Shortly after this incident, one paper commented on a review of Ward's engraving of Hudson that had appeared in the *Morning Post*, which among other things said that he looked 'well fed and contented'. This was, it mocked 'a pictorial libel. Like all ascetic philosophers, it is known that Hudson lives on pulse and dates; and – ere he addresses Parliament – drinks nought save waters from the well of Truth'.[121]

In 1849, Macaulay referred to Hudson as a 'bloated, vulgar, insolent, purse-proud, greedy, drunken blackguard'. This assessment does not appear to have been based on any particular incidents or personal encounter, but it does indicate his reputation in certain quarters.[122]

The contretemps with Hume seems to have been a turning point. Although the session continued until early September, Hudson's further contributions were few and his career as a serious Parliamentarian appeared to be over. Shortly after this incident, Lord Londonderry was even suggesting that his son, Lord Adolphus Vane (a guest at Hudson's victory dinner less than three years earlier) should replace Hudson in the Commons, and Joseph Wright 'had to assure [him] that his revised views of Hudson's worth were mistaken'. In Sunderland itself, the continuing work on the new dock meant that Hudson's position was still unassailable, but nationally his political stock was falling.[123]

7

Disgrace

On 20 February 1849, at 1 o'clock, Hudson took the chair at the regular twice-yearly meeting of the York and North Midland in the De Grey Rooms, York. The meeting was fairly straightforward. The dividend had been reduced to 6 per cent and Hudson gave a sensible, considered report. He warned the members that dividends might not remain at even this level; they would be well advised to decide whether current difficulties were due to their management or to trading conditions in general. He did not try to give them the answer to this, but most shareholders recognised that 6 per cent was a highly satisfactory return under the circumstances and no major concerns were expressed.

In line with normal practice, the York Newcastle and Berwick meeting followed on immediately afterwards. The members were to consider the accounts for the second half of 1848, which had been circulated a week earlier, and draft Bills for the leasing of the Newcastle and Carlisle and the Maryport and Carlisle lines. After discussing the Bills and commenting on the expensive, but strategically necessary, purchase of the Great North of England Railway, Hudson proposed a dividend of 6 per cent, down from the 8 per cent declared for the first half of 1848, but still entirely respectable, and then sat down.

The first shareholder to speak, Robert Prance of Hampstead, did not comment on the dividend or on the proposed Bills, but drew the attention of the meeting to an item in the accounts, the Great North of England Purchase Account. The York Newcastle and Berwick was committed to buying Great North of England shares on agreed terms on 1 July 1850 and in the autumn of 1846 the York and Newcastle had issued preference shares, guaranteeing 6 per cent, to create a fund to acquire the various classes of Great North of England shares in the market when the price seemed advantageous. Nearly £750,000 had been so spent, according to the latest accounts. Prance drew attention to the purchase of 3790 Great North of England £15 shares, at an average price of £35. This was not only significantly above the average price of £31 15s. according to the official lists of the London Stock Exchange but was an absurd transaction for the York Newcastle and Berwick, given the cost of its own funds.[1] Prance finished by saying that he

> disclaimed all animosity or hostility towards the directors in bringing this matter forward, which he had done from no other motive than a sense of duty (loud applause). The number of £15 shares stated by the directors to have been bought by the company was 3790, and when it was shown that they had been bought at £21 premium, certain explanations not at all complimentary to the directors were given; and I am sure that no more than the odd hundreds have been bought by the public, so that some one has received great benefit by selling them at this extravagant price to the company.

Prance sat down to loud burst of applause amid great excitement. Hudson, Chairman, replied

> I have not the books here and cannot therefore inform Mr Prance the names of all the sellers of Great North of England shares, as the company had bought a great many lots of different parties, But if there is any mistake, the books of the company are all open to the shareholders, and they can examine them as minutely and as fully as they thought proper. I would tell you candidly at once that I had 2800 of those £15 shares; that was all I had of them; and if I have disposed of them to the company at a larger price than I ought to have done, I should be prepared to do whatever the shareholders think would be just and fair. I had got the estimates of the prices from Mr Plews, I believe, and therefore the price was not of my own fixing and that is all I can say on the subject (partial applause and general disapprobation).

A shareholder from Liverpool commented:

> I think Mr Prance ought to be content with the assurances of the Chairman that whatever the averages might turn out to be, he was agreeable to abide by it (partial applause and general disapprobation).

> *Prance:*   I am not satisfied. The assurance of the Chairman does not answer my question. The question is not one of money, but of reputation (renewed excitement).

> *Hudson:*   I bought and sold the shares as I thought at a fair price, but if Mr Prance thinks himself entitled to a vote of censure, let him put it to the meeting and carry it.

> *Prance:*   I decline that course. Instead, I move the appointment of a Committee of Inquiry of five shareholders to examine the matter and report at an adjourned meeting (applause).

A shareholder questioned Prance's motives, and asked 'what interest [he] had in the undertaking'; the challenge to Hudson looked to him like 'a Stock Exchange job'. Prance replied that he was 'a large proprietor'.

Hudson: I do not know what the honourable proprietor requires more. I have told him that I have sold these shares and the question was whether I have done right in so selling them (cries of 'no, no', applause and excitement).

Prance: I admit that several hundreds have been sold at £21 premium in London but the inference on the Exchange was that that was an extravagant price given for them to get a quotation.

Hudson: That was an imputation of motive and was unfair. I bought large lots from private individuals which were never in the Exchange at all and if in some cases I got them lower than in others it made an average of them.

Mr H. Love, a shareholder, then seconded the motion for the appointment of a committee, at which point another shareholder condemned the proceedings as an 'insult to Mr Hudson', to 'loud cries of disapprobation'.

Hudson: I might have got wrong the early stage of these share transactions, but if I have made an error in this instance, I have been right in many others. I have never directed my attention to this particular transaction and relied on the data given me. If I have made an error, I will take all the shares back if the shareholders like and pay the interest on them (hear).

Mr Farsyde of Edinburgh, shareholder: The question is not one of money and no repayment can put a satisfactory end to the inquiry (loud applause).

Hudson: Repayment is the question because there is no doubt that I was perfectly justified in selling the shares like any other person and the only point was whether the price was more than it ought to have been (disapprobation and excitement).

Love: There is no doubt about the price being too high.

Hudson: Then let it be put right.

Other shareholders attempted to defend Hudson: one pronounced himself satisfied with Hudson's pledge to refund any excess payment; another contemptuously stated that he did not 'esteem as anything' the Stock Exchange list which Prance had produced; Robert Denison pointed out that 'there were seven other directors besides Mr Hudson [who] could have put their veto upon the transaction, had they thought there was anything wrong in it'.

Mr H. S. Thompson of Moat Hall, another shareholder: In order to clear the characters of the Chairman and the other directors, it is highly desirable that an investigation should take place (loud applause).

Love: It is as much due to the credit of Mr Hudson as it is to the shareholders, that an investigation take place [and be reported] without favour or affection towards any parties (hear).

Hudson: If the shareholders wish it, I have not the least objection to a committee.

A committee was appointed, consisting of Messrs Prance, Love, Denison, Clayton and Shield, with power to call for documents and report to an adjourned meeting.[2]

The meeting ended in great noise and excitement. It was clear to the members that this was no casual challenge; their chairman had been caught in a carefully prepared ambush. His challengers had rejected Hudson's apologies and offers of recompense; moreover, Farsyde's insistence that the question was not one of money was extremely ominous. The meeting had gone on to establish the Committee of Inquiry, as Prance and Love had intended from the outset, and they clearly meant serious business.

Two aspects of the meeting are very striking: it is clear that the feeling of the meeting was from the beginning in favour of Prance and against Hudson, an indication perhaps, of how badly confidence in the Chairman had been eroded. It is also astonishing that none of Hudson's fellow directors made any attempt to defend him. Equally noteworthy was the telling intervention from H. S. Thompson, who cleverly presented an inquiry as a means of exonerating the directors from any suspicion (a line quickly picked up by Prance's associate, Horatio Love), and so made it much more difficult for Hudson to oppose one. He did not become a member of the committee, but was soon a leading figure among those shareholders in both the York and North Midland and York Newcastle and Berwick who wanted Hudson's stewardship of these companies rigorously investigated and the Chairman himself brought to account.

In the 1840s, the setting up of a Committee of Inquiry was a statutory right of shareholders. These committees were usually established when the level of dividend payments had fallen to an unsatisfactory level, although they could be set up by shareholders whenever the situation warranted a detailed investigation on their behalf. In those days, the regular company audit did little to protect shareholders interests, limited in scope as it was and usually carried out by two or three of their own colleagues, rather than by independent accountants. Committees of Inquiry, on the other hand, had wide-ranging powers and might even hire professional accountants when the issues were sufficiently complex, so they were well equipped to carry out the most searching investigation. Although Hudson made no objection to a committee, he must have known that it would have been difficult to hold out against so basic a right. Instead, his friends at the

Yorkshire Gazette ran an obviously partisan account of the York Newcastle and Berwick meeting in which they said that the 'premeditated attack' on Hudson was 'met by that gentleman with the candour and openness which have ever characterised his conduct!'[3]

This challenge was only the beginning. Hudson went to attend a meeting of Protectionist MPs at Lord Edward Stanley's house in London. Just before the meeting began, Lord Stanley's secretary came to him with a message

> I regret to have to advise you, Sir, that His Lordship believes it advisable that you do not to make any appearance in public or among his legislative compeers, until matters have been satisfactorily settled.

This came as a shock to Hudson. He was to be ostracised by London society until matters at the York Newcastle and Berwick were resolved. Seriously disturbed, he left London immediately for Yorkshire.

He was due to attend a regular meeting of the Eastern Counties in London on 28 February 1849 but, on the 25th, he wrote from Newby Park to David Waddington, the Deputy Chairman at the Eastern Counties, in terms that show how severely discomposed he had now become:

> As I feel I cannot go thoroughly along with you in reference to the steamboat question, I have made up my mind not to attend the meeting on Wednesday next. I sincerely wish you well through it. I hope if any attack is made on me you will, if you can, defend me with reference to your company. I unfortunately hold a large stake, and bought at a very great price and lose terribly by the concern; they invited us, they were in a ruined condition both as to stock and credit.
> I shall resign whenever it may suit you and the Board. By not attending I shall avoid the Norfolk [amalgamation] question, which I could not but throw over.

Waddington immediately met other Eastern Counties directors living in London and wrote back to Hudson on 26 February:

> Upon receipt of your letter I convened a meeting of our directors residing in London and read your letter to them. It leaves us all in considerable difficulty as to the best course to be pursued; but my impression is, that as the steamboat matter is approved of in the report of the Board, and as no vote on the Norfolk amalgamation will have to be taken at the meeting, it is difficult to explain your absence from the meeting on any ground stated in your letter ... It appears therefore to us, that as you have determined on resigning your seat, it would be better for you to do this previous to the meeting. Should you concur to this and send me the resignation, to be at the Board prior to the meeting, you can give such reasons for the step as you wish, and I will make them known. The feeling of all is one of regret that we shall lose the valuable services your experience and knowledge enable you to give to every company with which you are associated.

To this letter, Hudson made no reply.

The members of the Eastern Counties Railway met in the meeting room of the London Tavern. Well before the meeting was due to start, some seven hundred people were present and others continued to arrive 'until the doors and passages leading to the room were literally choked up'. In an atmosphere of the greatest excitement, amidst mingled cheers, groans and hisses, at a few minutes after one o'clock, David Waddington, MP, Deputy-Chairman of the company entered the room with several other directors. When it became apparent that Hudson was not among them, 'a scene of the most tremendous tumult ensued, the directors being assailed on all sides with groaning, hissing and cries of "Where's Hudson?"'

Waddington reported the exchange of letters and assured those present that he and his colleagues were 'extremely anxious … that Mr Hudson should attend here this day', at which there were loud groans, hisses and cries of 'shame'. He explained that they had received no reply to their last letter to him, which they could not understand. When he said, rather lamely, that it might be that Mr Hudson was not at home, there were shouts of laughter and when he added that the Company Secretary 'could not get an answer either, being informed at the telegraph office that the wires [were] out of order', a great burst of laughter and repeated ironical cheers came from the audience.

A shareholder then spoke for many of those present when he said that his absence would 'convince the world that Mr Hudson had humbugged them from beginning to end'; under these circumstances, there could be no grounds for resisting the setting up of a Committee of Inquiry. The meeting then ended with 'three cheers for the Chairman, Mr Waddington and three groans for Mr Hudson'.[4]

The *Railway Times* applauded the 'manly way that Mr Waddington, deserted at his utmost need, unshrinkingly went through his work amidst a babel of confused voices', and expressed the opinion that that it was intolerable for a 'man to be wanting in nerve who had tried other men's nerves so severely'. Hudson's failings could have been more readily forgiven had he shown the pluck to 'come forward and beard the shareholders at the Eastern Counties meeting'.[5]

The partisan nature of the York press was again apparent. On the same day, 3 March 1849, that the *Yorkshire Gazette* described the accusations of the previous week as a 'malignant slander of Mr Hudson', the *Yorkshireman* 'confessed unaffectedly that on public grounds we rejoice at the fall of this man'. The *Times* had already concluded, in its first editorial comment on the Hudson's difficulties, that

> all things would seem to portend that this reign is over … The clay feet tremble beneath the image of brass, and all men foretell an impending ruin.[6]

Reports of the Eastern Counties meeting naturally excited suspicions at Hudson's other companies and demands were voiced for further inquiries. In the second week of March anonymous notices appeared in the press, inviting shareholders in the York Newcastle and Berwick to an unofficial meeting at the London Tavern on 19 March to press for 'the appointment of a Committee of Inquiry upon the general management of the affairs of the Company'. Harry Thompson, who had intervened so effectively at the York Newcastle and Berwick meeting, took the chair at a well-attended meeting and revealed that it was he who had placed the advertisements.

He then said he was convinced of the necessity of 'a thorough investigation into the management of the company', and explained that he had been concerned for some years that the 'statements of accounts were not sufficiently explicit', adding ominously that he 'was prepared to shew that very strong reasons existed for the appointment of a Committee of Investigation'. However, William Richardson, solicitor to the York Newcastle and Berwick and a substantial shareholder in his own right, had been asked by the Board to attend the meeting and explain that the directors were as anxious for an Inquiry as they were and would soon be convening a special shareholders' meeting to appoint a committee. This largely satisfied the meeting and Thompson stated that it was now undesirable to present the information he had, as this might be prejudicial to the interests of the company.[7]

At the Midland it was the 'Liverpool party' that took the initiative: an unofficial meeting was held in that city on 21 March, with A. H. Wylie (who had unsuccessfully moved for an inquiry in February) in the chair. He demanded the removal of Hudson and attacked the agreement he had entered into as Chairman of the York and North Midland with the Great Northern. This was a 'breach of confidence towards the Midland shareholders'. Presented with a requisition from the Liverpool shareholders, the Midland Board convened an extraordinary general meeting at Derby on 19 April.

This aroused enormous interest: the *Railway Times* reporter thought it the largest he had ever seen, estimating the attendance at nearly a thousand. Hudson did not attend, although he was present in Derby at the Midland Hotel, and during the meeting was 'within the precincts of the station, having expressed a readiness to come forward in the event of any explanations being required'. This proved unnecessary. John Ellis, Hudson's deputy, presided and read out Hudson's letter of resignation, in which he explained that, with the imminent opening of the Great Northern Railway, which he had always opposed, the interests of his various companies were no longer identical and, after due deliberation, he thought it 'might be more satisfactory to the shareholders of the Midland Company if he resigned the office of Chairman'. This was accepted with little further ado. A. H. Wylie proposed a Committee of Inquiry, and produced a list of seven names which he had agreed in negotiations with Ellis the previous evening. This was unanimously approved.[8]

The special meeting of the York Newcastle and Berwick to receive the report of the Prance Committee was held on 4 May and presided over by Robert Davies, the Deputy Chairman. The meeting was advertised to be held at the De Grey rooms, as usual, but had to be transferred to the city concert rooms 'in consequence of the numbers of shareholders present'. Davies read Hudson's letter of resignation, and the Prance Committee's report was received and adopted 'amidst loud cheers' with only two dissentients.

H. S. Thompson then moved the appointment of a Committee of Inquiry. He had acted as chairman of a grouping of York shareholders, and had invited important shareholders in five other towns where large numbers of shares were held (London, Edinburgh, Glasgow, Newcastle and Darlington) each to nominate a member, and proposed these five, who included Horatio Love (from London), together with his own committee's James Meek (currently Lord Mayor of York) and a board nominee, Ralph Phillipson. This proposal was adopted unanimously after some discussion, and a vote of thanks was given to 'the York Committee, presided over by Mr Thompson, of Moat Hall' for its role bringing about the Inquiry.[9]

Hudson was now Chairman only of the York and North Midland, but here too the Board decided, on 2 May, to convene an extraordinary meeting on 24 May to consider whether a Committee of Investigation should be appointed. By the time of the meeting, Hudson had sent a letter of resignation (dated 16 May), which was received by the Board the following day. This last resignation, from his first railway company, the springboard for his entire career, must have been peculiarly painful. His fellow directors, after hearing the letter read, merely 'resolved that Mr Hudson's resignation be accepted' and moved on to the next item of business.

The meeting on the 24 May was told of the resignation and appointed a committee of six to investigate the affairs of the company and elected four new directors: William Crawshay, Joseph Rowntree, his old enemy James Meek, and Harry Thompson. Hudson had 'at length been driven from the last citadel in his railway dominions', exulted the *Yorkshireman* two days later; 'not an inch of his iron crown remains intact, while his sceptre has been broken, and, in a divided shape, placed in the hands of others'.[10]

By the end of November 1849, the Committees of Inquiry at the four companies had produced a total of twelve reports, including four at the York and North Midland and six at the York Newcastle and Berwick, covering the last four or five years of Hudson's chairmanships. Two matters in particular stood out: Hudson's personal dealings with the companies he had chaired; and the manner in which their progress had been charted in the accounting statements. The evidence contained in these reports generated an extraordinary level of publicity, frequently taking over the entire front pages of some regional papers. Some editions had several pages devoted to the details and extraordinary editions of up to fifty pages were produced to cover the findings of an important committee report. Newspapers such as the *Yorkshireman* frequently had to be reprinted, when their normal runs sold out.

From this point, George Hudson's reputation was broken. His railways were still there, of course, for all to see, the lines and bridges, the networks and the station architecture, irrefutable evidence of his prodigious energies. And yet public perceptions of his almost alchemic powers as well as his standing among his peers, were irrevocably transformed by these twelve documents.

At both the York and North Midland and the York Newcastle and Berwick, so many of the directors were associates of Hudson and had been discredited by the ensuing scandal that Hudson's fall led to the near total reconstruction of their boards of directors. By the end of the year the two York-based companies were chaired by H. S. Thompson and George Leeman respectively, neither of whom had been directors or even notably active shareholders at the time Prance put his fatal question.

Harry Stephen Meysey Thompson (1809–74) was a country gentleman from a wealthy, although untitled family of North Yorkshire. He had been born, by a remarkable coincidence, at Newby Park, but was now living at Moat Hall, in Little Ouseburn, not far from Knaresborough. He studied entomology under Charles Darwin while a student at Cambridge and later achieved distinction as an agriculturalist. He wrote extensively on agricultural questions (including an admired survey of Ireland), developed or popularised a number of agricultural improvements and was a founder of the Royal Agricultural Society in 1838. He was always Liberal in his politics and had thought of a political career when a young man, but this had been vetoed by his father.[11]

He was a shareholder in both the York and North Midland and York Newcastle and Berwick, but does not appear to have played any active part in the affairs of either company until he supported Prance's motion for an inquiry. He later said he became convinced of the need for an investigation at the York Newcastle and Berwick in August 1848 when that company published its accounts for the first half of the year. He said nothing, however, at the meeting which approved those accounts, nor did he make any other public comment, although he may have discussed his concerns with other shareholders: if he did this may help to explain the hostility to Hudson shown at the York Newcastle and Berwick meeting. Thompson's motives are also unclear. He may have been primarily concerned with the value of his own investments – the *Railway Times* described him as 'a very large proprietor' in the York Newcastle and Berwick – although another source insists that he 'was not actuated by any motives of self-interest' as he had already taken steps to remove the greater part of the family interest from the suspect undertakings. Instead, he saw the property of innocent share-holders, 'unworldly clergymen, widows and orphans' alike, being 'devoured by the cruel demon of greedy speculation; ... there was wrong to be righted' and he was determined to see justice done.[12]

Thompson's contemporary George Leeman (1809–1882) was, like him, a lifelong Liberal, but his social background was utterly different. His was a classic Victorian story of self-improvement. He started work in a firm of solicitors as a simple clerk at the age of thirteen. By the time he was twenty-one, he had acquired the necessary means (£120) to become an articled clerk with the firm. After qualifying as a solicitor he started his own practice, prospered and acquired various business interests, including an investment in the London and York Railway. He was also active politically and by 1849 was one of the small anti-Hudson group on York Council.[13]

Thompson was one of four new directors elected to the board of the York and North Midland at the meeting on 24 May that appointed a Committee of Investigation. The Chair was taken by another new director, William Crawshay, but he soon retired through ill health and was replaced by James Meek. Meek in turn withdrew after suggestions from the committee that, as a director of the Great Northern, he was unfitted for the post. Thompson succeeded him at the end of October 1849.

At the York Newcastle and Berwick, Thompson's role was more indirect. He had led the campaign for a Committee of Investigation, helped to arrange its composition and almost certainly encouraged the appointment of George Leeman as the committee's secretary, the latter's first active involvement in the affairs of the York Newcastle and Berwick. Leeman attended subsequent meetings in that capacity and occasionally acted as a spokesman. At the half-yearly meeting on 23 August 1849, Thompson proposed that all directors resign, except Plews and Wood, and be replaced temporarily by members of the committee, pending a full reconstruction of the Board when the Committee of Investigation had completed its reports. This was carried with only one vote against, whereupon the directors immediately retired to another room for an impromptu meeting to effect the changes. James Meek was one of the new directors and served temporarily as Chairman (so that, for a period he was Chairman of both the York Newcastle and Berwick and the York and North Midland). The committee then proposed an extraordinarily cumbersome way of reconstructing the Board. Meetings of shareholders were held all over the country to appoint delegates, who in turn met in York on 12 October, with Thompson in the chair, and agreed a list of eight names (headed by Leeman) for a new Board. At a subsequent shareholders' meeting on 25 October, Thompson proposed the list, which was largely accepted by the meeting, and the new directors promptly elected Leeman as their Chairman.[14]

Involvement in the removal of Hudson assisted both Thompson and Leeman to long and illustrious careers as railway directors. They presided over their respective companies until 1854, when they amalgamated with the Leeds Northern to form the North Eastern Railway, one of the largest railway companies in Britain. Both became directors of the North Eastern Railway, and a year later Thompson was elected Chairman, with Leeman as his deputy, positions they held for twenty years until Thompson's retirement in 1874. Leeman then succeeded him, remaining in office until 1880. The two were closely associated politically and were already working together in 1849. Leeman had the technical expertise and performed well as the York Newcastle and Berwick committee secretary, but he could hardly have secured a place on the board, or the chairmanship of the York Newcastle and Berwick without the kind of influence that Thompson was able to wield. The latter was in a position to place his associate in control of the York Newcastle and Berwick, while he himself took over the York and North Midland. Thompson's new career was fateful for George Hudson: throughout he remained implacably, some might say vengefully, determined to exact full reparation from the former Railway King and was to pursue him unrelentingly for the next twenty years.

In Victorian times, individuals were expected to deal with their own financial problems. It was not the state's role to regulate transactions between them and men of business, both as shareholders and their directors, were hostile to any attempt to control their activities from the outside.

In the 1830s and 1840s, limited liability companies could not be formed by simple registration; those that did exist had either been established by the Crown or by formal permission of Parliament.[15] Most railway companies were established by private Act of Parliament that defined their powers in some detail. The government began to regulate the industry as a whole in 1840, when the Railway Department of the Board of Trade was set up, but this body was more interested in traffic levels and safety issues than in the powers and duties of directors. At first, the overall position of directors in

law was far from clear but this began to change in the 1840s as the wording
of the various private Acts was gradually standardised leading to the cod-
ifying Companies Clauses Consolidation Act of 1845 which then applied to
all newly established statutory companies.[16]

Hudson's powers as chairman, therefore, were defined by the individual
provisions of a number of private railway company Acts, although the York
Newcastle and Berwick, because it was formed by amalgamation in 1847,
was effectively governed by the Companies Consolidation Act of 1845.[17]
The directors of early railway companies were elected by their fellow
shareholders to act on their behalf, typically on a part-time basis. They
could not be employed by the company in any other capacity and were
usually major shareholders with experience of managing other businesses.[18]
They were expected to act as honest agents of the shareholders and as the
trustees or stewards of their property and to provide them with relevant
information in a number of ways, not least in the twice-yearly financial
statements.

The shareholders, for their part, were expected actively to defend their
own interests. They might elect or dismiss the directors and directly question
them at meetings. If the half-yearly accounts were audited, the auditors
were almost invariably themselves shareholders, elected by their colleagues.
Often, they might inspect the company books in person, as under the
Companies Consolidation Act 1845, section 117.

Above all, calling the directors to account was seen as a responsibility of
shareholders that could not be delegated to third parties such as the state
or a professional accountant. On the other hand, the extent to which
directors, acting as trustees of their shareholders' property, should, or should
not, profit from their position was not, at first, well defined, partly because
the legislature looked to improve the standards of behaviour of directors,
not by detailed prescription, but by strengthening the monitoring powers
of the shareholders.[19] Some attempt was made to see that directors did not
face conflicts of interest, with the Companies Consolidation Act 1845 (sections 85 and 86) stipulating that they could not also be employees of the
company or have an interest in any contract with the company, although
the only explicit sanction was removal from office as a director, which
might not be very onerous after the event.

Although Hudson's name in our day has been widely connected with false
accounting, the most damaging findings in the committee reports concerned
his personal dealings with the companies he had chaired.[20] It had been
suspicion of his dishonesty that had led to his social ostracism and to
his resignations from chair and board; when the reports confirmed these
doubts, he was quickly ruined as a public figure. Victorian society was

highly sensitive to such things. When an *arriviste*'s amazing success could be convincingly attributed to cheating, it could be quite merciless.

Society was quicker to condemn dishonesty then than now, but it had done little to define the legal position, perhaps relying too much on gentlemen to know right from wrong. Some forms of dishonesty, such as simple theft, were of course clearly defined and punished quite savagely during the nineteenth century, but what we might call 'white collar' crimes were far less straightforward. Many of Hudson's transactions raised complex questions about the function of directors vis-à-vis their shareholders, par-ticularly during the 'get-rich-quick' free-for-all of the railway mania, long before the legislature had confronted the contradictions.

The Committees of Inquiry found that Hudson had entered into many transactions that breached his responsibilities as a director in a number of ways. They also revealed that it was at the two York-based companies, the York and North Midland and the York Newcastle and Berwick, where his control was entrenched and absolute, that he really abused his position; at the Eastern Counties there had been only one minor problem while the Midland Committee found no misuse of company monies and effectively exonerated Hudson from any personal wrongdoing.[21] All of the instances cited took place in the five year period from February 1844; the committees did not investigate earlier periods, when the circumstances were simpler and the likelihood of dishonesty correspondingly lower.

The pervasive difficulty was Hudson's use of his position within the company to advance his own interests without making this apparent to his shareholders, yet the extent to which this actually represented a problem varied from instance to instance. In most cases, of course, his considerable abilities were used only to advance the interests of the shareholders but there were other cases in which there was an abuse of position. Sometimes this involved simple embezzlements of corporate monies. Here Hudson effectively confirmed his guilt by repaying his gains, with interest, to the railway company concerned, once the process of investigation began. Other cases ranged from clear breaches of trust to far more debateable issues concerning the position of shares 'left at the disposal of the directors' and Hudson's own contracts with companies he chaired.

There were five instances where Hudson clearly embezzled money from a railway company of which he was chairman, across the period from early 1844 until late 1847. In February 1844, the York and North Midland agreed to buy two thousand £25 shares in the North British Railway, then building the line from Berwick to Edinburgh, before selling them again in 1846–47. Some of the proceeds were pocketed by Hudson and, therefore, excluded from the books of the York and North Midland, but none of the other directors ever carried out any checks. Once the committee began its inquiries, Hudson repaid just over £60,000, this being the amount owed with interest.[22]

In December 1845, the Newcastle and Berwick charged £37,350 in its published accounts as expenditures on land acquisitions. This covered a series of cheques made out by the company to local landowners, but six of the cheques, totalling £31,000, did not reach their ostensible recipients, the Duke of Northumberland, the Earl of Tankerville, Earl Grey, Lady Mary Stanley, Sir W. M. Ridley and the Earl of Carlisle. Instead, in a flagrant breach of proper banking practice, they were paid into Hudson's personal account at the York Union Bank in January 1845. The cheques had all been signed by Hudson and countersigned by either Robert Davies or James Richardson, close friends of his; the cheques, as returned through the banking system, were the only vouchers presented to the auditors to evidence the transactions. Hudson refunded the monies to the York Newcastle and Berwick, with interest for the three-year period, within days of the Committee of Inquiry being appointed.[23]

At the end of July 1846, Hudson helped to negotiate the purchase of the Wisbech line on behalf of the Eastern Counties, which had agreed to buy their shares at a premium of £2 each. Neither Hudson nor Waddington, his Vice-Chairman, held any shares in the Wisbech and they decided it was time to acquire some at face value. On the day of the contract, Hudson told Mr Day, the solicitor of the Wisbech Company, that 'out of the unissued shares he must make out scrip for five hundred shares for himself and for Mr Waddington. Mr Day refused with indignation'. Hudson and Waddington instead each embezzled £1000 of Eastern Counties money in order to arrive at the position they would have achieved but for Day's refusal to cooperate.[24]

A special meeting of York Newcastle and Berwick shareholders on 26 October 1846, at Hudson's suggestion, agreed to issue stock with a guaranteed annual dividend of 6 per cent, in order to fund the purchase of the Great North of England shares as part of an agreed takeover. From that date, until January 1849, the York Newcastle and Berwick spent nearly £750,000 buying Great North of England shares on the open market by means of a share purchase fund controlled by Hudson. The York Newcastle and Berwick's Committee of Inquiry found that Hudson had simply appropriated almost £27,000 from the share purchase fund for his own use during the year from February 1848, although the Company Secretary, John Close, described the amounts removed as 'errors'. He also confirmed that Hudson had repaid the money with interest in March 1849.[25]

In December 1847, York Newcastle and Berwick cheques totalling £40,000 were drawn in favour of three contractors. Hudson again took the cheques and paid them into his own private bank account at the York Union Bank. As before, the 'vigilance of the auditors was [satisfied] by the mere production of the cheques, without any evidence of the sums having reached the parties to whom they purported to be payable'. On 15 May 1849, soon after the committee was appointed, Hudson refunded the money, with accumulated interest from the date of the misdemeanour.[26]

There were as many as eight instances in which Hudson acted in clear breach of the trust that shareholders were entitled to place in him as a director.

When the York and North Midland took over the Hull and Selby Railway in 1845, they initially leased the line, with an option to purchase Hull and Selby ordinary shares. The York and North Midland bought Hull and Selby shares on the open market, but 40 per cent of their acquisitions were from Hudson personally, of shares that he had bought only a few weeks earlier, for the very purpose of selling them on to the company at a profit. On 23 May 1849, the day before the Committee of Inquiry was established, Hudson returned the profits involved to the York and North Midland, together with the accumulated interest.

When the Hull and Selby takeover took place, all York and North Midland shareholders were entitled to purchase additional shares, which were trading at a good price on the market. Based on his shareholding, Hudson was entitled to buy just over two hundred shares at face value but he instead purchased nearly two thousand. He paid the York and North Midland for the shares he bought but gained the market premiums on far more shares than he was entitled to buy.[27]

On two occasions, loans to the York and North Midland from the Bank of England were diverted to Hudson's own use. The loans were properly repaid but Hudson left the company to pay the interest involved, which came to rather more than £2000.[28] After Hudson had acquired the twelve thousand acre Londesborough estate in East Yorkshire in the summer of 1845 from the Duke of Devonshire, some seventy or eighty acres were needed for the Market Weighton line of the York and North Midland. Hudson went to arbitration over the compensation and was awarded about £20,000 but saw to it that the York and North Midland paid him nearly twice that amount.[29]

Hudson was a partner in the Electric Telegraph Company, which installed its wires along one hundred and sixty miles of the York and North Midland's lines. The installation cost of almost £25,000 was borne by the York and

North Midland, although their only benefit was the free transmission of their own messages. Once the telegraph lines were working, there was a complete failure to differentiate the operations, costs and receipts of the two businesses, with no account ever having been rendered by the Telegraph Company to the York and North Midland for any of the receipts or expenses concerned.[30]

On the formation of the Newcastle and Berwick Railway Company in July 1845, shares in the new company were offered at face value in the first instance to shareholders in the Newcastle and Darlington Junction Railway, *pro rata* to their holdings. Hudson was entitled by his shareholding to buy just under a thousand shares but, on his own authority and without any approval from any shareholders or directors, he instead took up nearly eleven thousand, some of which were shown as being in the ownership of other people, a falsification carried out by Close, the secretary, on Hudson's confidential instructions. Again, Hudson paid for his shares but, with the shares selling at very high premiums, he gained approximately £145,000 on the additional shares.[31]

The day after the York Newcastle and Berwick shareholders agreed to purchase Great North of England shares as part of their agreed takeover, on 27 October 1846, the company bought nearly three thousand five hundred shares from Hudson personally for around £130,000, a price £8400 above their market value. Moreover, Hudson had only bought the Great North of England shares some three weeks before. None of the directors or auditors knew that the York Newcastle and Berwick had bought shares from Hudson personally, except for the two directors who signed the cheques, his close friends James Richardson and Robert Davies.[32]

Finally, by the time of Hudson's downfall, the arrears of call (or instalment) payments on shares at the York Newcastle and Berwick stood at the quite extraordinary level of £185,000. This had two causes. First, those who failed to pay were charged 5 per cent interest on outstanding calls but continued to receive dividend payments averaging about 8 per cent and, secondly, a small number of large debtors, including Hudson, were simply not pressed for payment. Indeed, two shareholders, Hudson and Nicholson, received dividends on shares on which they had paid nothing at all.[33]

Hudson was accused by the Committees of Inquiry of the York and North Midland and York Newcastle and Berwick of acting improperly in three instances where shares were left 'at the disposal of the directors' during the railway mania period of 1845–46. Although the phrase sounds ambiguous, the Committee of Inquiry members understood it to mean merely that the directors had discretion over the timing of the shares being offered to the public.

In order to finance the purchase of the Brandling Junction Railway, in February 1845, the shareholders of the Newcastle and Darlington Junction, which later became part of the York Newcastle and Berwick, agreed to issue a further 22,000 £25 shares. Twenty thousand were made available, at face value, to the existing shareholders *pro rata* to their holdings but the remainder were placed 'at the disposal of the directors'. At the meeting concerned, two shareholders suggested that the surplus shares be presented to Hudson in recognition of the services he had rendered the company, but this proposal was not adopted by the meeting. Instead, the resolution passed 'made it the duty of the directors to dispose of these surplus shares for the benefit of the whole proprietary'. The shareholders were not told that the directors had already promised five hundred of the new shares to Hudson as an appreciation for the way he had arranged the acquisition of the Brandling Junction. Neither were they informed that, on 5 March 1845, the directors decided to place the two thousand shares concerned, then standing at a premium of £21 per share, at the personal disposition of the chairman. Hudson for his part allocated three hundred and twenty of the shares to three of the directors, the company secretary and two company engineers and kept the remainder himself, at a personal profit of £35,000.[34]

In January 1846, when the York and North Midland's £25 shares were trading at a premium in excess of £10 each, the shareholders authorised a major issue of fifty thousand East and West Riding Extension shares. About three-quarters were offered to the shareholders at face value, in proportion to their existing holdings, but the remaining twelve thousand were again left 'at the disposal of the directors'. About half of these shares were allocated at face value to Hudson and his fellow directors, which the Committee found objectionable, given their value on the open market.[35] The allocations included:

1. Six hundred shares, distributed equally between six directors of the York and North Midland, including Hudson, as agreed at a board meeting on 5 October 1846. Two other directors had refused the shares, as they considered the allotment unethical, but they did not bring the matter to the attention of the members.

2. Nine hundred and fifty shares to investors in the Whitby Building Company, set up by Hudson in 1843 to develop the town as a resort and thereby also advance his chances of becoming MP for Whitby. Hudson, as the largest investor, took five hundred of the shares and the remainder were shared between his close colleagues at the York and North Midland: Nicholson, Richardson, Davies, Jennings, Close and Andrews.

3. Two thousand shares supposedly sold on behalf of the company in the second half of 1847, but where the gains of £16,000 could not be found in the York and North Midland's books.

4. Nine hundred and fifty shares apparently given by Hudson to 'various parties to advance the interests of the York and North Midland'. Hudson would not name the people concerned and said only that they had had 'a great fight in Parliament and ... one cannot very well tell all these transactions ... under similar circumstances I should be prepared to do the same tomorrow; I had no motive but to do what was right. I thought these parties were richly entitled to them for their services and friendly disposition to the company at a time when it was sorely assailed ... it's no use shutting one's eyes to the facts. A company at that time could not get on without allotting shares; we found we could not'.

5. Eleven hundred shares that Hudson admitted appropriating.[36]

The Committee called on the directors concerned to refund the premiums on shares they had appropriated and on Hudson personally to account for the shares allegedly sold or allotted to unknown third parties.[37]
Also in January 1846, the Newcastle and Berwick shareholders agreed to a further issue of 64,000 £25 shares. 52,000 of these were allotted rateably to the existing shareholders of the company and the remainder were once again left 'at the disposal of the directors'. Hudson took up nearly six hundred shares, then trading on the markets at a premium of about £9 a share. As soon as the Committee began its investigations, Hudson repaid the amounts involved of more than £5000 back to the York Newcastle and Berwick.[38]

Hudson contracted in 1845–46 with companies of which he was a director, for the sale of iron rails and shares in the Sunderland Dock Company contrary to sections 85 and 86 of the Companies Clauses Consolidation Act of 1845. Hudson often bought rails, apparently in his own name, when he thought the price was low, and later sold the rails when needed by the railway companies he managed, at the current market price.[39] Thus, early in 1845, he took out a contract for ten thousand tons of iron rails with Thompson and Foreman of London at £6 10s. per ton. Two weeks later, the Provisional Committee of the Newcastle and Berwick, chaired by Hudson, invited tenders for the supply of twenty thousand tons of rails and in March they bought fourteen thousand tons from Thompson and Forman at a price of £12 per ton. When the rails were supplied, half were in fact part of Hudson's consignment, on which he made a gain of nearly £40,000.[40]

The Newcastle and Berwick's own advert for twenty thousand tons of iron rails had done a good deal to quickly raise the price, as other contracts were being sought at the time and the market was already rising. Normal practice would have been to advertise for only five thousand tons, even if twenty were wanted, precisely in order to avoid inflating the market price. The rate at which iron rail prices had risen was most unusual and the ironmaster William Crawshay was highly critical of the way the Newcastle and Berwick had gone about things. He thought their approach thoroughly imprudent and quite unprecedented.[41]

In 1846, Hudson bought three thousand tons of rails at £9 a ton from the same supplier. These had been intended for the Leeds and Bradford line, which in fact did not need them, so they were allocated instead to the York and North Midland, which did. An invoice was sent by Thompson and Foreman to the York and North Midland but, following Hudson's instructions to Mr Close, a York and North Midland clerk made a copy of the statement from Thompson's, but changed the price from £9 to £12 a ton, that being the market price at the time. A cheque for the full amount was given to Close, who handed it to Hudson, who paid Thompson's their £9 a ton and kept the remaining £9000 himself.[42] Given the position in which Hudson had placed himself in dealing personally with the company of which he was chairman, the rail purchases should have been reported to the board of directors, and recorded in their minutes but 'unfortunately this was not done'. Thus, neither the increase in price from £9 to £12 a ton nor the supply by Hudson of his own rails to the company were known to the general body of directors, who believed that the York and North Midland had simply bought the rails themselves in the usual way.[43]

When Hudson became the Tory candidate for Sunderland in the summer of 1845 he promised, as an important part of his appeal to the electorate, to promote a new dock in the town. Subsequently the York Newcastle and Berwick, on the advice of their Chairman, Hudson, who by then was also Chairman of the Sunderland Dock Company, invested substantial sums of money in the Sunderland Dock Company, although the benefits were uncertain and only loosely connected with their railway business. The York Newcastle and Berwick also purchased more than two thousand Sunderland Dock Company shares from Hudson personally; he had never intended to buy them himself but, when concerns were expressed at a meeting on 27 February 1847 about the large discount at which the shares were then being quoted, he said rather grandly that he would 'take up the shares of any gentleman at par, who might be disposed to sell them'. Hudson doubtless meant this merely as a show of confidence that would stifle anxieties but, when he was offered shares at the end of the meeting, he could hardly refuse to buy them. Despite every indication that the offer was an impromptu, personal initiative, Hudson subsequently told the Committee of Inquiry that he had made his purchases on behalf of the York Newcastle and Berwick, which was why he had transferred the shares and the related losses to the company. The most that Hudson had done to inform his co-directors was to talk to two directors, Richardson and Wood, 'on the sands at Sunderland, on the morning of the dock meeting' concerned. No minute relating to the transaction appeared in the directors' minute-books for two years, until the appointment of a Committee of Investigation was imminent and then in terms that showed all too clearly that the Board had previously known nothing about it.[44]

Apart from the legal prohibition on contracting between directors and their companies, whenever contracts were not properly approved by the board, Hudson was able to benefit from a fundamental and important asymmetry; speculations that led to price increases could be treated as personal contracts, as in the case of the rail contracts, whereas unsuccessful speculations, such as the Dock Company, could instead be viewed as contracts of the railway company concerned.

Financial reporting was subject to very few controls in the first half of the nineteenth century. The statutory requirements were modest; directors were expected to appoint a bookkeeper and cause 'full and true accounts to be kept of all sums of money received or expended on account of the company' and see that the books were balanced half yearly, at least two weeks before each general meeting at which a balance sheet was to be presented, but very little was said in the legislation as to how the accounts themselves were to be drawn up and how the 'distinct view of the profit or loss which shall have arisen' was to be determined, beyond the basic requirement that no dividend was to be paid that would reduce the capital of the business.[45]

The protection afforded by the routine audits of the time was also very limited. The Acts establishing the Eastern Counties and the York and North Midland railways, in common with many other Acts of the 1830s, made no provision for the appointment of auditors. When they were appointed, which became common practice during the 1840s, they were typically shareholders acting on behalf of their colleagues. This was consistent with the pervasive rationale of the time, that it was the shareholders, rather than professional auditors or government regulators, who should hold directors to account, although in practice this could only provide very limited protection.[46]

In two ways, however, shareholders in Hudson's railway companies had more powers than their counterparts have nowadays. They did have the right to inspect the books of the company themselves at specified times and they were also able to set up committees of inquiry, sometimes called committees of investigation or inspection, when they were dissatisfied with the directors' handling of the company's affairs. These committees were capable of carrying out very detailed investigations and could, when necessary, employ accountants to help them with the more technical matters.[47]

As far as the Committee of Inquiry could tell, until 1845 the board of directors at the York and North Midland had functioned reasonably satisfactorily as a body, with each member having 'some voice in the administration of the company's affairs'. From that date onwards, however, with the government giving 'undue encouragement to new railway schemes', Hudson became the 'almost sole and absolute manager, the rest retaining little beyond the bare name of directors'.[48]

During the period 1846–8, when Hudson dominated the management of the company's affairs, there was a great deal of false accounting. The committee showed the falsifications in some detail both in the main body of their fourth report and in the accountant's appendices thereto. Their main conclusions, as regards the profit and loss accounts for the three years 1846–48, were that the profits of that period as a whole had been deliberately overstated by about £68,000 and that this had been brought about by three devices: by leaving expenditures out of the accounts (£28,000); by overstating traffic income (£26,000); and by treating expenses as assets (£14,000). To facilitate the latter, three special accounts had been opened in the company's books for construction, station and sundry expenditures, 'with no other view than as a cover to fictitious entries'. The end result was the distribution of the overstated profits in the form of dividends.[49]

Over the three-year period, almost exactly an eighth of the profits as reported were fictitious, 10 per cent of the profits in 1846, 8 per cent in 1847 and nearly 20 per cent in 1848. The falsehoods were not such as to convert losses into profits but they were sufficient to mask an increasing decline from the high profitability of the York and North Midland's earlier years.

Despite the poor state of the company's books, the committee was quite clear in its own mind that the accounts of the York Newcastle and Berwick Railway and its predecessor companies, particularly the Newcastle and Darlington Junction, had been systematically falsified by its officers from the time the Newcastle and Darlington had begun to operate as a railway in 1844. The total discrepancy was estimated at almost £122,000 and had been achieved by four mechanisms: by leaving expenditures out of the accounts (£60,000); by treating expenses as assets (£31,000); by the creation of fictitious assets (£16,000); and by overstating traffic income (£15,000).[50]

The largest items of expenditure omitted from the accounts were repairs to locomotives (£11,000), bills for fuel, gas and water (£11,000) and the company's Income Tax liability for 1848 (£5000). More than half the expenses treated as assets (some £18,000) consisted of loan interest that should have been charged against profits once the period of construction was over and the railway's lines were in use, while the remainder consisted of an extra-ordinary number of the most obvious revenue expenses that could not possibly have been confused with assets, including the costs of printing tickets, the costs of buying candles, and amounts paid to customers as compensation for the loss of their luggage. Amongst the fictitious assets that had been created was an amount of £11,630 shown as being due by a customer, a Mr Harrison, 'who did not owe the company any sum whatever'.[51]

The level of distortion in the published profit figures for the second half of 1844, for 1845 and for 1846, mainly concerning the Newcastle and Darlington Railway, was not substantial; just under 10 per cent of the published profits were fictitious. The level of misrepresentation in the published results of the York Newcastle and Berwick railways in 1847 and 1848 was far more serious, however; close on 20 per cent of the reported profits in 1847 and almost 30 per cent in 1848 were bogus. Once again this did not turn losses into profits but it did hide the fact that the great route to the north was earning only moderate profits when trading conditions deteriorated after the end of the railway mania. Thus, behind the optimistic facade that Hudson had erected, the viability of the projected route north was far from certain.

By way of contrast, the Midland Committee of Inquiry found that the published accounts of the company were in accordance with its books and that the accounting practices at the Midland were of similar standard to those of other well-run railway companies. Their report went on to consider a number of more optional accounting changes, concerning relatively technical aspects of railway operations, including rail replacement and upgrading, the treatment of engines awaiting repair and of light engines taken out of service to be replaced by heavier locomotives, the costs of wagon and carriage replacement and the depreciation of the permanent way.[52]

These parts of the report suggested that increased allowance be made for depreciation of the company's rolling stock and permanent way and, after a long discussion, the shareholders decided to set aside an extra £35,000 from accumulated profits for this purpose. The adoption of this more cautious position towards future uncertainties absorbed about 2 per cent of the published profits in the period from July 1844 to December 1848 but it was essentially discretionary and did not indicate any defects in the Midland's practices while Hudson had been Chairman.

At the Eastern Counties Railway, Hudson practised false accounting on an astonishing scale.[53] The details were set out in the single Committee of Inquiry report presented to the shareholders in late April 1849. The report confirmed that the company had never been able to escape the consequences of the hugely wasteful spending of the early years, which meant virtually all their capital had been used up in the construction of less than half the intended route. Not surprisingly, Hudson had not been able to turn around the company's fortunes, although he had clearly decided from the outset to give every appearance of having done so.

He made sure, throughout the time he was chairman, that the presentation of the accounting statements was subordinated to the payment of dividends that would make the company look far more successful than it had been previously. As early as 22 December 1845, for example, Hudson decided that a dividend of nine shillings per share would be paid for the second half of that year, three times as much as in the first half, even though the accounting period did not end until 4 January 1846. When the internal accounts were properly completed, they certainly did not show that any such dividend had been earned but they were altered prior to publication, with the traffic expenses 'squared to suit the dividend'.[54] This was not an isolated occurrence. The company accountant, Davis, confirmed that throughout the time Hudson was chairman, 'items of expenditure were diminished and those of receipts were increased' in the statements laid before the shareholders. Two employees alleged that Hudson had on occasions even written into the accounts the figures he wanted to see, although he strongly denied this.[55]

The Quilter Ball Report, which covered rather more than Hudson's term on the Eastern Counties Board, quantified the overall profit overstatement at more than £353,000, brought about by the misclassification of expenses as assets (£202,000), by the omission of expenses from the accounts (£93,000), and by the inclusion of fictitious revenues (£58,000).

There was no doubting the deliberate intention in this process: the overwhelming mass of the expenses that were treated as assets consisted of items that could not possibly have been thought of as anything other than operating expenses, such as wage payments to engine drivers, porters and other employees, office expenses, stationery, locomotive repairs, postage, bad debts

and even the costs of keeping the company's horses. Some two-thirds of
the omitted expenses consisted of arrears of interest, while the fictitious
revenues largely resulted from the deliberate overstatement of amounts
supposedly due to the Eastern Counties by other railway companies.[56] The
overstatement of profits was on an extraordinary scale; almost 40 per cent
of the published profits in 1845 were false, as were two-thirds of those in
1846, more than 40 per cent of those in 1847 and just over half of those
for 1848.[57]

The twelve reports produced by the various Committees of Inquiry put
information in the public domain that shocked investors and the general
public of the time and forced a reassessment of Hudson's methods and
achievements. The findings at the four main companies were not, however,
consistent; there were major differences between the way Hudson had
behaved at the two York-based companies and at the Midland and the
Eastern Counties.

Although Hudson's name in present times has often been associated with
false accounting, the revelations of personal malfeasance and other covert
ways of diverting company money to his own use mattered much more to
his contemporaries and did far more to ruin his reputation. Hudson did
not embezzle money from either the Eastern Counties or the Midland
railway companies but, at the York-based York and North Midland and
York Newcastle and Berwick, where his extraordinary initiative and enterprise had given him total control, numerous types of fraud and misdealing
took place, including clear breaches of trust and the diversion of very
substantial amounts of money to Hudson's pockets in what one newspaper
described as a 'vast aggregate of avaricious and flagitious jobbing for the
accumulation of wealth'.[58]

Despite this, Hudson was never prosecuted. In large part this was because
the laws of the time generally expected the shareholders to resolve their
own problems and to sue for any losses they had suffered. In those cases
where Hudson was most obviously culpable, as concerning the York Newcastle and Berwick cheques written out to landowners and contractors, the
shareholders did not need to take legal action as he had repaid the amounts
concerned, with interest, before the committee investigations began.

In other instances, however, the issues were more complex and took legal
action by the members to resolve. Some of the time, while it was clear that
Hudson had acted deceptively and covertly, it was less obvious exactly what
the company or its members had lost. Thus, when Hudson sold his rails
on to the York and North Midland, the company of which he was chairman,
he covertly charged them the then current market price of £12 per ton, his

profit on the transaction arising only because he had purchased the rails at an earlier market price of £9 per ton. Hudson was in breach of the statutory prohibition on directors having an interest in any contract with their company, had not acted openly and might have even helped to rig the market price, but the only statutory penalty was disqualification from office, which meant very little where Hudson had already resigned before the committee's inquiries began.[59] A number of share allotments had brought him major financial gains, but not by a process of simple misappropriation. When the York and North Midland was allocating its new extension shares to the existing shareholders at face value, each shareholder expected to gain market premiums in proportion to their holdings. Hudson gave himself a much larger share than he was entitled to, which earned him excess premiums, but the company had properly received the face value of the shares concerned. Equally clearly Hudson had acted improperly, but the identity of those who had lost was not so obvious. Moreover, he could justifiably claim to have been the main cause of the high premiums in the first place.

To defend himself against other accusations, Hudson juxtaposed two alternative doctrines, personal responsibility and more general stewardship obligations, in saying that 'so far from considering myself in the light of a trustee and therefore disqualified from acting in any other character, I may say with truth that I have never hesitated to take upon myself any amount of personal responsibility the interests of the company might require'.[60] His apparent inability to distinguish personal responsibility from legally defined directorial or stewardship duty was, however, ultimately disingenuous. He must have been aware that the lack of clarity concerning his personal role, either as an influential private individual or as a company representative, provided an extremely valuable asymmetry. If a speculation went well, it could be treated as Hudson's own, as in the case of some of the rail contracts; if it went badly, it could instead be treated as the company's contract, as in the case of the purchase of shares in the Sunderland Dock Company. Although Hudson sought to project himself as someone effectively indistinguishable from the company itself and who was bound to act in its members' interests, somewhat akin to a feudal lord, he actually practised the far more modern ability of advancing his own interests by misusing other people's money subscribed under the doctrine of limited liability.

The accounting statements provided by the four companies, while Hudson was their chairman, had also been subject to very different levels of manipulation. At the Eastern Counties, a venture almost ruined by spending decisions made before Hudson's arrival, more than half the published profits were false, as compared with a fifth at the York Newcastle and Berwick, one-eighth at the York and North Midland and at most a fiftieth at the Midland. Moreover, whereas the improvement in profitability at the Eastern Counties after Hudson took control was almost entirely due to his false accounting, at the York and North Midland and York Newcastle and Berwick accounting misrepresentations did not transform operational failure into apparent success but instead masked a relatively moderate decline in profits in the more difficult trading conditions that followed the ending of the mania period.

These differences are broadly reflective of the different pressures that Hudson faced at each of his four main companies. When he eventually agreed to become Chairman of the Eastern Counties, the company was already in difficulty. In order to achieve his own strategic objectives, he needed to effect a very rapid transformation in the apparent fortunes of the company. At the York-based companies the situation was very different. Hudson had been with them since they began. In particular he knew that the York and North Midland's core routes were highly profitable, even if returns on the new extensions to the coast and elsewhere were far lower. Much of his reputation had been built on the genuine 10 per cent dividends the York and North Midland had earned in the early 1840s and his false accounting was designed, as at the York Newcastle and Berwick, to maintain the impressive level of distributions even when operating performance began to fade. At the Midland, on the other hand, operating results and dividends remained at an entirely satisfactory level, without accounting manipulations, throughout the time Hudson was chairman.

It has often been asserted that 'questionable tactics' by railway company directors were commonplace during the first half of the nineteenth century, leading to the payment of dividends out of capital and that there were 'many instances ... of fraud on a grand scale' perpetrated by promoters during the mania,[61] although few other instances have actually been cited.[62] The reports of the Committees of Inquiry into Hudson's practices undoubtedly brought general discredit to an industry already struggling in the aftermath of the mania, but the level of fraud perpetrated by George Hudson was almost certainly unique, reflecting the importance of the companies he chaired and the amount of control he had over their affairs.[63]

During the early Victorian period, in which Hudson appropriated huge sums of money from the York Newcastle and Berwick and large sums from the York and North Midland without the knowledge of the shareholders or other directors, the personal incentives available to enterprising company directors were surprisingly meagre. Entrepreneurs who ran their own businesses, in an age of very low taxes, could make very substantial gains from their enterprise, but company directors generally received only modest fees.

Whereas many company directors in modern times have been encouraged to succeed by substantial share option schemes and profit-related bonuses, in early Victorian England directors were often treated as if they were custodians of a municipal office in which a strong sense of duty was their most important attribute. On occasions, it was said quite explicitly that directors should carry out their duties and not expect more than their allotted fees, which were typically modest. As a result, Hudson was effectively expected to earn large amounts for shareholders without receiving any major reward for his unusual enterprise, an expectation that he found increasingly vexing as the scale of his activities, and the benefits it brought to others, increased.

Inevitably, the revelations of wrongdoing caused Hudson's achievements as a businessman and promoter to be reassessed. No longer could he be seen as a man of almost alchemical powers. Clearly, he had not after all been able to achieve the impossible and transform the commercial fortunes of the Eastern Counties Railway. The mass of evidence in the York and North Midland committee reports also tended to confirm the view of the *Railway Times* that the company's success was really due to the fact that their main line was 'of easy and therefore cheap construction [and] it traverses a much-travelled district', rather than to 'any special merit in its managers'.[64] The York and North Midland's line extensions, beginning with the line to Scarborough, had in reality paid very poorly, as Captain Laws had predicted they would.[65]

Against this, even if the York and North Midland and the York Newcastle and Berwick had not survived the railway mania as well as Hudson had claimed, they were still in fairly good shape despite the difficult trading conditions of the late 1840s. Further, nothing he had achieved at the Midland, where he had pioneered a far-sighted amalgamation that anticipated coming trends in the railway industry, had been tarnished, even by a searching investigation. The ability and vision he had shown in bringing together a number of disparate interests to construct an east coast route to the north remains a hugely impressive achievement even when some of his ways of proceeding have been seen as disreputable. At the time, however, his shareholders felt utterly deceived and their retribution was swift and severe.

8

Holding On

It is ironic, or perhaps fitting, that the man who had so expertly manipulated the newspapers to catch the attention of investors from all over the country should now find those same organs of the press acting just as effectively to broadcast his own failings to a fascinated and incredulous readership.

Once the various committees of inquiry had completed their work, the accusations followed thick and fast. The consequent decline in his public standing was so precipitous that some of his former critics even became sympathetic. On 12 May 1849, for example, the day after the Eastern Counties shareholders had crowded into the large ballroom of the London Tavern to consider the report of the Cash Committee, *Herapath's Journal*, as always expressing the interests of the ordinary railway investor, said 'whatever may have been the errors or faults of Mr Hudson, there is no man but must feel for him, on account of the crowd of misfortunes which have lately come tumbling in upon him'.

Throughout that spring, the press paid enormous attention to his affairs. The publicity he received, as one report after another was published, was very bad indeed. The *Money Market Examiner* saw him as 'irrecoverably lost' and the *Yorkshireman*, always hostile to Hudson, felt itself thoroughly vindicated by the turn of events and lost no opportunity to condemn his behaviour.

Punch, on the other hand, took it all in its stride and merely included a mock advert in its columns

> To be disposed of (a Bargain), almost as good as new, albeit a little tarnished, an IRON CROWN that has been worn for a very few years, and is now disposed of, no longer fitting its late owner. Any Ex-King, disappointed of a diadem of the aforesaid metal, will find the Iron Crown in question a good, stout, serviceable article – apply at the Railway Station, York.[1]

There were a number of other journals and newspapers that avoided the obvious course of heaping personal blame on Hudson and brought the more complex aspects of the affair to the attention of their readers. The *Atlas*, for example was thoroughly puzzled by what had happened; surely Hudson, 'whose very nod could cause railway shares to rise 10 per cent in the market' could have found much safer ways of enriching himself. Whereas nothing could have veiled his chosen means of making money, the 'deep mist of figures in the hands of an accountant waiting beside the desk of the chairman' could have kept many other transactions entirely 'secure from the certainty of public reprobation'.[2]

The *Times*, never comfortable with the 'get-rich-quick' fervour in the railway industry, was not ungenerous towards Hudson, seeing in him a victim of unreasonable temptation, a casualty of the mood of the age. In an editorial published in mid-April 1849, it argued for greater understanding of his position, arguing that

> neither the other officials nor the shareholders must hope to escape censure under the cover of a personal onslaught upon Mr Hudson. The system is to blame. It was a system without rule, without order, without even a definite morality. In 1845, respectable men did monstrous things and were thought very clever. Thousands rejoiced in premiums which they believed to have been puffed up by mere trickery, collusion and imposture ... Now Mr Hudson's position was not only new to himself, but absolutely a new thing in the world altogether. His subjects exalted him to the position of those early kings who knew no difference between their own purse and the public exchequer ... between the aggrandisement of their family and the good of the people ... or between prerogative and law. Hudson was the William the Conqueror of railways and his system of government and of equity was rather intuitive than legal. His colleagues knew this. The shareholders knew it ... it was their own choice. They preferred a slovenly and irregular despotism. Parliament over and over again wished to give them the benefit of a public audit and they refused it. Why? Among other reasons, because they had a misgiving that there were things necessary to the success of railway operations which would not quite stand a stiff official scrutiny. We think the King and his subjects are much of a piece ... Mr Hudson found himself everything at once; a large shareholder, a comprehensive projector, a chairman, a trustee for shareholders, an agent for particular transactions, a broker, a contractor, a banker, a confidential friend of landowners and a good deal more besides. Had he discharged all these functions with perfect fairness, he would have been little less than an angel and that he certainly is not.[3]

A fortnight later, the paper again argued movingly against the hypocrisy of those who now sought to distance themselves from Hudson

> Hudson appeared to mankind in a good hat and a coat of the best Saxony cloth, corpulent and jolly, bustling and forward, rather rude of speech but said to be very quick at figures and with a remarkable show of that common sense which in these days is held to be a sufficient substitute for the spiritual gifts usually claimed by fanatics ... Hurrying about here and there, he sustained a sort of

ubiquity, attending numberless meetings of shareholders, making brief and not very intelligible addresses, snubbing questioners with very short replies ... There in the secretary's parlour sat Hudson and his trusty friend 'cooking' the accounts ... the last figure in the calculation was always written first ... We are not disposed to let the impostor off, but neither can we pardon his dupes. In fact they are dupes only now that the imposture is discovered and its profits have vanished. Everybody knew the contents of the cauldron seething in the company's kitchen. When a 3 per cent dividend had been declared at Midsummer and before the half-year's accounts could possibly be made out a dividend of 9 per cent was declared for Christmas, everybody who had a pair of eyes in his head must have known that the last dividend was arbitrary and fraudulent. It raised shares, however, in the market ... so long as Hudson was successful in keeping up the price of shares he enjoyed unlimited confidence.[4]

A few days later they returned to the same subject in their editorial columns and called for some understanding of the position in which Hudson now found himself

He no more caused the railway mania than Napoleon caused the French Revolution. He was its child, its ornament and its boast ... His talent for organisation was prodigious. No labour or speculation seemed too vast for his powers. He combined and systematised the attacks of a hundred bands upon the public purse; he raised all the fares, he lowered all the speed, he reduced all the establishments, he 'cooked' all the reports, and he trebled all the shares ... The shareholders wanted their dividends doubled, and their shares raised to a proportionate market value. They never calculated the extent to which these achievements were honestly practicable, or considered the measures to which it would be necessary to resort. They wanted the trick done at once, and Hudson was the man to do it. He promised impossibilities, but he gave a very good imitation of them ... in ancient times, a man ran into the city of Athens announcing to its excitable population the gain of a splendid victory. For twenty-four hours all was joy and congratulation. When the succeeding morning brought the real truth to light, and the author of the previous delusion was seized and maltreated. 'Am I to blame', said he, 'O Athenians, for having given you one happy day?'

Moreover, they also saw the incentives that Hudson was offered as simply inadequate to the situation

the companies had perhaps no title to monopolise Mr Hudson's cunning to the exclusion of his private interests. They had not bought him in full entirety and they seemed to have forgotten that he had his own fortunes to make as well as theirs.[5]

The *Illustrated London News* also pointed out the important general lessons to be learnt and condemned the way that the 'crowd of speculators who attempted to enrich themselves by gambling in shares [were] loud in the expression of their horror' at Hudson's recently revealed transactions. The truth was

> that Mr Hudson is neither better nor worse than the morality of 1845. He rose to wealth and importance in an immoral period; he was the creature of an immoral system and ... it is rather too much to expect of him that he should be purer than his time or his associates. Men who would have scorned to do a dishonest act towards any other real tangible living man, did not scruple to do acts against that great abstraction, the public, which no morality could justify ... Had there been no insane lust for unearned and unmerited wealth, there would have been no 'Railway King' ... the public made him and the public is to blame for him. Let Mr Hudson be condemned, therefore, where he has done wrong; but let the public not shut its eyes against its own folly, without which Mr Hudson would have been a very insignificant, but doubtless a most respectable person.[6]

As soon as the first accusations had been substantiated, Hudson's credibility suffered immediate and enormous damage. The shareholders in every enterprise he managed (and not only the railway companies) were on their guard and his business colleagues quickly scrutinised his various dealings in order to establish their own degree of exposure. Hudson soon found it necessary to resign all his railway chairmanships even though, at the Midland, his conduct appeared to have been blameless. In July 1849 he also left the Electric Telegraph Company, which had some dealings with the railway companies, with the full consent of the other partners, although he did receive back his capital plus another £500.[7]

Some of his most fraudulent railway dealings had involved the payment of cheques into the York Union Bank, where he had been chairman since August 1841. The other directors of the bank lost no time in carrying out their own internal investigations, mindful of Hudson's close working relationship with Wilkinson, manager of the York office, who had been forced to resign in December 1848 when his unauthorised and unsecured overdraft had become apparent. They discovered a number of irregularities and Hudson, who had continued to chair the weekly meetings, resigned by means of a letter read to and accepted by the board of the bank on 11 July 1849.[8] He owed huge sums to the bank, both in his own name and in the name of the Whitby Building Company, as well as to the York-based railway companies. The sale of most of his landed estates became inevitable.

At a special meeting of the Board in January 1850, the directors of the bank resolved to retain all available securities until Hudson paid the 'whole of the monies owing by him' and, on 16 January 1850, they were greatly relieved to receive a cheque for £200,000, from the sale of his Londesborough estate. This cleared much of his personal liability to the bank and enabled them, at the annual general meeting that took place the following month, to confront the accumulated bad news of the last eighteen months. They accordingly wrote off 'serious amounts of losses' (£25,700) from the reserve fund, most of which was to cover Wilkinson's unauthorised and irrecoverable overdraft. As they judged, the proposed dividend of eight per cent, with more than £5000 maintained in the reserve fund, provided sufficient reassurance to their members and spared the Board from the necessity of going into too many details on 'the long protracted difficulties and anxieties' to which they had been subject. The securities they held enabled them to avoid any discussion of the amounts owed by the Whitby Building Company or of Hudson's ability to meet the scheduled payments, even though these were to cause them problems for many years to come.[9]

With relief the directors of the York Union Bank were able to draw a line publicly under the 'extraordinary events' that had cost them the services of two directors in the past year.[10] They looked forward to better times. The same could not be said for their founder and former chairman, George Hudson.

Hudson's dishonest business dealings had no implications for the funds of York corporation but of course his political credibility was completely destroyed. He was now extremely unpopular with the many investors of York, whose shares had quickly lost much of their value, and he immediately dropped out of York politics. The Tories at first appeared to escape any substantial fall-out from his public disgrace. At the municipal elections of November 1849, although the Liberals campaigned vigorously on the theme of a Tory vote being a vote for Hudson, to everyone's surprise they gained only two of the twelve available seats, which hardly disturbed the comfortable Tory majority.[11]

Nonetheless, when the new council met there was a minor purge. Hudson's aldermanic seat was declared vacant, by unanimous decision, on the grounds that he had been absent for six months and had ceased to be a citizen of York. The council also agreed that Hudson Street be renamed Railway Street, although a proposal that Hudson's portrait be removed from the Mansion House was defeated by two votes, there being nine abstentions, including that of his long-standing Liberal adversary, George Leeman. The seat of Wilkinson (the disgraced manager of the York Union Bank), who no longer had a place of business in the city, was also declared vacant and, shortly afterwards, Robert Davies resigned from the council.[12]

The effects of Hudson's downfall were felt rather more in the municipal elections of November 1850, when eleven of the twelve retiring councillors were Tories. The Liberals combined anti-Hudson sentiment with an emphasis on the need to reduce the price of gas and water and won eight of the seats, to gain a majority (25–23) for the first time since the 1830s. Fortuitously, this gave them control over the aldermanic elections at a time when five of the six retirees were Tory, and provided them with the basis for a secure and lasting majority. By July 1852 they were in control of two-thirds of the municipal seats but this did not greatly influence the parliamentary election held that month. The Liberals fielded two candidates, the establishment Whig Milner and the Radical Vincent, the same two men who had fought each other at the by-election in 1848. Smyth, whom Hudson had proposed exactly five years before, distanced himself from Hudson, took a more reformist position, and entered a *de facto* alliance with the Whigs. He topped the poll (with 1871 votes), with Milner taking the second seat (1831 votes). Vincent was a distant third with 887 votes.

It was not only his associates in business and politics who broke their connections with Hudson. Society was just as quick to turn its back on him. As early as February 1849, at the house of Lord Edward Stanley, he was made to understand that his presence would not be welcome until certain matters had been sorted out. Of course, matters were anything but resolved and so Hudson found himself cut by many of those who had once enjoyed his lavish hospitality and valued his investment advice.[13]

If this was hard to take, worse was to come. On 8 May 1849 the body of his brother-in-law, Richard Nicholson, was pulled out of the River Ouse. The day after Hudson had been attacked in Parliament, Nicholson had been walking along the river towards the city centre, after dinner at about eight o'clock. He had not drunk heavily with his meal, but several passers-by had observed his low state of mind. His body was recovered from the river by two boatmen at about ten o'clock that same evening. The previous week he had been restless and less cheerful than usual. It was now widely assumed that he had committed suicide in a state of depression connected to the fact that some of the Great North of England shares resold by Hudson to the York Newcastle and Berwick had been taken out in his name.

This was a grievous blow to both the Hudsons. Elizabeth's brother had been the fifteen-year-old George Hudson's first employer at the draper's shop in Cathedral Street. Six years later they had become related by marriage and extended their close association into their many business connections. We know relatively little about Richard Nicholson's character but he was clearly very different from his brother-in-law, being described in his obituary as one who lived a quiet and unostentatious life, collecting fine paintings and obtaining great pleasure from promoting the happiness of those around him.[14]

For Hudson to lose such a close relative, knowing that the death was an indirect consequence of his own misdemeanours, was hard to bear. He retreated with his family to the seclusion of Newby Park, emerging only to give evidence to the various committees. He and Elizabeth remained very close and, during this time, he confided to a good friend that 'the greatest comfort he had when all the world seemed against him was his wife and he thought that if he had not received that comfort it would have been too much for him'.[15]

Life continued to be difficult for the Hudsons socially. In January 1851, Hudson let it be known that he and Elizabeth would attend a civic gathering at York's Assembly Rooms, perhaps as a means of 'testing out the waters', but the *Yorkshireman* was still as hostile as ever and openly advised the other guests to ostracise the couple. In the light of this, the Hudsons decided not to attend the gathering.[16]

In spite of these and other setbacks the ostracism was not total and he was able to maintain some of his public duties. In Sunderland and Whitby he remained a valued figure. Even in London he continued to attend the occasional function; in April 1851, for example, he and Lord Viscount Seaham were the official stewards for a public dinner at the London Tavern, Bishopsgate, to raise funds for the City of London and East London Dispensary. Nor did he forget his responsibilities. He continued to support worthy causes, being, for example, one of the largest donors to the Artists Benevolent Fund in May 1851.[17] George and Elizabeth were also encouraged when their son George completed his degree at Oxford in autumn 1851 and started his intended career as a barrister.

George Hudson had always loved to be at the centre of things. His enforced absence from the glittering ceremonies held to mark the completion of some of his greatest initiatives was thus particularly painful. But for his downfall, he would have been the focus of each occasion, basking in the recognition of his vision and acumen. Now, he was only the ghost at the party.

One of Hudson's most ambitious projects was the construction of the high-level bridge over the Tyne at Newcastle which was nearing completion when he fell from grace. The removal of the timber framing revealed the attractive and unusual design of a bridge that was thirteen hundred feet in length and would carry trains well over a hundred feet above the Tyne's high water mark. The ribs of the arches, arranged in pairs, each 125 feet in span, rested on piers of 'a peculiarly light construction', with wrought iron tension chains taking the lateral thrust. Square hollow pillars rose from the ribs to support a longitudinal trough girder, from which was suspended the lower roadway, twenty-two feet below the rails. On 15 August 1849, trains began to cross the new bridge and on 28 September 1849 the historic crossing of the Tyne was formally opened by Queen Victoria, on her way south from Scotland.[18]

Later that day, the Queen stopped at York en route from Scotland, to be received by James Meek, Lord Mayor and Chairman of the York Newcastle and Berwick. The royal engine, whose boiler bore the inscription 'Long Live the Queen', in large metal letters 'surmounted by an exquisitely wrought crown', drew into a York station lavishly decorated with flags and evergreens, in front of a crowd of some twenty thousand people. The Queen was given the keys of the city, a 'dutiful address from her loyal citizens' and an elegant lunch in the Banqueting Room, before she resumed her journey about an hour later. The Queen passed through York again a year later, on her way to Castle Howard, and she was met at Normanton by Harry Thompson, now Chairman of the York and North Midland.[19]

The completion of Newcastle Central was celebrated in two separate ceremonies. When the train shed was finished, it 'provided a fitting venue for a celebratory banquet to Robert Stephenson on 30 July 1850', although the formal opening by the Queen did not take place till a month later. The building she opened was most impressive, although Hudson's collapse had caused a substantial scaling-down of John Dobson's magnificent design of 1846. The need to make savings and the political necessity of accommodating the transfer of office staff from York meant the loss of the classic colonnade that would have extended the whole length of the building.[20] Nor was there a place for the pair of statues originally intended to grace the end bays of the arcade, one of George Stephenson and the other of George Hudson; although the former was eventually erected close to the station.[21]

On the same day, 29 August 1850, the Queen also formally opened the Royal Border bridge at Berwick-on-Tweed with more ceremony. Designed by Robert Stephenson, the bridge was more than seven hundred yards wide, consisted of twenty-eight semi-circular arches, springing from lofty piers and had taken over three years to build.[22]

None of the contemporary reports of these occasions make any mention of a conspicuous absence, the absence of the author of the enterprise they had come to celebrate. He should have been on their minds but, by their demeanour, he might never have existed. Although Hudson's position in the railway world, in York business and political circles and in London society was totally compromised, in the north east his position was less badly affected. He had lost his considerable influence as Chairman of the York Newcastle and Berwick Railway but he was still Chairman of the Dock Company, he carried on in business as a partner in Messrs Cookson's Old Glass Works in South Shields and, most important of all, he received an encouraging signal from his constituents to continue to act as MP for Sunderland.[23]

In early May 1849, a deputation from Sunderland visited him at Newby Park with an 'address signed by eight hundred electors, expressive of their confidence in [his] private and public character'. This support came when Hudson was under enormous pressure and he was genuinely moved by the knowledge that he still possessed the 'unshaken confidence and the kind feelings of [his] constituents'. This, he said with some feeling, 'imparts a consolation to my mind for which I can never be sufficiently grateful'.[24] The boost for his morale was timely as the remainder of that month was to prove a severe trial to him. On 7 May 1849, questions were asked in the House of Commons about the position at the Eastern Counties Railway, in particular whether MPs had been bribed in order to further the company's interests. The very next day, his domestic world was deeply shaken by the suicide of his brother-in-law, Richard Nicholson.

Meanwhile, public processes continued remorselessly. Little more than a week later, on 17 May 1849, a petition from some of the Eastern Counties shareholders was presented in Parliament which alleged that Hudson, as Chairman had 'from time to time, caused to be made out and published statements purporting to be true accounts of the receipts and disbursements of the company which he well knew to be false and untrue, whereby the public had been grossly deceived and the petitioners grievously injured'. The petitioners asked the House to inquire into their charges and, if they were proven, to expel Hudson from the House.

In the House, Hudson acknowledged that it was his duty, 'although labouring under considerable difficulty in consequence of domestic affliction', immediately to attend in his place in Parliament. He was given a reasonably sympathetic hearing, partly because of his domestic circumstances and his defence, although highly selective and only obliquely related to the charges, sufficed. He explained that he had become Chairman of the Eastern Counties only when he was pressed by a majority of the shareholders so to do and that, at that time, he had had no shares or other interests in the company. He complained about the processes of the Eastern Counties Committee of Inquiry, which did not give him proper notice of what was being considered. He also cited a number of the findings as inaccurate or unsound. He was shrewd enough to combine the statement that he was 'perfectly ready to bow to any decision the House may come to' with the reminder that 'if the House were by an express enactment, to determine what is capital and what is revenue, what ought to go to capital and what should go to revenue', directors would then have had no difficulty concerning such matters.[25]

He continued to attend Parliament from time to time and to vote, although the pressure of events took a considerable toll on his morale. In April 1849 he thought it politic to attend and vote against the Bill repealing the Navigation Laws, a question of great importance in Sunderland, but, as one observer noted, his public demeanour was now very different from his former bombast

> Instead of the round, burly, imperious-looking person, inflated with import-ance ... who used to roll down the centre of the chamber ... like an empty hogshead on an uneasy sea, until he came beside poor Lord George Bentinck, and brought himself to an anchor [he] slipped into the house under cover of a couple of members, edged along the side seats without attracting notice, and found a hiding-place in the extreme point of the back bench under the shade of the gallery, where he remained *incognito* until the time came for recording his vote ... Alas! That he who so short a time ago was the observed of all observers should be thus left, like the modest flower, to blush unseen in the obscurest corner of the house!

A year later another report described him as trying to steal unnoticed into the House of Commons, sitting in a remote seat as if to escape attention and receiving from his former acquaintances only a 'hurried shake of the hand [and] a distant hurried nod [as] no one can be prevailed upon to give more'.[26] He did in fact speak sometimes in debates, but without his former conceit. In 1850, for example, he spoke on the first reading of a Bill to repeal the duty on bricks, on the postponement of the Stamp Duties Bill and in a debate on the Customs Bill. He also made a speech on shipbuilding and presented a petition in June from Sunderland against the Burgess Lists Bill. In 1851, in April he presented another petition during the budget debates, signed by every shipbuilder in Sunderland, asking for the repeal of the timber duty as this was 'in fact a bonus to foreign shipbuilders'. He also spoke on the Smithfield Removal Bill.[27]

At least, back in Sunderland, he was still able to enjoy some good times. Few people in the town had lost much money over his railway company misdemeanours and his willingness to see to the building of the dock they badly needed ensured his popularity. The official opening of the new docks on June 20 1850 was one of the great days in the history of Sunderland and one that Hudson richly enjoyed. A crowd of around fifty thousand watched him lead a procession towards the river, as a regimental band played, guns fired, flags waved and the bells of the various churches rang out. As the first steamers entered the dock, the river itself was packed with all manner of craft, with their 'rainbow-hued flags' flying and every conceivable vantage point 'thronged with gaily dressed spectators'. Afterwards, at an immense banquet held in a 'capacious structure on the coal jetty', it was Hudson's 'extraordinary talents, indomitable energies and wonderful character' that were so roundly applauded. The main toast was to his health and prosperity and, at the ball, Mrs Christopher Bramwell, wife of the managing director of the Dock Company, led off the dancing with him. The *Sunderland Herald* thought it a day of 'such paramount interest and importance' to the town that all the rest of its history was 'tame and poor' in comparison. For George Hudson, it was just like old times again.[28]

Although the building of the south dock did a great deal to stimulate the level of trade in the town, the returns to the Dock Company's shareholders were altogether more modest. In August 1851, when the first annual general meeting was held, the dividend provided was only 2 per cent and the process for the re-election of outgoing directors, which Hudson controlled by means of proxy votes despite his absence, was condemned as 'a farce'.[29]

In 1852, with elections not far away, Hudson was taking a more active role in the House of Commons. In March, while expressing the gratitude of his constituents for the partial repeal of the timber duties, he urged the Chancellor to do more to reduce the distress in his constituency. In April, he spoke on the Corrupt Practices Bill and, on 1 May 1852, took a prominent part in the debate on the government's financial statement, advocating a 'mixed system of direct taxation and customs and excise duties' and opposing too great a reliance on direct taxation since, 'in times of excitement there would be great difficulty in collecting such taxes'.[30]

When Parliament went into recess, Hudson went back to Sunderland to speak on his political beliefs and on his work in the House representing the town's shipping interests. He showed good timing in announcing, shortly before the election, that additional contracts had been signed between the Dock Company and the York Newcastle and Berwick Railway that would further boost the level of trade. On nomination day, when he mounted the platform, he was hissed by Liberal supporters but a crowd of 'navvies' from the south docks cheered him vociferously, particularly when other speakers said that he had proved himself not only a staunch supporter of the town's interests but also a good 'friend to the working man'. In the election itself, on 8 July 1852, he was greatly helped by divisions within the Liberal party, and the fact that one of their candidates, William Digby Seymour, was an associate of Hudson and son-in-law to J. J. Wright, Hudson's political agent. These two were elected, well ahead of the other Liberal, Henry Fenwick.[31] When the result was known, he expressed his thanks to the electors of Sunderland, who had supported him through many trials; 'when all had forsaken me, Sunderland has remained firm to me. My right hand shall forget her cunning before I forget the favours I have received at your hands', he declared with some feeling.

Later that summer, improvements were being made to the south dock, to the half-tide basin and to the piers of the tidal harbour, although not everything was plain sailing; on one occasion, when Hudson was showing a visiting party of admiring dignitaries round the dock, the sluicing system jammed and they were all soaked by a backwash of filthy water. A junction was also constructed between the Marquess of Londonderry's Seaham Railway and the Durham and Sunderland line, so that more coal could be shipped through the dock. The volume of trade had increased considerably, with dock revenues up by 50 per cent in a year, but the dividend was still only two and a half per cent.[32]

Hudson's increasingly obvious weakness for drink and his financial situation were both beginning to cause him embarrassment in Parliament, where his opponents seized the opportunity for some easy sport. In December 1852, when he spoke out against Radical objections to the cost of the state funeral of the Duke of Wellington, which, he thought, should have been passed 'unanimously and without observation', his old parliamentary adversary, Joseph Hume, the Radical Member for Montrose, said mischievously that he had 'no objection if the honourable gentleman will take a cheque out of his own pocket'. Hudson's heated retort, that he would give a cheque for as much as Hume caused the House a good deal of unkind amusement. A few days later, on 10 December 1852, when he made an interjection, Mr Bernal Osborne played to an appreciative gallery when he said very pointedly that 'at such an early hour of the evening the honourable member for Sunderland had no excuse for interrupting'.[33]

Hudson was not prosecuted for any of his railway company frauds because the legal framework of the time generally assumed that company memberships would act when their own interests had been affected, and they would only be interested in civil actions to recover damages.

In 1849 shares in the Eastern Counties lost over 40 per cent, the Midland 55 per cent, the York Newcastle and Berwick 45 per cent and the York and North Midland over 70 per cent of their share values as the markets struggled to come to terms with the revelations of Hudson's misdemeanours. These losses fuelled the widespread anger against him but there were serious difficulties in establishing and then quantifying the extent of his personal responsibility for them. Instead, the shareholders' legal actions were confined to identifying the corporate monies and other assets that Hudson had misappropriated.

At the Midland there were no such problems and at the Eastern Counties only one transaction was questionable and for an amount that did not really justify legal action. It was the two York-based companies, the York and North Midland and the York Newcastle and Berwick that took civil proceedings against Hudson, based upon the evidence set out in their Committee of Inquiry reports. The actions did not concern the most obvious misappropriations, as Hudson had already made restitutions for these as soon as the committees were set up, in order to reduce his vulnerability to legal action.

Despite this, on 19 July 1849, at the special meeting of the York Newcastle and Berwick which received the Meek Committee's second report, Thompson proposed that the committee be empowered, pending the reconstruction of the Board, to begin legal proceedings against Hudson for the restitution of funds of theirs that he had misapplied, and this was unanimously agreed. However, he made it clear that he did not want to pursue other directors for the premiums on the relatively small numbers of shares they had received. At the time, he pointed out, 'it was considered the perquisite of the Chairman and the directors that shares should be allotted to them [and] if the shareholders had been aware of the transaction at the time ... they would not have been against it'. They should 'be just, and not put the directors in the same category with a man who took shares to the extent of several thousands, and never told his brother directors what he was doing'. Hudson had already repaid £90,000 to the company and, after discussions, he offered to compound with them at a figure to be decided by arbitration. It was agreed that close on £100,000 and the handing over of Hudson's holding of shares in the Sunderland Dock Company would lead to the 'quittance of all claims made upon him by the company'. The compromise, allowing payment in instalments, avoiding legal costs and not requiring any admission of guilt on Hudson's part, was agreed by a special meeting on 8 January 1850. There were objections, especially from A. H. Wylie of Liverpool, who felt that they were being rushed into an agreement too favourable to Hudson. They 'were giving away their character, and almost compounding a felony', but Leeman, chairing the meeting for the first time, explained that if they did not take the money now, they might find that 'the bird had flown' and that Hudson's resources had gone to other creditors. Another shareholder, Robert Clayton (a member of the Prance Committee) urged them to accept a smaller sum than their claims and avoid litigation; 'they might depend upon it that after twenty years' law they would have much less to receive and a very large sum to cash up for law expenses', which, as Hudson was to discover, was very sound advice. Hudson followed the settlement up by making a lengthy statement to the York Newcastle and Berwick's shareholders that was published in several newspapers and which sought to justify his previous actions at the company.[34]

Before the position at the York and North Midland could be resolved, matters were complicated by the decision of Hudson's close friend, business colleague and personal solicitor, James Richardson, to sue Mr Wodson, the proprietor of the *Yorkshireman*, for libel. On 30 August 1849 the *Yorkshireman* had published an anonymous letter, by 'One Behind the Scenes', probably written by the newspaper's editor, that described Richardson rather implausibly as the 'mainspring and originator of many of Mr Hudson's schemes' and suggested that he had written many of Hudson's business speeches and letters, as well as providing the legal and financial expertise that Hudson needed.[35] The *Yorkshireman* returned to these themes under its own name after B. T. Wilkinson was forced to resign from the York Union Bank for financial irregularities, and from his position as treasurer to York City Council. On 9 February 1850, in an article headed 'The Union Bank: Curious Exposures', the newspaper offered its own opinion that there appeared to be a 'charter for mismanagement, artifice and defalcations in every joint stock company over which Messrs George Hudson and James Richardson have had control'. It was suggested that 'no man should be trusted in a responsible situation who was narrowly associated with Mr Hudson; that man is not only corrupt himself, but corrupted every one around him'.

This convinced Richardson of the necessity of taking Wodson to court to protect his professional good name and he took out a writ to that effect on 21 February 1850. The case came to court on 17 July 1850, in a hearing that lasted ten hours. The defendants placed considerable emphasis on two sets of transactions at the York Newcastle and Berwick, where Richardson had been a director; first, the cheques payable to landowners and landlords that were instead paid into Hudson's own account at the York Union Bank, one of which Richardson had signed; and, secondly, the discretionary allocation by Hudson of a hundred railway company shares to Richardson. Although Hudson only appeared as a witness, he was richly abused by the defence counsel, who described Hudson as both the 'greatest enemy of mankind in his day' and as 'a blot on the commercial honour of the nation', causing Richardson's counsel to complain that the defence counsel had thereby exceeded his privileges and that Hudson was, in effect, being attacked through Richardson. The jury, after deliberating for an hour and a half, arrived at the conclusions that

> even if there was no evidence that Richardson had been personally corrupted, he had nonetheless received a hundred shares from Mr Hudson under very suspicious circumstances, there had been artifice, mismanagement and defalcations in every joint-stock company over which the plaintiff [Richardson] and Mr George Hudson had had control and the article complained of was not libellous.[36]

The verdict was a great disappointment for both Richardson and Hudson. They appealed against the judgement, in November 1850 and in February 1851, but without success.[37]

At this time, Hudson was trying very hard to re-establish his business career. An article in the *Sun* said that Hudson 'had gone a long way during the court case towards exonerating himself from the various charges' and copies of the article were circulated to provincial newspapers, although it turned out to have been written by William Digby Seymour, the son-in-law of J. J. Wright, Hudson's political agent in Sunderland. An article in the *Yorkshire Gazette*, also syndicated to the *Newcastle Journal*, conjured up the rather unlikely and highly sentimental picture of the 'gentlemen of the bar' having been so won over by Hudson's explanations in court that many of them 'hurried out of court to shake hands with and congratulate Mr Hudson on the very satisfactory evidence he had given'.[38] The *Times* reported rumours that Hudson was being sought by more than one railway company that hoped to make use of his considerable energy and experience and offered their own opinion that 'Hudson's retirement from railway affairs has been severely felt in more than one quarter and is beginning to excite a feeling of regret',[39] but two months later, correspondence in the same newspaper involving the two owners of the *Weekly Chronicle*, Robert Russell and John Doyle, revealed all too clearly that bribes had been offered in a clumsy attempt to rehabilitate Hudson's public reputation.[40]

The York and North Midland had also taken prompt legal action to recover all monies due to them. In October 1849 they wrote to Robert Davies, George Jennings, James Richardson and Sir John Simpson to demand repayment of the share premiums appropriated on the East and West Riding Extension shares and the Hull and Selby purchase shares, with some success.[41]

Discussions were also soon under way concerning the much larger amounts that Hudson owed. He had already repaid £75,000 in connection with cheques to landowners and contractors fraudulently diverted to his own bank account, and more than £70,000 in connection with the North British Railway shares.[42] The York and North Midland then offered to quit all claims against Hudson in return for a further £50,000. In probably the biggest misjudgement of his life, he refused their offer, believing that the claims were not sufficiently well founded to succeed.[43]

The York and North Midland promptly filed three suits in Chancery, which came to court in 1853. The cases were mainly concerned with the extent of a director's duties towards his shareholders and did a good deal to clarify the legal position in the area.[44] The first case, heard on 17 January 1853, dealt with the appropriations of East and West Riding Extension £25 shares. Most of the total allotment of fifty thousand shares had been taken

up by the existing shareholders, in proportion to their holdings, but just
over twelve thousand shares remained 'to be placed at the disposal of the
directors'. Nearly five thousand of these shares were never issued, while
others were allocated to landowners and other people important to the
company's business. Two other allocations, involving about two thousand
shares in all, to recipients that Hudson would not name and to himself,
were disputed by the York and North Midland. Hudson, for his part,
contended that he was entitled to the shares he had taken 'in consideration
of his services to the company'.[45]

Appearing for the York and North Midland, the then Solicitor-General,
Richard Bethell, was very hard on Hudson. He described his conduct as
'contrary to every principle of honour and fair dealing' and marvelled at
his effrontery in coming to the court, so as to 'express his own wonder at
his own peculiar morals, and his surprise that when he had so good a
chance of benefiting himself he did not make more by it than he did'.
Hudson's secondary argument that the shareholders had not previously
complained was also dismissed contemptuously:

> one of the great crimes of this man is that he carried on his plans so systematically
> and took precautions to pollute the fountain heads of the security of the com-
> pany ... the very auditors were his own solicitor and brother-in-law and these
> were the authorities the shareholders had to consult. The delinquency and iniquity
> of the defendant consisted not only in taking the shares improperly, but in
> corrupting the people about him, and appointing his own tools in the company
> for his own particular purposes.

The company claimed that the shares had only been placed with the directors
for the company's benefit, rather than that of the directors personally. The
judgement against Hudson confirmed a number of widely held principles:
that the office of director was a place of trust; that directors were bound
to give explanations to their shareholders; that they could not derive any
personal or pecuniary advantage from their chosen way of dealing with
shares; and, finally, that no person in a fiduciary position could retain any
remuneration for his services.[46]

In the second suit, on 20 January 1853, the York and North Midland
sought the repayment by Hudson of the proceeds of the sale of the North
British shares. Judgement was given in mid-February 1853, with the Master
of the Rolls concluding that the shareholders clearly meant Hudson to have
some shares, partly because he was one of the landowners over whose land
the York and North Midland's lines passed, although less than he took. He
also decided that, as a trustee of the York and North Midland, Hudson was
duty 'bound to account for the profits he had made'. He also criticised the

other directors for failing to sanction the distribution of the shares and for not keeping proper minutes relating to the transaction, although his main conclusions concerned the fundamental responsibilities of a director. These conclusions directly conflicted with Hudson's view. Thus, directors were trustees who were 'bound to manage the affairs of the company for the benefit of the shareholders'. When Hudson accepted office as chairman, he knew what the salary would be and it was his duty in return 'to devote his time and attention to the service of the company and to the functions of his office'. Clearly, he had no right to take shares or share premiums. Moreover, resolutions could not be used for personal advantage or as a secret trust without a clear and unambiguous expression by the shareholders to that effect; if Hudson's arguments were accepted, 'any clerk would be justified in detaining the property of his master to pay himself for any great or valuable services that he might suppose himself to have performed'. The judgement that Hudson should repay all the proceeds, with interest, included a punitive element, since the York and North Midland shareholders had always intended Hudson to have some of the shares. An appeal produced a small reduction in the amount he was to pay.[47]

The third suit on 20 July 1853 concerned the iron rail contracts, which the Master of the Rolls considered completely illegal when entered into by a director of one of the companies concerned. The York and North Midland thus obtained decrees against Hudson totalling £73,520, from which he was entitled to make one or two deductions, totalling nearly £4000. In November 1853 the Master of the Rolls made it clear that matters already decided by him in his chambers could not be reopened and argued again in court. At this point Hudson finally decided to abandon expensive court actions and settle with the York and North Midland although his error of judgement in taking them on was now all too clear. He had gone through an embarrassing and bruising series of court cases to establish a liability of nearly £70,000, some £20,000 more than he could have settled for out of court.[48]

Hudson was now in serious difficulties. The railway mania was over. The revelations in the various committee reports and the unsuccessful legal battles with the *Yorkshireman* had irrevocably broken the trust which had once encouraged the flow of investors' monies. No longer in the position to promote major projects, and unable, despite all his hard won expertise, to re-establish a career in the railways, he was now cut off from even a modest regular income.

He had made a small fortune from share dealings and speculations during the railway mania, when he held railway property to the value of £200,000 to £300,000, and his fraudulent dealings at the York and North Midland

and York Newcastle and Berwick had raised further sums of the order of £350,000. While he chaired the York Union Bank, and while Wilkinson was manager of the York office, he had also been able to borrow huge amounts to purchase land for development at West Cliff, Whitby, and for the purchase of his London house and his country seat, Newby Park. There were also three country estates that he had bought to settle his sons as gentlemen. He had also grown used to spending hugely on hospitality, something he enjoyed for itself and for the image it projected of a supremely successful man. His financial over-exposure was now apparent and very serious.

Against this, he had substantial assets to weigh in the balance. In the summer of 1849, the *Globe* estimated the value of his Londesborough Park estate at £470,000, the Baldersby estate at £108,000, Octon Grange at £89,000 and Albert Gate £18,000, a total of almost £700,000. He had further amounts tied up in land at West Cliff, Whitby, and at Hutton Cranswick, at least £100,000 in railway company shares and further amounts in more readily disposable assets: the *Morning Post* for example had once suggested that on some occasions Hudson's wife, Elizabeth, wore jewellery worth £60,000.[49]

The real value of these assets was less than it appeared, however, due to the very large mortgages and loans he had had to take out in order to acquire them. Thus, when he had to make the repayments to the York and North Midland and York Newcastle and Berwick, he realised that these holdings were quite beyond him. In November 1849, he was forced to sell Londesborough Park, Octon Grange and his Hutton Cranswick estate, comprising altogether about 16,000 acres of land in the East Riding, to Lord Albert Denison, Deputy Lieutenant of the West Riding and Liberal MP for Canterbury, who was related by marriage to Hudson's railway adversary, Edmund Beckett Denison.

His misjudgement of the strength of the York and North Midland's legal case against him meant that, even after his major assets had been sold, there was not enough to pay off the remaining amounts he owed the York Union Bank and the York and North Midland. His debt to the bank, in the name of the Whitby Building Company, was agreed in June 1850 at about £35,000. A schedule of payments was arranged that would clear this by February 1853 but, by October 1852, almost nothing had been paid and interest charges continued to accumulate.[50]

In the case of the York and North Midland, the court had ordered an initial instalment of £20,000 early in 1854, which Hudson was unable to pay, and he entered into a complex arrangement with the company that was to be the subject of legal argument for another seventeen years. Under this agreement, Hudson waived his right of appeal against the court's judgements and the York and North Midland, waiving its right to an immediate £20,000, agreed to accept £50,000 in full settlement of their claims (plus £1000 in costs), provided this was secured by a first mortgage on Hudson's property at Whitby. The agreement also stipulated that, in the event of Hudson's failure to adhere to the terms of the agreement, the company could revert to its full claim.

Hudson had agreed the sale of Newby Park (together with Baldersby) to the seventh Viscount Downe, for the very good price of £190,000, and a first instalment was to be paid to the York and North Midland out of the sale proceeds. In the meantime, Newby Park was transferred to Harry Thompson and another director of the York and North Midland, George Seymour, as trustees for the company.

When the sale of Newby Park was completed in October 1854, £33,000 was paid direct to the North Eastern Railway (of which the York and North Midland was now a constituent part) and Hudson's liability was reduced to about £15,000, which he was due to clear in two instalments in October 1855 and October 1856. The directors of the York and North Midland had initially described their arrangement with Hudson as the 'equitable and satisfactory settlement of a tedious and difficult question'. Now, despite further difficulties, it did seem as though its resolution was in sight.[51]

Hudson had balked at selling off the land he had bought in 1848 at Whitby, because of its development potential, which underpinned his standing in that town and because of his powerful desire to pass on some land there to his children when he died, but his freedom of manoeuvre was now severely limited by the legal charges the York Union Bank and the North Eastern Railway had established to protect their debts.

Although Hudson's position was very difficult, he did his best to get by. He tried to make a little money by dealing in iron, other metals and even wheat, from a room at the Royal Exchange Buildings, where other brokers had their offices.[52] Many of his dealings were with foreign railways but not all were successful and, on 18 February 1854, the French Count Seraincourt successfully sued Hudson for £4000 damages over their recent dealings in iron. Soon after this, Hudson was also sued by Davidson and Gordon, metal brokers, for his failure to deliver a hundred tons of copper. He settled the claim out of court.

He still enjoyed support from his constituents in Sunderland and he managed to resume some sort of parliamentary career. Further questions were asked in Parliament, on 7 February 1854, about the shares given to MPs by the York Newcastle and Berwick and Hudson successfully defended himself in the House the following day against accusations of bribery. He also spoke in the House on the Coasting Trade Bill and the Railway Traffic

Regulation Bill in March and April 1854 and again in June 1854 on the
Customs Duties (Sugar) Bill.

At the Sunderland Dock Company, revenues were up nearly 40 per cent
in a year, partly through the railway link with the Marquis of Londonderry's
pits, and in August 1854 Hudson was able to announce a dividend on the
ordinary shares of three and a half per cent. This was still only a modest
rate but Hudson was pleased that the rate had increased steadily since the
first payment in September 1851. Work was also well advanced on a sea
outlet that would enable ships to come and go during the winter and
generate additional business.[53]

It was now five years since the Committee of Investigation reports had
been published and Hudson's social position had recovered a little. His
younger brother Charles, who lived in Whitby, was a member of the local
Agricultural Society. In September 1854, Hudson was guest of honour at
the twenty-first annual meeting of Whitby Agricultural Show, where he was
received with 'loud and repeated bursts of applause'.[54] At the other end of
the scale, the willingness of Prince Albert to accept Hudson's invitation, as
host of the 1854 British Association meeting in York, was also very helpful
to his social standing. The Prince, having first met Hudson nearly ten years
before, was known genuinely to like him and to see in him a 'man of tact
and charm'. He was believed to have accepted the invitation, despite opposition from respectable social circles, in order to help Hudson 'rehabilitate
himself' after the scandals of 1849.[55]

On 12 August 1855, Hudson left the north east and went abroad for a
while, first to Hamburg, where his daughter Anne had gone to live after
marrying a Polish nobleman, Count Suminski, the year before. From there
he went to Paris, where he had spent family holidays in the past and then
on to Santander for three months to help promote a new trunk railway
line. In Marseille, later that year, he met his son John, on his way to India
to join his regiment, the 10th Hussars. He was confined to bed with gout
in St Sebastian until the end of June 1856, after which he went to a spa
town in Germany where his health was finally restored.[56]

As a result of these travels, he was not able to attend the meeting of the
Sunderland Dock Company in August 1856 at which the company's long-
term problems began to become apparent. The dividend was down to 3
per cent and, although trade and revenues continued to rise – revenues
were more than three times their level in 1851 – the profit margin on
revenues was so small that no one wanted to put new equity capital into
the business. The financing of successive expansions of the dock facilities
was now coming from loan capital requiring a return of 4 or 5 per cent
that did nothing to improve the returns to equity shareholders.[57]

He had also been absent from the House of Commons for some time, and in January 1857, the committee of the Sunderland Shipowners' Society thought about writing to him but decided not to as it was understood he would be retiring at the next election. Two months later, however, his friends affirmed that he would stand again and would soon be returning to Sunderland. The next day, a letter came from Paris, in which Hudson blamed his absence that year on severe illness and on his 'unavoidable attention to a large undertaking in Spain'. Free of this matter, he was 'again at full liberty to devote [his] time and exertions' to their service and hoped that they would give 'generous consideration' to these unusual circumstances.[58]

To the *Sunderland Herald*, Hudson had reduced the representation of Sunderland to a 'delusion and a sham' yet the townspeople still held him in great esteem and 'no greater or more enthusiastic meeting' was ever seen in Sunderland than that which greeted his address to the voters on 19 March 1857. His local constituency party openly regretted his absence during the last twelve months but pointed out that, at the east end of the town, stood the 'keystone of [their] prosperity' and suggested that that they 'owed him a debt of gratitude which we will scarcely ever be able to repay'. Pragmatically, his political position had gradually become a little more liberal and he was now able to assure the electors of his support for 'a judicious extension of the franchise', of his consistent support for the admission of Jews to Parliament, and for the removal of 'all paltry religious differences', as well as for 'economy and retrenchment in all our government departments' and the abolition of income tax. He was also shrewd enough to hold out hopes of further harbour improvements, by stating that 'the day is not far distant when I may again be further able to assist in extending the commercial enterprise of your port'.[59]

Informed opinion now expected him to top the poll comfortably, despite his absence. His very real need to retain his seat was made clear on 27 March 1857, when he was seized by a sheriff's officer and served with a debtor's writ, probably at the instigation of the Liberals. Hudson could not, as a sitting MP contesting his seat, be arrested but the officer was known to be watching the poll closely with every intention of arresting Hudson if he lost.

The election was, in fact, unusually peaceable and the local press regretted the passing of the good old times of electioneering, when 'flags and banners, cockades and party-coloured ribbons, street music and torchlight processions' had been much in evidence, although they were less sorry to see the absence of beer 'exercising its influence over the brains of the free and independent', of street rioting or of the 'election breakfast and payment of expenses'.[60]

The nominations took place at hustings erected in front of the Exchange. These were divided into sections, 'tastefully ornamented' in the pink and white of the Mayor as returning officer and in the colours of the three candidates; 'Mr Hudson's blue and white, Mr Fenwick's buff and blue and Mr Walter's green and white'. The crowd was no more than three thousand strong and 'on the whole conducted themselves extremely well'. The political temperature was held down by the establishment Whig, Fenwick, in an address that denied the existence of any 'coalition' but then made explicit the assumption that many electors would vote for both himself and Hudson, in recognition of their services to the borough. The 'ultra-liberal', Walters, was left 'out in the cold' by this manoeuvre and, even though Hudson polled fewer votes than expected, Fenwick and Hudson were duly elected.[61]

It seemed at last that Hudson had ridden out the storm, eight years after his spectacular downfall. He could have few complaints. His reputation had been savaged but he had, after all, been the author of most of his own misfortune. He had had to sell his landed estates in order to repay the ill-gotten gains from his railway promotions, but he still had some property in Whitby to pass on to his children. Though he had badly misjudged the offer of the York and North Midland to settle out of court his debts were now much smaller than they had been and his parliamentary seat protected him from imprisonment for debt and bought him time to settle outstanding claims. His name was too sullied for him to make a living in the more elevated business circles but he had recovered from long illness and still had his wits about him, so that he could expect to make a modest living. The loyalty of family and friends in the north of England, particularly in Sunderland and Whitby and the generous support of the Prince Consort, had even restored some social standing to him. After paying the price for his wrongdoing, he was down, but not out. Perhaps the corner had been turned.

9

Defeat

After his re-election, Hudson took up lodgings in Sunderland and returned to a more active role as MP, as he had promised. In May he spoke in the House on two shipping matters and in December 1857 he gave vigorous support to the Bank Issues Bill, which legitimised the recent suspension of the 1844 Bank Act 'a great boon to money-lenders but ... a scheme concocted for the purpose of raising the value of money and depressing the trade of the country'. He also hoped that the government would go further and remove the excessive limitations on the issue of bank notes.[1]

He was making steady progress, despite a number of difficulties but he now received a blow that he could hardly bear. His son John had been promoted to Lieutenant in the Crimea before receiving a commission with the 6th Dragoon Guards in India. In January 1858, George and Elizabeth received news of his death, aged twenty-five, from grapeshot wounds received while charging Indian guns during the Mutiny. Hudson was severely afflicted by the news and his health deteriorated again.

Other troubles beset him. The Sunderland Dock Company was struggling in the face of increased competition from other towns on the north east coast, such as Hartlepool, Middlesbrough and Jarrow. In August 1857, although the increase in revenue was the largest since the opening of the docks, the directors were still unable to increase the rate of dividend beyond 4 per cent. They had an admirable dock, they had succeeded in what some thought a 'desperate enterprise to contest with the North Sea', but, with the commissioners of the River Wear collecting dues of around £9000 a year, the 'poor shareholders were so well fleeced that very little was left for them'.[2] Hudson attended the meeting on 25 February 1858 to explain matters but he cut a sorry figure, on crutches with his limbs bandaged against gout. The dock had brought a great increase in the level of sea-borne trade to Sunderland but the dismal commercial returns had alienated the shareholders and damaged Hudson's reputation in the town. It was clear that the commissioners had outflanked him and they announced their takeover of the dock, which would lead to lower charges on vessels and dividends of three to five per cent, according to the level of traffic.[3]

In the second half of 1858, Hudson spent several months in France but otherwise he continued to attend Parliament and spoke on the Government of India Bill and on the Civil Service Estimates. In March 1859, he spoke in a number of debates, including those on the effects of the remaining timber duties on his constituency shipowners, on church rates and on the Reform Bill, which he thought 'placed the honourable members in a disagreeable and painful position'.[4] As he had suspected, the Reform Bill brought down the government and precipitated a general election. Hudson was hoping for a 'renewal of the confidence reposed in him for fourteen years' and there was some expectation that the sitting MPs, Hudson and Fenwick, would be returned unopposed, saving the considerable costs of polling. Nonetheless, the Liberals were well aware of Hudson's reduced effectiveness in Parliament and of the damage to his reputation from the persistently low dividends of the Dock Company; they decided the time was ripe to take both seats. Their second nominee, Lindsay, was a strong candidate; he was sitting MP for Tynemouth and, like Fenwick, a member of the Royal Commission on shipping. Hudson presented himself as 'an old tried friend, a man who has supported your town, who has spent his time, his money and his position in the advancement of your interests', but he had nothing new to offer and Liberal supporters jeered his unconvincing speeches. The contest took place in early May 1859 and 'from the outset it was seen that Mr Hudson's cause was utterly hopeless'. At lunchtime on polling day, Hudson withdrew and, when the votes were counted, he came a poor third. His parliamentary career was over.[5]

He made a dignified speech to his former constituents, emphasised his lack of ill feeling towards the gentlemen they had elected and his hope that they might give more efficient service to the borough than he had done. He finished by reminding them of his continuing interest in the 'welfare and prosperity of the town' and set off straightway for Paris, in order to escape imprisonment for debt.[6]

From Paris, he instructed his solicitors to write to the North Eastern Railway to see what could be done to settle his liability to the company. Hudson had been due to settle the £15,000 outstanding to the North Eastern in instalments in 1855 and 1856 but had paid nothing. The interest due on this had accumulated and he was eager to make a settlement and return to London. His solicitor's letter to George Leeman, the Deputy Chairman of the North Eastern, claimed that he had the means to make a settlement, if the payments could be spread over a period of three years. On this basis, he requested some 'abatement of the company's strict rights'. On 22 August Leeman replied that Harry Thompson, the Chairman, would not entertain such a proposal but was willing to listen to any immediate and reasonable offer of settlement. Hudson then wrote personally to Leeman on 31 August, from Meurice's Hotel in Paris, and appealed to the Board to overturn what he described as a 'severe and hard decision'.[7]

On 12 October 1859, Hudson's close friend Robert Stephenson died, aged fifty-six. This was sad news but, at the same time, it opened up possibilities that might restore his public position in England. Stephenson, like Hudson a staunch Tory and ardent protectionist, had been MP for Whitby since 1847.[8] Hudson had always been highly regarded there and, when he had attended the Agricultural Society's annual dinner in the town in the summer of 1858, he was described as the 'moving power' of everything in Whitby.

Hudson had a long-standing ambition to develop the West Cliff area. He had spent many a family holiday in Whitby and he had been left a small amount of property there by his greatuncle, Matthew Bottrill. With the support of close colleagues, he had formed the Whitby Building Company in 1843 with the intention of buying land to build fourteen or fifteen lodging houses. As Chairman of the York and North Midland Railway, he had promoted the coastal extensions to Scarborough and Whitby. With better railway links established, in October and November 1848, Hudson, James Richardson and Richard Nicholson bought the entire West Cliff fields site for nearly £20,000, fifty-five acres of land fronting the sea, with 'unbounded views of the German Ocean'.[9]

Hudson then took over the Royal Hotel, which his younger brother Charles managed on his behalf, but his main ambition was to provide an area of substantial classical terraces, facing the abbey ruins and the sea, a prospect 'entirely new to Whitby, at once voluminous and impressive with disciplined rows of three to four stories and balconied houses lining new streets wider than anything Whitby had been used to'. Some building work was carried out in the early 1850s, but the key development was the drawing up of plans in 1857 by John Dobson, the noted Newcastle architect, who, despite his railway work, 'remained a Georgian at heart'.[10]

The Conservatives had held Whitby since the seat was established in 1832 and the constituency party was keen that Hudson should represent them in the by-election. The Liberals responded by putting forward Harry Thompson, Chairman of the North Eastern Railway, as their candidate.

Hudson's liabilities to the North Eastern Railway now returned to haunt him. The North Eastern maintained that, as Hudson had failed to pay the outstanding £15,000 on the agreed dates, their agreement to accept £50,000 instead of the £70,000 awarded by the court no longer applied. They would press for the full amount, with interest. Worse still for Hudson, the North Eastern had gone much further while awaiting payment. While it had originally held only third mortgages on Hudson's various properties, in 1857 the company had spent a great deal of money on purchasing the prior claims so as to become first mortgagee. The North Eastern secretary accordingly wrote to Richardson, as Hudson's solicitor, to say that the full amount the company was entitled to claim, because of Hudson's failure to pay, was in fact in the region of £123,000. This Hudson was quite unable to pay.[11] At first, Hudson took this to be a manoeuvre to discourage him from standing against Thompson, rather than an amount he would actually be called upon to pay. He decided against standing for the seat, although he promised his supporters that he would be back to contest it at the next general election. Harry Thompson was then elected by a small majority on 22 November 1859.[12]

Hudson wrote to Leeman at the North Eastern Railway to see if a number of disputed items could be resolved. He was clearly anxious to reach a settlement with the railway, which he said had 'seized everything and left [him] without the means of subsistence'. He had been able to assist his wife with 'three hundred a year'; now even that was under threat.[13]

Leeman wrote back cordially on 3 December 1859 to deplore deeply the fact that he was 'reduced to the extremities to which you refer'. He also sent on a small balance, of just over a hundred pounds that had been standing to Hudson's credit in the Berwick Railway books since 1841, to provide a little short-term comfort.

At an official level, however, the company became ever more unyielding. The Company Secretary wrote to Hudson's solicitors on 2 December 1859 to express surprise that 'Mr Hudson should now seek to reopen questions which were settled ten years ago', to emphasise their refusal to discuss such issues and to formally confirm £123,000 as the amount that the North Eastern Railway were now claiming. The letter did indicate the directors' willingness to accept £100,000 in cash as a final settlement, in return for which they would hand over the securities to Hudson's various properties, including those at Whitby, but also emphasised that the Board would not agree to any settlement involving a larger abatement.[14]

On 10 December 1859, Hudson himself wrote back to the North Eastern Company Secretary, correctly identified the sum he had failed to pay, with accumulated interest, as £17,300 and offered forthwith to pay that sum. He complained of the 'severity, almost cruelty' with which he had been treated but added that, although his disappointments had been great and his struggles severe, he was confident that, 'with a little of your kind consideration I am about to surmount them'. The North Eastern board's reply of 23 December 1859 was briskly formal, rejecting Hudson's offer and even omitting seasonal good wishes.[15]

Hudson wrote twice in early January 1860 to ask for full details of the amounts claimed. He complained of his severe bereavement and his inability to spend Christmas with his family, which a settlement might have permitted, and finished with the lament that 'you get my money but you get it in such a cruel way that you make it a double loss'.[16]

The North Eastern's Company Secretary was sufficiently embarrassed by Hudson's letter to send a politer response but there was no substantive change of position. Hudson's subsequent letters in the winter months of 1860 to Leeman, with whom he remained on friendly terms, indicate that his grief over John's death in 1857 was acute and that he found separation from his wife and sons very difficult; the North Eastern Railway's intransigence had deprived him of 'all family enjoyments'. During this period he seems to have been close to breakdown, writing of his melancholic sense of a 'miserable existence with a weight that is too much to bear', of an anxiety to 'either swim or sink at once' and of his concerns as to whether one particular letter was legible, as he felt 'very nervous', although he also had moments of optimism in which he thought he would yet surmount his difficulties.[17] The North Eastern, nevertheless, confirmed their position on 12 March 1860. Having fully considered Hudson's letters, they 'saw no reason for altering their views or for accepting a less sum'. Hudson was extremely bitter at the North Eastern's position, given his earlier contributions to its wellbeing, but he came to accept that it could not be changed.[18]

He was well aware that his position was dependent on the attitude adopted by Harry Thompson, Chairman of the North Eastern Railway, who had assumed personal responsibility for handling the negotiations with Hudson.[19] There was some correspondence between them but no common ground was established. Partly a matter of self-interest (Thompson's position as MP for Whitby was far more secure with Hudson in France) style and disposition were also very important considerations. Thompson had little time for Hudson, despite the importance of his early work at the York and North Midland and had never admired the brash ebullience that contrasted so sharply with his own 'quiet, calm', rather formal manner. Thompson was an establishment figure with a deep sense of moral rectitude; he objected to Hudson's continual attempts to 'get away with things' and avoid his just desserts.[20]

Thompson hid his personal feelings behind the façade of duty to his shareholders and reiterated his position in a letter to Hudson written on 28 December 1861. He 'much regretted' Hudson's painful position but he had personally taken the stance that, when Hudson did not pay up at the time specified, the whole arrangement should be at an end and the company would revert to its previous position with its legal powers unaffected. The claims of the North Eastern exceeded by a considerable margin the value of the mortgaged property, on which there were other, subsequent claimants and Thompson could not recommend the North Eastern Railway to 'forego their due' because any abatement they offered would merely put money into the pockets of Hudson's other creditors.[21]

Hudson's approach to business and politics had made him friends and enemies in almost equal number. Part of his success had been due to the way that he maintained a loyal coterie of friends and colleagues. His confrontational style had alienated business rivals, such as Denison and Meek, and Liberals such as Elsley and Leeman, but this was all a long time ago. In general, his adversaries had taken things as 'part of the game' and Leeman in particular was far more reasonable now that Hudson's fortunes had fallen. Thompson was different. His enmity came from a deeper base and showed no signs of abating with the passing of time.

After this, Hudson's life gradually settled down a little. He stayed on the Continent for several years, living mainly in France but also in Spain and Germany. He was certainly in Santander for part of each year from 1856 to 1861 or 1862. For much of the time he was in France, he stayed at the Hotel Meurice in the Rue de Rivoli, Paris. This hotel was comfortably middle-class and particularly frequented by the English. It was 'comfortable, especially in winter, when you could have an English breakfast without going abroad, at the street end of the dark *salon*, with the *Times* or *Galignani* stuck up against the coffee pot'. In many of the old-fashioned Parisian hotels, there was 'neither light, nor sweetness, nor sociability', but it was said that 'the smoking-room at Meurice's was rather an exception; there was generally a lively group of English assembled of an evening and for a time Mr Hudson, the dethroned railway king of England, reigned there supreme'. Here he was remembered as a philosophical and good-humoured old gentleman who could 'easily be drawn into reminiscences of the days when he kept open house at Albert Gate and had half the impecunious aristocracy for his courtiers'.[22]

As his financial position deteriorated, he moved to the French coast and when Charles Dickens saw him in Boulogne in January 1863 he was in a distinctly impoverished state

> taking his leave of Manby, as he joined the Folkestone boat was a shabby man of whom I had some remembrance, but whom I could not get into his place in my mind. Noticing when we stood out of the harbour that he was on the brink of the pier, waving his hat in a desolate manner, I said to Manby, 'surely I know that man' – 'I should think you did', said he; 'Hudson!' He is living – just living

– at Paris … I asked Manby why he stuck to him and he said, because he [Hudson] had so many people in his power, and had held his peace, and because he [Manby] saw so many notabilities grand with him now, who were always grovelling for shares in the days of his grandeur.[23]

A correspondent for the *Hull Express* visited him in Calais, where he was living in lodgings, in a 'plain dwelling where he occupied a small sitting and bedroom, scantily furnished'. The reporter had been commissioned, as he passed through Calais, to deliver a letter to Hudson, which contained money. Hudson was moved to tears by this unexpected alleviation of his problems and he immediately paid his landlady what he owed and then went out and bought tea, bread and cold fowl, ready cooked. His visitor was astonished at Hudson's activity and simplicity and at the way he bustled round to lay the table and to make him feel at home. The two had a splendid evening, during which Hudson reminisced about the north of England and said that the assistance he had received since he had been in Calais had come from people who never received much favour from him. He was astonished at the kindness of people in York, Hull and Newcastle, who often sent him presents, and spoke well of George Leeman, who had been kind to him and would have settled matters readily had he been in charge at the North Eastern Railway.[24]

Mrs Hudson's marriage settlement helped her to get by respectably but quietly at 8 South Crescent, Bedford Square, before she found it necessary to move on to lodgings in Burton Street, near Euston Square. Unfortunately, very few people kept in touch with her, although among them were Algernon West's mother, Sir John Fowler and his wife, and Lord William Pitt Lennox. Fowler also visited Hudson in France several times.[25] By now, Hudson's children had moved on. George had been called to the Bar and he practised for some time on the north east circuit before he became a Factory Inspector. William graduated from Christ Church, Oxford, and then trained to become a doctor.

Charles Hudson tried again to get his brother to stand for Whitby and, in December 1863, in correspondence with the local Conservative Association, Hudson 'expressed his willingness to come forward if it was the wish of the party'. Charles died in December 1864 but the local party remained enthusiastic about Hudson's prospects.[26] Despite the death of his brother, which was fortunately 'without pain or suffering', Hudson was in better spirits and, on 24 December 1864, he wrote to Leeman to say that he was bearing up against his 'accumulated afflictions', although he rather unwisely added, with a touch of the old spirit, 'at all events you will not get the Whitby property!' Hudson had a very strong desire for the property at Whitby to be passed onto his children and on one occasion he confessed to 'an overpowering feeling for the possession of that property' as the last he held and thought he could 'die happy [were he] able to leave that property among my family and forget all my misery and distress'.[27]

As a prelude to the coming electoral contest in the borough, Hudson wrote to the directors of the North Eastern Railway on 24 February 1865 and sent a copy of his letter to the *Whitby Gazette*, thereby initiating a quite extraordinary series of exchanges. Harry Thompson wrote a very full letter to the paper on 3 March 1865. He went through the history of the various law suits and reminded readers that Hudson had been found guilty of a breach of trust when he 'wrongly appropriated to his own use' the premiums realised by the sale of York and North Midland shares. He denied that Hudson had been faced with 'penalty payments' and argued that he had instead merely been offered a 'heavy discount for prompt payment' at a time when the York and North Midland was 'at a low ebb'; when he still failed to pay, the company was perfectly entitled to recover the full amount due. He also set out a valuation of the various assets and claims thereon to substantiate his argument that, even if the North Eastern agreed to accept the £17,300 owed from the court cases of 1853, as Hudson proposed, there would still only be £10,000 left to be 'scrambled for by the other claimants'.

In a further letter, written from the Carlton Club and dated 14 March 1865, Hudson once again showed his ready grasp of political realities. He did not attempt to match Thompson's 'large array of figures', but simply rejected Thompson's valuation of the Whitby property and dismissed his arguments, saying that nearly all the 'other claimants' had been paid off. He reiterated that he had been willing to settle his debts to the railway company until the company had then demanded infinitely more. He tellingly likened Thompson to Shylock, always crying 'my bond! my bond!' and hoped that an honourable escape would be left for him, 'even from the demand of the pound of flesh'. Finally, he poured scorn on Thompson's claim that the Board was prosecuting the action. Thompson himself had long since claimed the 'privilege of the management of this suit', in pursuit of which he had allowed personal dislike to override considerations of sound judgement and fair dealing.[28]

Against this troubled background, on 5 June 1865, Hudson was adopted as the official Conservative candidate for Whitby for the forthcoming general election, to stand against Thompson as the sitting MP. The local Liberal election agent, Matthew Gray, immediately advised Leeman that Hudson's opposition should be taken very seriously, as he 'will get a mixed support of Conservatives and Liberals'. He was also aware that Hudson's supporters were confident he would soon overcome the legal obstacles to 'repossession of the West Cliff property' and that he was a man 'more calculated to benefit the port and harbour than Mr Thompson', who was widely believed to favour the development of nearby Scarborough. Thompson, in short, needed to try harder.[29]

These concerns were borne out on 8 June, when Hudson returned to Whitby by train to one of the most enthusiastic receptions ever seen in the town. Ten days later, he attended a service in York Minster and, on the following day, his speech from the windows of the Angel Hotel at Whitby was well received by a cheering crowd. He addressed another meeting that same evening in St Hilda's Hall, promising 'if returned, to take the West Cliff Estate back out of the hands of the railway company and develop it for the town'. During a long speech, full of half-truths and excuses, he won his audience over and claimed that, in the past, he had been a 'scapegoat for the sins of the people'.[30]

Thompson was judged a poor local MP. Many thought his persecution of Hudson had been spiteful and cruel and the hostility between the two candidates was all too apparent. On 27 June 1865, Thompson's address to his supporters in St Hilda's Hall turned into 'one of the largest and most riotous meetings ever held in Whitby'. Large numbers of Hudson supporters turned up 'for the evident purpose of creating a disturbance', causing a scene of the 'most indescribable confusion' when they tried to storm the platform. The poll was fixed for the second week in July and Hudson's position had improved so much that he was now expected to win.

In the early morning of 10 July, however, a sheriff's officer entered Hudson's bedroom and arrested him, after a firm of solicitors representing a creditor of Hudson, a Mr Sandeman, had produced a petition for debt. Hudson was immediately taken to the railway station and on to York, where he was committed to the Castle gaol.

The solicitors acting for Sandeman claimed that they had only presented the petition for debt at such a time to prevent it becoming unenforceable for the life of the coming Parliament, but almost everyone suspected Thompson, and possibly Leeman, as the real instigators of this legal manoeuvre. Feelings ran even higher when it emerged that, with the North Eastern Railway in possession of West Cliff, the claims of Sandeman as third mortgagee were virtually worthless, that his claims had 'lain dormant for years' until Hudson had announced his intention to stand, and that the relevant writ had been obtained in May 1865 and had been used only when the strength of Hudson's support had become apparent. As his solicitors said

it is the misfortune of Mr Hudson to have found united in the person of Mr Thompson a political adversary and electoral competitor and, as Chairman of the North Eastern Railway, the representative of claims against him susceptible alike of liberal adjustment or of unlimited, stringent and harsh enforcement.[31]

The Conservatives were outraged; they soon produced a replacement candidate, Charles Bagnall, who owned the local ironworks and who was connected by marriage with several of the leading families in the town. At the hustings, despite six years of service as MP for Whitby, Thompson was greeted with a 'perfect storm of cheers, hisses and waving of hats' whereas Bagnall was 'received in the most enthusiastic manner'. Thompson's whole campaign was now badly marked by the way Hudson had been treated and Bagnall beat him by 305 votes to 288, a result greeted with 'immense cheering'.

Afterwards, Thompson blamed his defeat on the 'mistaken idea on the part of a certain number of electors that Mr Hudson was victimised and persecuted by the North Eastern Railway Company, and that this arose from personal enmity on his part towards Mr Hudson'. He bore 'no personal ill-will whatever to Mr Hudson' and said that all the proceedings he had taken against Hudson were 'simple matters of duty' to the company of which he was chairman.[32]

Hudson remained in York gaol for just over three months. His imprisonment took a further toll on his already poor health until George Elliot, of Houghton Hall, a colliery owner and President of the Association of Mining Engineers, generously paid off his immediate debts. Released in mid October 1865, Hudson immediately returned to the continent to avoid any further trouble at the hands of the North Eastern Railway or his other creditors.[33]

In January 1863 the North Eastern Railway had begun legal proceedings to foreclose on the mortgages they held and the courts were asked to adjudicate on the validity of its claims. In 1866 Hudson came back to London in connection with the case and on 5 June, shortly after leaving the office of the Master of the Rolls, he was arrested yet again, outside the Carlton Club and taken to the debtors' prison in Whitecross Street in the City. Legal action had again been taken against him, this time by a Mr Bartlett to whom he owed £13,000. Hudson was supposed to have enjoyed immunity from arrest for a reasonable time after attending the meeting but he remained in prison for three weeks because of a misunderstanding over the time he had left the legal chambers. He was quite unnerved by the experience and fled back to France, remaining there even when the North Eastern Railway brought their case against him to court in July 1866. In November 1866, for example, he was certainly staying at, and writing letters from, a cheap hotel in Calais.[34]

The case between the North Eastern and Hudson was complex. It was agreed that Hudson had paid the North Eastern Railway or its predecessor companies what he owed, apart from a sum of nearly £15,000. When the Master of the Rolls heard the case, in July 1866, he decided that the North Eastern Railway were only entitled to recover the £15,000, with interest, and that their attempt to claim a much larger sum as a penalty for non-payment was unenforceable in equity.[35] The North Eastern appealed against this ruling, only to see it confirmed by the Court of Appeal in a judgement given in January 1867. They made their final appeal to the House of Lords, which decided early in 1869 that the arrangement was *not* a penal stipulation but merely a mutual agreement and that, as payment had not taken place on the due dates, reversion to the larger sum was, in fact, legal.[36] The House of Lords judgement confirmed the desperate nature of Hudson's position. He now owed the North Eastern Railway £107,000, plus the considerable legal costs involved. He dared not risk even the briefest of visits to England and the *Times* reported him as reduced by the judgement to a 'state of penury', living in France, 'utterly destitute'.[37]

Thompson had won. His claims had been upheld by the highest court in the land and his political adversary at Whitby had been banished to France. Better still, the wrongdoer had been thoroughly punished, losing possession of the last piece of property he had hoped to leave to his children as a mark of at least some achievement in a chequered career. Even so, Thompson showed no signs of relenting.

Thompson's motives remain something of a mystery. If simple duty was, as he claimed, his only motive for pursuing Hudson so zealously, it certainly led him into strange courses of action for a man of business. The North Eastern was owed £15,000. Their security as third mortgagee on the Whitby property was weak and Thompson chose to spend something of the order of £85,000 to pay off the first and second mortgages, so that the North Eastern would become virtually the sole claimant against Hudson, yet the property was worth no more than the additional sum spent to secure it. Why did Thompson risk his shareholders' funds in this way when the land had no great importance to the development of his railway?

As we have seen, Harry Thompson had been born in 1809 at Newby Park, the same Newby Park that was later acquired by Hudson in the glory days of the 1840s. This might have been grounds for friction, yet the Thompson family had long before moved on to even grander surroundings. Nor is there any record of slight or insult from Hudson toward Thompson or his family. The two men were very different, even in outward appearance – Thompson's refined and aquiline features could hardly contrast more sharply with Hudson's energetic, plebeian countenance. Thompson, though not an aristocrat, was landed gentry, the class to whose ranks Hudson strove to elevate his sons. Could the wealthy and successful Chairman of the North Eastern Railway have so resented Hudson's upstart ambitions?

By now, Thompson's implacable thirst for revenge had become an embarrassment. His colleagues at the North Eastern Railway, upright citizens themselves, were uncomfortable at the level of retribution visited on the wretched Hudson. A major shareholder of the North-Eastern Railway was known to be ready to ask his fellow members at their next meeting to provide Hudson with an annuity of £200 a year to meet his present needs, in the belief that he was as much 'sinned against as sinning'.[38] But this could not be done legally without the express sanction of Parliament; any such initiative would have to be a private one.

George Elliot, now Conservative MP for South Durham and Hugh Taylor, a coal and ship-owner from Chipchase Castle, had already shown their willingness to help. A meeting was held in Sunderland, in late May 1869, to try to raise a subscription of £3000 to buy Hudson, then aged sixty-nine, an annuity of £400 for the rest of his life. The *Sunderland Times* lent its support to the venture by reminding its readers, in an editorial, that their town was

> the place which above all others has profited largely by the works which that remarkable man set agoing ... Sunderland Docks will for ever remain a noble monument to George Hudson. It would have been scandalous to the town had the old man to end his days in sordid pinching penury. He has suffered enough for his sins. Let him be made comfortable for the rest of his life.[39]

In July a meeting was held in York, presided over by the Lord Mayor, and it was reported that 'great sympathy and kindness had been manifested towards Mr Hudson in his adversity by men of all classes and parties'. Collections in London, York, other parts of Yorkshire, Newcastle and in Sunderland raised nearly £6000 to provide an annuity of over £500 'in acknowledgement of his services in connection with public works'.[40]

On receiving news of his annuity, Hudson wrote to the Lord Mayor of York from Calais on 14 July 1869 to voice a 'gratitude which words cannot express ... that so many friends have united to express, in so substantial a manner, their sympathy towards me and their acknowledgement of my services in the promotion of public works'.

Within six months, on 1 January 1870, the Abolition of Imprisonment for Debt Act became law, so that no one could be arrested or imprisoned for defaulting on the payment of a sum of money. Hudson could now return safely to England and he rejoined his wife in London at 37 Churton Street, in Pimlico. He had always been regarded as 'good company when

he was relaxed, away from the Boardrooms and the House of Commons'
and he was still full of zest. Some courtesies were also paid to him, which
he seemed to greatly appreciate

> They've elected me chairman of the smoking-room of the Carlton again' he
> remarked to a friend soon after his return from exile, adding with genuine glee,
> 'my old position, sir, my old position' and 'Only this day sir, I was in Hyde Park
> and Lord —(naming one of the most distinguished statesmen in the Upper
> House) rode by. I saw him of course, but I didn't think he saw me, until he
> turned his pony's head and putting out his hand said, 'How do you do, Mr
> Hudson? I'm very glad to see you looking so hearty after all your troubles'–nothing
> could be kinder or more friendly, could it now? It touched me very much.[41]

Despite the passing of so much time and the changes in the legal position
of debtors, the North Eastern Railway had not put an end to their legal
claims against Hudson. On 31 January 1870 and again on 5 February 1870,
he accordingly wrote to Leeman in further attempts at a settlement that
would end the matter, so that the latter part of his days could be 'spent in
peace'.[42]

In April 1870, Hudson visited York, Newcastle and Sunderland, where he
was received by the Mayor, the Town Clerk and the Chairman of the Wear
Commissioners. On 15 April, there was a colourful gathering when he visited
the docks, where he was feted as in the old days with flags, banners and
streamers flying. A dinner followed at the Queen's Hotel, Sunderland in
'recognition of his past eminent and valuable services to the town and port',
attended by eighty of the town's leading businessmen and chaired by the
Mayor. Hudson was received with 'great cheering' and gave a long and
nostalgic speech to those present, in which he described some of his past
actions rather romantically as 'errors of the head and not of the heart'.
There was even some suggestion that he might be offered the post of
manager of Sunderland Docks at a salary of £2000 a year, although nothing
came of it.[43]

On 17 July 1871, he and Elizabeth were together for their golden wedding
anniversary and that autumn he visited the Earl of Lonsdale at Lowther
Castle and then went on to Whitby, where he stayed at the Royal Hotel.
Later he was the guest of the Sheriff in York and dined with the Lord
Mayor.[44]

One of the North Eastern Railway's largest shareholders, Joseph Mitchell
of London met Hudson by chance at the house of a friend and decided to
involve himself in Hudson's continuing liability. Thompson's position was
now increasingly eccentric, almost as if he had taken it upon himself to act
as the personal agent of the upper classes to ensure that Hudson the *arriviste*

was fully punished for his flawed standards. Mitchell wrote first to Leeman in concern that Hudson, who 'did good service in his time, has suffered some twenty-three years of disrepute and poverty' and then wrote to Thompson on 26 July 1871 in the following terms;

> I lately happened to meet Mr George Hudson and was sorry to learn from him that the North Eastern Railway Company were still litigating with him ... Of course, as chairman of a great company, you must protect the interests of the shareholders; but I venture to think that, consistent with that duty, you may be able to devise some means of putting a stop to that litigation. I understand that in 1854 a settlement was made, the terms of which he failed to implement on the day; might not the company revert to that settlement? The company might well act generously (seeing how flourishing under your able auspices it now is) towards one whose energy was formerly of such service to the railway interests of the country. Whatever were the faults and irregularities of that time, it is not my province to defend ... If the settlement I refer to cannot now be adopted, what would you say to referring the accounts ... to arbitration.

Thompson was not responsive, replying on 31 July to say only that 'the directors of the North Eastern Railway have good reasons for the course which they have taken in this matter and in which they will certainly persevere'.[45] Mitchell wrote again to reiterate his concerns, on the grounds that

> a litigation prolonged over a period of twenty-four years is not only discreditable to our Law Courts but ... indicates a degree of persistence on the part of the company, which I should have imagined might have been terminated before this time ... he is now experiencing the fruits of his [previous] autocracy by suffering obloquy and obscurity. Had Mr Hudson been wallowing in wealth there might have been a reason for this continued litigation; but you know that he has only been rescued from absolute want by the generosity of private friends.

He reminded Thompson of a series of decisions that Hudson had taken in the past that had greatly increased the value of the North Eastern Railway. Finally, on 1 September 1871, he asked for the matter to be placed before the shareholders, as 'lawyers sometimes pursue a case, when they get into it, with the keenness of our Highland sportsmen. As a measure of humanity, do settle it!'

When Hudson heard of Mitchell's initiative, he wrote on 19 August 1871 to thank him greatly for his trouble. Finally, on 30 November 1871, he was able to write again to Mitchell to say that he had at last arrived at a settlement with the North Eastern Railway. Following Leeman's intervention, Hudson met a deputation from the North Eastern and an agreeable position was arrived at for a settlement. Thompson opposed it to the last but then gave way, evidently because he was unwilling to bear the odium of a discussion that Mitchell threatened to bring before the shareholders and the general public.[46]

If this brought Hudson some belatedly peace of mind, he was not to enjoy it for long. Early the following month, December 1871, he was again visiting in the north of England. He arrived at York one Friday, intending to stay with his old friend J. L. Foster, by then proprietor of the *Yorkshire Gazette*, over the weekend before calling on the Lord Mayor at the Mansion House on the Monday. He had been suffering for some time from chest pains and on the Friday evening he had an attack of 'angina pectora', for which he received treatment. He was soon free of pain and decided to return home for rest. He wrote a cheerful letter to his friend Foster on 11 December 1871 but, on 13 December, he suffered a heart attack and died at 8.40 a.m. the following morning, with his youngest son William at his bedside.[47]

His body was taken by train to York station, where it rested in a carriage until the day of the funeral, 21 December 1871. On the shortest day of the year, in brilliant sunshine, a funeral cortège drawn by four horses left York station at 9.30 a.m. The hearse, containing an outer coffin of polished oak, with a silvered plate bearing the simple inscription of his name, date of death and age, and attended by bearers walking on either side, was followed by the mourning carriages. The procession passed through the streets of York in a simple, unostentatious manner, accompanied by the solemn tolling of the minute bells of the cathedral. Shops along the route were closed (as they were in Whitby) as the cortège headed for the long-established family grave in the grounds of the church in the small village of Scrayingham, close to Howsham on the Derwent, where they joined other mourners from Whitby, Malton and Howsham.[48]

The *Times* recorded his death in their editorial columns as of one

whose name has long been used to point the moral of vaulting ambition and unstable fortune [although] those to whom his face and figure and voice were familiar ... are to be found only among the middle-aged members of the House of Commons or the most seasoned frequenters of London society. There was a time when not to know him was to argue one's self unknown; now he is only a tradition ... he was dethroned, like so many other Sovereigns, in the revolutionary period which began with 1848 ... to the last he was energetic and enterprising, even to audacity ... a quarter of a century ago he turned all that he touched to gold; in after years his name was enough to wither the prospectus on which it was printed. The world which blindly trusted him, which cringed to him and flattered him, avenged itself by excessive and savage reprobation ... It would be ridiculous to apologise for him and to deny his faults merely because he is dead, but it is fair to notice that to the last he had warm friends ... Robert Peel decided on free trade in railway enterprise – unlimited competition between projectors and companies, fierce Parliamentary battles, useless branches, suicidal rivalry in traffic ... George Hudson was a creature of such a system; he made the best of it and turned it to account for himself and the nation ... he was a man who united largeness of view with wonderful speculative courage. He went in for bigger things than anyone else ... He showed his confidence by investing more largely than anyone else and taking upon himself all sorts of responsibilities. This is the kind of man who leads the world. Let him have one success and people will follow him anywhere. Mr Hudson was for two or three years looked upon as having the key to untold treasures. The world will court rich men, but there is one whom it will court still more and that is he who is supposed to be able to make all men rich. This was Mr Hudson's position.[49]

**

Hudson was survived by his wife and three children. His daughter Ann was the first member of his remaining family to die, only three years later in November 1874, in Berlin at the age of forty-four. She had no children. His younger son William trained and qualified as a doctor after leaving Oxford and lived close by his mother in Pimlico until his equally untimely death in February 1876, when he was hit by a train at Victoria underground station. He was unmarried. Elizabeth Hudson moved to Campden Hill, Kensington, and continued to live a quiet, blameless life until she died in January 1886, aged ninety-one. Their last surviving son, George, who had qualified as a barrister after leaving Oxford and practised on the north-eastern circuit, lived at Monkwearmouth Grange before becoming an Inspector of Factories. He married Hannah Singleton, youngest daughter of the Rev. W. R. Griesbach of Millington, near Pocklington in East Yorks, in 1879, and later they lived at Newby House (which may have been so named in memory of Newby Park), Sunninghill, Ascot, until his death in 1909. They had no children either, so George and Elizabeth were not survived by any grandchildren.[50]

The financial difficulties of his later years and the protracted struggle over the ownership of the properties at West Cliff, Whitby left Hudson very little property to pass on. His will was dated 24 February 1858, a month after learning of the death of his son John in India, and was signed and witnessed at the Carlton Club, where he had always been welcome despite his troubles. It bequeathed two-thirds of his property to his elder son George and the remaining one-third to William, after asking that due consideration be given to Ann's position, but in the event it was all relatively academic; his will was proved in July 1872 with personal effects of less than £200.[51]

George Hudson was a man of great influence who left more to the world in which he lived than family and personal property. Though some of the changes he brought about were transitory, others have endured: the development of Middlesbrough, Jarrow and Crook, and the existence of the great docks in Sunderland, the Tyne Bridge, Newcastle Central, Monkwearmouth station, the Royal Border Bridge at Berwick and a host of other railway buildings remain to mark his life.

He was particularly fond of Whitby. The development of the West Cliff area did go ahead broadly in line with his intentions, although the realisation of his ideas had to await the purchase of land from the North-Eastern Railway in May 1873 by his friend George Elliot. One of the streets behind the main crescent facing the sea is still called George Street and another Hudson Street.[52]

Many contemporary writers showed a good deal of understanding for his position, largely because they disliked the new commercial ethics. The *Times* argued that other officials and shareholders should not 'hope to escape censure under the cover of a personal onslaught upon Mr Hudson'; the system was to blame. The *Times* was also well aware of the failure of incentive mechanisms and pointed out that the companies had not bought out the 'full entirety' of his talents; they seemed to forget that he 'had his own fortunes to make as well as theirs'. The *Illustrated London News* saw Hudson as 'neither better nor worse than the morality of 1845. He rose to wealth and importance in an immoral period; he was the creature of an immoral system and ... it is rather too much to expect of him that he should be purer than his time or his associates'.[53]

His career also produced echoes in the literature of the nineteenth century. The hero in R. Bell's *Ladder of Gold*, written in 1850, for example, is a shop assistant who marries his late employer's widow and uses his newfound wealth (and an uncle's bequest) to speculate successfully on the railways. He acquires a country estate, a seat in Parliament and enters London society. He suffers from, but survives, the end of the Mania.[54]

He may have also provided some of the inspiration for Trollope's Augustus Melmotte, the swindling financier in *The Way We Live Now*, published in 1874–75, even though there are major differences between the two. Melmotte arrives in Britain already wealthy from business dealings in France, although he does hoodwink investors over a railway venture, the 'Great South Central Pacific and Mexican Railway' of which he is Chairman. Melmotte is a Conservative MP, gauche, rude and ignorant of procedure and, when his frauds are uncovered, he is cut by his former friends and finds solace in champagne. On the other hand, he is purely a swindler, with no intention of actually building the railway.[55]

Mr Merdle, the financier in Charles Dickens' *Little Dorrit*, also seems to be partly modelled on Hudson (whom Dickens disliked). From obscure origins, as a man of 'prodigious enterprise', he becomes immensely rich. Society worships his wealth and flocks to his dinners although he turns out to have been merely a swindler; 'the greatest Forger and the greatest Thief that ever cheated the gallows'.[56]

Disraeli's last novel, *Endymion*, features Peter Vigo, a Yorkshireman who transcends his origins as a tailor to become chairman and leading spirit of an important railway. His energy is certainly Hudsonian. At his peak, he obtains in one morning the consent of his shareholders to twenty-six Bills that he immediately introduces into Parliament, before moving to other pressing concerns. He becomes an MP and buys a splendid mansion in London where invitations to his banquets are looked upon 'almost as commands'. There is, however, no suggestion of shady dealing and Sir Peter has 'the wisdom to retain his millions'.[57]

By 1842, Hudson was recognised as the 'best railway manager in the kingdom' and went on to control a quarter of the lines in operation in Britain. His most common nickname, the 'Railway King', he liked but he was knowledgeable, not technically gifted, very different in that sense from Brunel and the Stephensons. His extraordinary powers of visualisation and organisation and the capacity to make things happen were the gifts of a great capitalist and entrepreneur.

Hudson's contribution to the founding of a tolerably rational railway system, through the promotion of lines that had a genuine commercial rationale and by means of pioneering amalgamations and other structural innovations, has also been widely recognised by contemporary authorities.[58]

Hudson's name is now widely associated with two types of fraud; false accounting and the unwarranted appropriation of corporate assets. His use of false accounting was more limited than has often been alleged; at the Midland there was no misrepresentation and at the York and North Midland and the York Newcastle and Berwick it was relatively limited in scope. Only at the Eastern Counties did he totally misrepresent the underlying situation and, even here, the subterfuge required the effective complicity of the shareholders. As the *Times* said, 'everybody knew the contents of the cauldron seething in the company's kitchen'.[59]

As for the appropriation of corporate assets, it might have been obvious to a judge that Hudson should have expected no more than his director's fee of fifty guineas a year for his endeavours but contract law does not always provide a reliable basis for moral judgement. Hudson was proud of the fact that his enterprise provided a great deal of employment and he often chided his Liberal opponents for their empty talk about helping the common man. His appropriations were certainly a fraud on other share-holders but Hudson was well aware that his projects made investors wealthy; as the person providing the initiative, he expected to do well out of the situation himself. As the North Eastern Railway's historian, Tomlinson, wrote

> it was the time of the railway mania. Everyone was looking out for shares and would have them in one line or another, as Mr Hudson said, either for you or against you. Many services were rewarded by an allotment of shares: directors, engineers, secretaries and managers participated in this indirect mode of payment. Naturally, Mr Hudson, who was labouring from morning to night on behalf of the companies with which he was connected – planning, organising, negotiating and beating down opposition with an energy almost unparalleled – felt himself entitled to a large share of the benefits accruing from his efforts. The value of his services it would be difficult to exaggerate. No professional man would have undertaken many of the duties which Mr Hudson performed without a very large remuneration. By his judgement and foresight, Mr Hudson must have saved the York and North Midland and York Newcastle and Berwick companies enormous sums of money'.[60]

In 1849, *Tait's Edinburgh Magazine* was already aware that the question of whether Hudson was a man or a myth would be asked many years hence, 'when people talk of our railways as we speak of the Pyramids'. They were not at all certain how posterity would treat him but foresaw a time when the 'biography of George Hudson would sell in thousands.'

This book is now his fifth biography, following those written by Lambert in 1934, Peacock in 1988–9, Bailey in 1995 and Beaumont in 2002.[61] In it, we argue that Hudson's importance is wider than railways because he was a great capitalist and one whose practices and experiences form an important part of the evolution of capitalism. Unlike Lambert, we argue that he is important precisely because he did things that other people did not do, at a time that was particularly important in the evolution of capitalism towards its present form.[62]

In many ways he was the first modern capitalist, using publicity as a means to develop a cult of personality and attract huge amounts of scattered savings to his schemes. He was a major influence on the most modernising industry of his age, yet unlike many other entrepreneurs of his time he was no urban, Liberal, nonconformist, free-trade radical but someone rooted in the country, espousing traditional Anglican, High Tory land-owner politics consistent with his own ambitions towards gentrification and his own instinctive belief in protectionism.[63]

George Hudson was unique and, in both the manner of his rise and the depths of his decline, his experiences tell us a great deal about the times in which he lived and which he marked so signally.

APPENDIX 1

Parliamentary Acts Promoted
by George Hudson

Description	Act	Date
EASTERN COUNTIES RAILWAY		
Branches	9 & 10 Vic. c. 76	1846
Epping to Ilford branch	9 & 10 Vic. c. 205	1846
Enlarge Stratford station etc.	9 & 10 Vic. c. 258	1846
Amendment to Ely to Huntingdon line	9 & 10 Vic. c. 270	1846
Exemption from Cambridge Improvement Tolls	9 & 10 Vic. c. 345	1846
Wisbech, St Ives & Cambridge Jnct[a]	9 & 10 Vic. c. 356	1846
Edmonton to Enfield[a]	9 & 10 Vic. c. 357	1846
Thames Junction etc.	9 & 10 Vic. c. 367	1846
Purchase of Maldon, Witham and Braintree	10 & 11 Vic. c. 92	1847
Purchase of the North Woolwich Railway etc.	10 & 11 Vic. c. 156	1847
Enlargement of London and Stratford Stations etc.	10 & 11 Vic. c. 157	1847
Cambridge to Bedford	10 & 11 Vic. c. 158	1847
Wisbech to Spalding	10 & 11 Vic. c. 235	1847
MIDLAND & LEEDS AND BRADFORD RAILWAYS		
Midland Railway Act (Amalgamation)	7 & 8 Vic. c. 18.	1844
Leeds and Bradford Act (L&B)	7 & 8 Vic. c. 59	1844
Leeds and Bradford: Extension to Colne (L&B)	8 & 9 Vic c. 38	1845
Nottingham to Lincoln	8 & 9 Vic. c. 49	1845
Syston (Leicester) to Peterborough	8 & 9 Vic. c. 56	1845
Acquisition of the Sheffield & Rotherham and new works	8 & 9 Vic. c. 90	1845
Leeds and Bradford – mistake (L&B)	8 & 9 Vic c. 181	1845

Description	Act	Date
Erewash Valley[b]	8 & 9 Vic c. 189	1845
Alterations and branches	9 & 10 Vic. c. 51	1846
Erewash Valley Extension	9 & 10 Vic. c. 102	1846
Nottingham to Mansfield	9 & 10 Vic. c. 103	1846
Branches from Erewash Valley	9 & 10 Vic. c 156	1846
Clay Cross to Newark (Junction with Nottingham and Lincoln)	9 & 10 Vic. c 157	1846
Nottingham to Mansfield	9 & 10 Vic. c 163	1846
Burton to Nuneaton Branch and purchase of Ashby canal	9 & 10 Vic. c 203	1846
Acquisition of the Leicester & Swannington	9 & 10 Vic. c. 243	1846
Extension to Birmingham	9 & 10 Vic. c. 254	1846
Purchase of Oakham Canal	9 & 10 Vic. c. 255	1846
Alteration of levels (L&B)	9 & 10 Vic. c. 272	1846
Junction with Midland (L&B)	9 & 10 Vic. c. 301	1846
Connection of Leicester and Swannington to the Midland	9 & 10 Vic. c. 311	1846
Acquisition of Bristol and Gloucester and Birmingham and Gloucester	9 & 10 Vic. c. 326	1846
King's Norton to Hales Owen branch of the B'ham and Gloucester	9 & 10 Vic. c. 340	1846
Vale of Neath line	9 & 10 Vic. c. 341	1846
Chesterfield to Trent consolidation etc.	9 & 10 Vic. c. 358	1846
Alteration to Leicester & Swannington line etc.	10 & 11 Vic. 122	1847
Hitchin, Northampton and Huntingdon extension	10 & 11 Vic. 135	1847
Enlargement of Masborough and Normanton stations etc.	10 & 11 Vic. 150	1847
Purchase of Mansfield and Pinxton etc.	10 & 11 Vic. c. 191	1847
Lincolnshire extensions	10 & 11 Vic. c. 214	1847
Syston-Peterborough deviations	10 & 11 Vic. c. 215	1847
Alterations in Hitchin, Northampton, and Huntingdon	11 & 12 Vic. 21	1848
Ripley Branches etc.	11 & 12 Vic. c. 88	1848
Gloucester to Stonehouse	11 & 12 Vic. c. 131	1848

Description	Act	Date
YORK, NEWCASTLE & BERWICK, AND PREDECESSOR COMPANIES		
Incorporation of N&DJ and transfer of authorisation from Great North of England	5 & 6 Vic. c. 80	1842
Deviation of line	6 & 7 Vic. c. 8	1843
Purchase of Durham Jctn, authorisation of Gateshead Station and Tyne Bridge (N&DJ)	7 & 8 Vic. c. 27	1844
Purchase of Brandling Junction Railway (N&DJ)	8 & 9 Vic. c. 92	1845
Incorporation of Newcastle and Berwick (N&B) and amalgamation with the Newcastle and North Shields Railway	8 & 9 Vic. 163	1845
Malton to Hemsley (nr Thirsk) (N&DJ)	9 & 10 Vic. c. 58	1846
Boroughbridge branch (N&DJ)	9 & 10 Vic. c. 95	1846
Bedale branch (N&DJ)	9 & 10 Vic. c. 96	1846
Branch lines (N&B)	9 & 10 Vic. c. 207	1846
Purchase of Durham & Sunderland and Monkwearmouth Dock (N&DJ)	9 & 10 Vic. c. 235	1846
Acquisition of the Great North of England (N&DJ, which becomes the York and Newcastle (Y&N))	9 & 10 Vic c. 242	1846
Branches (N&DJ)	9 & 10 Vic. c. 264	1846
Purchase of Pontop and S Shields (N&DJ)	9 & 10 Vic. c. 330	1846
Wearmouth Dock enlargements	10 & 11 Vic. c. 117	1847
Y&N, N&B amalgamation	10 & 11 Vic. c. 133	1847
Pelaw Branch etc	10 & 11 Vic. c. 134	1847
Tyne Docks	10 & 11 Vic. c. 263	1847
Main line improvements (borrow £690,000) and abandon 11m of Bishop Auckland branch	11 & 12 Vic. c. 24	1848
Deviation in Thirsk and Malton	11 & 12 Vic. c. 55	1848
Lease of Hartlepool Dock and Railway Company and Great North of England, Clarence and Hartlepool Jctn	11 & 12 Vic. c. 81	1848

Description	Act	Date

YORK AND NORTH MIDLAND

Description	Act	Date
Original Leeds-York line	6 & 7 Wm. IV c. 81	1836
Deviation to line	7 Wm. IV & 1 Vic. c. 68	1837
Authorisation of additional capital	4 & 5 Vic. c. 7	1841
Purchase of the Leeds and Selby	7 & 8 Vic. c. 21	1844
York to Scarborough and Pickering	7 & 8 Vic. c. 61	1844
Alteration to York-Scarborough line	8 & 9 Vic. c. 34	1845
Purchase of the Whitby and Pickering	8 & 9 Vic. c. 57	1845
Bridlington branch	8 & 9 Vic. c. 58	1845
Harrogate branch	8 & 9 Vic. c. 84	1845
East Riding branches (No 1)	9 & 10 Vic. c. 65	1846
East Riding branches (No 2)	9 & 10 Vic. c. 66	1846
Extension to Whitby and Pickering	9 & 10 Vic. c. 77	1846
York to Leeds direct line	9 & 10 Vic. c. 89	1846
Lease or purchase of the Hull and Selby	9 & 10 Vic. c. 241	1846
Widening main line	9 & 10 Vic. c. 247	1846
Harrogate Extension	10 & 11 Vic. c. 140	1847
Knottingley branch	10 & 11 Vic. c. 141	1847
Purchase of Market Weighton & other canals	10 & 11 Vic. c. 216	1847
Hull station and branches	10 & 11 Vic. c. 216	1847
Boroughbridge and Knaresborough branch	10 & 11 Vic. c. 216	1847

SUNDERLAND DOCK COMPANY

Description	Act	Date
Creation and authorisation of works	9 & 10 Vict. c. 13	1846
Authorisation of further share issue etc.	12 & 13 Vict. c. 31	1849

Notes:
[a] Lines promoted by nominally independent companies, but whose Acts contained powers to enable the Eastern Counties Railway to acquire them.
[b] The Erewash Valley had been promoted independently, but the Midland agreed to acquire it in February 1845, before the Act was passed.
L&B Acts promoted by the Leeds and Bradford
N&DJ Acts promoted by the Newcastle and Darlington Junction
N&B Acts promoted by the Newcastle and Berwick
Sources: Report of the Royal Commission on Railways (1867), Appendix EK; Scrivenor (1849).

APPENDIX 2

Main Railway Lines
of Hudson's Companies

Table 1: Lines Constructed, Acquired and Leased by the York and North Midland (YNM), 1836–48

Description	Act	Length (miles)	Opened/(acquired)
York to Leeds	1836	27	1839–40
Leeds & Selby	1841	20	(October 1840)
York–Scarborough	1844	49	July 1845
Church Fenton to Spofforth	1845	14	August 1847
Spofforth to Harrogate	1845	5	July 1848
Whitby–Pickering [a]	1845	23	(July 1847)
Seamer–Filey	1845	7	October 1846
Filey–Bridlington	1845	13	October 1847
Hull & Selby	1846	31	(July 1845)
York–Market Weighton	1846	22	October 1847
Selby–Market Weighton	1846	16	August 1848
Hull and Bridlington	1845	31	October 1846
Hull Station	1846	5	May 1848
Total mileage		263	

Note: [a] Acquisition and upgrading of previously horse-drawn line.
Sources: Tomlinson, (1987), YNM Third Report (1849), Scrivenor, (1849).

Table 2: Lines Constructed, Acquired and Leased by the York
Newcastle and Berwick and Predecessor Railways, 1842–48

Description	Act	Length (miles)	Opened/(acquired)
Darlington to Gateshead (N&DJ) [a]	1842	26	Apr-June 1844
Durham Junction (N&DJ)	1844	5	(November 1843)
Brandling Junction	1845	27	(September 1844)
Newcastle to North Shields (N&B)	1845	8	(July 1845)
York to Darlington (N&DJ) [b]	1846	48	(July 1845)
Durham to Sunderland (N&DJ)	1846	17	(October 1845)
Hartlepool Dock (N&DJ)	1848	26	(July 1846)
Pontop and South Shields (N&DJ)	1846	24	(October 1845)
Newcastle to Berwick (N&B) [c]	1845	65	Mar-July 1847
Boroughbridge branch	1846	7	July 1847
Bedale branch	1846	5	March 1848
Others		12	
Total mileage		270	

Notes:

[a] The Newcastle and Darlington Junction Railway was formed in July 1842 and became the York and Newcastle in July 1846, after taking over the Great North of England Railway.

[b] The Great North of England (opened in April 1841).

[c] The Newcastle and Berwick was formed in July 1845. It merged with the York and Newcastle to become the York, Newcastle and Berwick Railway as of 1 July 1847.

Sources: Tomlinson (1987); Scrivenor (1849).

Table 3: Lines Constructed, Acquired and Leased by the North Midland and the Midland Railways, 1836–48

Description	Act	Length (miles)	Opened/(acquired)
Derby to Leeds [a]	1836	73	May-July 1840
Derby to Hampton [b]	1836	38	August 1839
Derby to Rugby and Nottingham [c]	1836	58	1839–40
Hampton to Birmingham	1840	10	February 1842
Midland Railway at its formation	1844	179	
Sheffield to Rotherham	1845	9	(Oct 1844) [d]
Erewash Valley	1845	16	Sept 1847
Bristol to Birmingham	1846	88	(July 1845) [d]
Leicester to Swannington	1846	16	(Aug 1845) [d]
Leeds to Bradford	1844 [e]	15	July 1846
Nottingham to Lincoln	1845	36	Aug 1846
Syston to Peterborough	1845	48	1846–48
Nottingham to Mansfield	1846	13	1848
Bradford to Colne etc.	1845 [e]	28	1847–48
Others		10	
Total mileage (open at 31 December 1848) [f]		458	

Notes:

[a] The North Midland Railway.

[b] The Birmingham and Derby Junction Railway.

[c] The Midland Counties Railway.

[d] Acquisition of existing line.

[e] The Leeds and Bradford was promoted independently of the Midland, but the Act of incorporation (and the subsequent Act for the extension to Colne, passed in 1845) explicitly allowed the line to be leased by the Midland, which was agreed in July 1845, before the original line was completed.

[f] A further 40 miles of line were under construction at this date. Hudson was not made a director of the North Midland until late 1842.

Sources: Lewin (1925); Scrivenor (1849); Stretton (1901).

Table 4: Lines Constructed, Acquired and Leased by the Eastern Counties Railway, 1845–48

Description	Act	Length (miles)	Opened/(acquired)
London to Colchester (ECR)	1836	51	1839–43
London to Bishop's Stortford (N&E)	1836	29	1840–42
Broxbourne to Hertford (N&E)	1841	6	October 1843
Bishop's Stortford to Newport (N&E)	1843	10	July 1845
Newport–Brandon (ECR)	1844	45	July 1845
The ECR at Hudson's accession		141	
Ely to Peterborough	1844	28	Jan 1847
March to Wisbech	1844	8	May 1847
Cambridge to St Ives	1845	12	Aug 1847
Stratford to North Woolwich	1844	5	June 1847
St Ives to March	1846	18	Feb 1848
Brandon–Norwich–Reedham–Yarmouth[a]	n/a	58	(May 1848)
Wymondham to Dereham[a]	n/a	12	(May 1848)
Reedham to Lowestoft[a]	n/a	12	(May 1848)
Chesterford to Newmarket[b]	n/a	18	(Oct 1848)
Maldon to Braintree	1847	12	Oct 1848
Total mileage (at 31 Dec 1848)[c]		324	

Notes:
[a] Norfolk Railway, leased from May 1848.
[b] Newmarket Railway, leased from October 1848.
[c] A further 17 miles of line were under construction at this date.
Hudson did not become Chairman until 30 October 1845.
Sources: Lewin (1925), Scrivenor, (1849), Allen, (1968).

APPENDIX 3

Share Capital and Profits of Hudson's Companies

Date	Share capital[a] £'000	Profits £'000	Divi rate [ord shares] Annual %age	Ord share (Nom) £–	Ord share (Paid up) £–	Ord share (Price) £–
NORTH MIDLAND						
30 June 1842		30	2	£100	£100	57
31 Dec	2487	49	3.25			63
30 June 1843		44	3			70
31 Dec	2510	65	4			90
30 June 1844		56	2.2			94
MIDLAND						
31 Dec 1844	4511	152	6	£100	£100	116
30 June 1845		151	6			188
31 Dec	4967	199	7.3			156
30 June 1846		165	7			149
31 Dec	6151	211	7			130
30 June 1847		240	7			130
31 Dec	7556	295	7			109
30 June 1848		205	6			100
31 Dec	10425	284	5			85
YORK & NORTH MIDLAND						
31 Dec 1839	198	9	7	50	30	40.5
30 June 1840		7	7		50	71
31 Dec	329	14	7			68
30 June 1841		16	9			71
31 Dec	433	24	10			92

Date	Share capital[a] £'000	Profits £'000	Divi rate [ord shares] Annual %age	Ord share (Nom) £–	Ord share (Paid up) £–	Ord share (Price) £–
30 June 1842		22	10			86
31 Dec	464	26	10			93.5
30 June 1843		22	10			98.5
31 Dec	466	22	10			120
30 June 1844		24	10			106.5
31 Dec	790	40	10			103
30 June 1845		42	10			111.5
31 Dec	1078	75	10			109
30 June 1846		68	10			98
31 Dec	1834	118	10			94.5
30 June 1847		109	10			88
31 Dec	2632	162	10			72.5
30 June 1848		118	8			67
31 Dec	3484	132	6			54.5

NEWCASTLE AND DARLINGTON JUNCTION

Date	Share capital[a] £'000	Profits £'000	Divi rate [ord shares] Annual %age	Ord share (Nom) £–	Ord share (Paid up) £–	Ord share (Price) £–
30 June 1844				25	21	41
31 Dec	474	21	8		24	61.5
30 June 1845		37	8		25	55
31 Dec	889	43	9			59
30 June 1846		39	9			46
31 Dec	1298	44	9			38.5
30 June 1847	1532	70	9			38.25

NEWCASTLE & BERWICK

Date	Share capital[a] £'000	Profits £'000	Divi rate [ord shares] Annual %age	Ord share (Nom) £–	Ord share (Paid up) £–	Ord share (Price) £–
30 June 1846			n/a	25	15	24.25
31 Dec	1123	3	n/a		20	34.6
30 June 1847	1178	3	n/a		20	30

'YORK, NEWCASTLE & BERWICK'

Date	Share capital[a] £'000	Profits £'000	Divi rate [ord shares] Annual %age	Ord share (Nom) £–	Ord share (Paid up) £–	Ord share (Price) £–
31 Dec 1847	3427	129	9	25	25	33.25
30 June 1848		89	8			31.75
31 Dec	5584	110	6			28.75

Date	Share capital[a] £'000	Profits £'000	Divi rate [ord shares] Annual %age	Ord share (Nom) £–	Ord share (Paid up) £–	Ord share (Price) £–
EASTERN COUNTIES						
31 Dec 1845	2012	64	6			22.75
30 June 1846		59	6			24.1
31 Dec	4922	99	6.7			23.1
30 June 1847		122	5			21.25
31 Dec	6570	144	4			15.5
30 June 1848		137	4			14.25
31 Dec	8386	198	0			11.9
YORK UNION BANK						
31 Dec 1833	54	1	0			
31 Dec 1834	54	5	7			
31 Dec 1835	57	6	8			
31 Dec 1836	63	8	9			
31 Dec 1837	64	9	10			
31 Dec 1838	66	9	10			
31 Dec 1839	66	8	10			
31 Dec 1840	66	9	10			
31 Dec 1841	66	9	10			
31 Dec 1842	66	8	10			
31 Dec 1843	66	6	8			
31 Dec 1844	66	8	8			
31 Dec 1845	66	16	10			
31 Dec 1846	99	20	10			
31 Dec 1847	99	23	10			
31 Dec 1848	99	15	10			

Note: [a] Share capital includes preference and guaranteed shares.

Notes

Notes to Chapter 1: First Steps

1. Baptismal entry, parish register of Scrayingham, Y923.8, York Reference Library.

2. The office passed initially to George's brother John, who resigned it to his brother William. The title lapsed on the latter's death in 1868.

3. *English Gentleman*, 20, 6 September 1845, p. 313; *Fraser's Magazine*, August 1847, p. 216; *Bankers' Magazine* (December 1851), p. 747; *A Complete Report of the Recent Trial for Libel, Richardson v. Wodson* (London, 1850), p. xiii.

4. In the early part of the nineteenth century, despite the effects of the industrial revolution, most people in Britain still lived in rural areas; see J. H. Clapham, *An Economic History of Modern Britain, the Early Railway Age, 1820–1850* (second edition, Cambridge, 1967), p. 66.

5. It has also been suggested that Hudson was a Methodist for part of his life. See for example, A. Vaughan, *Railwaymen, Politics and Money: The Great Age of Railways in Britain* (London, 1997), p. 103. He denied being a Methodist and maintained instead that he was a supporter of the Church of England. In 1847, for example, when his past as an alleged 'Methodist exhorter and prayer leader' was alluded to in the House of Commons, he said 'he never had that honour', and had only presided at meetings of the Methodist missionary society when Lord Mayor of York (*Times*, 7 July 1847, p. 2). On the other hand, a decade later, in a political speech in Sunderland in March 1857, he said that he thought Methodists had 'done an immense deal of good to the Church of England by stirring her ministers up to greater exertions' and that, although he generally preferred the Church of England, he 'would as freely go and frequently did go to a Methodist chapel and with as much pleasure as to the church', *Sunderland Times* 19 March 1857, p. 1. In the early 1820s, he had also been one of the secretaries to a Sunday School largely under the control of the followers of Wesley but also supported by the 'members of various churches', J. Lyth, *Glimpses of Early Methodism in York* (York, 1885), p. 218.

6. W. B. Rubinstein, *Britain's Century: a Political and Social History 1815–1905* (London, 1998), p. 7; F. Crouzet, 'Wars, Blockade and Economic Change in Europe, 1792–1815', *Journal of Economic History*, 24 (1964) p. 567.

7. S. G. Checkland, *The Rise of Industrial Society in England, 1815–1885* (London, 1964), p. 8.

8. At the start of the nineteenth century, York was the sixteenth largest city in England. E. Royle, 'York in the Nineteenth Century: A City Transformed', in P. Nuttgens (ed.), *The History of York from Earliest Times to the Year 2000* (Pickering, 2000), p. 244; A. Armstrong, *Stability and Change in an English County Town: A Social Study of York, 1801–51* (London, 1974), pp. 16–17, 96; Victoria County History, ed. P. M. Tillott, *A History of Yorkshire: the City of York* (London, 1961), pp. 266–67.

9. *Yorkshire Gazette*, 25 September 1817, 2 October 1819, 12 May 1849; R. Beaumont, *The Railway King: A Biography of George Hudson* (London, 2002), p. 14.

10. W. Parson and W. White, *Directory of the Borough of Leeds and the County of York, etc.* (Leeds, 1830); Deed of co-partnership, accession 135, box 7, York City Archives. There is a suggestion that Elizabeth put up a thousand pounds of Hudson's capital; see the notes in Knowles Scrap Book, 1852–91, p. 93, York Reference Library Y040; Stephen, L. and Lee, S. (eds) (1959–60), *Dictionary of National Biography X* (London, 1959–60), pp. 145–47; *English Gentleman*, 20, 6 September 1845, p. 313; *Fraser's Magazine*, August 1847, pp. 216–17.

11. Marriage entry, parish register of Holy Trinity, Goodramgate, York. The Hudsons paid thirty-five pounds a year to the partnership for the 'dwelling house and premises adjoining the said shop for the residence of himself and family'; deed of co-partnership, York City Archives.

12. Armstrong, *Stability and Change*, p. 31.

13. Knowles Scrap Book, 1852–91, pp. 93–94, 108–9.

14. An obituary of Hudson quotes him as saying that the business made a profit of some £7500 a year, of which he would have half, although this seems an extraordinary figure; *Daily News*, 18 December 1871, p. 3. Under his will, Matthew Bottrill left various annuities of £20 to £50 each to a number of people, including his brother, James, Eleanor Brennard, a 'female servant' and her son James; Borthwick Wills, York Prerogative 176/200. See also A. J. Peacock, 'Another Look at George Hudson's Legacy', in A. J. Peacock (ed.), *Essays in York History* (York, 1997), pp. 348–52.

15. Bottrill left Hudson his house in Monkgate, York and land in nearby Osbaldwick and Huntington, in Westow near Malton, a large farm in the east Yorkshire village of Hutton Cranswick and other land at Newton-on-Derwent and at Whitby. Beaumont says that the land at Whitby was in the West Cliff area although, if so, the holding can have been only a modest one as Hudson's major acquisitions in that area were not made until 1848; see Beaumont, *The Railway*, pp. 17–18, 27–28; Deeds of conveyance for land at Whitby; Register of Deeds NRRD HQ 178146 and 179147, North Yorkshire County Record Office; R. B. Martin, *'Enter Rumour': Four Early Victorian Scandals* (London, 1962), p. 190.

16. C. B. Knight, *A History of the City of York* (York, 1944), p. 617.

17. Hudson bought 42 Monkgate for £500. The deed of conveyance, dated 17/18 April 1828, allowed Richard Nicholson to use the house during Hudson's lifetime; E98, fos 61v–62v, York City Archives. G. T. Andrews, a partner in the York-based architects, Robinson and Andrews, who became one of Hudson's

closest friends, was appointed by him in 1830 to carry out the extensive remodelling of his two houses in Monkgate; B. Fawcett, *A History of North Eastern Railway Architecture*, i , *the Pioneers* (Hull, 2001), p. 48; Royal Commission on Historical Monuments in England, *Inventory of the Historical Monuments in the City of York*, iv (London, 1975), pp. 90–91.

18. In York business circles Whig beliefs were dominant.

19. The average price of wheat fell from 96s. 11d. in 1817 to 56s. 1d. in 1821, for example; see also Checkland, *Rise of Industrial Society*, pp. 11–12; B. C. Hunt, *The Development of the Business Corporation in England 1800–1867* (Cambridge, Massachusetts, 1936), pp. 30–31. Wheat was not the only protected commodity; malt was very heavily taxed and duties on imported butter and cheese were also increased in 1816. Several industries, such as whale and herring fishing, linen and silk manufacture and sugar re-exporting were subsidised. The French recovery after the Napoleonic wars was based on the introduction of highly protectionist tariffs; see Checkland, *Rise of Industrial Society*, pp. 10, 333–34.

20. Rubinstein, *Britain's Century*, p. 9.

21. Checkland, *Rise of Industrial Society*, pp. 9–10.

22. The death of the monarch required the holding of an election; E. J. Hobsbawm, *Industry and Empire* (London, 1969), p. 77.

23. Fitzwilliam patronage took many forms, including contributions to benevolent and charitable societies, local schools, the York races, the maintenance of the city hounds, the upkeep of prisoners in the city goal, the establishment of soup kitchens in times of economic distress and more specific projects such as the building of the Ouse Bridge; P. Brett, *The Rise and Fall of the York Whig Club, 1818–1830*, Borthwick Paper 76 (York, 1989), pp. 7–8.

24. Freemen could engage in trade, have a voice in the management of their city and could also vote in parliamentary elections; R. Y. Hawkin, *A History of the Freemen of the City of York* (York, 1955), p. 8. George Hudson's name does not appear in the standard list of the freemen of York. In general, one needed to be a freeman to carry on a trade but certain areas within the city were unaffected by the regulations concerning freemen: 'around the Minster ... in particular, any person could carry on trade without being a freeman'; J. Malden, *Register of York Freemen* (York, 1989), p ii.

25. *Yorkshire Gazette*, 10 July 1830; *Times*, 5 July 1830, p. 3; 31 July 1830, p. 4, 10 September 1830, p. 3.

26. Hudson was openly anti-papist and was one of a number of the 'local gentry' who attended a meeting in the city's concert rooms to promote a branch of the Protestant Association in York on 23 April 1840. Local interest in the Association, however, soon declined; M. Eames, 'Anti-Catholicism in York from the General Election of 1826 to the Opening of the New St Winifred's Church in 1864', unpublished MA thesis (York, 1996), pp. 33–34.

27. *York Herald*, 17 July 1830; *Times*, 31 July 1830, p. 4.

28. The parliamentary voting figures throughout the chapter are as shown in G. R. Park, *Parliamentary Representation of Yorkshire* (Hull, 1886), pp. 59–61.

29. See *Times* 21 March 1831, p. 6; 24 March 1831, p. 6; 2 May 1831, p. 6.

30. *Yorkshire Gazette*, 19 May 1832; *York Courant*, 22 May 1832.

31. The city's sanitation problems stemmed from its position at the centre of great flats that stretched for miles. Drainage into the River Foss was particularly problematic, due to a badly handled canalisation of the river in the late eighteenth century that left large areas of stagnant water. Armstrong, *Stability and Change*, p. 118.

32. M. Durey, *The First Spasmodic Cholera Epidemic in York, 1832*, Borthwick Paper 46 (York, 1974), pp. 7–8; Knight, *A History of the City*, p. 622.

33. *York Courant*, 10 July 1832.

34. Durey, *The First Spasmodic*, pp. 21–22; *Yorkshire Gazette*, 11 August 1832.

35. *Times*, 18 September 1832, p. 3.

36. Petre 1505 votes, Bayntun 1141 votes, Lowther 884 votes, Dundas 872 votes. *York Herald*, 10 November 1832; *Yorkshire Gazette*, 15 December 1832.

37. See Rubinstein, *Britain's Century*, p. 51.

38. *Times*, 6 January 1835, p. 5.

39. Lowther gained 1499 votes and John Dundas was also elected with 1301 votes. Barkley obtained only 919 votes.

40. This did not change until 1872.

41. *Times*, 10 January 1835, p. 3.

42. *York Herald*, 10 January 1835; *Yorkshireman*, 24 January 1835.

43. *Yorkshireman* 24 January 1835; *Yorkshire Gazette*, 14 February 1835.

44. *Times*, 1 July 1835, p. 1.

45. A guinea was usually paid to a voter who had split his vote between two candidates or two guineas to a voter who had voted for him alone.

46. Bayntun was badly off as a result of over expenditure in the 1831 election.

47. *Times*, 12 September 1835, p. 4.

48. *Times*, 9 September 1835, p. 3; 12 September 1835, p. 4.

49. Anon., *Stranger's Guide through the City of York* (York, 1832), p. 19; Armstrong, *Stability and Change*, p. 23; J. B. Morrell and A. G. Watson (eds), *How York Governs Itself* (London, 1928), pp. 4–8.

50. Knight, *A History of the City*, p. 636.

51. *Yorkshireman*, 5 December 1835.

52. *York Courant*, 21 January 1836.

53. Those of the twelve least supported councillors plus two other seats where councillors had resigned.

54. J. F. C. Harrison, *Early Victorian Britain, 1832–51* (London, 1988), pp. 24–25; Checkland, *Rise of Industrial Society*, p. 18.

55. *Yorkshire Gazette*, 20 February 1836.

56. Private papers confirm that Lowther's supporters undertook to make amends to Atcherley at a later election as they were 'sensible of their injustice to [him] at the last election'. They also reveal that bribery and treating took place; 'freemen and electors were taken and treated with as much liquor as they could or would drink'. Atcherley papers re 1837 election, accession 93/7–8, York City Archives.

57. Of twenty-five (twenty-two councillors and three aldermen) to twenty-three (fourteen councillors and nine aldermen). *Yorkshire Gazette*, 4 November 1837.
58. *Yorkshireman* 4 November 1837, p. 5.
59. The Lord Mayor of York, an office dating back to the twelfth century, ranked equal in the order of precedence with London's Lord Mayor. Hawkin, *A History of the Freemen*, p. 10.
60. R. S. Lambert, *The Railway King* (London, 1934), pp. 42–43.
61. *York Courant*, 27 January 1838.
62. Davies had been Town Clerk since December 1827. He trained as a solicitor and was also a clerk to the magistrates. He married into the local Cattle family before becoming known as a collector, antiquarian and publisher of many works on the history of York. His maternal grandfather, Robert Rhodes, had been Lord Mayor of York in 1808.
63. *Yorkshire Gazette*, 12 October 1839; *York Chronicle* 31 October 1839.
64. Leeman, a staunch Liberal, was close friends with the editor of the *Yorkshireman*, the newspaper that proved to be Hudson's fiercest critic. S. M. Jenvey, 'George Leeman and the Virtue of Independence', unpublished PhD thesis, York University, 1969.
65. *York Courant*, 14 November 1839.
66. *York Courant*, 13 February 1840; Clapham, *Economic History*, p. 219.
67. *Times*, 30 December 1839, p. 5; 28 July 1840, p. 5.
68. Politics did not, of course, necessarily extend to business matters; two years later, at a meeting of the Newcastle and Darlington Railway in February 1843 the same C. H. Elsley proposed 'a cordial vote of thanks not only for the services [Hudson] had rendered this company during the time that he had been its Chairman, but also for the talent and zeal he had always brought to bear upon railway interests'. *Railway Times* (1843), p. 230.
69. Copies of the Bill were given to the committee members only on the Saturday before a meeting on the Tuesday, the day before the full meeting of the council.
70. *Yorkshire Gazette*, 3 July 1841.
71. 1842 has been seen as 'the worst year of distress and disorder that Britain experienced in the nineteenth century'. Rubinstein, *Britain's Century*, p. 75.
72. This was eventually used as an officer's mess for the Yorkshire Hussars and for various other events, including the regular meetings of the York-based railway companies.
73. *Times*, 30 September 1844, p. 6.
74. *York Herald*, 22 February 1845; D. Brooke, 'The Origins and Development of Four Constituent Lines of the North-Eastern Railway, 1824–54', unpublished MA thesis, University of Hull (1972) pp. 64–65; A. J. Peacock, 'York in the Age of Reform', unpublished PhD thesis, University of York (1973), p. 497.
75. *Yorkshireman*, 5 December 1846.
76. L. T. C. Rolt, *George and Robert Stephenson* (London, 1984), p. 324.
77. *Yorkshire Gazette*, 3 July 1847.

78. Smyth was ex-Eton and Trinity College, Cambridge, a protectionist and anti-papist. His father had previously been MP for Cambridge University. It was widely suggested that the commercial monies of the York and North Midland had been used to pay its men to march to the hustings in support of the political interests of the local Tory party. *Yorkshireman*, 5 April 1849.
79. Andrews was a close business colleague of Hudson. *Times*, 29 July 1847, p. 5.
80. Wilkinson, the son of a Hull merchant, had begun business in York as an 'accountant and commission merchant' in 1827 and also acted as a wine merchant.
81. Hopwood's 261 votes were 175 less than the second Tory. *Yorkshireman*, 6 November 1847.
82. Milner 1506 votes, Henry Vincent 860, Charles Wilkins 57 votes. A. J. Peacock, 'George Leeman and York Politics 1833–1880', in C. H. Feinstein (ed.), *York, 1831–1981: 150 Years of Scientific Endeavour and Social Change* (York, 1981), pp. 236–37.
83. *Yorkshire Gazette*, 12 August 1848, p. 6. This was the second of two portraits of Hudson to be painted by Francis Grant, later Sir Francis. The other showed Hudson in business clothes, holding a Railway Bill and is now displayed at Monkwearmouth Station Museum, Sunderland.
84. Once the Council was back in session, Hudson confirmed that the York and North Midland would meet all its obligations towards the city of York over the Lendal Bridge.

Notes to Chapter 2: Banker and Promoter

1. At first the maximum shareholding was one hundred shares, raised in 1843 to two hundred and in 1847 to four hundred shares. The capital was provided in the form of one hundred pound shares although much of this remained uncalled, as a form of security. The bank was registered under the Banking Act of 1826, with its powers and arrangements defined in its deed of settlement, University of London Rare Books Collection, 28073. It would later be the bank of the York and North Midland, the Newcastle and Darlington and the Newcastle and Berwick railways, M. Phillips, *A History of Banks, Bankers and Banking in Northumberland, Durham and North Yorkshire* (London, 1894), pp. 410–11; see also P. W. Matthews, *History of Barclays Bank* (London, 1926), pp. 235–37.
2. In 1840, the managing directors' remuneration was increased to two hundred and fifty pounds each and, in 1847, with profits booming, to five hundred pounds apiece. The assistant director fee was doubled in 1846.
3. York Union Bank, Minute Books of the Board of Directors, 1833–62, Barclays Bank Archives, 0003–0392/3.
4. C. B. Knight, *A History of the City of York* (York, 1944), pp. 618, 623–24.
5. *Yorkshireman* 18 February 1837.
6. *York Courant* 24 November 1836.

7. By 1837 there were five other banks in York, M. Phillips, *A History of Banks*, pp. 410–12.
8. York Union Bank, correspondence files, Barclays Bank Archives, 0003–3881.
9. W. W. Tomlinson, *Tomlinson's North Eastern Railway* (third edition, Newton Abbot, 1987), pp. 5–14.
10. See, for example H. G. Lewin, *Early British Railways* (London, 1925), p. 4.
11. H. Parris, *Government and the Railways in Nineteenth-Century Britain* (London, 1965), pp. 1–3; J. H. Clapham, *An Economic History of Modern Britain, the Early Railway Age, 1820–1850* (second edition, Cambridge, 1967), p. 86; J. Simmons and G. Biddle (eds), *Oxford Companion to British Railway History* (Oxford, 1997), p. 134.
12. Clapham, *Economic History*, pp. 87, 90; see also G. R. Hawke, *Railways and Economic Growth in England and Wales, 1840–1870* (Oxford, 1970), p. 157. The railways reduced the rates of carriage on the canals by from one-third to one-half and put an end to canal construction, S. G. Checkland, *The Rise of Industrial Society in England, 1815–1885* (London, 1964), pp. 13, 82.
13. In the line's early years, passengers still travelled by horse-drawn coaches adapted for use on the rails. M. C. Reed, *Investment in Railways in Britain, 1820–1844: A Study in the Development of the Capital Market* (Oxford, 1975), pp. 3–4; Lewin, *Early British Railways*, p. 3; Tomlinson, *Tomlinson's*, pp. 15–16, 30–31.
14. Clapham, *Economic History*, pp. 381–82; G. R. Hawke and J. P. P. Higgins, 'Transport and Social Overhead Capital', in R. Floud and D. McCloskey (eds), *Economic History of Britain since 1700*, i (Cambridge, 1981), p. 235.
15. S. and D. Dugan, *The Day the World Took Off: the Roots of the Industrial Revolution* (London, 2000), pp. 34–7; see also Reed, *Investment*, pp. 3–5.
16. Parris, *Government*, pp. 3–4; J. Foreman-Peck and R. Millward, *Public and Private Ownership of British Industry 1820–1990* (Oxford, 1994), p. 13; J. Simmons, *The Victorian Railway* (London, 1995), p. 373.
17. Reed, *Investment*, pp. 6–7.
18. Tomlinson, *Tomlinson's*, pp. 382–83.
19. H. A. Shannon, 'The Coming of General Limited Liability', *Economic Journal* (*Economic History Supplement*), 2 (1931), p. 267; G. Todd, 'Some Aspects of Joint Stock Companies, 1844–1900', *Economic History Review*, old series 4 (1932), p. 46; P. L. Cottrell, *Industrial Finance, 1830–1914* (London, 1980), p. 39–43.
20. Under the Limited Liability Act of 1855 (18&19 Vict. c. 133).
21. Hunt, *Development*, p. 16.
22. M. Freeman, *Railways and the Victorian Imagination* (New Haven, 1999), pp. 31–32.
23. See Parris, *Government*, pp. 18, 29; Hawke and Higgins, 'Transport and Social', p. 237; Foreman-Peck and Millward, *Public and Private*, pp. 14–15; Simmons and Biddle, *Oxford Companion*, p. 185.
24. J. B. Baskin, 'The Development of Corporate Financial Markets in Britain and

the United States, 1600–1914: Overcoming Asymmetric Information', *Business History Review*, 62 (1988), p. 209; J. B. Baskin and P. J. Miranti, *A History of Corporate Finance* (Cambridge, 1997), p. 132.

25. J. F. Wilson, *British Business History, 1720–1994* (Manchester, 1995), p. 46; Cottrell, *Industrial Finance*, p. 10.

26. J. R. Edwards, 'Depreciation and Fixed Asset Valuation in Railway Company Accounts to 1911', *Accounting and Business Research*, 16 (1986), p. 252. Note Hawke's conclusion that railways were the main element in both the booms of 1835–6 and 1838–40 and in the depression of 1841–42; Hawke, *Railways*, p. 364.

27. In 1801, for example, York's population was only 16,000.

28. This certainly worked as far as coal was concerned. A few weeks after the opening of the first section of the line, to South Milford, on 30 May 1839, the price of coal in York fell from 14s. to 8s. per ton and by 1846, it was nearer 5s. *Railway Magazine* (1839), p. 439. More generally, however, the railways had no 'revolutionary consequences' on York, which remained a city of small enterprises until the 1880s. In 1851, the glass manufacturer James Meek was still the largest employer (with 220 employees) and was one of only four firms employing more than fifty people, Victoria County History, ed. P. M. Tillott, *A History of Yorkshire: The City of York* (London, 1961), pp. 272–4.

29. Newton later wrote that 'Mr Hudson, who took such an active part afterwards did not at first join so heartily', in a letter to Henry Pease dated 15 September 1875, in connection with the fiftieth anniversary of the opening of the Stockton and Darlington Railway. PRO RAIL 770/44.

30. The Leeds and Selby had been formed in 1829, after a more ambitious scheme for a line from Leeds to Hull had failed to attract enough support. C. J. Allen, *The North Eastern Railway* (London, 1964), p. 50.

31. *Yorkshire Gazette*, 21 June 1834.

32. *Railway Times* (1839), p. 460.

33. *Yorkshire Gazette*, 17 October 1835.

34. H. H. Meik, 'The York and North Midland Railway', *Railway Magazine*, 38 (1916), p. 320.

35. Their Act stipulated that a majority of the directors should be residents of York and that all general meetings were to be held there. It also specified voting rights that favoured the small shareholder. D. Brooke, 'The Origins and Development of Four Constituent Lines of the North-Eastern Railway, 1824–54', unpublished MA thesis, University of Hull (1961), p. 34; *Railway Times* (1839), pp. 98, 461; York and North Midland Railway Act (1836), sections 3, 98, 101 and 105.

36. Initially, £153,500 came from York residents; Brooke, 'The Origin', pp. 236–38, 248. The York Union Bank had needed only £54,000 of initial capital.

37. *Lord Howden* v. *Simpson and Others*, Queen's Bench, 1839; *Railway Times* (1839), pp. 107, 124–25, 481; see also *Times*, 4 July 1837, p. 7; *Railway Times* (1838), p. 45.

38. Cost control generally was good and, despite the problem with Lord Howden,

even the land costs were slightly below the UK average; see H. Pollins, 'A Note on Railway Construction Costs, 1825–50', *Economica*, 19 (1952), p. 407.

39. He held 420 of the £50 shares, although in early 1838 he had needed to pay calls or instalments of only £2500; *Railway Times* (1838), p. 45.

40. *Railway Times* (1838), p. 382.

41. *Railway Times* (1839), p. 227.

42. Allen, *North Eastern*, p. 61.

43. *Railway Times* (1839) p. 442.

44. The pattern of Sunday line working varied greatly from one company to another, although the Post Office could insist on the provision of Sunday mail trains. Once these were running, it was a small step to running Sunday passenger services as well. J. Simmons, *The Victorian Railway* (London, 1995), p. 282.

45. *Railway Times* (1839), pp. 530–31.

46. *Railway Times* (1839) p. 779; see also Freeman, *Railways*, p. 82.

47. *Railway Times* (1840), p. 78.

48. G. W. J. Potter, *A History of the Whitby and Pickering Railway* (London, 1906), p. 41.

49. *Railway Times* (1839), p. 460; (1840), pp. 581–83.

50. Brooke, 'The Origin', pp. 42–44, 46; Tomlinson, *Tomlinson's*, p. 341.

51. It also enabled the York and North Midland to reach an agreement with the North Midland to rationalise the lines used for both companies passenger and freight traffic. Meik, 'The York' p. 326.

52. *Railway Times* (1840), p. 916.

53. Allen, *North Eastern*, p. 54; Tomlinson, *Tomlinson's*, pp. 233, 337; *Railway Magazine* (1841), p. 224; Brooke, 'The Origin', pp. 47–49.

54. *Railway Times* (1840), pp. 976, 997–98. The carriages were, of course, very small by modern standards; the first-class carriages consisted of three compartments, each holding six passengers and the second-class carriages carried forty people. Meik, 'The York', p. 324.

55. The city was willing to move the inmates of its House of Correction to another site in return for a compensation fee of £5000.

56. Cabry had begun his working life under George Stephenson at Killingworth Colliery.

57. In the 1840s, the railways were also allowed into four other historic towns: Chester, Conway, Shrewsbury and Newcastle. Fawcett, B., *A History of North Eastern Railway Architecture*, i, *The Pioneers* (Hull, 2001), p. 49; York City Archives, Council Minutes, ii, p. 63; Royal Commission of Historical Monuments in England, *Inventory of the Historical Monuments in the City of York*, iii (London, 1972), pp. 53–56. The old station should not be confused with the present York station built in the 1870s. Hudson Street was renamed 'Railway Street' from 1849–1971.

58. *Herapath's Journal* (1841), p. 130.

59. *Times*, 13 September 1842, p. 5; 19 September 1842, p. 6.

60. *Railway Times* (1841), p. 887.

61. *Railway Times* (1841), pp. 160, 882; (1842), p. 1046.

62. Tomlinson, *Tomlinson's*, p. 429.

63. The Act establishing the Newcastle and Darlington Junction Railway Company was obtained in July 1842.

64. *Railway Times* (1843), p. 1275.

65. To raise the £260,000 needed to build the new line, 10,400 of the £25 shares would have to be issued. On the assumption that all the shareholders exercised their options, they would take up 10,050 shares, leaving a further 350 shares to be sold to raise the necessary sum.

66. *Railway Times* (1843), pp. 1275–76.

67. *Railway Times* (1843), pp. 1084, 1313.

68. This was public knowledge by early 1844; see *Railway Times* (1844) p. 189.

69. Many railways were of course built to seaside towns including Brighton in 1840–41 and Weston-super-Mare in 1841, well before the line to Scarborough was built in 1845. In the years 1846–49, lines were built to serve fourteen more seaside resorts, including Blackpool, Southport, Eastbourne and Torquay. J. Simmons and G. Biddle (eds), *Oxford Companion to British Railway History* (Oxford, 1997), p. 207.

70. *Railway Times* (1843), p. 1325.

71. The witness was Captain Laws of the Manchester and Leeds Railway. Report of the Select Committee on Railways, *Parliamentary Papers* (1844) vol. xi, p. 525 (Q6106)).

72. A. J. Peacock, *George Hudson, 1800–1871, The Railway King*, i (York, 1988), p. 127; *Railway Times* (1844), p. 302.

73. *Railway Times* (1844), pp. 131, 186.

74. *Railway Times* (1844), p. 523.

75. This permission was given in November, 1845; see also Tomlinson, *Tomlinson's*, p. 461.

76. The construction of public buildings in London and other cities provided a large and expanding market for the stone, while there was an unsatisfied demand for ironstone in Middlesbrough, at least until the richer ores of North Cleveland were successfully mined.

77. The trains were horse-drawn, except on the Goathland incline, where they were cable-drawn.

78. Allen, *North Eastern*, pp. 54–56; Simmons and Biddle, *Oxford Companion*, p. 563.

79. Andrews's buildings included the stations at Scarborough, Beverley, Whitby and Hull. He was noted for his classical facades and small plain 'house-type' wayside stations. He also built nine churches in Yorkshire in the period 1834–55. Simmons, *Victorian*, pp. 34, 159.

80. See A. White, *A History of Whitby* (Chichester, 1993), p. 59. The sitting (Tory) MP, Aaron Chapman, had stated his intention to retire at the next election.

81. *Railway Times* (1845), pp. 379, 634, 655; Tomlinson, *Tomlinson's* pp. 456–57.

82. A. Smith, *The Bubble of the Age, or The Fallacies of Railway Investments, Railway Accounts and Railway Dividends* (London, 1848), p. 53.

83. The line from South Milford to Doncaster was rather different to the others and had greater value to Hudson's long-term plans than to the future revenues of the company, designed as it was to link up with the Midland line from Lincoln and counter the threat of a direct London to York line by rival promoters, then under consideration by a Parliamentary Committee. *Railway Times* (1844), pp. 1258–9; (1845), pp. 729–31.

84. *Railway Times* (1845), pp. 1008–9. The York and North Midland's first eight locomotives, all six-wheeled single engines, were supplied by Robert Stephenson and Co. of Newcastle in 1838–40. The first was named 'Lowther' and two of the others were named 'Stephenson' and 'Hudson'.

85. L. T. C. Rolt, *George and Robert Stephenson* (London, 1984), pp. 65–67.

86. Rolt, *George*, pp. 251–53.

87. *Evening Sun* (London), 16 October 1845, based on an earlier report in the *Sunderland Times*.

88. In fact, the proposed line from Selby to Goole failed to obtain parliamentary approval in 1846.

89. In a letter to Miss Wooler, written on 30 January 1846. C. K. Shorter, *Charlotte Bronte and her Circle*, p. 132, cited in Tomlinson, *Tomlinson's* p. 493.

90. The additional forty-nine miles of track on the Scarborough line had been built, under Robert Stephenson as engineer, within a year at a cost of less than £6000 a mile. Simmons and Biddle, *Oxford Companion*, p. 576; *Herapath's Journal* (1846), p. 1366.

91. Hotels and boarding-houses were later built in large numbers on part of the site, G. H. J. Daysh (ed.), *A Survey of Whitby and the Surrounding Area* (Eton, 1958), p. 67.

92. *Railway Times* (1847), p. 189; Allen, *North Eastern*, p. 57.

93. Allen, *North Eastern*, pp. 93–94. The terms of the agreement were modified after Hudson's downfall, in favour of the Great Northern, but the agreement did operate. The Knottingley branch was opened to local traffic in April 1850. In August 1850, Great Northern trains began running into York. Tomlinson, *Tomlinson's*, p. 503.

94. Andrews had worked on contracts for the York and North Midland, from August 1839 until late 1848, with an estimated total value of £515,000; Fawcett, *A History*, p. 49.

95. *Railway Times* (1847), pp. 1023–24.

Notes to Chapter 3: The Way North

1. T. R. Gourvish, *Railways and the British Economy, 1830–1914* (London, 1980), p. 20.

2. Apart from the Great Northern, built in the 1850s, and the Great Central,

built much later in the nineteenth century; G. R. Hawke, and J. P. P. Higgins, 'Transport and Social Overhead Capital', in R. Floud and D. McCloskey (eds), *Economic History of Britain since 1700*, i (Cambridge, 1981), p. 235.

3. In the peak year, 1847, over 250,000 (4 per cent of the male workforce) were employed in railway construction. In that year, investment in railway construction amounted to nearly 7 per cent of the gross national product. Collectively, in 1850 the fifteen largest companies controlled three-quarters of the UK's gross traffic revenue and 60 per cent of its paid-up capital. Each of these companies had a capital of more than £3 million at a time when few industrial companies had a capitalisation of even £500,000. The London and North Western Railway was the largest business enterprise in the world in the 1840s and 1850s, Gourvish, *Railways*, pp. 10, 20.

4. The index, which was 61.7 in 1830 then rose from 60.2 in June 1835 to 129.4 in May 1836 (where June 1840 = 100), A. G. Kenwood, 'Railway Investment in Britain, 1825–1875', *Economica*, 32, new series (1965), p. 316.

5. The share index by December 1837 had fallen back to 82.2; Kenwood, 'Railway', p. 316; B. C. Hunt, *The Development of the Business Corporation in England, 1800–1867* (Cambridge, Massachusetts, 1936), p. 101.

6. *Economist* (1845), p. 310; *Railway Times* (1842), p. 549; Hunt, *Development*, p. 102; M. C. Reed, *Investment in Railways in Britain, 1820–1844: A Study in the Development of the Capital Market* (Oxford, 1975), pp. 10, 24.

7. W. B. Rubinstein, *Britain's Century: A Political and Social History, 1815–1905* (London, 1998), p. 68; J. Foreman-Peck and R. Millward, *Public and Private Ownership of British Industry, 1820–1990* (Oxford, 1994), p. 13; S. and D. Dugan, *The Day the World Took Off: The Roots of the Industrial Revolution* (London, 2000), pp. 36–37; J. H. Clapham, *An Economic History of Modern Britain, the Early Railway Age, 1820–1850* (second edition, Cambridge, 1967), p. 390.

8. Gourvish, *Railways*, p. 27. In 1835–45, the railways had concentrated on passenger traffic, which provided three-quarters of their gross revenues at that time.

9. *Morning Chronicle*, 12 October 1844.

10. *Economist* (1848), p. 1297; Hunt, *Development*, p. 102.

11. The railway share index, which had averaged 98.2 in 1843 and 121.3 in 1844, climbed to its peak of 167.9 in July 1845 and remained above 140 for most of 1846. Kenwood, 'Railway', p. 316; L. T. C. Rolt, *George and Robert Stephenson* (London, 1984), p. 291; Hunt, *Development*, p. 106.

12. Hunt, *Development*, pp. 73, 104–5; Kenwood, 'Railway Investment', p. 317; B. R. Mitchell and P. Deane, *Abstract of British Historical Statistics* (Cambridge, 1962), p. 225; Gourvish, *Railways*, pp. 130–31.

13. J. Simmons, *The Victorian Railway* (London, 1995), p. 239.

14. Simmons, *Victorian*, p. 346; E. J. Hobsbawm, *Industry and Empire* (London, 1969), p. 110.

15. *Economist* (1845), p. 601; Gourvish, *Railways*, p. 17; J. F. Wilson, *British Business History, 1720–1994* (Manchester, 1995), p. 49; Hunt, *Development*, p. 107;

J. R. Killick and W. A. Thomas, 'The Provincial Stock Exchanges, 1830–1870', *Economic History Review*, second series 23 (1970), pp. 96, 104.

16. There was only one large cutting, one major embankment and two bridges, one across the Tees and the other over the Ouse. M. W. Kirby, *The Origins of Railway Enterprise: The Stockton and Darlington Railway, 1821–1863* (Cambridge, 1993), pp. 124–25; C. J. Allen, *The North Eastern Railway* (London, 1964), p. 67.

17. *Railway Times* (1841), p. 406; Kirby, *The Origins*, p. 125.

18. The scheme was entirely feasible; on the assumption that costs were contained to the budgeted £500,000, the 6 per cent guarantee effectively required the payment of a combined rent of £30,000 per annum. The York and North Midland was willing to pay £8000, the North Midland £6000, the Manchester and Leeds £3000 and the Midland Counties £3000, leaving £10,000 to be contributed jointly by a number of northern lines, such as the Newcastle and Carlisle, the Durham Junction and the Brandling Junction. *Railway Times* (1841), pp. 1108–10; Fawcett, *A History*, p. 47.

19. See Rolt, *George*, pp. 262–76, and Tomlinson, *Tomlinson's*, pp. 433–38. The Stanhope and Tyne was later reorganised as the Pontop and South Shields Railway.

20. *Railway Times* (1841), pp. 551, 1108.

21. *Railway Times* (1841), pp. 1108–10.

22. *Railway Times* (1841), pp. 1161, 1178.

23. *Railway Times* (1841), pp. 1305–6.

24. For example, see R. S. Lambert, *The Railway King* (London, 1934), p. 66.

25. *Railway Times* (1841), pp. 1305–6; Rolt, *George*, p. 273.

26. *Railway Times* (1842), p. 433. The Newcastle and Darlington Junction Act gave it powers to raise £500,000 in share capital and one-third of that sum in the form of loans.

27. Andrews was to design most of the buildings on the Newcastle and Darlington Junction; Fawcett, *A History*, p. 48.

28. Hudson was thought to have made an initial investment of £5000; *Railway Times* (1842), pp. 1058–59; (1843), p. 14.

29. *Railway Times* (1843), p. 230. The 'abuse' referred to was not the eccentric comment of Captain Watts, but the more considered view of the prolific 'Veritas Vincit' on the way Hudson was running the North Midland, which attracted the editorial support of the *Railway Times*.

30. *Railway Times* (1843), pp. 968, 991.

31. The Newcastle and Darlington Junction referred the dispute with the Dean to a jury, who decided largely in favour of the company, Tomlinson, *Tomlinson's*, p. 439.

32. *Railway Times* (1844), pp. 678–79; Rolt, *George*, p. 253. Contemporary newspaper adverts show that the fast train from London, leaving at 9 a.m., was due to arrive into Newcastle at 9.30 p.m.

33. The purchase took effect on 1 September 1844 and was at an agreed price of

£550,000, the money being raised by a rights issue to the existing shareholders of the Newcastle and Darlington Junction. Allen, *North Eastern*, p. 78; *Yorkshire Gazette*, 10 August 1844; *Railway Times* (1845), pp. 269–70.

34. Prospectus of the Northumberland Railway, issued 16 August 1844; Early British Railways collection, chiefly of press cuttings, maps and other printed matter compiled by Septimus Bell, vol. 8, Newcastle and Darlington, item 6; London School of Economics Archives, Misc. 189; Tomlinson, *Tomlinson's*, pp. 454–55.

35. *Railway Times* (1844), p. 870. *Herapath's Journal* agreed with Hudson's view.

36. Newcastle and Berwick Railway: correspondence, financial records and legal papers, PRO RAIL 506/8.

37. Newcastle and Berwick Railway, PRO RAIL 506/8.

38. Early British Railways collection, vol. 8, Newcastle and Berwick, item 42a.

39. B. Bailey, *George Hudson: The Rise and Fall of the Railway King* (Stroud, 1995), p. 53.

40. See, for example, J. Simmons and G. Biddle (eds), *Oxford Companion to British Railway History* (Oxford, 1997), p. 192.

41. Great North of England Railway, correspondence, financial records and legal papers, PRO RAIL 232/78; D. Brooke, 'The Origins and Development of Four Constituent Lines of the North-Eastern Railway, 1824–54', unpublished MA thesis, University of Hull (1961), pp. 156–57.

42. Allen, *Great Eastern*, pp. 89–90; Early British Railways collection, vol. 6, Great North of England, item 140; Brooke, 'The Origins', pp. 156–9.

43. Fawcett, *A History*, p. 47.

44. *Railway Times* (1845), p. 1228.

45. *Railway Times* (1844), p. 870.

46. *Railway Times* (1845), pp. 1451–52.

47. Dobson (1787–1865) built widely in the north of England, mostly on public buildings. His work included Newcastle's Eldon Square, Grainger Markets and Royal Arcade. He was the first President of the Northern Society of Architects and also worked closely with Hudson on the development of Whitby. T. Faulkner and A. Greg, *John Dobson: Architect of the North East* (Newcastle, 2001), p. 7.

48. Fawcett, *A History*, p. 149.

49. Newcastle came to be seen by many as the 'best designed large city in England'. The importance of Hudson's contribution to the redesign of Newcastle was widely recognised in the city. Unfortunately Newcastle Central was not built to Dobson's first design, because of the later need for economies. Faulkner and Greg, *John Dobson*, pp. 46–47, 102–4, 144; Fawcett, *A History*, pp. 149, 153; Simmons and Biddle, *Oxford Companion*, pp. 128, 161, 345–46.

50. A. Rivett, 'The Building of the South Dock at Sunderland 1846–1856', unpublished dissertation, Sunderland Training College (1964), pp. 35–36.

51. S. T. Miller, *Sunderland Past and Present* (Sunderland 1983), p. 18.

52. The main acquisitions were the takeover of the Wearmouth Dock, the purchase of the Durham and Sunderland and the Pontop and South Shields Railways

and the leasing of the Hartlepool Dock and Railway. The Stockton and Darlington, however, remained determinedly independent. *Herapath's Journal* (1846), p. 960.

53. Hudson's claim was that the average at that point in time was just under £30,000 a mile, a figure that was expected to fall to no more than £14,000, leaving aside the bridge over the Tyne. Instead it was argued the true figure to date was just over £60,000 a mile. *Herapath's Journal* (1846), pp. 961, 1497.

54. *Herapath's Journal* (1846), p. 1194.

55. *Herapath's Journal* (1846), p. 1311.

56. The York and Newcastle branches under construction were to Boroughbridge, Thirsk, Malton and Bedale; *Railway Times* (1847), p. 478.

57. Fawcett, *A History*, p. 153.

58. *Railway Times* (1847), pp. 268–70, 355–56; (1848), pp. 1116–17.

59. *Railway Times* (1847), p. 1004. According to his biographer, Dobson the architect was often to be found 'seated in company with engineers, architects, builders, barristers and solicitors and sometimes King Hudson himself ... at the Queen's Head' or some other inn famed for its 'bountiful larder', Faulkner and Greg, *John Dobson*, p. 102.

60. *Herapath's Journal* (1846), p. 118; *Railway Times* (1847), pp. 1024–26.

61. Sir Nikolaus Pevsner thought that, 'if one does not mind a railway station looking like a Literary and Scientific Institution or provincial Athenaeum ... Monkwearmouth is one of the most handsome stations in existence'. Its architect, Moore specialised in theatres and banks. The line was not extended over the Wear until 1879, when Sunderland Central was built. Monkwearmouth then became a through station, not a terminus and, being so close to Sunderland Central, it quickly lost much of its importance. G. L. Dodds, *A History of Sunderland* (Sunderland 1995), pp. 59, 63; G. E. Milburn and S. T. Miller (eds), *Sunderland, River, Town and People: A History from the 1780s* (Sunderland, 1988), pp. 17, 26; N. T. Sinclair, *Railways of Sunderland* (Newcastle, 1985), pp. 9–10; T. Corfe (ed.), *The Buildings of Sunderland, 1814–1914* (Sunderland, 1983), p. 18; Miller, *Sunderland Past*, p. 17.

62. Maryport and Carlisle Railway Prospectus (1836), University of London Rare Books Collection, I1.825. Stephenson had a strong preference for easy gradients, so that locomotive power could be used to carry heavy loads and not be wasted on steep gradients, although this sometimes led him to choose routes that were circuitous and strategically weak. Rolt, *George*, p. 254.

63. Under certain conditions the percentages payable were to be slightly higher. *Railway Times* (1848), pp. 967, 1042; (1849), pp. 283, 330; *Railway Intelligence*, 30 September 1848; J. S. Maclean, *The Newcastle and Carlisle Railway* (Newcastle, 1948), pp. 55–56.

64. Tomlinson, *Tomlinson's*, pp. 453, 488.

65. It seems that the Stockton and Darlington Board only made their suggestion because their line's excessive dependence on local mineral traffic had become a major problem. The Stockton and Darlington then suffered exceptionally

poor profitability, until the happy discovery of the main seam of the Cleveland ironstone on 8 June 1850. Kirby, *The Origins*, pp. 139, 143, Tomlinson, *Tomlinson's*, pp. 507–10. The York Newcastle and Berwick in fact rejected the arrangements Hudson had made, the Bill for the York Newcastle and Berwick never became law and the Newcastle and Carlisle and the Maryport and Carlisle both regained their independence again in 1850. The Newcastle and Carlisle was eventually taken over by the York Newcastle and Berwick's successor, the North Eastern Railway, but not until 1862. After a financial reorganisation in 1850, the Maryport and Carlisle became a prosperous line that paid good dividends. Simmons and Biddle, *Oxford Companion*, pp. 316, 345; G. Whittle, *The Newcastle and Carlisle Railway* (Newton Abbot, 1979), pp. 55–58.

Notes to Chapter 4: The Great Amalgamator

1. L. T. C. Rolt, *George and Robert Stephenson* (London, 1984), p. 253.
2. Robert Stephenson became Resident Engineer of the North Midland. E. G. Barnes, *The Rise of the Midland Railway, 1844–1874* (London, 1966), p. 51. Rolt, *George*, pp. 288–89.
3. The actual costs amounted to more than £40,000 a mile, as against £26,000 on the Midland Counties and under £20,000 on the Birmingham and Derby Junction and the York and North Midland; see also Rolt, *George*, p. 253.
4. *Railway Times* (1842), p. 264.
5. *Railway Times* (1842), pp. 255–58.
6. Although most of the directors were local, the members of the committee came from Liverpool, Bradford, Huddersfield, Sheffield, Leeds and York. *Railway Times* (1842), pp. 887, 933–36.
7. *Railway Times* (1842), pp. 1090, 1137–40.
8. After legal action, the North Midland had to pay a week's wages to the men who were sacked, in lieu of proper notice.
9. Letters to the *Railway Times* more often than not used pseudonyms such as 'a suffering shareholder', 'John Bull' and the like.
10. They were later published as a book, V. Vincit, *Railway Locomotive Management, in a Series of Letters by Veritas Vincit* (Birmingham, 1847). The author's identity was never proved but he was probably John Robertson, the editor of the *Railway Times*; see M. Robbins, 'The North Midland Railway and its Enginemen', *Journal of Transport History*, 4 (1960), pp. 180–86.
11. Cabry acted in this role until March 1843 and was paid fifty guineas for this by the North Midland. B. Lewis, *The Cabry Family: Railway Engineers* (Mold, Clwyd, 1994), pp. 22–25.
12. *Railway Times* (1843), p. 198; Vincit, *Railway Locomotive*, p. 12. Edward Jenkins was tried for manslaughter but acquitted. The *Railway Times* said it was pleased at the verdict but thought that Hudson and company, not Jenkins, should have been in the dock; (1843), p. 377.

13. *Railway Times* (1843), p. 198; H. Parris, *Government and the Railways in Nineteenth-Century Britain* (London, 1965), pp. 47–48. The North Midland's letter was signed by their secretary although it gave every appearance of having been composed by Hudson.

14. Parris, *Government*, pp. 48–49.

15. *Railway Times* (1843), p. 222; Vincit, *Railway Locomotive*, p. 13.

16. *Railway Times* (1843), pp. 275–80.

17. *Railway Times* (1843), p. 264.

18. *Railway Times* (1843), pp. 198, 449, 796, 873.

19. Vincit, *Railway Locomotive*, p. 13.

20. £5000 had been charged for depreciation in 1842; Robbins, 'The North Midland', p. 180.

21. *Railway Times* (1843), p. 223.

22. *Railway Times* (1843), pp. 1029–30.

23. J. Simmons and G. Biddle (eds), *Oxford Companion to British Railway History* (Oxford, 1997), pp. 12–13.

24. C. R. Clinker, *The Birmingham and Derby Junction Railway* (Weston-super-Mare, 1982), pp. 13–16; P. S. Stevenson, *The Midland Counties Railway* (Mold, Clwyd, 1989), pp. 66–68; see also *Railway Times* (1843), pp. 249, 423, 545, 872.

25. For expressions of support for amalgamation see, for example, *Railway Times* (1842), p. 1078; (1843) pp. 368, 417, 500–1, 523, 662–63, 715; for outright opposition to the inclusion of the North Midland see *Railway Times* (1843), p. 537.

26. R. Williams, *The Midland Railway: A New History* (Newton Abbot, 1988), p. 37.

27. *Railway Times* (1843), p. 876.

28. Except that the Birmingham and Derby Junction shareholders were to receive only 95 per cent of the value of their shares and would also be entitled to a slightly smaller dividend. C. E. Stretton, *The History of the Midland Railway* (London, 1901), p. 71.

29. *Railway Times* (1843), pp. 1026, 1030.

30. *Railway Times* (1843), pp. 1042–44.

31. *Railway Times* (1843), pp. 1084, 1313.

32. 'Amalgamation as a more or less continuous process really began in 1844' with the creation of the Midland, W. Simnett, *Railway Amalgamation in Great Britain* (London, 1923), p. 5. It is interesting to note that there was no comparable progress on the London-Brighton and London-Dover amalgamation that had been much discussed in the railway press.

33. *Railway Times* (1838), p. 745; (1843), p. 871; A. J. Peacock, *George Hudson, 1800–1871: The Railway King*, i (York, 1988), p. 127.

34. See C. E. Stretton, *History of the Leeds and Bradford, and Leeds and Bradford Extension Railways* (second edition, Leeds, 1901); *Railway Times* (1843), p. 131.

35. *Railway Times* (1844), pp. 62, 173–74.

36. *Railway Times* (1844), p. 190.

37. *Railway Times* (1844), pp. 192–94.

38. *Railway Times* (1844), p. 328.

39. *Railway Times* (1844), p. 826.
40. Stretton, *History of the Midland,* pp. 72–74.
41. Barnes, *The Rise,* p. 66; *Railway Times* (1844), p. 680.
42. After Hudson's downfall, Ellis was to become Chairman from 1849 until 1858. Simmons and Biddle, *Oxford Companion,* p. 145.
43. *Railway Times* (1844), p. 793.
44. C. H. Grinling, *The History of the Great Northern Railway* (London, 1966), pp. 10–27.
45. The Cambridge and Lincoln was certainly under Hudson's influence and both the Midland and Eastern Counties had nominees sitting on its committee. The members also approved the leasing of the unfinished Sheffield to Manchester line, although that company later withdrew from the agreement. In addition, Hudson proposed building from Nottingham to Lincoln via Newark, and from Syston (north of Leicester) to Peterborough, as well as the acquisition of a Sheffield and Rotherham line that would complete the route from London to Sheffield.
46. 30 November 1844 was the last date for the submission of Bills to be considered in the 1845 parliamentary session.
47. *Railway Times* (1844), pp. 1160–61; Barnes, *The Rise,* p. 71; Grinling, *The History,* p. 27; D. I. Gordon, *A Regional History of the Railways of Great Britain,* v, *The Eastern Counties* (third edition, Newton Abbot, 1990), pp. 106–9.
48. The Midland's victory was also a defeat for the Great Western's broad gauge. The lease offer, at 6 per cent on a capital of £1,800,000, with an option to purchase after two years, was ratified by a special meeting in April 1845; *Railway Times* (1845), pp. 522–23; F. S. Williams, *Williams's Midland Railway: Its Rise and Progress* (Newton Abbot, 1968), pp. 64–66.
49. The extensions were from Ely to March, Spalding, Boston and Lincoln, from Nottingham to Newark and Lincoln, from Swinton to Doncaster and Lincoln (which would run counter to the direct London to York proposal), from Syston in Leicestershire to Peterborough, a line along the Erewash Valley and, finally, the taking over of the Sheffield and Rotherham Railway. *Railway Times* (1845), p. 672.
50. Grinling, *The History,* p. 30; *Railway Times* (1845), p. 290; *Times,* 22 February 1845, p. 7.
51. Grinling, *The History,* pp. 33–41; Williams, *Williams's Midland,* pp. 73–77.
52. *Railway Times* (1845), p. 1115.
53. Grinling, *The History,* pp. 42–45.
54. *Railway Times* (1846), p. 121.
55. Detailed in Stretton, *History of the Midland,* pp. 91–93.
56. A. J. Peacock, *George Hudson, 1800–1871: The Railway King,* ii (York, 1989), pp. 215–16; Barnes, *The Rise,* pp. 80–84; Report of the Committee of Investigation to the Shareholders of the Midland Railway ('Midland Report'), *Derby Mercury* (extraordinary edition), 15 August 1849, pp. 35–36.
57. The rate was to be only 5 per cent until three months after the opening of

the Leeds and Bradford's extension to Colne; *Herapath's Journal* (1846), pp. 8–9, 648, 948; *Railway Times* (1844), pp. 1010, 1070, 1113.

58. At the time of the meeting, Manchester and Leeds £100 shares, with £76 paid, were trading at around £135, i.e. at a premium of £59; by June, with £82 paid the value had fallen to around £120, a premium of only £38; *Railway Times* (1846), pp. 25–26, 46, 894.

59. Stretton, *History of the Leeds and Bradford*, pp. 11–16; *Railway Times* (1846), pp. 1042–46.

60. *Railway Times* (1846), p. 1046; *Herapath's Journal* (1846), p. 1381; Peacock, *George Hudson*, ii, pp. 216–17.

61. *Herapath's Journal* (1846), pp. 1364–65.

62. A line between Leeds and Bradford should have had good prospects, but it was expensive to build. If the purchase of the line was, then, a 'bargain' it was undoubtedly of a strategic rather than an operational nature; the Committee of Investigation could not determine, from the books of the Midland, what were the profits on the line (as Hudson indeed had 'no statistics' on his railway) but their own calculations showed a considerable loss for the first year after it opened fully in October 1848. During this time the receipts were less than the guaranteed rent, so the Manchester and Leeds probably had a fortunate escape.

63. *Railway Times* (1847), pp. 187–89.

64. These are detailed in Stretton, *The History of the Midland*, pp. 124–25.

65. The Midland had carried 1,750,000 passengers in the previous six months 'without accident or bruise to any one of them'.

66. The three Acts had involved additional capital of only £234,000. *Railway Times* (1847), pp. 1026–28; H. Scrivenor, *The Railways of the United Kingdom* (London, 1849), p. 125.

67. *Railway Times* (1848), pp. 249–52.

68. *Railway Times* (1848), p. 540.

69. *Railway Times* (1848), pp. 899–901.

70. Williams, *Williams's Midland*, pp. 90–91; Stretton, *The History of the Midland*, pp. 132–33; *Railway Times* (1849), pp. 17, 166–67.

71. Grinling, *The History*, p. 82.

Notes to Chapter 5: High Stakes

1. J. Simmons, *The Railways of Britain* (third edition, London, 1990), p. 15; *Eastern Counties Railway Prospectus* (1834), University of London Rare Books Collection, I1.825.

2. No tunnelling was anticipated, nor any embankments of a height of more than thirty feet, *Proceedings of the First General Meeting of the Eastern Counties Railway* (London 1888), pp. 13–14, 39; *Eastern Counties Railway Prospectus*.

3. Simmons, *The Railways*, pp. 14–15. The Eastern Counties's accounts for 30 June 1843 showed capital expenditure of £2,700,000, *Railway Times* (1843),

p. 907. Land and compensation, at £750,000, represented 27.7 per cent of the total construction cost as against a UK average of 13.3 per cent; H. Pollins, 'A Note on Railway Construction Costs, 1825–50', *Economica*, 19 (1952), p. 407. The decision to halt the line at Colchester was taken as early as April 1839, even before the first section of line between Mile End and Romford was opened in June of that year; D. I. Gordon, *The Eastern Counties* (third edition, Newton Abbot, 1990), p. 41.

4. 'The legacy of the construction stage for companies such as the Eastern Counties was such that no traffic manager could produce satisfactory profits, however gifted he was', T. R. Gourvish, 'Railway Enterprise', in R. A. Church (ed.), *The Dynamics of Victorian Business: Problems and Perspectives to the 1870s* (London, 1980), pp. 138–39.

5. J. A. Francis, *A History of the English Railways: Its Social Relations and Revelations, 1820–45* (Newton Abbot, 1968), p. 242; H. Frith, *The Flying Horse: The Story of the Locomotive and the Railway* (London, 1893), pp. 64–67.

6. Directors' report for the six months to 30 June 1843, *Railway Times* (1843), pp. 906–7.

7. Gordon, *The Eastern*, pp. 28, 105–10; C. J. Allen, *The Great Eastern Railway* (fifth edition, London, 1968), pp. 11–12.

8. Gordon, *The Eastern*, pp. 111–12; C. H. Grinling, *The History of the Great Northern Railway* (London, 1966), p. 19.

9. Grinling, *The History*, pp. 46–47.

10. *Railway Times* (1845), pp. 40–48.

11. The 'Liverpool party' was important from the outset in the company's affairs. Investors from that city put up about one third of its capital and naturally expected their interests to be represented on the Board.

12. *Railway Times* (1845), pp. 1371–79.

13. Hints in Scott's remarks at the August meeting and in some of Duncan's subsequent comments that indicate that Scott, very sensibly, had been in contact with Hudson before speaking out in public.

14. Gordon, *The Eastern*, pp. 29, 113; Grinling, *The History*, pp. 47–48; *Railway Times* (1845), pp. 140, 1967–71.

15. Hudson insisted that the rival line would cost over £10,000,000, not the £6,500,000 estimated by its Engineer.

16. *Railway Times* (1845), pp. 2141–43.

17. *Railway Times* (1845), pp. 2138–39.

18. *Railway Times* (1845), pp. 2294–95.

19. *Railway Times* (1845), p. 2304.

20. *Railway Times* (1845), p. 2366.

21. These advertisements cost the Eastern Counties about £340; *Report of the Select Committee into Expenditure of Certain Sums under the Head of Parliamentary Expenses, Parliamentary Papers* (1849, Cmd 366), x, pp. 676, 693.

22. *Railway Times* (1845), p. 2446. The letter appears there as an advertisement inserted by the London and York; see also Grinling, *The History*, p. 50.

23. *Response of the Directors of the Eastern Counties Railway to the Eastern Counties Report* (London, 1849), pp. 3–4. *Report of the Committee of Investigation to the Shareholders of the Eastern Counties Railway* ('EC Report'), reproduced as Appendix 'A' of the Second Report of the House of Lords Select (Monteagle) Committee on the Audit of Railway Accounts, *Parliamentary Papers* (1849, Cmd 371), x, p. 104.

24. Cabry received a hundred guineas for his services on this occasion; *EC Report*, p. 104; Anon., 'The Centenary of the Eastern Counties Railway', *Locomotive, Railway Carriage and Wagon Review*, 45 (1939), p. 206; B. Lewis, *The Cabry Family: Railway Engineers* (Mold, Clwyd, 1994), p. 30.

25. *Railway Times* (1846) p. 39.

26. Orders were placed for forty-five new locomotives and two hundred carriages, a 'very substantial' quantity, given the size of the Eastern Counties at that time; E. Doble, 'History of the Eastern Counties Railway in Relation to Economic Development', unpublished PhD thesis (London, 1939).

27. *Railway Times* (1846), pp. 201–4.

28. The Select Committee that investigated the activities of the Size Lane committee in 1849 concluded that Duncan acted with the approval of Eastern Counties Deputy Chairman Waddington but that the latter acted 'without the knowledge or authority of the other Directors'. This seems hard to believe. The total cost of the committee included £168 paid to a Mr Davis, who had acted as secretary to the committee, 'to purchase his silence'; Grinling, *The History*, pp. 50–52; *Report of the Select Committee into Expenditure*, pp. 677, 696; *Railway Times* (1846), pp. 594, 604, 635–36, 667.

29. Grinling, *The History*, pp. 52–55; *Railway Times* (1846), pp. 667, 791–92.

30. *Railway Times* (1846), p. 882.

31. *Punch*, 11 (1846), pp. 52, 180. There had been four deaths and more than forty injuries in the Board of Trade report period of 1 January 1846 to 20 July 1846, *Times*, 26 August 1846, p. 5.

32. Frith, *The Flying Horse*, p. 67; *Herapath's Journal* (1846), p. 977; *Times*, 7 August 1846, p. 5.

33. *Times*, 7 August 1846, p. 5; *Herapath's Journal* (1846), p. 1091.

34. *Railway Times* (1847), p. 18.

35. *Railway Times* (1847), pp. 199–200, 211

36. Gordon, *The Eastern*, p. 29.

37. The Stratford works became a central part of the Eastern Counties operation after the locomotive works were moved there from Romford in 1848. The company also built three hundred houses for its employees in an area just south of the station that was popularly known as 'Hudson's Town'. Allen, *The Great Eastern*, pp. 17–18.

38. Hudson's putting forward of the proposal only to quickly drop it may have been intended merely to 'soften up' the shareholders for the remaining schemes, which he did want, or it may have been part of some more complex political gesture towards the Great Northern.

39. *Railway Times* (1847), pp. 199–200, 211; Grinling, *The History*, pp. 59–60, 68–69; Gordon, *The Eastern* pp. 150, 154, 234; *Times*, 16 January 1847, p. 5. See also the *Cambridge Advertiser* and the *Yorkshireman* of 28 March 1846.

40. *Cambridge Chronicle and Journal and Huntingdonshire Gazette*, 10 July 1847, p. 2; *Cambridge Independent Press*, 10 July 1847, p. 3; R. Fulford, *The Prince Consort* (London, 1949), pp. 196–97; *Illustrated London News*, 10 July 1847, pp. 20–8; H. Murray, 'Queen Victoria, York and the Royal Myths', *York History*, 11 (1994), pp. 56–68; *Oxford and Cambridge Review*, 5 (1847), pp. 264–66.

41. Allen, *The Great*, p. 17.

42. *Railway Times* (1847), pp. 1037–40.

43. *Railway Times* (1848), pp. 266–69.

44. *Railway Times* (1848), pp. 508–10.

45. The fastest London to Norwich train was now scheduled at 305 minutes instead of 260, for example, Gordon, *The Eastern*, pp. 172, 191; Allen, *The Great*, p. 30.

46. *Railway Times* (1848), pp. 868–71.

47. J. Simmons and G. Biddle (eds), *Oxford Companion to British Railway History* (Oxford, 1997), p. 138.

Notes to Chapter 6: The Heights

1. *Illustrated London News*, 24 February 1844.

2. The 'Railway Mania' was only a year away. F. E. Hyde, *Mr Gladstone at the Board of Trade* (London, 1934), pp. 153–81 esp. p. 172); J. Prest, 'Gladstone and the Railways', in P. J. Jagger (ed.), *Gladstone* (London, 1998), pp. 197–99. See also W. C. Lubenow, *The Politics of Government Growth: Early Victorian Attitudes Toward State Intervention, 1833–48* (Newton Abbot: 1971), pp. 107–36.

3. Report of the Select Committee on Railways, *Parliamentary Papers* (1844) vol xi; Glyn's evidence is at pp. 253–71 (Q2963–3151), see especially Q2967–70.

4. Report of the Select Committee; Laing's evidence is at pp. 45–173 (Q1–1809), see especially Q1370.

5. Evidence of Joseph Baxendale to the Select Committee, quoted in Hyde, *Mr Gladstone*, p. 159. Baxendale was the Chairman of the South-Eastern Railway (London to Dover), which had a more enlightened attitude than most. Their third-class carriages had seats and high sides, affording some protection from the elements, although no roof. Baxendale claimed he himself travelled third-class on the line, if the weather was 'at all tolerable'. The company charged less than 1*d.* per mile for third-class tickets; Report of the Select Committee, Q3207–9.

6. Lower fares would of course promote higher traffic volumes so that revenues would not necessarily fall. Running costs would, however, be higher.

7. Report of the Select Committee, Q1372-Q1716, 1736–57.

8. Report of the Select Committee, Q1411–13, 1608–10, 1682–91, 1744–46.

9. Report of the Select Committee, Q1412.

10. Report of the Select Committee, Q4382–83.

11. Report of the Select Committee, Q4217, 4228–29, 4255, 4347.

12. Report of the Select Committee, Q4351.

13. Report of the Select Committee; Hudson's evidence is at pp. 362–85 (Q 4175–520).

14. Railway Regulation Bill (1844) *Parliamentary Papers* (1844) Cmd 397, vol. iv, sections 1–24. Cf. Third Report of the Select Committee, pp. 5–11 [1–7].

15. *Railway Times*, 1844, pp. 712, 727, 713–14, 737. The paper argued that the Bill was a 'breach of faith' because it gave existing railway companies no explicit protection against competition. In April it had published the Third Report of the Select Committee, containing the revision and purchase proposals and commented (p. 437) that it was 'impossible to bestow too great praise upon the moderate and rational tone of the last Report of the Select Committee'.

16. 'My temper was moved by the proceedings of the railway people today and a kind of sediment of anger remained long after'; H. C. G. Matthew, *The Gladstone Diaries*, iii (Oxford, 1978), pp. 386–87, entry dated 3 July 1844. See also a letter dated 5 July referring to the 'blind and unreasonable conduct' of the railway companies in Hyde, *Mr Gladstone*, p. 177.

17. *Times*, 9 July 1844, pp. 3–4; Lubenow, *The Politics*, pp. 114–15.

18. *Times*, 11 July 1844, p. 7.

19. Matthew, *The Gladstone Diaries*, pp. 389–90; *Railway Times*, 1844, p. 801.

20. W. B. Rubinstein, *Britain's Century: A Political and Social History 1815–1905* (London, 1998), p. 76; J. Simmons and G. Biddle (eds), *Oxford Companion to British Railway History* (Oxford, 1997), pp. 155, 177, 369.

21. Regulation of Railways Act (1844) 7 & 8 Victoria, c. 85, sections 1–3, 6; Railway Regulation Bill, preamble and sections 1, 7; Hyde, *Mr Gladstone*, pp. 159, 177–81.

22. B. Bailey, *George Hudson, The Rise and Fall of the Railway King* (Stroud, 1995), p. 45.

23. *Railway Times*, 1844, pp. 62, 328.

24. *Railway Times*, 1844, pp. 764, 826.

25. Hudson liked to tell this story although it is not clear that Smith, who could be far less complimentary about Hudson, really saw things in these terms. *Daily News*, 18 December 1871, p. 3; see Smith on Hudson in C. Nowell Smith, *Letters of Sydney Smith*, ii (Oxford, 1953), pp. 852–53, 857.

26. J. Simmons, *The Victorian Railway* (London, 1995), p. 147.

27. W. W. Tomlinson, *Tomlinson's North Eastern Railway* (third edition, Newton Abbot, 1987), p. 464; *Times*, 21 July 1845, p. 6.

28. N. McCord and P. A. Wood, 'The Sunderland Election of 1845', *Durham University Journal*, new series, 21, pp. 11–21.

29. Thompson was an alderman, was elected Lord Mayor in 1828 and was also Chairman of Lloyd's and a director of the Bank of England and of a number of railway and other companies. G. E. Milburn and S. T. Miller (eds), *Sunderland River Town and People: A History from the 1780s* (Sunderland, 1988), p. 95. The Hudsons attended a dinner in London given by Thompson in May 1834; V. B. Ponsonby, *Lady Charlotte Guest: Extracts from her Journal, 1833–1852* (London, 1950), pp. 27–28.

30. S. T. Miller, 'More a Work of Art than Nature: The Story of the Development of Sunderland Harbour', *Port of Sunderland Millennium Handbook* (Sunderland, 2000), pp. 12, 26; S. T. Miller, *Sunderland Past and Present* (Sunderland, 1983), p. 16; S. T. Miller, *The Book of Sunderland* (Buckingham, 1989), p. 39.

31. Williamson reputedly controlled two to three hundred votes in Sunderland (in an electorate of around 1500) and David Barclay, Lord Howick's fellow MP, was his brother-in-law. Milburn and Miller, *Sunderland*, pp. 16–17, 94; Miller, 'More a Work', pp. 30–31; F. Rivett, 'The Building of the South Dock at Sunderland, 1846–1856' (Sunderland College dissertation, 1964), pp. 26–27.

32. Milburn and Miller, *Sunderland*, p. 94; Miller, *Sunderland*, p. 18; Miller, 'More a Work', p. 30; Miller, *The Book*, p. 39.

33. His 'Catechism on the Corn Laws' had first appeared in 1827 and he was known as the 'Father of Free Trade Agitation'.

34. Bagshaw was a director of the Eastern Counties Railway, which invited Hudson to become their Chairman a few months later; Milburn and Miller, *Sunderland*, pp. 99–100; McCord and Wood, 'The Sunderland Election', pp. 13–14.

35. *Times*, 21 July 1845, p. 5; 23 July 1845, p. 6; 24 July 1845, p. 6; *Newcastle Journal*, 26 July, 1845.

36. L. G. Johnson, *General T. Perronet Thompson* (London, 1957), p. 253.

37. Johnson, *General*, p. 256; *Times*, 25 July 1845, p. 5.

38. *Times*, 30 July 1845, p. 3.

39. See J. R. Morrison, 'Perronet Thompson, 1783–1869: A Middle-Class Radical', unpublished D.Phil. thesis (University of York, 1994), pp. 233–37; *Times*, 1 August 1845, p. 3; 4 August 1845, p. 6; 11 August 1845, p. 5.

40. *Sunderland Herald*, 23 March 1849. The reference to the York Newcastle and Berwick is an error; the Newcastle and Darlington is meant.

41. The population of the borough was 53,335 in the census 1841, and 66,618 ten years later; Milburn and Miller, *Sunderland*, p. 222; *Newcastle Journal*, 26 July 1845; *Times*, 7 August 1845, p. 7; 28 July 1845, p. 3.

42. Collection of election material, ref. 1/F LB HUD, Sunderland City Archives.

43. *Times*, 11 August 1845, p. 5; 13 August 1845, p. 6; R. S. Lambert, *The Railway King* (London, 1934), p. 151; A. J. Peacock, *George Hudson, 1800–1871 The Railway King*, i (York, 1988), p. 12 n. 16.

44. *Newcastle Journal*, 26 July 1845.

45. *Sunderland Herald*, 15 August 1845, p. 5; *Times*, 15 August 1845, pp. 5–6; 16 August 1845, p. 6; 18 August 1845, p. 6; P. J. Storey, 'Mayors of Victorian Sunderland', in *Sunderland's History*, vi, pp. 17–40, pp. 36–37.

46. *Times*, 16 August 1845, p. 4; 18 August 1845, p. 6; Lambert, *Railway King*, pp. 153–54; Tomlinson, *North Eastern* p. 464.

47. *Times*, 18 August 1845, p. 6; (unidentified) local newspaper cuttings dated 23 August and 26 August 1845 and November 1847, Hudson family papers; information leaflet of the church of St John the Evangelist, parish of East Darlington.

48. *Times*, 18 August 1845, p. 6.

49. *Standard*, 15 August 1845, p. 2; *Railway Times* (1845), p. 1259; *Times*, 15 August 1845, p. 4; McCord and Wood, 'The Sunderland Election', p. 16; *Yorkshireman*, 16 August 1845; *Sunderland Herald*, 12 September 1845, p. 5; *English Gentleman*, 6 September 1845, p. 313. This last article is anonymous, but was in fact written by the editor of the *Yorkshireman*, John Duncan; see Richardson versus Wodson, booklet on the trial published by the *Yorkshireman*, with additional material, Sect 2, p. xvi.

50. *Illustrated London News*, 25 October 1845, p. 263; *Times*, 24 October 1845, pp. 8–9.

51. Miller, 'More a Work', pp. 33–35; Rivett, 'The Building', pp. 32–34; *Times*, 30 October 1845, p. 7.

52. McCord and Wood, 'The Sunderland Election', pp. 18–19; *The Sunderland, Seaham and Hartlepool General Review and Advertiser*, 10 December 1853.

53. R. B. Martin, *'Enter Rumour': Four Early Victorian Scandals* (London, 1962), pp. 202–3.

54. An anonymous correspondent, 'Binks the Bagman', went further and alleged that the entire line, on which 'the passenger receipts barely [paid] for the engine grease', was constructed for Hudson's personal convenience, *Yorkshireman*, 26 May 1849, p. 5.

55. W. Page (ed.), *The Victoria History of the County of York: North Riding*, ii (London, 1986), pp. 70, 75; N. Pevsner, *The Buildings of England: Yorkshire, The North Riding* (London, 1966), p. 71; *Railway Express*, 10 October 1845. After Hudson's time the house was known as Baldersby Park.

56. N. Pevsner, *The Buildings of England: London*, i (London, 1973), p. 594; G. H. Cunningham, *London* (London, 1927), p. 8; B. Weinreb and C. Hibbert, *The London Encyclopædia* (second edition, London, 1989), p. 11; Martin, *'Enter Rumour'*, p. 204; *Punch*, 9, 'The Monster House', p. 136. The two buildings were later known as 'Scylla and Charybdis', and the house on the west side of the gate was eventually subdivided. Hudson actually purchased a seventy-five year lease, under which he was obliged, amongst other things, to 'paint the outside wood and ironwork every fourth year with two coats of paint and, at the same time, re-colour and re-joint in imitation of Bath stone all the outside stucco work'; North Eastern Railway, correspondence, financial records and legal papers; sundry files, PRO RAIL 1021/39.

57. Lambert, *Railway King*, p. 191.

58. The day concerned was Friday 8 May 1846; *Railway Times*, 16 May 1846, pp. 692.

59. D. A. Wilson, *Carlyle at His Zenith, 1848–53* (London, 1927), p. 93; *Daily News*, 18 December 1871, p. 3.

60. *Fraser's Magazine*, August 1847, p. 222; T. Martin, *Helena Faucit* (Edinburgh, 1900), p. 194.

61. D. Brooke, 'The Origins and Development of Four Constituent Lines of the North-Eastern Railway, 1824–54', unpublished MA thesis (University of Hull,

1961), p. 82; (unidentified) local newspaper cuttings dated October and November 1848, Hudson family papers.

62. *The Monthly Chronicle of North Country Lore and Legend*, November 1887, p. 395; *Hunt's Merchants' Magazine*, 29, July 1853, p. 43.

63. A. J. Peacock, *George Hudson, 1800–1871: The Railway King*, i (York, 1988), p. 132.

64. *Yorkshireman*, 6 February 1847; Early British Railways collection, chiefly of press cuttings, maps and other printed matter compiled by Septimus Bell, vol. iii, item 15.

65. Simmons, *Victorian Railway*, pp. 198, 237.

66. *Herapath's Journal* (1846), p. 53. The *Railway Times* was never, in fact, consistently hostile to Hudson; it was indisputably critical at times but it also sometimes praised his conduct.

67. *Herapath's Journal* (1846), p. 1195.

68. *Gateshead Observer*, 20 March 1847, 3 April 1847; *Sunderland Herald*, 26 March 1847, p. 4; *Yorkshireman*, 27 March 1847.

69. (Unidentified) newspaper cutting dated 26 August 1845, Hudson family papers; *Times*, 21 January 1847, p. 7; *Sunderland Herald*, 8 October 1847; W. P. Lennox, *Celebrities I Have Known: with Episodes, Political, Social, Sporting and Theatrical* (London, 1877), p. 188.

70. *Yorkshire Gazette*, 19 February 1848, p. 5; Report of the Commissioners of Railways (1848), PRO RAIL 1053/17, pp 91–92.

71. Some said he used it to purchase Albert Gate. Lambert, *Railway King*, p. 144; *Times*, October 6 1845, p. 3; October 6 1845, p. 5; *Railway Times*, 1845, p. 1971; *Railway Express*, 10 October 1845; 17 October 1845.

72. W. O. Skeat, *George Stephenson: The Engineer and his Letters* (London, 1973), p. 225.

73. *Standard*, 19 December 1846, p. 2.

74. J. Ingamells, 'Jackson and Grant at York', *Preview*, 101, p. 910; *Yorkshire Gazette*, 20 November 1847, p. 4.

75. *Times*, 23 March 1846, p. 5; *Sunderland Times*, quoted in the *Railway Times*, 1846, p. 500. This meeting is the subject of an even more colourful story, in an article published shortly after Hudson's death: 'Amid the constellations of celebrities, there were two men [Prince Albert and Hudson] round whom the crowds circled [who] looked like rival monarchs, each with his obsequious courtiers round him'. After the introduction, Albert, 'ever anxious to increase his stock of knowledge', asked Hudson's opinion on atmospheric railways. 'The oracle spoke freely, "I think they're a Humbug, your Royal Highness!" was the bluff reply. Its idiomatic directness was almost too much for the gravity of the Prince himself', who burst out laughing; *Daily News*, 18 December 1871, p. 3. Another version of the story has the two men meeting on a station platform and in this Hudson 'was heard to snort loudly, "It's a 'umbug, Your Royal 'Ighness, a 'umbug!" The word baffled Albert', who looked it up in his dictionary ... under the letter U!; E. E. P. Tisdall, *Restless*

Consort (London, 1952), p. 85. In a third version the meeting takes place at the original location, but Hudson's diction deteriorates even further as he 'burst out ... "Hit's a 'umbug, Your Royal 'Ighness!"'; Martin, *Enter Rumour*, p. 211. The story is almost certainly apocryphal.

76. *York Courant*, 26 March 1846, p. 4; *Times*, 20 March 1846, p. 5.

77. *Newcastle Journal*, 5 June 1847; E. D. Bancroft, *Letters from England, 1846–49* (London, 1904), p. 114.

78. R. Nevill, *The Reminiscences of Lady Dorothy Nevill* (London, 1906), pp. 103–4.

79. W. Gregory, *Sir William Gregory* (London, 1894), p. 132.

80. Absalom Watkin, quoted by Martin, *Enter Rumour*, p. 206; F. H. Grundy, *Pictures of the Past* (London, 1879), p. 128; *English Gentleman*, 6 September 1845, p. 313; Anon., 'The Railway Potentates', *Fraser's Magazine*, August 1847, p. 221.

81. *Fraser's Magazine*, August 1847, p. 219.

82. *Northern Star*, 14 April 1849, p. 4; Lennox, *Celebrities*, p. 189; Martin, '*Enter Rumour*', p. 206.

83. *Times*, 21 December 1846, p. 7; 22 December 1846, p. 4; *Standard*, 19 Decenber 1846, p. 3.

84. F. L. Gower, *Bygone Years: Recollections by the Hon. F. Leveson Gower* (London, 1905), p. 46 (Gower was a nephew of the Duke of Devonshire); T. H. S. Escott, *City Characters under Several Reigns* (London, 1922), p. 34; Martin, *Enter Rumour*, p. 204; Lennox, *Celebrities*, p. 187; Ponsonby, *Lady Charlotte*, pp. 27–28; A. Gilchrist, *Life of William Etty, RA* (London, 1855), p. 99.

85. According to Lennox, 'the Railway Queen certainly interlarded her conversation with many French words, spoken with a pure Yorkshire accent'. Referring to a well-known singer, she described her as 'tut-a-fa (*tout-à-fait*), marvelluxe (*merveilleux*); but ... she dresses in le plus movey goo (*le plus mauvais goût*)', Lennox, *Celebrities*, pp. 185; 187; see also Gower, *Bygone Years*, p. 46.

86. The 'Marcus' story is in Martin, *Enter Rumour*, p. 207; Lennox, *Celebrities*, p. 192; Tisdall, *Restless Consort*, p. 85. The 'butter' story is in R. H. Nevill, *Under Five Reigns by Dorothy Nevill* (London, 1910), p. 148; Escott, *City Characters*, p. 37.

87. G. N. Ray, *Thackeray: The Age of Wisdom, 1847–1863* (London, 1958), p. 29; Gower, *Bygone Years*, pp. 45–46; Milburn and Miller, *Sunderland*, p. 104, n. 33.

88. (Unidentified) newspaper cuttings dated October 1847, Hudson family papers.

89. *Times*, 10 July 1848, p. 7; 13 July 1848, p. 6; 14 July 1848, p. 8; Bancroft, *Letters*, pp. 189–94.

90. C. R. Dod, *The Parliamentary Pocket Companion for 1850* (London, 1850), p. 196; (unidentified) newspaper cuttings dated October 1848, Hudson family papers; E. Bogg, *From Edenvale to the Plains of York: or A Thousand Miles in the Valleys of the Nidd and Yore* (Leeds, 1894), p. 307.

91. *Times*, 27 January 1846, p. 3; *Hansard*, vol. 83, pp. 199–202.

92. *Times*, 27 January 1846, p. 5; *Standard*, January 27 1846, p. 4; *Yorkshire Gazette*, 7 February 1846.

93. *Times* 28 October 1845, p. 4; Rubinstein, *Britain's Century*, p. 81.

94. Edward Stanley was the son of the Earl of Derby, but had already been raised to the peerage by Peel as Baron Stanley of Bickerstaffe in 1844. He succeeded as Earl of Derby in 1851. Bentinck had apparently been the last MP to appear in the House 'in pink', i.e. wearing his scarlet hunting coat. He sold all his horses to devote himself to politics, and was mortified when one of them won the Derby in 1848, his own (unfulfilled) life's ambition; B. Disraeli, *Lord George Bentinck: A Political Biography* (London, 1905), pp. 226, 350.

95. R. J. Cruickshank, *Charles Dickens and Early Victorian England* (London, 1949), p. 103.

96. *Hansard*, vol. 83, pp. 1133–44; *Times*, 18 February 1846, p. 4.

97. *Hansard*, vol. 83, p. 1193; vol. 84, pp. 205–6, 568;

98. *Hansard*, 19 March 1846, vol. 84 pp. 1239–45.

99. Rubinstein, *Britain's Century*, p. 83; J. McCarthy, *Sir Robert Peel* (London, 1906), p. 156; W. D. Jones, *Lord Derby and Victorian Conservatism* (Oxford, 1956), pp. 120–23.

100. *The Observer*, 12 July 1846; Jones, *Lord Derby*, p. 119.

101. Anon., 'The Railway', p. 215.

102. The government would make long-term loans over thirty years of twice the amount of share capital put in by proprietors, bearing interest at 3.5 per cent; Disraeli, *Lord George*, pp. 223, 242–58.

103. *Hansard*, vol. 89, pp. 826–29; *Times*, 5 February 1847, p. 3; *Yorkshireman*, 20 February 1847.

104. *Morning Post*, 4 March 1847.

105. *Hansard*, Vol. 93, pp. 747–8, 1096, 1101, 1282–5; *Times*, 7 July 1847, p. 3; *Yorkshire Gazette*, 10 July 1847, p. 6.

106. *Times*, 2 July 1847, p. 4.

107. Anon., 'The Railway', p. 222.

108. *Yorkshire Gazette*, 7 February 1846.

109. *Yorkshireman*, 21 February 1846; *Fraser's Magazine*, August 1847, p. 222.

110. *Times*, 31 July 1846, p. 2; *Gateshead Observer*, 1 August 1846.

111. *Yorkshireman*, 20 Feb 1847.

112. Construction of the protective groynes for the south dock, to test their efficiency, had started even before the Act was passed in May 1846; Miller, 'More a Work', p. 35; *Times*, 22 July 1847, p. 3; 23 July 1847, p. 8; *Sunderland Herald*, 25 June 1847.

113. The meeting is reported in a handbill published by the Hudson campaign; Hudson family papers; Disraeli, *Lord George*, p. 271; Jones, *Lord Derby*, p. 126. Even the description of the Bank Charter Act as a 'fair weather' law was borrowed from Bentinck.

114. The result was Hudson 878 votes, Barclay 646 and Wilkinson 569 votes; whereas 532 electors had voted for both Hudson and Barclay, only fifty-three people had voted for the two Liberal candidates. Shortly after the election Barclay resigned because of severe financial problems; Sir Hedworth Williamson, who

controlled many of the Whig votes, himself stood in the ensuing by-election, defeating Wilkinson in a straight fight in December 1847 which the Tories did not contest. *Times*, 4 August 1847, p. 3; *Sunderland Herald*, 6 August 1847, pp. 6–8; Milburn and Miller, *Sunderland*, p. 223.

115. *Times*, 27 November 1847, p. 2; *Hansard*, vol. 95, pp. 243–48; for the reports of the Select Committee, see *Parliamentary Papers* 1847–48, vol. viii, pt 1; Bailey, *George Hudson*, pp. 76–77.

116. R. Blake, *Disraeli* (London, 1966), pp. 258–63; the *Gateshead Observer* of 29 May 1847 noted Rothschild's presence at a 'grand' dinner given at Albert Gate; *Hansard*, vol. 95, pp. 1352–53. In 1847 Hudson gave a job to one of Disraeli's former business associates, who claimed to be owed money; Blake, pp. 268–69.

117. Report in the *Sunderland Herald*, quoted in Rivett, 'The Building', pp. 52–53; *Illustrated London News*, 12 February 1848, p. 83; (unidentified) local newspaper cuttings dated 5 February 1848, Hudson family papers; Miller, 'More a Work', p. 35; Milburn and Miller, *Sunderland*, p. 17.

118. *Hansard*, vol. 96, pp. 450, 841–46, 1305–6; vol. 97, p. 503; vol. 98, p. 827; vol. 99, pp. 273–80, 705–6.

119. Hume had been a member of a committee that had raised a loan of £800,000 in 1824 for Greek insurgents fighting for independence from Turkey. V. Chancellor, *The Political Life of Joseph Hume* (London, 1986), pp. 35–36; *Times*, 17 June 1848, p. 4; reports in the *Morning Chronicle* and *Liverpool Albion*, quoted by the *Gateshead Observer* of 24 June 1848. Hudson does seem to have had a taste for champagne with his dinner, which is not incongruous as the drink was 'particularly favoured' as an accompaniment to a meal at that time. Anon., *Sketches of Public Men of the North* (London, 1855), pp. 53–54; Ray, *Thackeray*, p. 29.

120. *Yorkshireman*, 7 August 1847; 24 June 1848; *Hansard*, vol. 93, p. 1179.

121. The newspaper reference to Raphael Ward's engraving (of a portrait of Hudson by Francis Grant) published on 26 June 1848 indicates a publication date a few days later; (unidentified) newspaper cutting, Hudson family papers; Ingamells, 'Jackson and Grant', p. 910.

122. Ray, *Thackeray*, p. 32.

123. He wrote to Londonderry on 25 July 1848 to say that 'Your Lordship never was further wrong than in the opinion you entertain of Mr Hudson'; Milburn and Miller, *Sunderland*, p. 96.

Notes to Chapter 7: Disgrace

1. The total consideration was £747,785. Other denomination Great North of England shares had also been purchased; £100 shares at £234 14s. per share; £40 shares at £94 6s. 6d. and £30 shares at £70 3s. 3d. The £15 shares were created with a small deposit of £1 10s. and their holders were to receive dividends at 5 per cent on the various instalments up to June 1849, then 10 per cent until 1 July 1850 when the York Newcastle and Berwick was committed

to purchasing them for £37 10s. Paying £35 for these shares in October and November 1846 was 'something so extraordinary as to induce him [Prance] to ask for further explanation'.

2. *Railway Times* (1849), pp. 160, 183–84, 226–27; *Yorkshireman*, 24 February 1849, p. 7; *Yorkshire Herald*, 24 February 1849, p. 7; *Yorkshire Gazette*, 24 February 1849, p. 3.

3. *Yorkshire Gazette*, 24 February 1849, p. 5. It seems as though Hudson, his close friend James Richardson and the latter's brother Henry were amongst the larger stakeholders in the *Gazette*.

4. *Railway Times* (1849), pp. 227–28, 233.

5. *Railway Times* (1849), p. 258.

6. *Yorkshire Gazette*, 3 March 1849, p. 5; *Yorkshireman*, 3 March 1849, p. 5; *Times*, 1 March 1849, p. 5.

7. *Railway Times* (1849), pp. 272, 308–9.

8. *Railway Times* (1849), pp. 309–10, 402–3.

9. *Railway Times* (1849), pp. 467–69.

10. *Railway Times* (1849), pp. 449; 522–24; York and North Midland Railway, correspondence, financial records and legal papers; Directors' Minutes 1846–50, PRO RAIL 770/3; *Yorkshireman*, 26 May 1849, p. 5. Later Crawshay said that it had been the 'great anxiety' of himself and his colleagues to 'get Mr Thompson into the Direction and into the chair'; *Railway Times*, 1849, p. 1107.

11. The biographical information is from L. Stephen and S. Lee (eds), *Dictionary of National Biography*, xix (London, 1959–60), pp. 691–93; Cathcart (Earl of), 'Sir Harry Stephen Meysey Thompson, Bart: A Biographical Sketch', *Journal of the Agricultural Society of England* (second series), 10 (1874), pp. 519–41.

12. *Railway Times* (1849), p. 468; Cathcart, 'Sir Harry', p. 536.

13. The biographical information is from A. J. Peacock, 'George Leeman and York Politics, 1833–1880', in C. H. Feinstein (ed.), *York, 1831–1981: 150 Years of Scientific Endeavour and Social Change* (York, 1981), pp. 234–54.

14. *Railway Times* (1849), pp. 860–64, 1060, 1082–89. The meeting also agreed, on Thompson's proposal, a presentation of a hundred guineas to each committee member and gave a separate vote of thanks to Leeman for his work as the committee's secretary.

15. Companies could be formed by simple registration under the Joint Stock Companies Act of 1844, but they did not have the important protection of limited liability until 1855.

16. Unless specifically varied; H. Pollins, 'Aspects of Railway Accounting before 1868', in A. C. Littleton and B. S. Yamey (eds), *Studies in the History of Accounting* (London, 1956), pp. 337–39.

17. The York and North Midland Railway Act 1836, the Eastern Counties Railway Act 1836, the Midland Railway Act 1844 and the York, Newcastle and Berwick Railway Act 1847. The York and North Midland Committee of Investigation recommended that the company introduce bye-laws to bring its governance into line with the provisions of the Companies Consolidation Act; Third

Report of the Committee of Inquiry to the Shareholders of the York and North Midland Railway ('York and North Midland First Report'), York, 1849, p. 51; Goldsmith's Library of Economic Literature, University of London.

18. The Companies Clauses Consolidation Act 1845, section 85, merely required directors to be shareholders, but private Acts would often prescribe a substantial minimum holding; e.g. the Midland Railway Act of 1844 required directors to hold shares with a nominal value of £2000 (section 91).

19. See, for example, T. Chambers and A. T. T. Peterson, *A Treatise on the Law of Railway Companies in their Formation, Incorporation and Government* (London, 1848), p. 435. The digest of law reports for 1845–50 also lists cases concerned with the powers of directors, but none relating to their fiduciary duty towards shareholders; F. T. Streeten and H. J. Hodgson, *An Analytical Digest of the Cases Published in the New Series of the Law Journal Reports etc., 1845 to 1850* (London, 1852).

20. See also S. McCartney and A. J. Arnold, '"A Vast Aggregate of Avaricious and Flagitious Jobbing"? George Hudson and the Evolution of Early Notions of Directorial Responsibility', *Accounting, Business and Financial History*, 11 (2001), pp. 117–43.

21. Report of the Committee of Investigation to the Shareholders of the Midland Railway ('Midland Report'), *Derby Mercury (Extraordinary Edition)*, 15 August 1849, p. 2.

22. A further £2000 also remained under dispute; York and North Midland Second Report (1849), p. 5.

23. Further Report of the Committee of Investigation to the shareholders of the York, Newcastle and Berwick Railway ('Second Meek Report' et seq.), *Railway Times* (1849), p. 730.

24. Report of Eastern Counties shareholders' meeting, *Railway Times* (1849), p. 610; see also Report of the Committee of Investigation to the Shareholders of the Eastern Counties Railway ('Eastern Counties Report'), reproduced as appendix 'A' of the Second Report of the House of Lords Select (Monteagle) Committee on the Audit of Railway Accounts, *Parliamentary Papers* (1849, Cmd 371), x, p. 108.

25. Report of the Committee appointed by the proprietors of the York, Newcastle and Berwick Railway, to investigate the Great North of England Purchase Account ('Prance Report'); attached as appendix 'B' to the Second Report of the House of Lords Select (Monteagle) Committee on the Audit of Railway Accounts, *Parliamentary Papers* (1849, Cmd. 371), x, pp. 428–61; Second Meek Report (1849), p. 730.

26. Second Meek Report (1849), p. 730.

27. The committee considered him 'unquestionably liable to the Company' for the premiums received on the extra shares; York and North Midland First Report (1849), pp. 5–8; York and North Midland Second Report (1849), p. 9.

28. York and North Midland Second Report (1849), pp. 13–14.

29. York and North Midland Third Report (1849), p. 26.

30. York and North Midland Third Report (1849), p. 29.

31. Second Meek Report (1849), p. 729.

32. Prance Report (1849), pp. 428–61.

33. Third Meek Report (1849), p. 7.

34. Second Meek Report (1849), p. 729.

35. Five thousand shares were not issued and a thousand were transferred to officers, landowners and others connected with the York and North Midland for proper business reasons.

36. York and North Midland Second Report (1849), pp. 8–9, 23.

37. The latter was to form the subject of legal action in *York and North Midland Railway Company* v. *Hudson* in 1853.

38. Second Meek Report (1849), p. 729.

39. York and North Midland Second Report (1849), p. 14.

40. Hudson had already supplied the first three thousand tons to the Newcastle and Darlington Junction and the York and North Midland. On the remaining seven thousand, he made a profit of £5 10s. per ton, or £38,500 in total.

41. York and North Midland Second Report (1849), pp. 51–52, 54–55.

42. York and North Midland Second Report (1849), pp. 45–46, 48.

43. York and North Midland Second Report (1849), pp. 14–16, 39. There is some evidence to suggest that it was well known that Hudson dealt in iron rails on his own account, although this did not absolve him of responsibility to inform his fellow directors that particular consignments of rails were his property; see (unidentified) newspaper cutting for 30 September 1845 in Hudson family private papers.

44. Second Meek Report (1849), pp. 727–28.

45. Companies Clauses Consolidation Act, 1845, sections 115, 121–23.

46. Companies Clauses Consolidation Act, 1845, section 117; see also sections 102, 85. The York Newcastle and Berwick Committee claimed that the auditors had not done their duty in 'limiting their examination to a comparison of the bank book, in which are entered the directors' cheques with the entries in the journal ledger; they have neither required the production of vouchers nor original contracts, a mode of examination which it is obvious must be utterly worthless'. One of the auditors, Mr Barstow, claimed that they had done their duty, not on the grounds that they had in fact done more work than the committee had suggested, but on the grounds that they had not breached their duties as defined by the relevant Act of Parliament. *Railway Times* (1849), p. 467.

47. As stipulated in the Eastern Counties Railway Act (1836), section 170, the York and North Midland Act (1836), section 122, and the Midland Railway Act (1844), sections 113 and 126.

48. *Railway Times* (1849), p. 911.

49. Accountant's Report, York and North Midland Fourth Report (1849), pp. viii–ix.

50. Fifth Meek Report; *York Herald Extraordinary Edition*, 22 October 1849; PRO RAIL 772/15, p. 3.

51. Fifth Meek Report (1849), p. 19.

52. Midland Report (1849), pp. 5–8, 13–14, 47.

53. See S. McCartney and A. J. Arnold, 'George Hudson's Financial Reporting Practices: Putting the Eastern Counties Railway in Context', *Accounting, Business and Financial History*, 10 (2000), pp. 293–316.

54. Eastern Counties Report (1849), p. 104.

55. Eastern Counties Report (1849), pp. 104, 109; *Railway Times* (1849), pp. 607–8.

56. Eastern Counties Report (1849), pp. 127–45.

57. Virtually all the Eastern Counties's published profits were paid out to the shareholders as dividends during this period.

58. *Yorkshireman*, 10 March 1849, p. 5.

59. York and North Midland Railway Act 1836, section 110.

60. *Economist*, 14 April 1849, pp. 402–3.

61. R. P. Brief, 'Nineteenth-Century Accounting Error', *Journal of Accounting Research* (Spring 1965), p. 16; J. J. Glynn, 'The Development of British Railway Accounting, 1800–1911', *Accounting Historians' Journal*, 11 (1984), p. 107; see also Pollins, 'Aspects of Railway', pp. 339–44; J. R. Edwards, 'The Origins and Evolution of the Double Account System: An Example of Accounting Evolution', *Abacus* 21 (1985), pp. 26, 34; G. A. Lee, 'The Concept of Profit in British Accounting, 1760–1900', *Business History Review*, 49 (1975), pp. 21–22; J. R. Edwards, *A History of Financial Accounting* (London, 1989), pp. 144, 167; T. A. Lee, 'Company Financial Statements: An Essay in Business History', in *The Evolution of Corporate Financial Reporting*, T. A. Lee and R. H. Parker (eds) (London, 1979), p. 17; S. G. Checkland, *The Rise of Industrial Society in England, 1815–1885* (London, 1964), p. 37.

62. Simmons and Biddle cite only two promoters as being 'scandalous manipulators', Hudson and William Chadwick; J. Simmons and G. Biddle (eds), *Oxford Companion to British Railway History* (Oxford, 1997), pp. 5–6, 119, 214.

63. See also T. R. Gourvish, *Mark Huish and the London and North Western Railway: A Study in Management* (Leicester, 1972), pp. 25, 104.

64. *Railway Times* (1843), p. 1343.

65. See S. McCartney and A. J. Arnold, '"Capital Clamours for Profitable Investment, Confidence has Become Eager and May Shortly Become Blind": George Hudson and the "Railway Mania" Extensions of the York and North Midland Railway', *Journal of Industrial History*, 4 (2001), pp. 94–116. Regarding railway profits in general during this period, see A. J. Arnold and S. McCartney, 'Were they ever "Productive to the Capitalist"? Rates of Return on Britain's railways, 1830–55', *Journal of European Economic History* (forthcoming).

Notes to Chapter 8: Holding On

1. *Punch*, 16, April 7 1849, p. 137.

2. *Atlas*, 3 March 1849, p. 137.

3. *Times*, 10 April 1849, p. 5.

4. *Times*, 1 May 1849, p. 4.
5. *Times*, 10 May 1849, p. 5.
6. *Illustrated London News*, 14 April 1849, pp. 233–34.
7. Unidentified newspaper cutting dated 27 July 1849; Hudson family papers.
8. Apart from a lengthy gap from 12 February until 29 March 1849, when he was busy trying to deal with the problems at his various railway companies.
9. York Union Bank, Minute Books of the Board of Directors, 1833–62, 0003–0392/3, Barclays Bank Archives.
10. The other director was Richard Nicholson, who drowned himself in May 1849.
11. Half the contested seats had been previously held by the Tories and half by the Liberals. After the election, the Tories had a majority of twelve (twenty-one councillors and nine aldermen to the Liberals' fifteen councillors and three aldermen).
12. *Yorkshire Gazette*, 10 November 1849.
13. *Yorkshireman*, 14 April 1849.
14. *Darlington and Stockton Times*, 12 May 1849; *Yorkshire Gazette*, 12 May 1849, p. 5.
15. T. Mackay, *The Life of Sir John Fowler* (London, 1900), p. 119.
16. B. Bailey, *George Hudson: the Rise and Fall of the Railway King* (Stroud, 1995), p. 117.
17. He donated £20; *Daily News*, 25 April 1851 p. 115.
18. W. W. Tomlinson, *Tomlinson's North Eastern Railway* (third edition, Newton Abbot, 1987), p. 501. The suspended roadway was opened six months later. More than five thousand tons of iron went into the construction of the bridge, which cost £243,000 to build, in addition to the costs of land and the necessary compensation payments.
19. H. Murray, 'Queen Victoria, York and the Royal Myths', *York History*, 11 (1994), pp. 59–61, 63.
20. The station, in its final agreed form, was not completed until 1863, when Thomas Prosser added the present simplified version of the original portico, built by the North Eastern Railway as part of the agreed amalgamation with the Newcastle and Carlisle line. T. Faulkner and A. Greg, *John Dobson: Architect of the North East* (Newcastle, 2001), pp. 102–6; B. Fawcett, *A History of North Eastern Railway Architecture*, i, *The Pioneers* (Hull, 2001), p. 155
21. Stephenson's statue was erected in 1862, in Westgate Street, facing the station, Fawcett, *A History*, pp. 160, 182.
22. The bridge cost £120,000 to build and was first worked by goods traffic on 20 July 1850, Tomlinson, *Tomlinson's* pp. 506–7.
23. Hudson family papers.
24. *Illustrated London News*, 5 May 1849, p. 282; *Sunderland Herald*, 4 May 1849, p. 8. Outraged shareholders took a different view. A Liverpool shareholder in the Eastern Counties referred to the 'fulsome and nauseous address from his Sunderland subjects [which] ought to be sufficient to disfranchise the place'; *Railway Times*, 1849, p. 463.

25. *Hansard*, vol. 105 (1849), pp. 1112–13; *Times*, 18 May 1849, p. 3.

26. *The Atlas*, reported in the *Railway Times* (1849), p. 526; *Dumfries Courier*, as reported in the *Times*, 2 March 1850, p. 8.

27. *Hansard*, vol. 115 (1851), pp. 1112–13.

28. G. L. Dodds, *A History of Sunderland* (Sunderland, 1995), pp. 64–68; *Sunderland Herald*, 21 June 1850, p. 5; G. E. Milburn and S. T. Miller (eds), *Sunderland, River, Town and People: A History from the 1780s* (Sunderland, 1988), p. 97; *Port of Sunderland Millennium Handbook* (London, 2000), p. 35.

29. Nearly nine hundred ships had used the dock in the previous six months, with over a hundred and eighty thousand tons of coal being shipped, *Times*, 7 August 1851, p. 6.

30. *Hansard*, vol. 119 (1852), p. 1423; vol. 120 (1852), pp. 769–70; vol. 121 (1852), pp. 84–85; *Times*, 1 May 1852, p. 4.

31. Hudson 866 votes, Seymour 814 votes, Fenwick 654 votes; Milburn and Miller, *Sunderland*, p. 223.

32. *Times*, 7 August 1852, p. 8; *Port of Sunderland Millennium Handbook*, p. 37.

33. *Hansard*, vol. 121 (1852), p. 1242–43; *Times*, 7 December 1852, pp. 4–5; Sir W. Fraser, *Disraeli and his Day* (London 1891), pp. 279–80.

34. *Railway Times* (1849), pp. 727–32; (1850), pp. 26–28; York, Newcastle and Berwick Railway, correspondence, financial records and legal papers; sundry files, PRO RAIL 772/82.

35. *Yorkshireman*, 30 August 1849, p. 6. The same anonymous correspondent also wrote a similar letter on the activities of another of Hudson's close friends, Peter Clarke. *Yorkshireman*, 28 September 1849, p. 6.

36. *Richardson v. Wodson*, *Times* 19 July 1850, p. 7; *Report of the Evidence of George Hudson on the Trial of the Cause of Richardson v. Wodson* (London, 1850); *A Complete Report of the Recent Trial for Libel, Richardson v Wodson* (London, 1850).

37. *Times*, 7 November 1850, p. 7; 10 February 1851, p. 6.

38. *Newcastle Guardian*, 3 August 1850; Hudson family papers.

39. *Times*, 8 October 1850, p. 5.

40. *Times*, 3 December 1850, p. 8; 4 December 1850, p. 3; 5 December 1850, p. 3. One of Seymour's articles appeared in the *Weekly Chronicle* of 15 September 1850.

41. York and North Midland Railway, correspondence concerning law suits, PRO RAIL 770/64.

42. An initial payment of more than £60,000 was made in March 1849 and a further payment of £10,700 in spring 1851.

43. In March 1850, at a meeting of the York and North Midland, Thompson had said that, according to the 'best legal advice in the land', the claims on Hudson were £66,000, *Railway Times*, 2 March 1850, p. 223.

44. See F. T. Streeten and H. J. Hodgson, *An Analytical Digest of the Cases Published in the New Series of the Law Journal Reports etc., 1850 to 1855* (London, 1857), p. 167; C. F. F. Wordsworth, *The Law of Mining, Banking, Insurance and General*

Joint Stock Companies (sixth edition, London, 1854), p. 301–2; (tenth edition, London, 1865), pp. 159, 438–39.

45. During the appeal proceedings, Hudson did give details of the share recipients in private to the presiding judge, the Master of the Rolls, who made it clear in his case summary that the recipients had all been members of Parliament.

46. *York and North Midland v Hudson*, 1853, p. 529; *Times* 20 January 1853, p. 6.

47. *Times*, 12 February 1853, p. 7.

48. *Times*, 3 August 1853, p. 8; 10 December 1853, p. 8; Directors' Report for the York and North Midland at 31 December 1853; York and North Midland Railway, legal opinions on liabilities of George Hudson to the company, PRO RAIL 770/65.

49. *Newcastle Journal*, 28 July 1849. The Baldersby estate had cost £125,000, plus a further £20,000 for improvements and Newby Park £20,000; A. J. Peacock, *George Hudson: 1800–1871, The Railway King*, ii (York, 1989), p. 375. In July 1850, at the *Richardson v. Wodson* trial, Hudson stated that he held £12,000 of stock in the Eastern Counties, £18,000 in the Midland, £26,000 in the York and North Midland, and £40–50,000 in the York Newcastle and Berwick. *Illustrated London News*, 24 November 1849, p. 347; *Times* 19 July 1850, p. 7; *Report of the Evidence of George Hudson*, p. 43.

50. York Union Bank, Minute Books of the Board, 1833–62.

51. Hudson had not, however, been unable to clear the existing mortgages on the Whitby estate so, to persuade the North Eastern Railway to accept a third mortgage as security, Hudson had to agree to transfer Albert Gate, his shares in the Sunderland Dock Company and the land at Whitby, all of which were already mortgaged, to Thompson and Seymour, as trustees for the North Eastern Railway; North Eastern Railway; correspondence, financial records and legal papers; files concerning the lawsuits of George Hudson and the North Eastern Railway, PRO RAIL 527/1120; York and North Midland Railway, legal opinions on liabilities of George Hudson to the company, PRO RAIL 770/65; *Yorkshire Gazette*, 5 November 1853, p. 6; *Monthly Chronicle of North Country Lore and Legend*, November 1887, p. 397. The arrangements between Hudson and the York and North Midland and the North Eastern Railway are explained in detail in reports of later legal cases; see *Thompson* v. *Hudson* (1866), *Law Reports*, 2 Eq. 612; *Thompson* v. *Hudson* (1866–67), *Law Reports*, 2 Ch. App. 255.

52. An unidentified newspaper cutting, dated 5 May 1854, reports Hudson's purchase of forty thousand quarters of wheat; Hudson family papers.

53. *Times*, 2 September 1854, p. 7.

54. North Eastern Railway files, PRO RAIL 527/1120/3.

55. D. Bennett, *King without a Crown* (London, 1977), p. 236.

56. North Eastern Railway files, cuttings of 3 November 1864, PRO, RAIL 527/1121; *Sunderland Times*, 19 March 1857, p. 1.

57. *Times*, 29 August 1856, p. 6.

58. *Times*, 17 January 1857, p. 12; 11 March 1857, p. 12; 12 March 1857, p. 12.
59. *Times*, 20 March 1857, p. 9; 21 March 1857, p. 12; *Sunderland Times*, 19 March 1857, pp. 1–2; 21 March 1857, p. 5.
60. *Sunderland Times*, 28 March 1857, p. 5.
61. Fenwick polled 1123 votes, Hudson 1081 and Walters 863, *Sunderland Times*, 4 April 1857, p. 2.

Notes to Chapter 9: Defeat

1. *Hansard*, vol. 147 (1857), pp. 209, 1001; vol. 148 (1857), pp. 425–41; *Times*, 10 December 1857, p. 6.
2. *Times*, 27 August 1857, p. 10.
3. Over the period 1851 to 1858, the amount of coal exported from the Wear rose by 56 per cent, *Port of Sunderland Millennium Handbook* (London, 2000), p. 35; *Times*, 2 March 1859, p. 11; 12 August 1859, p. 8.
4. *Times*, 1 April 1859, p. 6; *Hansard*, Vol. 151 (1859), pp. 773, 1199–1202.
5. The final votes were Fenwick 1524, Lindsay 1291 and Hudson 788, *Times*, 8 April 1859, p. 5; 27 April 1859, p. 12; 2 May 1859, p. 8; *Sunderland Herald* 22 April 1859, p. 7; 6 May 1859, p. 7; G. E. Milburn and S. T. Miller (eds), *Sunderland. River, Town and People: A History from the 1780s* (Sunderland, 1988), p. 223.
6. *Sunderland Herald* 6 May 1859, p. 7.
7. North Eastern Railway; correspondence, financial records and legal papers; letters from Hudson concerning his debts, PRO RAIL 1155/15.
8. L. T. C. Rolt, *George and Robert Stephenson* (London, 1984), p. 324.
9. The acquisition of the land at West Cliff seems to have been envisaged in 1843 and was a firm intention by 1846; (unidentified) newspaper cutting dated 22 August 1846, Hudson family papers. See also North Eastern Railway; files concerning the lawsuits of George Hudson and the North Eastern Railway, PRO RAIL 527/1120 and sundry files, PRO RAIL 527/1129–30; York and North Midland Railway, legal opinions on liabilities of George Hudson to the company, PRO RAIL 770/65; deed of conveyance for land at Whitby; register of deeds, NRRD HQ 178146, North Yorkshire County Record Office; A. White, *A History of Whitby* (Chichester, 1993), p. 59.
10. Large numbers of hotels and boarding houses were later built on part of the site; T. Faulkner and A. Greg, *John Dobson: Architect of the North East* (Newcastle, 2001), pp. 111–12; G. H. J. Daysh (ed.), *A Survey of Whitby and the Surrounding Area* (Eton, 1958), pp. 67, 70; G. W. J. Potter, *A History of the Whitby and Pickering Railway* (London, 1906), p. 44; W. W. Tomlinson, *Tomlinson's North Eastern Railway* (third edition, Newton Abbot, 1987), p. 486; North Yorkshire County Record Office plan 2W(M) 1/95; Whitby Literary and Philosophical Society, plan 399.
11. North Eastern Railway files, PRO RAIL 527/1110/4; 527/1120/6.
12. Harry Thompson polled 218 votes, the Conservative Thomas Chapman 190.

13. North Eastern Railway letters, PRO RAIL 1155/15.

14. North Eastern Railway letters, PRO RAIL 1155/15.

15. North Eastern Railway files, PRO RAIL 527/1110/4.

16. North Eastern Railway letters, PRO RAIL 1155/15; files, PRO RAIL 527/1110/4.

17. North Eastern Railway letters, PRO RAIL 1155/15.

18. North Eastern Railway letters, PRO RAIL 1155/15.

19. R. Beaumont, *The Railway King: A Biography of George Hudson* (London, 2002), p. 167.

20. See for example, Thompson's letter of 3 March 1865 to the *Whitby Gazette*.

21. North Eastern Railway files, PRO RAIL 527/1110/4; PRO RAIL 527/1121.

22. A. I. Shand, *Old-Time Travel: Personal Reminiscences of the Continent Forty Years Ago Compared with Experiences of the Present Day* (London, 1903), pp. 368–70.

23. J. Forster, *The Life of Charles Dickens*, iii (London, 1874), pp. 243–44;

24. Meeting with George Hudson, newspaper extract, York Reference Library Y923.8.

25. T. Mackay, *The Life of Sir John Fowler* (London, 1900), p. 119; Sir A. West, *Recollections, 1832 to 1886* (London, 1900), p. 117; Lord W. P. Lennox, *Celebrities I Have Known: With Episodes, Political, Social, Sporting and Theatrical*, second series, i (London, 1877), pp. 190–92.

26. The election of a Liberal, Thompson, in 1859, had been unprecedented; North Eastern Railway letters, PRO RAIL 1155/15; files, PRO RAIL 527/1121.

27. North Eastern Railway letters, PRO RAIL 1155/15.

28. North Eastern Railway files, PRO RAIL 527/1121; *Thompson* v. *Hudson* (1870) L.R.10 Eq. 497.

29. *Whitby Gazette*, 4 March 1865; supplement to *Whitby Gazette*, 10 June 1865, p. 1; North Eastern Railway letters, PRO RAIL 1155/15. The 'scoffs' of Thompson's campaign adviser, Leeman, at the prospects of a Scarborough and Whitby Coast Railway had also given 'great umbrage to the people of Whitby and the neighbourhood', *Whitby Gazette*, 17 June 1865.

30. *Yorkshire Gazette*, 10 June 1865.

31. North Eastern Railway files, PRO RAIL 527/1121.

32. A little of the shine was taken off things for Hudson supporters by the news that Leeman (along with Lowther) had been returned as MP for York, *Times*, 15 July 1865, p. 8.

33. *Times*, 18 October 1865, p. 7.

34. *Times*, 30 June 1866, p. 12.

35. Curiously, the position of the North Eastern Railway was made much more difficult by the way the agreement was actually drafted, which made the reinstatement of their full claim in the event of a default by Hudson look like a penalty; see *Thompson* v. *Hudson* (1866), *Law Reports*, 2 Eq. 612, *per* Lord Romilly, at p. 623.

36. *Thompson* v. *Hudson* (1866–67), *Law Reports*, 2 Ch. App. 255; *Thompson* v. *Hudson* (1869–70), *Law Reports*, 4 H.L.1.

37. He was in real poverty, living in cheap hotels in the coastal towns of Belgium and France.

38. *Newcastle Daily Chronicle*, 5 March 1869; *Times*, 19 April 1869, p. 11.

39. *Times*, 28 May 1869, p. 12; *Sunderland Times*, 29 May 1869.

40. The subscription was administered by a trust, in order to keep the money safe from his creditors. The initial annuity of £520 was raised to £635 in 1870; *Times*, 14 July 1869, p. 12; 20 September 1870, p. 10.

41. *Daily News*, 18 December 1871, p. 3.

42. *Times*, 19 July 1869, p. 9; North Eastern Railway files, PRO RAIL 527/1121.

43. *Times*, 26 April 1870, p. 11; *Yorkshire Gazette*, 23 April 1870, p. 2.

44. *Yorkshire Gazette*, 7 October 1871, p. 9; 21 October 1871, p. 7.

45. Even after the House of Lords judgement, the North Eastern Railway had been involved in two further cases concerning the dispute with Hudson. The first in June 1870 revealed that, when Albert Gate had been sold in 1861, the North Eastern had not set the sum against Hudson's overall debt, but had simply banked the money and continued to charge interest on the debt as if the money had not been received, a practice which the court, not surprisingly, found against. The second case, in 1871, was part of a dispute between the North Eastern Railway and the 'other claimants' over the £33,000 paid by Hudson to the North Eastern Railway out of the sale of Newby Park in 1854; *Thompson* v. *Hudson* (1870), *Law Reports*, 10 Eq. 497; *Thompson* v. *Hudson* (Appropriation of Payments) (1870–71), *Law Reports*, 6 Ch. App. 320.

46. J. Mitchell, *Reminiscences of My Life in the Highlands* (Newton Abbot, 1971), pp. 241–51; North Eastern Railway files, PRO RAIL 527/1120/6; PRO RAIL 527/1121.

47. *Yorkshire Telegraph*, 16 December 1871, p. 8.

48. *Times*, 22 December 1871, p. 3; *Yorkshire Telegraph*, 23 December 1871; *Yorkshire Herald*, 23 December 1871. The family grave was renovated in 1935 by members of the Hudson family and by a 'few admirers of George Hudson, known as the Railway King', possibly as a result of Lambert's biography of Hudson. The vault was closed with a massive sarcophagus of polished grey granite, enclosed by a decorative railing, also inscribed with the names of other members of his family including his wife Elizabeth, his young children Matthew Bottrill and Richard Nicholson Hudson, his sister Ann and his parents John and Elizabeth.

49. *Times*, 16 December 1871, p. 9.

50. *Yorkshire Gazette*, 26 February 1876; 3 January 1880; 6 February 1909; Mackay, *The Life*, p. 119.

51. R. S. Lambert, *The Railway King* (London, 1934), p. 291; B. Bailey, *George Hudson: The Rise and Fall of the Railway King* (Stroud, 1995), pp. 134–35.

52. The purchase consideration was £75,000; *Whitby Gazette*, 17 May 1873, p. 4; 19 June 1875, p. 4; 22 April 1876, p. 4.

53. *Times*, 10 April 1849, p. 5; 10 May 1849, p. 5; *Illustrated London News*, 14 April 1849, pp. 233–4.

54. R. Bell, *The Ladder of Gold* (London, 1850).

55. A. Trollope, *The Way We Live Now* (London, 1951), i , pp. 31, 80–81, 205, 217–18, 331; ii , pp. 357–58.

56. C. Dickens, *Little Dorrit* (London, 1994), pp. 246–47, 390, 571, 710.

57. B. Disraeli, *Endymion* (London, 1882), pp. 66–67, 357–58.

58. See, for example, M. W. Kirby, *The Origins of Railway Enterprise: the Stockton and Darlington Railway, 1821–1863* (Cambridge, 1993), p. 98, M. Robbins, *The Railway Age* (London, 1962), p. 33.

59. *Times*, 1 May 1849, p. 4.

60. Tomlinson, *Tomlinson's*, p. 497.

61. *Tait's Edinburgh Magazine*, Vol. XVI, No. 185 (May 1849), pp. 319–20.

62. See, by way of contrast, Lambert, *Railway King*, pp. 18, 27.

63. C. J. Allen, *The Great Eastern Railway* (fifth edition, London, 1968), p. 58.

Bibliography

PRIMARY

Atcherley papers re 1837 election; accession 93/7–8, York City Archives, York

Atlas

Bankers' Magazine

Banking Act (1826) 7 Geo. IV c. 46

Baptismal entry, Parish Register of Scrayingham; Y923.8, York Reference Library, York

Cambridge Advertiser

Cambridge Chronicle and Journal and Huntingdonshire Gazette

Cambridge Independent Press

Companies Clauses Consolidation Act (1845) 8 & 9 Vict. c. 16

Complete Report of the Recent Trial for Libel, Richardson v Wodson (1850), London: Mitchell

Council Minutes; York City Archives, York

Daily News

Darlington and Stockton Times

Deeds of conveyance for land at Whitby; Register of Deeds NRRD HQ 178146 and 179147, North Yorkshire County Record Office, Northallerton

Deed of conveyance for land at Monkgate; E98 ff 61v–62v, York City Archives, York

Deed of co-partnership; accession 135, box 7, York City Archives, York

Early British Railways collection, chiefly of press cuttings, maps and other printed matter compiled by Septimus Bell, Vols. III, VI, VIII; London School of Economics Archives, Misc. 189

Eastern Counties Railway Act (1836) 6 & 7 Wm. IV c. 106

Economist

English Gentleman

Evening Sun (London)

Fraser's Magazine

Gateshead Observer

Great North of England Railway; correspondence, financial records and legal papers, PRO RAIL 232/78, Public Records Office, Kew

Hansard

Herapath's (Railway and Commercial) Journal

Hudson family private papers

Hunt's Merchants' Magazine (New York)

Illustrated London News

Knowles Scrap Book 1852–91, Yo40, York Reference Library, York

Limited Liability Act (1855) 18 & 19 Vict. c. 133

Lord Howden v. Simpson and others, Queen's Bench, 1839

Marriage entry, Parish Register of Holy Trinity, Goodramgate, York

Meeting with George Hudson; newspaper extract, Y923.8, York Reference Library, York

Midland Railway Act (1844) 7 & 8 Vict. c. 18

Monthly Chronicle of North Country Lore and Legend

Morning Chronicle

Morning Post

Newcastle and Berwick Railway Act (1847) 10 & 11 Vict. c. 133

Newcastle and Berwick Railway; correspondence, financial records and legal papers, PRO RAIL 506/8, Public Records Office, Kew

Newcastle Daily Chronicle

Newcastle Journal

Newcastle Guardian

North Eastern Railway; correspondence, financial records and legal papers; letters from Hudson concerning his debts, PRO RAIL 1155/15; files concerning the lawsuits of George Hudson and the North Eastern Railway, PRO RAIL 527/1110 and 1120–21; and sundry files, PRO RAIL 527/1129–30, PRO RAIL 1021/39, Public Records Office, Kew

Northern Star

Observer

Oxford and Cambridge Review

Plan of the proposed development of Westcliff, Plan 399, Whitby Literary and Philosophical Society, Whitby

Plan of Whitby Westcliff shewing the Intended Streets & Buildings, 1859 [by John Dobson], Plan 2W(M) 1/95, North Yorkshire County Record Office, Northallerton

Proceedings of the First General Meeting of the Eastern Counties Railway (1888), London: Eastern Counties Railway (reprint of original of 1836)

Punch

Railway Express

Railway Intelligence

Railway Magazine

Railway Regulation Bill (1844) P.P. (1844, Cmd. 397), Vol. IV

Railway Times

Joint Stock Companies Act (1844) 7 & 8 Vict. c. 110

Regulation of Railways Act (1844) 7 & 8 Vict. c. 85

Report of the Commissioners of Railways (1848); PRO RAIL 1053/17, Public Records Office, Kew

Report of the Committee of Investigation to the Shareholders of the Eastern Counties Railway ('Eastern Counties Report'), reproduced as Appendix 'A' of the Second Report of the House of Lords Select (Monteagle) Committee on the Audit of Railway Accounts, P.P. (1849, Cmd. 371) Vol. X, pp. 99–145

Report of the Committee of Investigation to the Shareholders of the Midland Railway ('Midland Report'), Derby Mercury (Extraordinary Edition), 15 August 1849, pp. 1–62; Derby City Reference Library

Reports of the Committee of Inquiry to the Shareholders of the York and North Midland Railway ('YNM First Report' et seq.); First, Second, Third, and Fourth Reports, York, 1849; Goldsmith's Library of Economic Literature, University of London

Report of the Committee appointed by the proprietors of the York, Newcastle and Berwick Railway, to investigate the Great North of England Purchase Account ('Prance Report'); attached as Appendix 'B' to the Second Report of the House of Lords Select (Monteagle) Committee on the Audit of Railway Accounts; P.P. (1849, Cmd. 371) Vol. X, pp. 428–61; Second Report of the Committee of Investigation to the shareholders of the York, Newcastle and Berwick Railway ('Second Meek Report'); *Railway Times* (1849), pp. 727–31; Third Report of the Committee of Investigation to the shareholders of the York, Newcastle and Berwick Railway ('Third Meek Report'); PRO RAIL 772/15; Fifth and Final Report ... ('Fifth Meek Report'); *York Herald Extraordinary Edition*, 22 October 1849; PRO RAIL 772/15, Public Records Office, Kew

Report of the Evidence of George Hudson on the Trial of the Cause of Richardson v Wodson (1850), London: John Hearne

Report of the House of Lords (Monteagle) Select Committee on the Audit of Railway Accounts; First, Second and Third Reports; P.P. (1849, Cmd. 371, 421), Vol. X

Report of the Royal Commission on the Railways, Appendix EK ('General List of Railway Acts passed from 1801 to the end of the Session of 1866'), P.P. (1867, Cmd. 3844), Vol. XXXVIII, Part II, pp. 363–423

Report of the Select Committee into Expenditure of Certain Sums under the Head of Parliamentary Expenses; P.P. (1849, Cmd. 366) Vol. X

Report of the Select Committee on Commercial Distress, P.P. (1847–48, Cmd. 395, 584), Vol. VIII

Report of the Select Committee on Railways, P.P. 1844, Vol. XI

Response of the Directors of the Eastern Counties Railway to the Eastern Counties Report (1849), London; LSE Reference Library

Standard

Sunderland Herald

Sunderland Times

Tait's Edinburgh Magazine

Times

Thompson v Hudson (1866) L.R.2 Eq. 612

Thompson v Hudson (1866–67) L.R.2 Ch. App. 255

Thompson v Hudson (1869–70) L.R.4 H.L.1

Thompson v Hudson (1870) L.R.10 Eq. 497

Thompson v Hudson (Appropriation of Payments) (1870–71) L.R.6 Ch. App. 320

University of London Rare Books Collection

Weekly Chronicle

Whitby Gazette

Will of Matthew Bottrill; Borthwick Wills, York Prerogative 176/200, Borthwick Institute of Historical Research, York

York Chronicle

York Courant

Yorkshire Gazette

Yorkshire Telegraph

York Herald

York and North Midland Railway Act (1836) 6 & 7 Wm. IV c. 81

York and North Midland Railway, correspondence, financial records and legal papers; Directors' Minutes 1846–50, PRO RAIL 770/3; (Capital) Receipts and Payments accounts, 1836–45, PRO RAIL 770/13; Revenue Accounts 1839–45, PRO RAIL 770/13; Letter of Henry Newton to Henry Pease, PRO RAIL 770/44; Correspondence concerning law suits, PRO RAIL 770/64; Legal opinions on liabilities of George Hudson to the company, PRO RAIL 770/65; Ledgers 1836–45, PRO RAIL 770/91; Public Records Office, Kew

York and North Midland Railway Company v. Hudson (1853) *Law Journal Reports*, Vol. XXII, pp. 529–38

York Newcastle and Berwick Railway Act (1847) 10 & 11 Vict. c. 133

York Newcastle and Berwick Railway, correspondence, financial records and legal papers; Committee of Investigation minutes and Reports (4 vols), PRO RAIL 772/15; sundry files, PRO RAIL 772/82; Public Records Office, Kew

Yorkshireman

York Union Bank; Correspondence files 1848–1872, 0003–3881, Individual Ledgers

1833–40, 0595–0004/5; Minute Books of the Board of Directors, 1833–62, 0003–0392/3; Private Ledgers 1833–68, 0081–0014; Barclays Bank Archives, Manchester

SECONDARY

Allen, C. J. (1964), *The North Eastern Railway* (third edition), London: Ian Allan.

Allen, C. J. (1968), *The Great Eastern Railway* (fifth edition), London: Ian Allan.

Anon. (1832), *Stranger's Guide through the City of York*, York: Bellerby.

Anon. (1847), 'The Railway Potentates', *Fraser's Magazine*, August 1847, pp. 213–27.

Anon. (1855), *Sketches of Public Men of the North*, London & Newcastle-upon-Tyne: William Gridley.

Anon. (1939), 'The Centenary of the Eastern Counties Railway', *The Locomotive, Railway Carriage and Wagon Review*, Vol. XLV, No. 563, pp. 203–6.

Armstrong, A. (1974), *Stability and Change in an English County Town: a Social Study of York 1801–51*, London: Cambridge University Press.

Arnold. A. J. and McCartney, S. (2004), 'Were They Ever "Productive to the Capitalist"? Rates of Return on Britain's Railways, 1830–55', *Journal of European Economic History* (forthcoming).

Bailey, B. (1995), *George Hudson: the Rise and Fall of the Railway King*, Stroud: Allan Sutton.

Bancroft, E. D. (1904), *Letters from England 1846–49*, London: Smith Elder.

Barnes, E. G. (1966), *The Rise of the Midland Railway 1844–1874*, London: Allen & Unwin.

Baskin, J. B. (1988), 'The development of corporate financial markets in Britain and the United States, 1600–1914: overcoming asymmetric information', *Business History Review*, Vol. 62, pp. 199–237.

Baskin, J. B. and Miranti, P. J. (1997), *A History of Corporate Finance*, Cambridge: Cambridge University Press.

Beaumont, R. (2002), *The Railway King: a Biography of George Hudson*, London: Review.

Bell, R. (1850), *The Ladder of Gold. An English Story* (in 3 volumes), London: Richard Bentley.

Bennett, D. (1977), *King without a Crown*, London: Heinemann.

Blake, R. (1966), *Disraeli*, London: Eyre & Spottiswoode.

Bogg, E. (1894), *From Edenvale to the plains of York: or, A thousand miles in the valleys of the Nidd and Yore*, Leeds: published by the author.

Brett, P. (1989), *The Rise and Fall of the York Whig Club 1818–1830*, Borthwick Paper No. 76, York: University of York.

Brief, R. P. (1965), 'Nineteenth century accounting error', *Journal of Accounting Research*, Spring, pp. 12–31.

Brooke, D. (1961), 'The Origins and Development of the Four Constituent Lines of the North-Eastern Railway, 1824–54', Unpublished MA thesis, University of Hull.

Cathcart, Earl of (1874), 'Sir Harry Stephen Meysey Thompson, Bart: a Biographical Sketch', *Journal of the Agricultural Society of England* (Second series), Vol. 10, pp. 519–41.

Chambers, T. and Peterson, A. T. T. (1848), *A Treatise on the Law of Railway Companies in their Formation, Incorporation and Government*, London: William Benning.

Chancellor, V. (1986), *The Political Life of Joseph Hume*, London: published by the author.

Checkland, S. G. (1964), *The Rise of Industrial Society in England, 1815–1885*, London: Longman.

Clapham, J. H. (1967), *An Economic History of Modern Britain, the Early Railway Age, 1820–1850* (second edition), Cambridge: Cambridge University Press.

Clinker, C. R. (1982), *The Birmingham and Derby Junction Railway*, Weston-super-Mare: Avon-Anglia. (First published in 1956).

Corfe, T. (ed.) (1983), *The Buildings of Sunderland 1814–1914*, Sunderland: Tyne and Wear Museums.

Cottrell, P. L. (1980), *Industrial Finance 1830–1914*, London: Methuen.

Crouzet, F. (1964), 'Wars, blockade and economic change in Europe, 1792–1815', *Journal of Economic History*, Vol. XXIV, pp. 567–90.

Cruickshank, R. J. (1949), *Charles Dickens and Early Victorian England*, London: Sir Isaac Pitman.

Cunningham, G. H. (1927), *London*, London: J. M. Dent.

Daysh, G. H. J. (ed.) (1958), *A Survey of Whitby and the Surrounding Area*, Eton: Shakespeare Head Press.

Dickens, C. (1994), *Little Dorrit*, London: Penguin (first published in book form in 1857).

Disraeli, B. (Earl of Beaconsfield) (1905), *Lord George Bentinck: A Political Biography*, London: Archibald Constable & Co. (first published in 1851).

Disraeli, B. (Earl of Beaconsfield) (1882), *Endymion*, London: Longmans, Green and Co.

Doble, E. (1939), 'History of the Eastern Counties Railway in relation to Economic Development', Unpublished PhD thesis, University of London.

Dodds, G. L. (1995), *A History of Sunderland*, Sunderland: Albion.

Dugan, S. and D. (2000), *The Day the World Took Off: the Roots of the Industrial Revolution*, London: Channel 4 Books.

Durey, M. (1974), *The First Spasmodic Cholera Epidemic in York, 1832*, Borthwick Paper No. 46, York: University of York.

Eames, M. (1996), 'Anti-Catholicism in York from the General Election of 1826 to the Opening of the New St Winifred's Church in 1864', Unpublished MA thesis, York University.

Edwards, J. R. (1985), 'The origins and evolution of the double account system: an example of accounting evolution', *Abacus*, Vol. 21 (1), pp. 19–43.

Edwards, J. R. (1986), 'Depreciation and fixed asset valuation in railway company accounts to 1911', *Accounting and Business Research*, Vol. 16 (63) (Summer), pp. 251–63.

Edwards, J. R. (1989), *A History of Financial Accounting*, London: Routledge.

Escott, T. H. S. (1922), *City Characters under Several Reigns*, London: Effingham Wilson.

Faulkner, T. and Greg, A. (2001), *John Dobson: Architect of the North East*, Newcastle: Tyne Bridge.

Fawcett, B. (2001), *A History of North Eastern Railway Architecture, Vol 1: the Pioneers*, Hull: North Eastern Railway Association.

Foreman-Peck, J. and Millward, R. (1994), *Public and Private Ownership of British Industry 1820–1990*, Oxford: Clarendon Press.

Forster, J. (1874), *The Life of Charles Dickens* (Volume 3), London: Chapman and Hall.

Francis, J. A. (1968), *A History of the English Railways: its Social Relations and Revelations 1820–45*, Newton Abbot: David and Charles. (first published in 1851).

Fraser, Sir W. (1891), *Disraeli and his Day*, London: Kegan Paul.

Freeman, M. (1999), *Railways and the Victorian Imagination*, New Haven: Yale University Press.

Frith, H. (1893), *The Flying Horse: The story of the Locomotive and the Railway*, London: Griffith and Farran.

Fulford, R (1949), *The Prince Consort*, London: Macmillan.

Gilchrist, A. (1855), *Life of William Etty, R. A.*, London: David Bogue.

Glynn, J. J. (1984), 'The development of British railway accounting 1800–1911', *Accounting Historians' Journal*, Vol. 11, pp. 103–18. Reprinted in R. H. Parker and B. S. Yamey (eds) (1994), *Accounting History: some British Contributions*, Oxford: Clarendon Press, pp. 327–42.

Gordon, D. I. (1990), *A Regional History of the Railways of Great Britain, Vol. 5: The Eastern Counties* (third edition), Newton Abbot: David and Charles.

Gourvish, T. R. (1972), *Mark Huish and the London and North Western Railway; a Study in Management*, Leicester: Leicester University Press.

Gourvish, T. R. (1980), *Railways and the British Economy 1830–1914*, London: Macmillan/Economic History Society.

Gourvish, T. R. (1980), 'Railway Enterprise', in R. A. Church (ed.), *The Dynamics of Victorian Business: Problems and Perspectives to the 1870s*, London: Allen & Unwin, pp. 126–41.

Gower, F. L. (1905), *Bygone Years, Recollections by the Hon. F. Leveson Gower*, London: John Murray.

Gregory, W. (1894), *Sir William Gregory*, London: J. Murray.

Grinling, C. H. (1966), *The History of the Great Northern Railway*, London: Allen & Unwin. (Reprint of work first published in 1898, with additional material on the period from 1898 to 1922.).

Grundy, F. H. (1879), *Pictures of the Past*, London: Griffith and Farran.

Harrison, J. F. C. (1988), *Early Victorian Britain, 1832–51*, London: Fontana.

Hawke, G. R. (1970), *Railways and Economic Growth in England and Wales 1840–1870*, Oxford: Clarendon Press.

Hawke, G. R. and Higgins, J. P. P. (1981), 'Transport and social overhead capital', in R. Floud and D. McCloskey (eds), *Economic History of Britain Since 1700*, Vol. 1, Cambridge: Cambridge University Press, pp. 227–52.

Hawkin, R. Y. (1955), *A History of the Freemen of the City of York*, York: Burdekin.

Hobsbawm, E. J. (1969), *Industry and Empire*, London: Pelican.

Hunt, B. C. (1936), *The Development of the Business Corporation in England 1800–1867*, Cambridge, Mass.: Harvard University Press.

Hyde, F. E. (1934), *Mr Gladstone at the Board of Trade*, London: Cobden-Sanderson.

Ingamells, J. (1973), 'Jackson and Grant at York', *Preview* (quarterly publication of the York City Art Gallery), Vol. XXVI, No. 101, pp. 907–11.

Jenvey, S. M. (1969), 'George Leeman and the Virtue of Independence', unpublished PhD thesis, York University.

Johnson, L. G. (1957), *General T. Perronet Thompson*, London: George Allen & Unwin.

Jones, W. D. (1956), *Lord Derby and Victorian Conservatism*, Oxford: Basil Blackwell.

Kenwood, A. G. (1965) 'Railway investment in Britain, 1825–1875', *Economica*, Vol. XXXII (new series), pp. 313–22.

Killick, J. R. and Thomas, W. A. (1970), 'The provincial stock exchanges 1830–1870', *Economic History Review*, Second series Vol. XXIII (1), pp. 96–111.

Kirby, M. W. (1993), *The Origins of Railway Enterprise: the Stockton and Darlington Railway, 1821–1863*, Cambridge: Cambridge University Press.

Knight, C. B. (1944), *A History of the City of York*, York: Herald.

Lambert, R. S. (1934), *The Railway King*, London: George Allen & Unwin.

Lee, G. A. (1975), 'The concept of profit in British accounting, 1760–1900', *Business History Review*, Vol. XLIX (1), pp. 6–36.

Lee, T. A. (1979), 'Company financial statements: an essay in business history', in T. A. Lee and R. H. Parker (eds), *The Evolution of Corporate Financial Reporting*, London: Nelson, pp. 15–39.

Lennox, Lord W. P. (1877), *Celebrities I have known; with Episodes, Political, Social, Sporting and Theatrical*, Second Series (Vol. 1), London: Hurst and Blackett.

Lewin, H. G. (1925), *Early British Railways*, London: Locomotive Publishing Company.

Lewis, B. (1994), *The Cabry Family, Railway Engineers*, Mold, Clwyd: Railway and Canal Historical Society.

Lubenow, W. C. (1971), *The Politics of Government Growth: Early Victorian Attitudes Toward State Intervention, 1833–48*, Newton Abbot: David and Charles.

Lyth, J. (1885), *Glimpses of Early Methodism in York*, York: Sessions.

McCartney, S. and Arnold A. J. (2000), 'George Hudson's financial reporting practices: putting the Eastern Counties Railway in context', *Accounting, Business and Financial History*, Vol. 10, pp. 293–316.

McCartney, S. and Arnold A. J. (2001), '"A vast aggregate of avaricious and flagitious jobbing"? George Hudson and the evolution of early notions of directorial responsibility', *Accounting, Business and Financial History*, Vol. 11, pp. 117–43.

McCartney, S. and Arnold A. J. (2001), '"Capital clamours for profitable investment, confidence has become eager and may shortly become blind:" George Hudson and the "railway mania" extensions of the York and North Midland Railway', *Journal of Industrial History*, Vol. 4, pp. 94–116.

McCartney S. and Arnold A. J. (2002), 'Financial reporting in the context of crisis: did the "mania" change the conceptual basis of early railway accounting?' *European Accounting Review*, Vol. 11, No. 2, pp. 401–17.

McCarthy, J. (1906), *Sir Robert Peel* (fourth edition), London: Dent.

McCord, N. and Wood, P. A. (1959), 'The Sunderland election of 1845', *The Durham University Journal*, Vol. XXI (N.S.), No. 1, pp. 11–21.

Malden, J. (1989), *Register of York Freemen*, York: privately published.

Mackay, T. (1900), *The Life of Sir John Fowler*, London: John Murray.

MacLean, J. S. (1948), *Newcastle and Carlisle Railway*, Newcastle: Robinson.

Martin, R. B. (1962), *'Enter Rumour': Four Early Victorian Scandals*, London: Faber and Faber.

Martin, Sir T. (1900), *Helena Faucit*, Edinburgh: Blackwood.

Matthew, H. C. G. (1978), *The Gladstone Diaries, Vol III 1840–47*, Oxford: Clarendon Press.

Matthews, P. W. (1926), *History of Barclays Bank*, London: Blades, East & Blades.

Meik, H. H. (1916), 'The York and North Midland Railway', *Railway Magazine*, Vol. XXXVIII, pp. 320–7, 398–402.

Milburn, G. E. and Miller, S. T. (eds) (1988), *Sunderland, River, Town and People: a History from the 1780s*, Sunderland: Reed.

Miller, S. T. (1983), *Sunderland Past and Present*, Sunderland: Waterloo Press.

Miller, S. T. (1989), *The Book of Sunderland*, Buckingham: Barracuda.

Miller, S. T. (2000), 'More a Work of Art than Nature: The Story of the Development of Sunderland Harbour', in *Port of Sunderland Millennium Handbook*, Sunderland: Port of Sunderland, pp. 12–47.

Mitchell, B. R. and Deane, P. (1962), *Abstract of British Historical Statistics*, Cambridge: Cambridge University Press.

Mitchell, J. (1971), *Reminiscences of My Life in the Highlands*, Newton Abbot: David and Charles (first published in 1883/4).

Morrell, J. B. and Watson, A. G. (eds) (1928), *How York Governs Itself*, London: Allen & Unwin.

Morrison, J. R. (1994), 'Perronet Thompson, 1783–1869: a Middle-class Radical', unpublished D. Phil. thesis, University of York.

Murray, H. (1994), 'Queen Victoria, York and the Royal Myths', *York History*, Vol. 11, pp. 56–68.

Nowell Smith, C. (1953), *Letters of Sydney Smith*, Vol. II, Oxford: Clarendon Press.

Nevill, R. (ed.) (1906), *The Reminiscences of Lady Dorothy Nevill*, London: Edward Arnold.

Nevill, R. (ed.) (1910), *Under Five Reigns. By Lady Dorothy Nevill. Edited by her son*, London: Methuen & Co.

Page, W. (ed.) (1986) *Victoria History of the County of York. North Riding (Vol. 2)*, London: Oxford University Press (reprint of the first edition of 1923).

Park, G. R. (1886), *Parliamentary Representation of Yorkshire*, Hull: Barnwell.

Parris, H. (1965), *Government and the Railways in Nineteenth-Century Britain*, London: Routledge and Kegan Paul.

Parson, W. and White, W. (1830), *Directory of the Borough of Leeds, and the County of York, etc*, Leeds: Parson and White.

Peacock, A. J. (1973), 'York in the Age of Reform', unpublished PhD thesis, University of York.

Peacock, A. J. (1981), 'George Leeman and York Politics 1833–1880', in C. H. Feinstein (ed.), *York 1831–1981: 150 Years of Scientific Endeavour and Social Change*, York: Sessions, pp. 234–54.

Peacock, A. J. (1988), *George Hudson 1800–1871 The Railway King*, Vol. I, York: Peacock.

Peacock, A. J. (1989), *George Hudson 1800–1871 The Railway King*, Vol. II, York: Peacock.

Peacock, A. J. (1997) 'Another look at George Hudson's Legacy', in A. J. Peacock (ed.), *Essays in York History*, York: York Educational Settlement, p. 348–52.

Pevsner, N. (1966), *The Buildings of England. Yorkshire, The North Riding*, London: Penguin.

Pevsner, N. (1973), *The Buildings of England. London, Vol. 1, The cities of London and Westminster* (third edition), London: Harmondsworth/Penguin Books.

Phillips, M. (1894), *A History of Banks, Bankers and Banking in Northumberland, Durham and North Yorkshire*, London: Effingham Wilson.

Pollins, H. (1952), 'A note on railway construction costs, 1825–50', *Economica*, Vol. 19, pp. 395–407.

Pollins, H. (1956), 'Aspects of railway accounting before 1868', in A. C. Littleton and B. S. Yamey (eds), *Studies in the History of Accounting*, London: Sweet and Maxwell, pp. 332–55.

Ponsonby, V. B. (Earl of Bessborough) (ed.) (1950), *Lady Charlotte Guest. Extracts from her journal, 1833–1852*, London: John Murray.

Potter, G. W. J. (1906), *A History of the Whitby and Pickering Railway*, London: Locomotive Publishing.

Prest, J. (1998), 'Gladstone and the Railways', in P. A. Jagger (ed.), *Gladstone*, London: Hambledon, pp. 197–211.

Ray, G. N. (1958), *Thackeray: The Age of Wisdom, 1847–1863*, London: Oxford University Press.

Reed, M. C. (1975), *Investment in Railways in Britain, 1820–1844: A Study in the Development of the Capital Market*, Oxford: Oxford University Press.

Rivett, A. (1964), 'The Building of the South Dock at Sunderland 1846–1856', unpublished dissertation, Sunderland Training College.

Robbins, M. (1960), 'The North Midland Railway and its Enginemen', *Journal of Transport History*, Vol. IV (3), pp. 180–6.

Robbins, M. (1962), *The Railway Age*, London: Routledge Kegan Paul.

Rolt, L. T. C. (1984), *George and Robert Stephenson*, London: Penguin.

Royal Commission on Historical Monuments in England (1972), *Inventory of the Historical Monuments in the City of York*, Vol. III, London: H.M.S.O.

Royal Commission on Historical Monuments in England (1975), *Inventory of the Historical Monuments in the City of York*, Vol. IV, London: H.M.S.O.

Royle, E. (2000), 'York in the Nineteenth Century: a City Transformed', in P. Nuttgens (ed.), *The History of York from Earliest Times to the Year 2000*, Pickering: Blackthorn, pp. 244–99.

Rubinstein, W. B. (1998), *Britain's Century: a Political and Social History 1815–1905*, London: Arnold.

Scrivenor, H. (1849), *The Railways of the United Kingdom*, London: Smith Elder.

Shand, A. I. (1903), *Old-Time Travel: Personal Reminiscences of the Continent Forty Years Ago Compared with Experiences of the Present Day*, London: John Murray.

Shannon, H. A. (1931), 'The coming of general limited liability', *Economic Journal (Economic History Supplement)*, Vol. II, pp. 267–91.

Simmons, J. (1990), *The Railways of Britain* (third edition), London: Sheldrake Press.

Simmons, J. (1995), *The Victorian Railway*, London: Thames and Hudson.

Simmons, J. and Biddle, G. (eds) (1997), *Oxford Companion to British Railway History*, Oxford: Oxford University Press.

Simnett, W. (1923), *Railway Amalgamation in Great Britain*, London: Railway Gazette.

Sinclair, N. T. (1985), *Railways of Sunderland*, Newcastle: Tyne and Wear Museums.

Skeat, W. O. (1973), *George Stephenson: the Engineer and his Letters*, London: Institute of Mechanical Engineers.

Smith, A. (1847), *The Eastern Counites Railway Viewed as an Investment*, London: Smith Elder.

Smith, A. (1848), *The Bubble of the Age; or, The Fallacies of Railway Investments, Railway Accounts and Railway Dividends*, London: Sherwood, Gilbert & Piper.

Stephen, L. and Lee, S. (eds) (1959–60), *Dictionary of National Biography* (22 vols), London: Oxford University Press. (Reprint of original publication of 1885–1901.).

Stevenson, P. S. (ed.) (1989), *The Midland Counties Railway*, Mold: Railway and Canal Historical Society.

Storey, P. J. (1992), 'Mayors of Victorian Sunderland', *Sunderland's History*, Vol. 6, pp. 17–40.

Streeten, F. T. and Hodgson, H. J. (1852), *An Analytical Digest of the Cases Published in the New Series of the Law Journal Reports etc., 1845 to 1850*, London: Edward Bret Ince.

Streeten, F. T. and Hodgson, H. J. (1857), *An Analytical Digest of the Cases Published in the New Series of the Law Journal Reports etc., 1850 to 1855*, London: Edward Bret Ince.

Stretton, C. E. (1901), *The History of the Midland Railway*, London: Methuen.

Stretton, C. E. (1901), *The History of the Leeds and Bradford, and Leeds and Bradford Extension Railways* (second edition), Leeds: Goodall and Suddick.

Tillott, P. M. (ed.) (1961), *A History of Yorkshire: the City of York* (Victoria County History), London: Oxford University Press.

Tisdall, E. E. P. (1952), *Restless Consort: The Invasion of Albert the Conqueror*, London: Stanley Paul.

Todd, G. (1932), 'Some aspects of joint stock companies, 1844–1900', *Economic History Review* (old series) Vol. IV, pp. 46–71.

Tomlinson, W. W. (1987), *Tomlinson's North Eastern Railway* (third edition), Newton Abbot: David and Charles (originally published as *'The North Eastern Railway, its Rise and Development'* in 1914).

Trollope, A. (1951), *The Way We Live Now*, London: Oxford University Press (first published in book form in 1875).

Vaughan, A. (1997), *Railwaymen, Politics and Money: The Great Age of Railways in Britain*, London: John Murray.

Vincit, V. (1847), *Railway Locomotive Management, in a Series of Letters by Veritas Vincit*, Birmingham: privately published.

Weinreb, B. and Hibbert, C. (1989), *The London Encyclopædia* (second edition), London: Macmillan.

West, Sir A. (1900), *Recollections, 1832 to 1886*, London: Smith Elder.

White, A. (1993), *A History of Whitby*, Chichester: Phillimore.

Whittle, G. (1979), *The Newcastle and Carlisle Railway*, Newton Abbot: David and Charles.

Williams, F. S. (1968), *Williams's Midland Railway: Its Rise and Progress*, Newton Abbot: David and Charles. (Originally published as 'The Midland Railway: Its Rise and Progress' in 1876. Reprint of the fifth edition of 1888.).

Williams, R. (1988), *The Midland Railway, a New History*, Newton Abbot: David and Charles.

Wilson, D. A. (1927), *Carlyle at His Zenith, 1848–53*, London: Kegan Paul, Trench, Trubner.

Wilson, J. F. (1995), *British Business History 1720–1994*, Manchester: Manchester University Press.

Wordsworth, C. F. F. (1854), *The Law of Mining, Banking, Insurance and General Joint Stock Companies* (sixth edition), London: W. G. Benning.

Wordsworth, C. F. F. (1865), *The Law of Mining, Banking, Insurance and General Joint Stock Companies* (tenth edition), London: W. G. Benning.

Index